Business performance measurement

The field of performance measurement has evolved rapidly in the last few years with the development of new measurement frameworks and methodologies, such as the balanced scorecard, the performance prism, economic value added, economic profit, activity-based costing, and self-assessment techniques.

This multi-disciplinary, international book draws together the key themes to provide an up-to-date summary of the leading ideas in business performance measurement, theory, and practice. It includes viewpoints from a range of fields including accounting, operations management, marketing, strategy, and organizational behavior.

The book will appeal to graduate students, managers, and researchers interested in performance measurement, whatever their discipline.

Andy Neely is Director of the Centre for Business Performance at Cranfield School of Management and Professor of Operations Strategy and Performance and has been researching and teaching in the field of business performance measurement since the late 1980s. He was chair of the international academic conference on performance measurement in 1998, 2000 and 2002 and has authored over 100 books and articles on the subject, including *Measuring Business Performance*, The Economist Books, 1998. He has consulted to and worked with numerous organizations including 3M, Accenture, British Airways, DHL, KPMG and Rolls Royce Aerospace.

Business performance measurement

Theory and practice

Edited by

Andy Neely

Cranfield School of Management, UK

PUBLISHED BY THE PRESS SYNDICATE OF THE UNIVERSITY OF CAMBRIDGE
The Pitt Building, Trumpington Street, Cambridge, United Kingdom

CAMBRIDGE UNIVERSITY PRESS
The Edinburgh Building, Cambridge CB2 2RU, UK
40 West 20th Street, New York, NY 10011-4211, USA
477 Williamstown Road, Port Melbourne, VIC 3207, Australia
Ruiz de Alarcón 13, 28014 Madrid, Spain
Dock House, The Waterfront, Cape Town 8001, South Africa

http://www.cambridge.org

© Cambridge University Press 2002

First published 2002
Fifth printing 2005

Printed in the United Kingdom at the University Press, Cambridge

Typeface Minion 11/14pt   *System* QuarkXPress™   [SE]

A catalogue record for this book is available from the British Library

ISBN 0 521 80342 X hardback

Contents

v

Part VI   Performance measurement – emerging issues and trends

Contributors

Chris Adams
Accenture

Thomas Ahrens
The London School of Economics
UK

Tim Ambler
London Business School
UK

Rob Austin
Harvard Business School
Boston, MA
USA

Umit Bititci
University of Strathclyde
UK

Mike Bourne
Cranfield School of Management
UK

Allan Carrie
University of Strathclyde
UK

Chris Chapman
Saïd Business School
University of Oxford
UK

Bruce Clark
Northeastern University
USA

Clive Emmanuel
University of Glasgow
UK

Ken Euske
Naval Postgraduate School
Monterey
USA

Graham Francis
Open University Business School
UK

Bruno S. Frey
University of Zurich
Switzerland

Jody Hoffer Gittell
Harvard Business School
USA

Rich Goodkey
Alberta Treasury
Canada

Lars Grønholdt
Copenhagen Business School
Denmark

Matthew Hinton
Open University Business School
UK

Jackie Holloway
Open University Business School
UK

Neha Kapashi
Accenture

Riitta Katila
Helsinki University of Technology
Finland

Mike Kennerley
Cranfield School of Management
UK

Flora Kokkinaki
London Business School
UK

Kai Kristensen
The Aarhus School of Business
Denmark

Pat Larkey
Carnegie Mellon University
USA

Michel Lebas
Groupe HEC
France

Bernard Marr
Cranfield School of Management
UK

Anne Martensen
The Aarhus School of Business
Denmark

David Mayle
Open University Business School
UK

Marshall W. Meyer
The Wharton School
USA

Elspeth Murray
Queen's University
Canada

Mohammed Al Najjar
Cambridge University
UK

Andy Neely
Cranfield School of Management
UK

Ken Ogata
Alberta Treasury
Canada

Margit Osterloh
University of Zurich
Switzerland

David Otley
Lancaster University Management
    School
UK

Peter Richardson
Queen's University
Canada

Trevor Turner
University of Strathclyde
UK

Preface

Performance measurement is on the agenda. New reports and articles on the topic have been appearing at a rate of one every five hours of every working day since 1994. A search of the World Wide Web reveals over 12 million sites dedicated to it, up from under 200000 in 1997. Since 1994 Business Intelligence, a professional conference organizing company based in the UK, has organized some 90 separate events on business performance measurement (BPM). Some 2700 delegates from over 1400 different firms attended these conferences. In terms of delegate fees alone, Business Intelligence has accrued over $5 million. Add to this, the revenues received by other conference organizers, publishers, market research firms, software vendors, and consultants and it is clear that business performance measurement is a multi-million dollar industry.

Like many multi-million dollar industries developments are rapid. Recent years have seen the introduction of new methods of measurement, such as activity-based costing, throughput accounting, and shareholder value analysis. New measurement frameworks, most notably the balanced scorecard and the business excellence model, have taken the business community by storm. Data collected by the US research firm, Gartner, suggest that 40 percent of firms will be using balanced scorecards to measure business performance by the end of 2000. Other data, such as those collected by the US consulting firm Towers Perrin, indicate that the majority of firms have introduced their balanced scorecards during the last five years. Similar trends can be observed in the field of quality management. Self-assessment frameworks, such as those underpinning the Baldridge Award and European Foundation for Quality Management Award, have generated significant industrial interest and activity. Increasingly authors and commentators are discussing the multiple roles of measurement; it is now recognized that measures allow managers to do far more than simply check progress; the behavioral consequences of measures are frequently discussed; the value of benchmarking and external comparisons is widely understood; and the question of what data should be disclosed to external parties – especially shareholders – is actively debated. Organizations, such as Skandia, the Swedish Insurance company, and Shell have begun producing supplements to their annual reports. Skandia's supplement discusses the value of the firm's intangible assets, while Shell's 2000 supplement, entitled "People, planet and profits: The Shell Report," describes the company's environmental performance. Other organizations, such as the UK's Cooperative Bank, have moved even further and structured their annual report around the "inclusive" framework, proposed by the Royal Society of Arts, Manufacturers and Commerce following their Tomorrow's Company Inquiry. The Cooperative Bank's "Partnership Report," for the 2000 financial year, reviews the bank's performance through the eyes of its seven partners: (i) shareholders, (ii) customers, (iii) staff and their families, (iv) suppliers, (v) local communities, (vi) national and international society, and (vii) past and future generations of "Cooperators."

In the academic community people from a wide variety of different functional backgrounds are researching the topic of performance measurement. Experts in accounting, economics, human resource management, marketing, operations management, psychology, and sociology are all exploring the subject, and one of the major problems with the field is that they are all doing so independently. The accountants discuss their ideas with other accountants. The operations managers talk to other operations managers. Rarely is knowledge generated in one functional academic silo assimilated by another, and, of course, the end result is a massive duplication of effort. In 1998 the first multidisciplinary conference on performance measurement was held at Churchill College in Cambridge. Between them the 94 papers presented at the conference cited some 1246 different books and articles. Of these, less than 10 percent were cited more than once and only 0.3 percent were cited more than five times. These figures are symptomatic of a field with vast richness, but unmanageable diversity.

A significant problem is that there appears to be no agreement as to which are the important themes and theories in the field. Everyone writing about the topic has his/her own preferred references and freely cites them. While this diversity is appealing, it also hinders development, because it makes it almost impossible for generations of researchers to build upon the work of others. If the field of performance measurement is to develop as an academic discipline then it is essential that some boundaries are identified and some theoretical foundations agreed. It is hoped that this book will make some small contribution to facilitating this process.

Deliberately the book draws on authors from a variety of functional disciplines, all of whom are working in the field of performance measurement. Deliberately it presents a variety of perspectives on performance measurement. The book opens with a part on functional perspectives, in which eminent authors from the accounting, marketing, operations management, and psychology fields offer their views on measurement.

The book continues, in the second part, by exploring some of the philosophical questions underpinning the topic of performance measurement, including the issues associated with the behavioral consequences of measurement and reward systems.

The third part of the book is devoted to a review of frameworks and methodologies. Undoubtedly the balanced scorecard and the business excellence model are the best known of these, but there are numerous other measurement frameworks and methodologies, each with their own strengths and weaknesses and it is on these that the third part concentrates.

In the fourth part practical applications of measurement are discussed. Once again this part draws upon multiple disciplines and the applications of measurement systems in a wide variety of contexts – including both the public and private sectors – are discussed.

The fifth part concentrates on specific dimensions of performance and explores the issues associated with the measurement of customer satisfaction, employee satisfaction, and innovation.

The sixth and final parts offer some views on emerging issues and trends in performance measurement, including a summary of recent research into what the "dot.coms" should measure and what they are measuring.

The breadth of the book means that it should appeal to a wide audience, encompassing measurement scholars and practitioners. Deliberately the book draws on work being undertaken by a diverse group of researchers, diverse in the sense of both geographical location and functional persuasion. The resultant richness illustrates well the diversity inherent in the topic of performance measurement, but it is hoped that the text also offers a reasonable foundation on which future generations of researchers can draw. By bringing together these diverse works in a single volume it is hoped that at least a start has been made on the process of unifying theory and practice in performance measurement.

Andy Neely
Cranfield School of Management

Part I

Performance measurement – functional analyses

By its nature performance measurement is a diverse subject. Researchers with functional backgrounds as diverse as accounting, operations management, marketing, finance, economics, psychology, and sociology are all actively working in the field. As discussed in the Preface this incredible diversity brings with it both challenges and opportunities. The diversity results in a fascinating richness, but makes it extremely difficult for generations of researchers to build on each other's work. A significant barrier stems from the fact that traditionally the way academic careers develop is through functional specialization. Accountants talk to accountants. Operations managers meet with operations managers. Marketing specialists network with other marketing specialists. The result is deep and rich streams of functionally specialized research, with little cross-fertilization. The aim of this first part is to begin the process of redressing this shortcoming by drawing together several functionally based reviews of performance measurement.

The part contains four chapters. The first by Professor David Otley reviews measurement from an accounting perspective and explores the different roles of measurement. Otley argues that implicitly the accounting community recognizes that measurement systems have three fundamentally different roles in organizations. First they provide a tool for financial management. Second they provide information on overall business performance. Third they provide a means of motivation and control. A key theme in Otley's contribution is that far too often academics and practitioners do not recognize these three different roles and the result can be confusion, especially when a measurement system designed to fulfil one role is used to fulfil another.

The second contribution comes from Professor Bruce Clark, who provides an extensive review of marketing performance measurement through the ages. He argues that, while the early work on marketing measurement concentrated on marketing productivity, more recent developments have resulted in massive interest in marketing orientation, customer satisfaction, customer loyalty, and brand equity. Clark ends his contribution by exploring some of the challenges facing marketing academics, including the difficulties of coping with feedback loops, the changing nature of reporting requirements, and the need to cope with the conflicting demands of multiple stakeholders.

The third contribution is based on the operations management perspective and is provided by Andy Neely and Rob Austin. They explore operations performance measurement and argue that three broad phases of evolution in the field can be identified. The first phase, which ran up until the late 1970s, was concerned with productivity measurement. The second, which ran from the early 1980s through to the late 1990s, was concerned with how to develop measures consistent with modern manufacturing management thinking. In the third phase, which is currently ongoing, Neely and Austin argue that the key operations management measurement issues are measures for the new economy and for inter- and intra-operational alliances.

The fourth, and final contribution, in this first part is provided by Professor Marshall Meyer, who argues that performance has the potential to become a new management discipline. Starting with the question – what is performance – Meyer argues that performance measurement, if used correctly, offers the potential for managers to understand which of the activities undertaken generate revenues that exceed costs. Building on this theme he introduces the notion of activity-based revenue as a measurement methodology and illustrates how this approach has the potential to overcome some of the shortcomings encountered in the measurement systems used by organizations today.

1 Measuring performance: The accounting perspective

David Otley

Introduction

Accounting measures of performance have been the traditional mainstay of quantitative approaches to organizational performance measurement. However, over the past two decades, a great deal of attention has been paid to the development and use of non-financial measures of performance, which can be used both to motivate and report on the performance of business (and other) organizations. The impetus for such developments has come from both the bottom and the top of the organization. Much performance management at the operational level is carried out using specific indicators of performance, which are usually not measured in financial terms. At the most senior levels, although financial performance is inevitably a major consideration, there has been increasing recognition that other important factors in the effective running of the organization cannot be well captured by such measures. Thus, non-financial performance measures have undergone significant development, to the relative neglect of the development of improved financial measures. However, the recent publicity surrounding the marketing of economic value added (EVA®) as an overall measure of company performance by management consultants Stern Stewart can be seen as a sign of a new emphasis on the financial aspects of performance.

The purpose of this contribution is to review the roles and functions of financial measures of organizational performance, and to outline the major features of their development, particularly in the latter half of the last century. It will be argued that there are three different major functions for financial performance measures, and that, although these functions overlap to some extent, major confusion can be caused by applying measures developed for one function to a different one. The three main functions involved are:

1 Financial measures of performance as tools of financial management. Here the focus is on the functional specialism of finance and financial management. This is concerned with the efficient provision and use of financial

resources to support the wider aims of the organization, and to manage the effective and efficient operation of the finance function.

2 Financial performance as a major objective of a business organization. Here an overarching financial performance measure, such as profit, return on investment, or EVA®, is used to signify the achievement of an important (perhaps the *most* important) organizational objective.

3 Financial measures of performance as mechanisms for motivation and control within the organization. Here the financial information provides a 'window' into the organization by which specific operations are managed through the codification of their inputs and outputs in financial terms.

Clearly, there is some overlap between these different functions. Efficient financial management is a component of efficient overall management, but it does not subsume the latter. Performance may be managed, in part, by the transmission of corporate objectives (in financial form) downwards as part of the process of strategy implementation, and financial measures may provide substantial insight into the overall impact of operational activities, but other, more specific, measures are generally needed to fully understand and manage the "drivers" of performance. This contribution will therefore first consider each of the major functions independently, and then examine the linkages between them.

What follows is by no means a comprehensive review of how functions of financial performance measures have been used over the past 50 years. Rather, it is a brief report on the highlights, which attempts to draw out the lessons that have been learned and to limit the confusion that can be caused by not recognizing the different functions involved.

A tool of financial management

Any organization, whether public or private, has to live within financial constraints and to deliver perceived value for money to its stakeholders. The role of the finance function is to manage the financial resources of the organization, and to ensure that the financial constraints it faces are not breached. Failure to do this will lead to financial distress, and ultimately, for many organizations, to financial failure or bankruptcy.

Thus, financial planning and control is an essential part of the overall management process. Establishment of precisely what the financial constraints are and how the proposed operating plans will impact upon them are a central part of the finance function. This is generally undertaken by the development of financial plans[1] that outline the financial outcomes that are necessary for the organization to meet its commitments. Financial control can be seen as the process by which such plans are monitored and necessary corrective action proposed where significant deviations are detected.

There are three main areas of focus for financial plans. Most basically, cash flow planning is required to ensure that the cash is available to meet the financial obligations of the organization. Failure to manage cash flows will result in technical insolvency (the inability to meet payments when they are legally required to be made). For business organizations, the second area requiring attention is profitability, or the need to acquire resources (usually from revenues acquired by selling goods and services) at a greater rate than using them (usually represented by the costs of making payments to suppliers, employees, and others). Although over the life of an enterprise, total net cash flow and total profit are essentially equal, this can mask the fact that in the short-term they can be very different.[2] Indeed, one of the major causes of failure of new small business enterprises is not that they are unprofitable in the long term, but that growth in profitable activity has outstripped the cash necessary to resource it. The major difference between profit and cash flow is the time period between payments made for capital assets which will generate income in the future and the actual receipt of that income which is needed as working capital. This highlights the third area of focus, namely on assets and the provision of finance for their purchase. In accounting terms, the focus of attention is on the balance sheet, rather than the profit and loss account or the cash flow statement.

In overall terms, financial management therefore focuses on both the acquisition of financial resources on terms as favorable as possible, and on the utilization of the assets that those financial resources have been used to purchase, and on the interaction between these two activities. The single most powerful tool of reporting on these matters is the so-called "pyramid of ratios."

The apex of the pyramid of ratios (see figure 1.1) is an overall measure of profitability that divides profit by the assets used in generating that profit, namely return on capital employed. Traditionally, this is broken down into two major secondary ratios, namely the profit margin on sales and the capital turnover. Clearly, return on capital employed is equal to the product of these

---

[1] Such financial plans are often referred to as budgets and are widely used as a means of management control. However, this use is more concerned with management than financial control, and will be discussed in later sections.

[2] If "clean surplus" accounting is used, total net cash flow and total profit are identical, in aggregate.

two items. Each of the secondary ratios can be broken down into tertiary ratios based on the fact that profit is equal to sales revenue less cost of sales, and capital employed can be split into fixed assets (long term) and current assets (short term). However, it is evident that the concept becomes more strained the further down the pyramid one proceeds, and, although the pyramid provides a clear connection between the values of each of its component ratios, a more focused approach can be more beneficial than attempts to create a totally integrated "pyramid."

This can be provided by considering the purpose of calculating each ratio. Thus, if the concern is with cash flows and liquidity, a range of ratios based on working capital are appropriate. Thus, five key ratios are commonly calculated, i.e.
- current ratio, equal to current assets divided by current liabilities;
- quick ratio (or acid test), equal to quick assets (current assets less inventories) divided by current liabilities;
- inventory turnover period, equal to inventories divided by cost of sales, with the result being expressed in terms of days or months;
- debtors to sales ratio, with the result again being expressed as an average collection period;
- creditors to purchases ratio, again expressed as the average payment period.

Each of these ratios addresses a different aspect of the cash collection and payment cycle. There are conventional values for each of these ratios (for example, the current ratio often has a standard value of 2.0 mentioned, although this has fallen substantially in recent years because of improvements in techniques of working capital management, and the quick ratio has a value of 1.0) but in fact these values vary widely across firms and industries. More generally helpful is a comparison with industry norms and an examination of the changes in the values of these ratios over time that will assist in the assessment of whether any financial difficulties may be arising.

If the concern is more with long-term profitability than with short-term cash flows, a different set of ratios may be appropriate. Profit to sales ratios can be calculated (although different ratios can be calculated depending whether profit is measured before or after interest payments and taxation); value-added (sales revenues less the cost of bought-in supplies) ratios are also used to give insight into operational efficiencies. A general principle is that each part of the ratio should be relevant to the audience being addressed, and that the overall ratio should reflect the interests of the specific user of the information it provides.

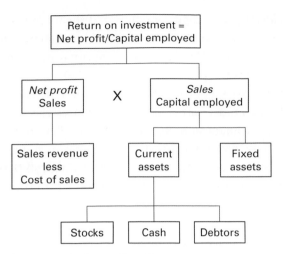

Figure 1.1. Outline pyramid of accounting ratios.

Finally, if it is desirable to consider the raising of capital, as well as its uses, a further set of ratios based on financial structure can be calculated. For example, the ratio of debt to equity capital (gearing or leverage) is an indication of the risk associated with a company's equity earnings (because debt interest is deducted from profit before profit distributable to shareholders is obtained). It is often stated that fixed assets should be funded from capital raised on a long-term basis, whilst working capital should fund only short-term needs. Again, this may seem to be a logical and prudent rule of thumb, but it is necessary to be aware that some very successful companies flout this rule to a very considerable extent. For example, most supermarket chains fund their stores (fixed assets) out of working capital because they sell their inventories for cash several times before they have to pay for them (i.e., typical inventory turnover is three weeks, whereas it is not uncommon for credit to be granted for three months by their suppliers). Thus, the values of these ratios indicate the potential riskiness of such an arrangement, but this does not necessarily preclude such a financial strategy being adopted.

It is of note that the overall return on investment ratio can be calculated in a variety of different ways. For example, return (profit) may be before or after payment of debt interest. Capital employed may be measured as total capital employed in the business, or just as the equity (shareholders') capital alone. Which measure is appropriate depends upon the use to which the ratio is being put. If the focus of interest is in the efficient use of financial resources by the firm as an entity, then profit before interest and taxation (PBIT) may be appropriately divided by total capital employed. If the interest is in the use of shareholders' capital, then the return attributable to shareholders (i.e., profit after interest and taxes (PAIT)) divided by equity capital alone may be the more meaningful measure.

There is thus no definitive set of financial ratios that can be said to measure the performance of a business. Rather, a set of measures can be devised to assess different aspects of financial performance from different perspectives. Although some of these measures can be derived from annual financial reports, and can be used to assess the same aspect of financial performance across different companies, care needs to be taken to ensure that the same accounting principles have been used to produce the accounting numbers in each case. As company directors are well aware that such analyses may be performed, it is not uncommon for "window dressing" to occur so that acceptable results are reported. A considerable amount of such manipulation is possible within generally acceptable accounting principles (GAAP), although it will occasionally stray into the realm of more "creative accounting" which may fall foul of the auditors. More importantly, such ratios allow financial managers to keep track of a company's financial performance (perhaps in comparison with that of its major competitors), and to adjust the activities of the organization, both operating and financial, to keep within acceptable bounds.

From this perspective, the role of financial performance measurement is to help keep the organization on the financial "straight and narrow" track. The measures are used primarily by financial specialists, and the action taken as a result of such analysis may also be exclusively financial (e.g., raising more capital to ensure that debts can be paid on time). Nevertheless, it is also clear that evidence of financial problems may occur because of deficiencies in other areas of business operations. In this case, the ratios can provide the finance director with the information necessary to convince other managers that operating action needs to be taken in order to avoid financial distress. However, the primary role served by this type of performance measurement lies within the province of the finance function, and is concerned with the effective and efficient use of financial resources.

An overall business objective

The second major role of accounting performance measures is connected with the financial objectives of the business. In particular, measures are addressed to meeting the needs of the external suppliers of capital, both debt and equity. It is this need that external financial reporting addresses. An organization's annual report and financial accounts are primarily produced for the shareholders, although some use may be made of them by bankers and other providers of debt capital. In some ways, these external financial reports can be seen as mirroring the internal measures and ratios discussed above, in that they cover the same three main areas of cash flow (rather obliquely), operating profit, and asset values. Also, the two differing foci of the performance of the business (financed by both debt and equity capital) and the return to its shareholders (i.e., the return on equity capital alone) are also apparent. However, by far the major attention is focused on reporting to shareholders.

The whole area of external financial reporting, in particular, and the debate surrounding corporate governance, more generally, is structured around the usefulness of audited financial statements (and other mandatory disclosures) to shareholders. At one level, this is captured by the agency theory formulation whereby owners (shareholders) seek to control managers, but are restricted in their ability to do this because they possess much less detailed information than the managers. Mandatory accounting statements represent one means of attempting to redress this balance by providing shareholders with an annual externally audited review of the financial outcomes associated with the business activities undertaken. This is very much of a "backstop" position, and active investors (e.g., institutional shareholders, for example) generally seek to obtain more frequent and prospective information than financial reports can provide. However, the acquisition of prospective information is restricted by the need to make all such information public, in order to preserve an equitable trading market in which all players have similar access to information. The whole area of "insider trading" and the legislation governing stock market operations is an example of the complexity of the rules needed to preserve such an open market. Thus, this brief review will restrict itself to information provided by annual financial accounts to the shareholders of a business, and the measures of performance that are used in this respect.

The legal constitution of shareholder-owned enterprises puts the shareholders in the position of being the residual owners of any financial benefits (profit) that the organization may create through its activities. The profit and loss account eventually arrives at a figure of profit after the deduction of all expenses including debt interest and taxes (PAIT). There may be other parties who have a legal right to certain fixed payments (e.g., supplier invoice payments, employees wages) but any excess over these expenses represents profit, without any upper limit. This profit will generally be partly distributed in the form of a dividend to shareholders, and partly retained in the business (retained earnings) to finance future expansion. If an organization fails to make a profit, dividends may still be paid out of previously retained earnings, but ultimately this will become exhausted and the business will become bankrupt. In such a case, it is likely that the shares will be valueless, and the shareholders will lose their investment, up to the amount they invested. There is no provision for the recovery of any further losses from shareholders (i.e., their liability is limited to the amount they paid for their shares).

Thus earnings (profit) is the central performance indicator for shareholders. A very common measure of performance is EPS (earnings per share) which divides total annual earnings by the number of shares in issue. Earnings essentially represent the (cum dividend) increase in the accounting book value of the company due to its previous year's activities. However, the share price of a company depends not only on its past achieved performance, but also on expectations of its future prospects. In technical terms, the share price "impounds' such information and conceptually represents both the historical value of the assets it possesses and the expectation of future performance, discounted by an appropriate time-value of money. The results of these future expectations is illustrated in the commonly calculated price/earnings (P/E) ratio, which divides the current share price by the last reported earnings figure. A high value of this ratio indicates an expectation of a high level of growth in future earnings; a low value an expectation of stability or even decline.

Annual reported earnings thus represent only one component of the return to shareholders, and one of only secondary importance. More formally, in any period of ownership, the return to a shareholder is comprised of the dividends received plus the increase in share price (or minus the decrease in share price) that has taken place during the period, divided by the initial share price. By way of a practical example, the average growth in share price over the past five years on the UK stock market has been somewhat in excess of 15 percent per annum, whereas dividends have been paid at a rate of around 3–4 percent per annum. Thus, the bulk of the return to shareholders is generally in the form of capital growth rather than dividend payments, and a period's dividend payment is only loosely related to the earnings in that period. Furthermore, the computation of actual returns to shareholders require no accounting information whatsoever, being comprised of cash dividend payments and the change in the market price of the shares.

What is a reasonable rate of return that may be expected by shareholders in a particular business? This question can only be answered by reference to past experience, and only in average terms. Essentially the computation that is being performed is an assessment of the opportunity cost of capital to the investor (i.e. what return might a shareholder expect if he had invested in alternative, but similar, investments?). The capital asset pricing model (CAPM) has been a popular method of making this assessment, and concludes that the return that can be expected depends upon (a) the risk-free rate of return that can be obtained from investing in an interest-bearing investment, such as a government bond, and (b) the riskiness of the particular investment being considered. This riskiness (represented by the coefficient beta in the model) is assessed by comparing the sensitivity of the returns from the particular investment with the returns from the market portfolio (i.e., a composite of all available investments, such as a stock market tracking fund). The relationship is assumed to be linear in form, so knowledge of a firm-specific beta and the risk-free and market portfolio expected returns allows an estimate of the cost of a company's equity capital to be made. This provides a benchmark against which future returns can be assessed. If returns in excess of this benchmark are expected, the share price is likely to rise such that new investors will obtain a return exactly in line with the benchmark figure.

However, most commonly used measures of company performance do not match this model. Earnings are the fundamental component of many performance measures. To the extent to which such earnings-based performance measures are assumed to capture information about the values of a business, these measures implicitly assume that past earnings are a good predictor of future returns and are thus associated with share price. As future values are much more dependent upon expectations of future performance, it is not necessarily the case that an historical measure of past performance is likely to be strongly associated with share price. Moreover, the current share price of a company already impounds all the publicly available information (and possibly a deal of private information, as well) about its future prospects. The market has therefore already taken into account all such information in setting the current share price. In a world of perfect information, the past history of company performance is irrelevant to predicting future share price movements.

Accounting measures of performance are largely restricted to providing confirmatory evidence that the beliefs of investors concerning current earnings are based on auditable "fact." But it must also be recognized that the calculation of accounting earnings is a matter of judgment as well as fact. For example, a charge representing the depreciation in value of capital assets forms a major cost item in the accounts of most companies. However, this requires an assessment to be made of the expected future life of these assets, and their likely residual value at the end of this life. Clearly, this requires a considerable degree of judgment to be exercised, and different accountants might well form a different opinion as to the amount of profit to be reported. Less legitimately, the whole arena of "creative accounting" indicates the lengths to which accounting judgments can be stretched in the cause of reporting profit figures which are helpful to directors and others.

Thus, paradoxically, even if the delivery of returns to shareholders is seen as the overall aim and objective of a business enterprise, reported accounting earnings provide only a weak surrogate for overall shareholder returns. There is a considerable body of empirical literature that demonstrates the relatively low level of correlation between reported profitability and share price movements.[3] But, even in the absence of such evidence, it is clear on conceptual grounds that no such relationship is likely to be strong. In terms of assessing performance from an investor's perspective, accounting measures provide only background and confirmatory evidence. Even economic value added, which will be discussed in detail in the following sections, is essentially an accounting-based performance measure and, as such, cannot be expected to do more than imperfectly mirror shareholder returns.

A mechanism for motivation and control

The third major function of accounting performance measurement lies in its internal use as a means of motivating and controlling the activities of managers so that they concentrate on increasing the overall value of the business or, at least, the value attributable to the shareholders. In short, the role of managers is often presented as "increasing shareholder value." Even if this is accepted as the over-riding objective of the business, there is a complicated chain of means–end relationships that now need to be considered. That is, how can shareholder value be increased?

At the first level of analysis, controllable aspects of performance can be partly captured in accounting performance measures, both earnings and balance sheet values. Here, the accounting information is concerned not just with financial performance, but rather uses financial indicators to represent the underlying activities that are being managed. In an organization of any

---

[3] See Lev (1989) for a summary of evidence from the first two decades of "market-based" accounting research.

size or complexity, there is a need to be able to represent a variety of different activities in terms of a common language or unit of measurement. Accounting provides such a common language, so that the impact of very different activities can be aggregated into overall measures, such as sales revenue, costs, and profitability.

At the next level of analysis, it may be realized that measures of outcomes are an insufficient mechanism for controlling performance. What is required in addition are measures that represent the "drivers" of performance; that is, those activities that it is believed it is necessary to undertake so that desired outcomes (financial and other) are attained. At this level, accounting measures alone become inadequate, and over the past ten years alternative approaches, such as the balanced scorecard, have been developed to supplement solely accounting measures of performance.

The two sets of approaches based on these differing models are likely to be complementary, but the development of performance measurement has tended to divorce them. We shall therefore first consider the development of accounting-based performance management techniques, and then go on to review the wider approaches that have been developed more recently.

Accounting approaches to control

The basic accounting approach to motivation and control is to divide an organization into "responsibility centers." These are organizational units which are as self-contained as possible, and which are responsible for defined aspects of performance. At the highest level, these are defined as investment centers, where managers have responsibility both for investing in business assets and in using the assets entrusted to them effectively. A typical performance measure for an investment center manager would be return on capital employed, as this involves both profit and asset value components. At a lower level, profit centers are defined. Here managers are responsible for generating sales revenue and for managing the costs involved in production or service delivery. Thus profit is an appropriate performance measure. Finally, the lowest level of responsibility is the cost center, where the results of the units of activity cannot be assessed in terms of revenue earned, and managers are held responsible (in accounting terms) only for costs.[4] Clearly, in performance

---

[4] A further form of responsibility center, the revenue center, is sometimes used. This is where the unit generates sales revenues, but is responsible only for the marketing costs not the costs of producing the products sold. Here the net revenue figure can be used as a measure of the success of the unit.

management terms, cost centers require other (non-accounting) measures to be associated with them to capture the outputs that result from expenditure on inputs.

To operate control based primarily on accounting measures requires profit or investment centers to be established. Indeed, there has been a tendency to create "pseudo-profit centers" where revenues are somewhat artificially attributed to responsibility centers in order to gain the advantages associated with control of profit centers. These advantages are primarily those of having only to consider accounting measures of performance, expressed as an overall profit measure and its components. In particular, if a profit center is indeed generating profits, it can potentially be left alone to continue the good work, with control exercised in a relatively decentralized manner. However, to construct profit statements for an organizational unit requires revenues as well as costs to be attributed to it. This is not an issue where products are sold to an external customer and sales revenues generated, but it is more problematic where intermediate products are transferred internally within a larger organization, or in the public sector where services may be provided at no cost to the immediate user.

Here a value has to be attributed to the transferred goods and services, the so-called "transfer price." A great deal of attention has been paid in the accounting literature to the setting of transfer prices which will motivate managers to act in the interest of the overall organization whilst maximizing their own reported profit measure. This can be achieved under certain circumstances, but it is more common for transfer prices to generate more heat than light. If they are mis-set, there is considerable potential for managers to appear to be performing well in local terms, but to be acting dysfunctionally from a more global perspective. An extreme example was the case of the motor car manufacturer which set transfer prices on a full cost plus basis. That is, each component plant, and the assembly plant had transfer prices set on the basis of their full costs plus a percentage addition for profit margin. Not surprisingly, all the units reported healthy profits; the only black spot was the marketing division which reported heavy losses, as it was unable to sell the vehicles at anything like the costs which had been transferred to it. Clearly, in this case, the problem did not lie only in the marketing area, but also in high production costs in all the other areas. Inappropriate setting of transfer prices, and the tendency to attempt to create profit centers where they do not really exist, is responsible for a great deal of dysfunctional activity.

Even where the transfer pricing issue has been satisfactorily dealt with, there is a further issue of motivation that can arise. In a profit center, a manager can

be targeted to improve his/her profit target. But because the conventional calculation of profit excludes any assessment of the return required by the providers of equity capital, maximization of reported profits is not an appropriate
objective. For example, it can be achieved by using excessive investment in
working capital to produce a low, but positive, rate of return. Conversely, in
an investment center, the use of return on investment as a performance
measure can lead to under-investment. For example, a manager currently
achieving a high rate of return (say 30 percent) may not wish to pursue a
project yielding a lower rate of return (say 20 percent) even though such a
project may be desirable to a company which can raise capital at an even lower
rate (say 15 percent). Both these potentially dysfunctional motivational effects
can be overcome by the use of residual income as a performance measure.

Residual income is defined as accounting profit less a charge for the equity
capital used in its generation. That is,

Residual income = Accounting income *less* (capital employed × cost of capital %)[5]

This overcomes the problems described above. Any project which increases
residual income over the life of an asset is desirable; any project which
decreases residual income is undesirable. In principle, the potential for dysfunctional motivation is removed, and residual income is thus a better overall
measure of performance than either profit or return on investment. However,
rather surprisingly, over the last 30 or more years since residual income was
introduced in the academic literature it has been surprisingly little used in
practice. But, recently, this lack of use has radically changed, especially in the
USA. During the 1990s the US management consultants Stern Stewart introduced a performance measure they named economic value added (EVA®)
which is conceptually identical to residual income and have very successfully
marketed it as an overall performance measure for companies, and as a device
for measuring the performance of individual business units. They argued that
all other performance measures in common use, including profit, return on
investment, and earnings per share potentially created dysfunctional motivations for managers. To encourage managers to focus on creating shareholder
value (rather than, for example, pursuing growth for its own sake, or because
of the advantages growth can bring to the managers themselves) they argued

---

[5] Note that this can be computed either by taking accounting income after interest charges and using the
equity capital employed and its cost, or alternatively by taking profit before interest and using the total
capital employed and the weighted average cost of capital (WACC). The numerical result should be identical; however, the latter approach is usually more easily applied in practice because capital employed can
be measured by valuing the assets involved.

that EVA® provided the one and only measure that would unambiguously provide the appropriate motivation.

To do this, they recommend that a considerable number of adjustments are made to the conventional financial accounts produced by companies. Most of these adjustments attempt to replace conventional financial reporting practices with recognition and measurement procedures which produce a more meaningful estimate of the capital committed to an enterprise by its investors. They claim to show, in a series of studies, that EVA® correlates more closely with share price than any other accounting measure. However, it still needs to be recognized that, even if this claim is substantiated, no historical measure of performance will be a perfect predictor of share price, in that much of the price of a share is determined by future expectations rather than past results.

Not only do they recommend the use of EVA® at the highest levels of the organization, they also strongly recommend that it is driven as far down the organization as possible, so that managers at every level are given the task of improving their reported EVA®. They also argue that managerial rewards should be closely matched to this performance measure. In such a way, they argue, managers will be motivated to improve shareholder value.

Although much can undoubtedly be achieved in this way, there are also some limitations to the effectiveness of this approach. First, accounting performance measures for a single period cannot accurately reflect the impact of decisions which may have repercussions over several accounting periods. For example, it has been shown that capital investment decisions which have a positive net-present value (NPV) (and which should therefore add value to the firm) do not necessarily yield positive accounting profits (or returns on investment, or EVA®) in every period of the project's life. The only way to ensure such an outcome would be to value the assets concerned at the NPV of their future expected cash flows. Although this is acceptable in economic decision-making terms, it is not feasible from the viewpoint of reporting on performance, as such estimates would be overly subjective. For example, a manager could improve on his reported performance merely by making slightly optimistic estimates of the outcome of future events. Second, even when multiple periods are considered, historical earnings only represent the true growth in value of a business if the assets it possesses are valued in terms of future expectations rather than historical attainments. That is, GAAPs would have to be cast aside and assets valued at the NPV of their expected future cash flows. At the very least, such an approach requires a great deal of subjective judgment on the part of managers, and is thus open to significant manipulation. There are therefore fundamental limitations as to what can be achieved by using historical accounting numbers to measure and assess managerial and organizational performance.

Performance drivers

The complementary approaches that have been developed move away from a concentration on accounting measures alone, and add consideration of a wider range of factors which are believed to drive future economic performance. The most popular of these approaches in the 1990s has been the balanced scorecard approach, developed at the Harvard Business School. Although this will be discussed in some detail in this section, it should be recognized that other similar approaches exist, including the European Foundation for Quality Management scheme, which is in many ways similar to the Harvard approach. Moreover, these approaches are not new. The General Electric Company developed a set of performance measures for its departments in the 1950s which incorporated the following elements:

- short-term profitability,
- market share,
- productivity,
- product leadership,
- personnel development,
- employee attitudes,
- public responsibility,
- balance between short-range objectives and long-range goals.

However, the balanced scorecard approach has a number of features which make it a good vehicle for structuring an array of performance measures. First, it makes an explicit link between the espoused strategies of an organization and the performance measures it uses to monitor and control strategy implementation. This key feature makes it very clear that there is not necessarily a universal set of performance measures that are appropriate for all organizations in all circumstance (as seems to be assumed in many accounting approaches), but that specific measures need to be devised for specific circumstances. Second, the four major areas in which performance measures are to be devised (financial, customer, business process, and innovation and learning) closely match the main stakeholders of the organization (especially as the employees tend to be discussed in the fourth, innovation and learning, area). It would not be difficult to extend the balanced scorecard approach into a more fully developed stakeholder model. Third, there is a clear attempt to model the main drivers of future performance, as each area requires the question "What must we do in order to satisfy the expectations of our . . .?" to be considered, and appropriate responses generated. Finally, the requirement that there are no more than four performance measures in each area, requires a focus on the "key success factors" that are believed to operate. This can help to compensate for the tendency to construct ever-increasing numbers of performance indicators. The difficulty in constructing a balanced scorecard is not in generating enough performance measures, but rather in selecting down to a very small number of centrally important measures.

In this formulation, the balanced scorecard uses measures of financial performance to ensure that the requirements of financiers are addressed. This closely matches the financial management use of accounting information, and may also incorporate some concept of an overall objective. Thus, it would seem that EVA® could quite appropriately be used as one of the financial measures in a balanced scorecard formulation. Interestingly, financial measures may appear in other areas. For example, the proportion of revenue generated by new products is cited as a learning and innovation measure. Clearly, a measure derived from financial components is being used to assess the long-run future prospects of a business unit. In a similar way, customer satisfaction might be assessed by repeat business, again measured by sales revenues. Such an approach perhaps gives greater insight into the development of appropriate accounting performance measures than the more universalistic approaches that accountants have tended to espouse.

Connections between the approaches

Although three major functions of accounting performance measures have been distinguished in the preceding sections, it is also common for any particular accounting measure to be used for more than one of these functions. For example, return on investment may be seen as the peak of the financial effectiveness pyramid of ratios, as a major business objective in its own right, and as a key performance target used to motivate and monitor operating performance.[6]

The most studied accounting technique in this regard has been the process of budgetary control. Although a budget is comprised of a whole set of accounting numbers, the "bottom line" (i.e., either total costs or operating

---

[6] Advocates of EVA would no doubt argue that EVA is an even better measure to use for these purposes.

profit) forms a single performance measure in its own right. Two major functions of budgets have been distinguished. First, a budget can be used as a financial plan, utilized by the finance department to ensure that the organization stays within its operating constraints. Second, it is much more widely used in most organizations as a tool of overall management control. Here budget targets are set for individual responsibility centers and their operating managers, so that operating performance can be monitored and controlled. The aggregate of all the responsibility center budgets becomes the overall operating objective of the organization, expressed in financial terms. The budgeting literature is very clear that budgets can be used for these two, and other, major purposes within an organization. It is equally clear that a single budget system cannot serve all these diverse purposes equally well, and that decisions need to be made as to which purposes should be prioritized.

The most acute conflict is often between the two functions outlined above, where the same budget estimates are used for both financial planning and management control. This often results in neither purpose being adequately served. Financial planning estimates need to be "best estimates" of likely outcomes, or even conservative estimates, given the unpleasant consequences of becoming unexpectedly illiquid. By contrast, management control is often best served by budget estimates being set as motivational targets which are "challenging, yet attainable." In practice, such targets may often fail to be achieved, yet may have served their purpose of motivating maximum managerial effort.

It is of interest to note that some of the more recent literature on budgetary control (see Bunce, Fraser, and Woodcock, 1995) indicates a widespread dissatisfaction by users of traditional budgetary control techniques, because they are seen to be failing as adequate control devices. This is partly because of the levels of uncertainty faced by organizations and the difficulties of making accurate forecasts of future events; the budget is often regarded as being out-of-date even before the budget period has begun. In such organizations, the primary role of budgeting is reverting to that of financial planning, with management control being assisted by a variety of measures of operating performance that are non-financial in nature, perhaps organized using a balanced scorecard framework. In this context, it is also of interest that Stern Stewart's views of budgeting are quite clear; it is a useful financial planning technique, but should not be used as a basis for issuing incentives and rewards.

However, the main point made in this section is still valid. That is, the use made of a particular performance measure should determine its operationalization and measurement. Different uses may require (sometimes subtle) differences in definition, and measurement techniques need to be made robust against likely attempts at manipulation. The framework proposed by Otley (1999) provides one schema against which any system of performance measures used for management control purposes can be assessed.

Conclusions

Financial and accounting measures of performance often appear to have an objectivity, particularly to unsophisticated users, that turns out to be illusory. The components of any accounting ratio, for example, can be defined in a variety of different ways. No way is objectively correct or incorrect, but rather assessments have to be made concerning appropriateness for a specific use. Even when a ratio has been defined in a conceptually appropriate way, there remain issues of measurement. Again, the non-accountant generally has a sense of the objectivity of an accounting measurement that is unsupported in practice. Accounting measures of both cost and profit require a myriad of subjective judgments to be made. For example, the activity-based costing literature is replete with examples of the grossly different cost estimates that are produced by traditional and ABC-based cost accounting systems, which may have led to inappropriate product pricing decisions being made. More recently, the EVA literature has proposed well over 100 accounting adjustments that might be made to convert traditional financial accounting numbers, prepared under GAAP, into the most appropriate numbers to be used in the calculation of EVA, where EVA is to be used as a motivational target for operating managers.

Accounting was once defined, borrowing from a definition of art, as "an attempt to wrest coherence and meaning out of more reality than we ordinarily deal with" (Weick, 1979). Far-fetched as such a comparison may seem, this definition does provide a sense of the complexity of the task undertaken by much accounting measurement. Financial statements provide, within the confines of a few pages of numerical data, an account of the (financial) outcomes of a complex web of activities undertaken over a period of time. When used for management control purposes, the task becomes even more complex, for these accounting measures are intended to help ensure that operating managers will be continually motivated and challenged to exercise their managerial skills in the interests of the overall organization. In such a way, the accounting numbers provide a "window" into the organization which gives an (albeitly imperfect) image of the activities being undertaken and their consequences.

From such a perspective, the management control function clearly requires an amalgam of both financial and non-financial performance measures, and frameworks for integrating these have been proposed (e.g., the balanced scorecard, the European Foundation for Quality Management framework, and so on). However, accounting performance measurements should not be treated as a universal "given", which can be applied in a formulaic manner to any specific situation. Rather, they are like all other performance measures used for a particular purpose. As such, considerable attention needs to be paid to both their conceptual definition and to the methods used in their construction.[7] Thus, accounting performance measures should be neither dismissed nor privileged in the attempt to construct systems of performance management that encourage managers to strive to achieve organizational objectives.

REFERENCES

Bunce, P., Fraser, R., and Woodcock, L. (1995). Advanced budgeting: A journey to advanced management systems. *Management Accounting Research*, **6**, 253–65.

Lev, B. (1989). On the usefulness of earnings and earnings research: Lessons and directions from two decades of empirical research. *Supplement to Journal of Accounting Research*, 153–92.

Otley, D.T. (1999). Performance management: A framework for management control systems research. *Management Accounting Research*, **10**, 363–82.

Weick, K.E. (1979). *The Social Psychology of Organizing*, 2nd edn. London: Addison-Wesley.

[7] Again, the EVA literature provides an excellent case study of how a particular accounting performance measure was adapted and refined from the more basic accounting data found in annual corporate reports.

2 Measuring performance: The marketing perspective

Bruce Clark

Introduction

Assessing marketing performance is an increasingly important task for managers and other corporate stakeholders. First, many firms are looking to provide fresh growth in profit through increasing sales after years of downsizing (Sheth and Sisodia, 1995). Second, multi-disciplinary perspectives on performance measurement, such as the balanced scorecard (Kaplan and Norton, 1992) are increasing the attention given to non-financial measures of performance in general, raising the issue of which marketing measures, if any, should be included in such schemes. Third, investors and analysts are increasingly asking for information on the marketing performance of firms (Haigh, 1998; Mavrinac and Siesfeld, 1997).

Unfortunately, assessing marketing performance is also very difficult to do. Unlike purely internal measures of performance, such as defects per million, marketing performance depends on external, largely uncontrollable actors, such as customers and competitors. Further, it acts as a mediator between these external actors and various internal corporate processes, such as accounting, manufacturing, research and development, and finance. Bonoma and Clark (1988, p. 2) observe that these factors make "marketing's outputs lagged, multivocal, and subject to so many influences that establishing causes-and-effect linkages is difficult."

This contribution is intended to introduce the reader to the long history of measuring the performance of marketing, reviewing representative samples of each research tradition. I begin with a discussion of the marketing productivity paradigm, which dominated much of the first 40 years of work in this area, and move on to illustrate expanded conceptions of marketing outputs and inputs, particularly in the distinction between marketing activities and assets. This expansion, in turn, has led to the development of four important recent measures of the health of an organization's marketing: market orientation, customer satisfaction, customer loyalty, and brand equity. The conclusion of the contribution examines current challenges to the accurate measurement and understanding of marketing performance.

Historical approaches: Marketing productivity

From the earliest studies through the 1970s, the vast majority of work on measuring the performance of marketing looked at marketing productivity. Drawing on earlier work in economics and manufacturing productivity, these efforts typically looked at measuring output per unit of input as a means of assessing marketing's contribution to the success of firms and industries.

Industry-level studies

Early US work in this area (e.g., Twentieth Century Fund, 1939) focused on measuring the productivity of marketing as a whole in the economy. "Marketing" at this point in time was defined as distribution. A goal of these studies was to compare marketing productivity to that of manufacturing, both to gain managerial insight and to answer public policy questions regarding whether distribution made a positive contribution to the economy.

The Twentieth Century Fund (1939) study is a representative example of this type of research. Examining US Census and Internal Revenue Service data, among others, the Fund study concluded that labor productivity of distribution grew far more slowly than manufacturing productivity in the period 1870–1930. They further found that most of the cost of finished goods came from distributive activities, but that distributors themselves remained less profitable than manufacturing firms. Barger's (1955) work confirmed these general findings while examining unit volume shipped per man-hour and gross margins, derived from a broader range of data. Beckman (1961) expanded this approach to cover total-factor productivity (i.e., capital and labor). In the UK, George (1966) examined retail productivity in 160 British towns, finding many moderating factors that explained variance in productivity from town to town.

Bonoma and Clark (1988), in their review of industry-level productivity studies, found that the most common output variables used were, in order of frequency, services provided, dollar sales, units shipped, and value added. The most common input measures were man hours, capital, and number of persons employed. Further, they noted some 17 moderating factors on the input–output relationship, including demographic, economic, and industry-specific variables.

Firm-level studies

While economists have continued examining productivity at the industry level, later marketing work moved the productivity paradigm to the firm level, looking to provide guidance to marketing managers regarding how to most effectively allocate their marketing resources (e.g., advertising, sales force, promotion, product development) to maximize financial return. Work in this area explicitly attempted to integrate finance and accounting perspectives, especially cost accounting, into evaluating the marketing function.

Charles Sevin's *Marketing Productivity Analysis* (1965) is a small master-piece of the marketing productivity literature, spending a little over 100 pages to lay out detailed profitability analysis for products and marketing programs. Feder (1965) borrowed from the microeconomic literature to discuss comparing marginal revenues to marginal costs as a way of better allocating marketing resources. Goodman (1970, 1972) followed in Sevin's footsteps by examining profitability and the return on investment of marketing activities, but made perhaps his most intriguing contribution to the literature in his advocacy of establishing the position of "marketing controller" within firms (Goodman, 1972). At an even more sophisticated level, Buzzell and Chussil (1985) and Day and Fahey (1988) advocate the use of discounted cash flows as a way of calculating the net present value (NPV) of marketing strategies, an approach that continues to be discussed to this day.

Bonoma and Clark (1988) found that the most frequent measures of output in firm-level productivity studies were, in order, profit, sales (unit and value), market share, and cash flow. The most common inputs were marketing expense, investment, and number of employees. They also noted a large number (26) of moderating factors, which they grouped by market, product, customer, and task characteristics.

Non-pecuniary measures of output

From the late 1970s through the late 1980s, there was a move to expand the consideration of output measures from the purely pecuniary to non-monetary measures. Unit market share attracted tremendous attention as an output variable in this period. Work by the Boston Consulting Group (Henderson, 1973) and the Profit Impact of Market Strategies (PIMS) project (Buzzell and

Gale, 1987) concluded that market share was a strong predictor of cash flow and profitability. An especially interesting perspective on market share as a performance measure was taken by Mehrotra (1984) and Hawkins, Best, and Lillis (1987), who advocated weighting unit market share by relative price, on the theory that a given level of market share for a product that commands a price premium is a qualitatively different performance than the same level of market share sold at a discount. Unfortunately, in retrospect the market share–profitability relationship has proven both complicated and controversial (Jacobson, 1988; Szymanski, Bharadwaj, and Varadarajan, 1993), making its use as a performance measure problematic. There is some evidence that the competitive focus market share measures engender can be counterproductive to profitable decision making (Armstrong and Collopy, 1996).

In his elegant exegesis of marketing productivity, Bucklin (1978) is particularly adamant that the quality of services provided must be included in any marketing productivity measure. Rather than consider only the benefit to a customer of using a product, Bucklin attempts to account for the services that add to simple form utility, discussing logistical services (e.g., delivery), informational services (e.g., product information), and product functional services (e.g., warranties, packaging).

A third measure of performance advocated at this time, and receiving continuing attention, is the adaptability or innovativeness of a firm's marketing (Bhargava, Dubelaar, and Ramaswami, 1994; Walker and Ruekert, 1987). Typically cast in terms of the firm's new product or marketing innovations, the idea behind measuring adaptability as an output of marketing is that, in the face of a changing environment, firms unable to adapt will fail (Walker and Ruekert, 1987). Organizations may, for example, measure the percentage of sales accounted for by new products, or the number of successful new product launches in a given period.

Productivity today

Productivity research has continued into the 1990s, typically with more elegant analytic techniques as an aid. Data envelopment analysis has attracted particular attention as a way of mapping different organizations' efficiency at reaching a multi-dimensional performance frontier (e.g., Bhargava, Dubelaar, and Ramaswami, 1994). Sheth and Sisodia (1995) combine several approaches to suggest that true marketing productivity should reflect the amount of *desirable* output per unit of input, a point to which I will return below.

Refocusing on good marketing inputs: activities and assets

In the last 15 years, there has been increasing interest in better specifying "good" marketing inputs, as opposed to continuing to emphasize the productivity paradigm. Partly, this reflects marketing managers' increasing frustration with traditional financial and accounting output measures (e.g., quarterly earnings) that – they believe – under-estimate the long-term value of what marketing does for the firm. Research in this area has focused on two types of marketing inputs: marketing activities and marketing assets. The measure of marketing, by this approach, lies in whether marketing managers engage in appropriate marketing activities and create valuable marketing assets, both of which should lead to improved financial performance in the long term.

One of the earliest performance assessment tools to refocus on inputs is the "marketing audit" (Brownlie, 1993; Rothe, Harvey, and Jackson, 1997). Borrowing from the concept of an accounting audit, the goal of a marketing audit is to systematically evaluate the activities and assets a firm uses in marketing, given the firm's situation. A seminal work in this area is Kotler, Gregor, and Rodgers (1977), who lay out a six-part framework for auditing. They advocate an evaluation of the environment, to understand the situation the firm is in, and then examination of strategy, organization, systems, and productivity of marketing, concluding with examination of specific marketing functions. Rothe, Harvey and Jackson (1997) note that there appear to be many successful case studies of marketing audit use in organizations. However, there is little systematic research indicating how widespread this use is; many components of a marketing audit are logical parts of any marketing planning process, whether the word "audit" is used or not. Even when used explicitly, Brownlie (1996) suggests that audits produce diagnostic suggestions more than they do specific performance numbers.

Bonoma (1985, 1986; Bonoma and Crittenden, 1988) also weighs in on the issue of what constitutes good marketing practices. He focuses on the firm's marketing skills and marketing structures (e.g., systems and procedural support), and argues that good marketing is the product of the interaction between the two.

Finally, there has been recent and continuing attention paid to the notion of developing good marketing assets (Piercy, 1986; Srivastava, Shervani, and Fahey, 1998). Piercy defines an asset as a "value-producing resource" for the firm, and notes marketing assets are generally outside the scope of financial evaluation except as "goodwill" (Piercy, 1986, pp. 9–10). Srivastava, Shervani, and Fahey (1998) suggest that assets can be divided into relational and intellectual assets, the former covering relationships with current external stakeholders (e.g., customers, channels) and the latter covering knowledge the firm has about its environment. The most valuable assets typically take time to develop; if inimitable, they can represent a significant advantage in the marketplace. An asset-based perspective on marketing suggests that good marketing develops good marketing assets, which in turn can be leveraged to generate superior business performance over the long term.

Recent innovations in performance measurement

In the past decade, four concepts have commanded extensive attention as representing good marketing inputs. All, to a varying extent, adopt the perspective that marketing needs to focus less on completing the individual transaction and more on developing long-term relationships with profitable customers. This section briefly reviews each of the following concepts: market orientation, customer satisfaction, customer loyalty, and brand equity.

Market orientation

The market-orientation perspective – also variously described as marketing oriented and market driven (Jaworski and Kohli, 1996; Wrenn, 1997) – suggests that good marketing involves activities that develop and use intelligence about the market. The market knowledge developed should be an important asset to future marketing efforts. While definitions across studies vary (e.g., Day and Nedungadi, 1994; Kohli and Jaworski, 1990; Narver and Slater, 1990), common components of being market oriented include systematic gathering, analysis, dissemination, and use of market information within the organization. Day and Nedungadi (1994) in particular note the importance of maintaining a balanced perspective between customers and competitors in this context.

Empirical evidence on the relationship between overall business performance and market orientation is mixed (Han, Kim, and Srivastava, 1998). Various studies have indicated a positive, mixed, or no relationship at all between the two constructs (Day and Nedungadi, 1994; Diamantopoulos and Hart, 1993; Greenley, 1995; Jaworski and Kohli, 1993; Narver and Slater, 1990). Empirical generalizations on this subject are particularly complicated due to the varying operationalizations of both market orientation and business performance. Some scholars have also explored the role of possible moderating variables in this relationship (Han, Kim, and Srivastava, 1998; Narver and Slater, 1994). Beyond its effect on overall performance, Wrenn (1997) also reviews studies suggesting a host of benefits as perceived by customers and employees.

It is difficult to tell how well the market-orientation practice has penetrated managerial practice, especially as related to the various definitions of particular scholars. Day and Nedungadi (1994) are not encouraging in this regard; only 16 percent of their sample qualified as market-driven by their definition. Many of the market-oriented activities suggested by the measures of orientation used (e.g., "We have interdepartmental meetings at least once a quarter to discuss market trends and developments," Kohli, Jaworski, and Kumar, 1993) may have been adopted by firms in response to the general admonition "pay attention to the market!" As with the marketing audit, these firms may use market-oriented activities without ever letting the words "market-oriented" pass their lips. Some have debated whether market orientation represents a set of behaviors or a culture in this regard (Deshpande and Farley, 1998a; Narver and Slater, 1998).

Customer satisfaction

Perhaps no recent measure of business performance has attracted as much attention as customer satisfaction. With a large and continuing academic research stream (see Halstead, Hartman, and Schmidt, 1994; Yi, 1990 for reviews) and substantial adoption by industry (the 1997 *Marketing News* Customer Satisfaction Research Directory listed over 200 research firms with satisfaction practices), customer satisfaction measures have become important benchmarks in many industries, and have been suggested as plausible measures to include in a balanced scorecard (Kaplan and Norton, 1996).

The basic notion behind customer satisfaction is that customers have expectations about the products and services they buy, and are more or less satisfied depending on how well the consumption experience meets or exceeds those expectations. Having a satisfied customer base is considered an important marketing asset because it should lead to increased loyalty, with its consequent revenue implications – see below – and lower marketing costs. Measurement of satisfaction is typically accomplished by surveys, often extensive, of the customer base.

Unfortunately, the ultimate payoff from satisfaction measures has been uneven. First, at least in North America, most customers are satisfied.

Peterson and Wilson (1992) review a large number of studies where the distribution of customer satisfaction responses is highly skewed towards the positive. In a well-developed economy, this makes sense – poor products do not survive for long, so the remaining products all tend to be at least adequate. This finding presents two problems, however. Managerially, a high satisfaction rating may have little consequence if customers are equally satisfied with competing products; if everyone gets an 85 percent score, then no firm has a competitive advantage. Jones and Sasser (1995) suggest that the impact of an advantage in customer satisfaction will vary dramatically with the competitive nature of the industry. Academically, Peterson and Wilson (1992) observe that the highly skewed distribution reduces the likelihood that a significant correlation between satisfaction and other performance variables will be observed; low variance in the satisfaction measure makes it unlikely that any clear relationship with other variables will be revealed.

Beyond the measurement issues, satisfaction ratings have also proven difficult to implement. Firstly, they are more subject to manipulation than accounting rule-based measures, such as profit. Once customer contact personnel (e.g., salespeople) or organizations (e.g., retailers) know they will be graded on satisfaction, there is a tremendous incentive to manipulate the ratings by such tactics as making sure dissatisfied customers do not receive the survey (Hauser, Simester, and Wernerfelt, 1994). Piercy and Morgan (1995) note that many organizations face substantial obstacles to an effective implementation of a customer satisfaction measurement system.

Finally, empirical research on the disconfirmation-of-expectations paradigm has produced mixed results, leading to multiple competing satisfaction frameworks (e.g., Anderson and Sullivan, 1993; Teas, 1993; Voss, Parasuraman, and Grewal, 1998). Controversy has arisen around the correct measurement of expectations (Teas and Palan, 1997), and whether one must measure multiple aspects of satisfaction with a product, either in terms of multiple processes (Spreng, MacKenzie, and Olshavsky, 1996) or individual product attributes (Donaher and Mattson, 1994; Halstead, Hartman, and Schmidt, 1994).

Customer loyalty

Financially, advocates of loyalty observe, it is not whether customers are satisfied that affects cash flow, it is whether they stay a customer of the firm over time. Reichheld (1994), suggests that good marketing attracts the right customers: ones whose loyalty the firm is able to earn and keep.

A loyal customer base should be an important marketing asset for several reasons (Dick and Basu, 1994). Loyal customers are easier to retain, so marketing costs for these customers should be lower; they should be less likely to search out information on competing products, and more resistant to persuasion efforts by competitors. Given retention, over time firms hope to obtain more business per loyal customer, as the customer's favorable initial impression of the firm leads to a willingness to try other products. Loyal customers may be willing to pay a price premium. Finally, having loyal current customers may reduce the acquisition cost for new customers through positive word-of-mouth.

A common financially based measure of the worth of a loyal customer base is to calculate the "lifetime value" of the customers in this base. Valuing customers in this fashion involves measuring or estimating three things (Wyner, 1996): the revenue generated from a customer in each time period, the cost of serving/retaining that customer in each time period, and the length of the customer's relationship with the firm. Once these three items have been estimated, one can construct cash flows for each customer over time, and, after subtracting the initial cost of acquiring the customer, can discount these cash flows to produce a NPV for each customer. Good marketing should produce customer bases with high lifetime values. Measurement of this kind is clearly useful, but is also difficult to do, especially for small firms or large firms in new businesses for which they have little customer history. This relates to the general point that loyalty research, to some extent, has been better at describing what to do once one has a loyal customer base than it has at describing how to obtain such a base.

Brand equity

Many researchers and managers believe that a powerful brand is among the most important marketing assets a firm can manage (see Barwise, 1993; Keller, 1998 for reviews). Strong brands, it is argued, (1) allow firms to charge price premiums over unbranded or poorly branded products; (2) can be used to extend the company's business into other product categories (e.g., the Ivory brand name, originally used on soap, was extended to introduce Ivory shampoo); and (3) reduce perceived risk to customers (and, perhaps, investors). Good marketing should produce brands with high equity.

The strength of a brand represents its "equity" in the marketplace. Measuring this strength has typically taken two different approaches. The behavioral approach looks at customer response to the brand, either in terms of perceptions or purchases. A representative definition of behaviorally based brand equity is the differential effect of brand knowledge on customer response to marketing of the brand (Keller, 1993). Customers in these studies typically respond more favorably to strong brands than to unbranded or poorly branded products. The financial approach to brand equity attempts to define the financial value of the brand to firms and their investors. A widely cited approach in this area was developed by Simon and Sullivan (1993), who define brand equity as the incremental cash flows that accrue to branded products over and above the cash flows that would result from the sale of unbranded products.

There is little question that brands and brand extensions can make a powerful difference to how customers respond. (Barwise, 1993; Keller, 1998), and growing evidence that brand equity has an influence on investors as well (Aaker and Jacobson, 1994; Simon and Sullivan, 1993). Barwise (1993) notes, however, that we actually know relatively little about the impact of a brand on the branded product's long-term profitability. Clearly it *should* make a difference, but it would help to have more evidence to back the anecdotes in this area. Further, the relationship between the behavioral and financial approaches to brand equity are at present not well-integrated (see Ambler and Barwise, 1998, for a discussion of recent measurement issues). Finally, while brand equity appears a powerful measure of performance, it also is one that is hard to use as a short-term performance measure for managers. It can take years and huge marketing expenses to create a powerful brand; conversely, barring public relations disasters, this asset can take substantial time to dissipate even in the face of reduced marketing support.

Current challenges

Several challenges lie before researchers and managers regarding how to best assess marketing performance. Following are issues that are likely to be important in measuring marketing performance in the future.

Feedback loops

One complicating factor in all performance measures lies in the existence of feedback loops (March and Sutton, 1997). Activities not only create assets and outcomes, but are created by them. Indeed, the point of creating a marketing asset is to then exploit it. At the end of each calendar year, automobile companies in the US regularly grant rebates and discounts to capture the highest volume of sales for the year so that in the next year they can claim they sell "the best-selling car in America." A frequently stated goal of mergers in the financial services industry such as the Citicorp-Travelers Group merger is to create one gigantic customer base to which both partners can cross-sell their products. Further, psychologically, previous success or failure can have profound consequences for further managerial behavior (Miller, 1994). Examining the effect of marketing performance measures on management behavior has been discussed in terms of sales force compensation and economic models (e.g., agency theory, Bergen, Dutta, and Walker, 1992), but feedback effects deserve more general empirical treatment.

Managers and other stakeholders

Related to this point, measures of marketing performance reviewed here have generally been developed by researchers or consultants and then "applied" to the management community. Measures have been curiously free of any consideration of how practicing managers see the performance measurement challenge. Separate research in the US and the UK suggests that, for all the schemes researchers and consultants have developed, managers continue to rely heavily on financial measures in practice (Ambler and Kokkinaki, 1998; Clark, 1998). Further, Clark (1998) suggests that managers seem to apply a version of the customer satisfaction paradigm. They compare their results to their expectations – results that exceed expectations are more satisfying and are seen as better performance. As managerial perceptions drive decisions, understanding the measure–perception link for the many diverse measures reviewed here would be very helpful.

Translating multiple measures into practice

Partly reflecting the different interests of different stakeholders, measures of marketing performance have become increasingly multi-dimensional in nature (e.g., Bhargava, Dubelaar, and Ramaswami, 1994; Dunn, Norburn, and Birley, 1994; Kumar, Stern, and Achrol, 1992). This reflects both theoretical and psychometric perspectives that suggest performance cannot be summarized in a single measure, a standard that applies not only to marketing but to virtually all business performance measures. Managerially, however, a plethora of measures can overwhelm any decision maker (Meyer, 1998). Further, theoretically, many of these measures appear likely to be correlated with one another for either causal or coincident reasons; Selnes (1993), for example, outlines inter-relationships among customer satisfaction, brand reputation, and customer loyalty. While relatively orthogonal constructs can be extracted by multivariate statistical techniques, these techniques seem unlikely to be part of everyday management. More generally, while various scholars have demonstrated reliable objective measures of performance, it is less clear that management is interested in elegant multi-dimensional schemes. Even academic researchers seem to rely on simple, tried and true measures, such as sales, profit, and market share, when using performance as a dependent variable (Ambler and Kokkinaki, 1997). The challenge is to present management and researchers with a handful of measures that are simple enough to be usable, but comprehensive enough to give an accurate performance assessment. Research on reducing the number of measures of marketing performance would be very helpful (e.g., Deshpande and Farley, 1998b).

Unit of analysis

Assuming a reasonable set of measures is available, it will be important to measure performance at different levels of the firm's organization. Notably, many of the early views of measuring marketing performance focused on evaluating the performance of the marketing department or function, but, as Piercy (1997) observes, the marketing department is becoming less important in many firms as market-driven activities become the responsibility of units throughout the organization. Rather than measuring the marketing department, two units of analysis seem likely to be important. First, one should examine marketing performance at the level of marketing programs, which I define as a combination of marketing activities and assets targeted at a particular product market. Second, one should evaluate overall corporate marketing. The combination of these two measures should lead to more effective resource allocation.

Subjective versus objective measures

The debate between using subjective and objective measures of performance remains unresolved. As noted earlier, asking managers their perceptions of performance is probably a better predictor of their future behavior than is a given objective measure. However, these subjective perceptions are likely to be prone to retrospective bias and other attributional phenomena (March and

Sutton, 1997). Published objective measures such as profit are not prone to bias in this fashion, but are the product of reporting rules that may or may not give accurate portraits of performance. The best advice in this area may be to measure both types and try to understand the correlation between the two (Katsikeas and Morgan, 1998)

Reporting issues

Given that one of the units with which we might measure marketing performance is at the corporate level, this raises the issue of whether corporations should engage in more detailed reporting of their marketing activities and assets. If marketing activities and assets do have long-term financial consequences, then it seems logical that investors would want to have information on these marketing dimensions as part of regular reporting by the corporation. Indeed, selected studies have revealed increasing demands by the investment community for non-financial information, such as marketing activities and success (Haigh, 1998; Mavrinac and Siesfeld, 1997). Herremans and Ryans (1995) point out that annual reports in the US typically include far more information on capital expenditures than marketing expenditures. They provide examples of and suggestions for appropriate marketing performance reports in annual reports. The critical questions in this area involve what will be reported regarding marketing to whom, and how compliance will be monitored. Would there be, for example, independent marketing auditors in the way that we now have independent accounting auditors? An additional complication arises as reporting standards diverge across countries; for example, valuations of brands on balance sheets now differ in the US versus the UK.

Stakeholder incompatibility

Beyond investors and managers, one can speak more broadly of the existence of many stakeholder groups who might emphasize differing performance measures. Governments, community groups, and activists, for example, might all demand that firms increase performance on different, possibly incompatible measures. How, then, does one decide which firm performs "the best"?

Efficiency versus effectiveness

A handful of scholars have noted the importance of the distinction between efficiency and effectiveness in marketing performance (Bonoma and Clark,

1988; Drucker, 1974; Sheth and Sisodia, 1995), which I will repeat here. The main point is that any performance measure must take into account the goals and objectives of the decision makers. Efficiency, in Drucker's (1974) definition, is "doing things right," while effectiveness is "doing the right things" to meet the organization's objectives (p. 45). Much of the research I review above is avowedly objective in nature, but managers are subjective creatures, attempting to maximize performance on the measures they deem important. To evaluate their performance on measures about which they do not care is questionable at best. What this means is that research must take into account how well marketing produces the desired outputs of the firm (Sheth and Sisodia, 1995). In turn this means that studies examining performance of multiple firms may (and should) evaluate different firms on different measures.

What to do while we're waiting

Managers will rightfully be impatient with the list of challenges here. Research to resolve these issues will take many years, while managers must decide what to do tomorrow. Following is advice for managers who need to know what to do while waiting for researchers to come up with results.

First, begin systematically collecting data on measures that seem likely to apply to your industry. It is important to move beyond sole reliance on financial measures, such as profit or sales. In many industries, measuring customer satisfaction, *relative to that of competitors*, will be helpful. See Piercy (1997) for advice on doing this correctly. If you believe your brand is an important asset for your company, begin measuring brand awareness and attitude toward the brand as psychological measures of brand equity. Purchase intention measures can give a (probably optimistic) sense of likely customer loyalty in the future. Try some creative sales-based measures, too, for example, market share weighted by relative price (Hawkins, Best, and Lillis, 1987).

Second, track these data to develop leading indicators. The initial measures you take on non-financial metrics are mainly useful as baselines. Once you have good baseline data, typically at least a year's worth, you can start trying to relate non-financial measures to future financial performance. Does brand equity in June, for example, predict sales in December? Examining these leading indicator relationships can both provide forecasting information and suggest problem or opportunity areas.

Finally, develop measures by market segment. Knowing how customer satisfaction, for example, varies across different market segments can provide powerful management insights. Conversely, consider segmenting markets by some of these measures. What, for example, does your loyal customer segment look like when compared to your non-loyal segment?

Progress, confusion, and hope

Marketing as a field has made tremendous progress in aiding better understanding of the "lagged, multivocal" nature of marketing performance, discussed at the beginning of this article. Compared to simple financial measures of marketing, we have far richer and more sophisticated measures of performance. Unfortunately, this richness brings with it confusion as researchers and managers struggle to find a set of measures that is comprehensive enough to be accurate, yet simple enough to be usable. The hope is that the history and challenges outlined here will stimulate further research and practice to make marketing performance measurement better in the future.

REFERENCES

Aaker, D.A. and Jacobson, R. (1994). The financial information content of perceived quality. *Journal of Marketing Research*, **31** (May), 191–201.

Ambler, T. and Barwise, P. (1998). The trouble with brand valuation. *The Journal of Brand Management*, **5**(5) 367–77.

Ambler, T. and Kokkinaki, F. (1997). Measures of marketing success. *Journal of Marketing Management*, **13**, 665–78.

Ambler, T. and Kokkinaki, F. (1998). Marketing performance measurement: Which way is up? In *Performance Measurement – Theory and Practice*, ed. A.D. Neely and D.B. Waggoner, Vol. I, pp. 31–8. Cambridge University, Cambridge: Centre for Business Performance.

Anderson, E.W. and Sullivan, M.W. (1993). The antecedents and consequences of customer satisfaction for firms. *Marketing Science*, **12**(2), 125–43.

Armstrong, J.S. and Collopy, F. (1996). Competitor orientation: Effects of objectives and information on managerial decisions and profitability. *Journal of Marketing Research*, **33** (May), 188–99.

Barger, H. (1955). *Distribution's Place in the American Economy Since 1869*. Princeton, NJ: Princeton University Press.

Barwise, P. (1993). Brand equity: Snark or boojum? *International Journal of Research in Marketing*, **10**, 93–104.

Beckman, T.N. (1961). Measuring productivity in marketing. In *1960 Proceedings of the Business and Economic Section of the American Statistical Association*. Washington, DC: American Statistical Association.

Bergen, M., Dutta, S., and Walker, O.C. (1992). Agency relationships in marketing: A review of the implications and applications of agency and related theories. *Journal of Marketing*, **56**(3), 1–24.

Bhargava, M., Dubelaar, C., and Ramaswami, S. (1994). Reconciling diverse measures of performance: A conceptual framework and test of a methodology. *Journal of Business Research*, **31**, 235–46.

Bonoma, T.V. (1985). *The Marketing Edge: Making Strategies Work.* New York: Free Press.

Bonoma, T.V. (1986). Marketing Subversives. *Harvard Business Review*, **64**(6), 113–18.

Bonoma, T.V. and Clark, B.H. (1988). *Marketing Performance Assessment.* Boston, MA: Harvard Business School Press.

Bonoma, T.V. and Crittenden, V.L. (1988). Toward a model of marketing implementation. *Sloan Management Review*, **29**(2), 7–14.

Brownlie, D. (1993). The marketing audit: A metrology and explanation. *Marketing Intelligence and Planning*, **11**(1), 4–12.

Brownlie, D. (1996). Marketing audits and auditing: Diagnosis through intervention. *Journal of Marketing Management*, **12**, 99–112.

Bucklin, L.P. (1978). *Productivity in Marketing.* Chicago, IL: American Marketing Association.

Buzzell, R.D. and Chussil, M.J. (1985). Managing for tomorrow. *Sloan Management Review*, **26**(4), 3–14.

Buzzell, R.D. and Gale, B.T. (1987). *The PIMS Principles: Linking Strategy to Performance.* New York: Free Press.

Clark, B.H. (1998). Managerial perceptions of marketing performance. Working paper, College of Business Administration, Northeastern University.

Day, G.S. and Fahey, L. (1988). Valuing market strategies. *Journal of Marketing*, **52**(3), 45–57.

Day, G.S. and Nedungadi, P. (1994). Managerial representations of competitive advantage. *Journal of Marketing*, **58** (April), 31–44.

Deshpande, R. and Farley, J. (1998a). The market orientation construct: Correlations, culture, and comprehensiveness. *Journal of Market-Focused Management*, **2**(3), 237–9.

Deshpande, R. and Farley, J. (1998b). Measuring market orientation: Generalization and synthesis. *Journal of Market-Focused Management*, **2**(3), 213–32.

Diamantopoulos, A. and Hart, A.S. (1993). Linking market orientation and company performance: Preliminary work on Kohli and Jaworski's framework. *Journal of Strategic Marketing*, **1**, 93–122.

Dick, A.S. and Basu, K. (1994). Customer loyalty: Toward an integrated conceptual framework. *Journal of the Academy of Marketing Science*, **22**(2), 99–113.

Donaher, P.J. and Mattson, J. (1994). Customer satisfaction during the service delivery process. *European Journal of Marketing*, **28**(5), 5–16.

Drucker, P. (1974). *Management: Tasks, Responsibilities, Practices.* New York: Harper and Row.

Dunn, M.G., Norburn, D. and Birley, S. (1994). The impact of organizational values, goals, and climate on marketing effectiveness. *Journal of Business Research*, **30**, 131–41.

Feder, R.A. (1965). How to measure marketing performance. *Harvard Business Review*, **43**(3), 132–42.

George, K.D. (1966). *Productivity in Distribution*, London: Cambridge University Press.

Goodman, S.J. (1970). *Techniques of Profitability Analysis.* New York: Wiley-Interscience.

Goodman, S.J. (1972). *The Marketing Controller.* New York: AMR International.

Greenley, G.E. (1995). Market orientation and company performance: Empirical evidence from UK companies. *British Journal of Management*, **6** (March), 1–13.

Haigh, D. (1998). The future of brand value reporting. London: Brand Finance Limited.

Halstead, D., Hartman, D. and Schmidt, S.L. (1994). Multisource effects on the satisfaction formation process. *Journal of the Academy of Marketing Science*, **22**(2), 114–29.

Han, J.K., Kim, N., and Srivastava, R.K. (1998). Market orientation and organizational performance: Is innovation a missing link? *Journal of Marketing*, **62**(4), 30–45.

Hauser, J.R., Simester, D.I., and Wernerfelt, B. (1994). Customer satisfaction incentives. *Marketing Science*, **13**(4), 327–50.

Hawkins, D.I., Best, R.J., and Lillis, C.M. (1987). The nature and measurement of marketing productivity in consumer durables industries: A firm level analysis. *Journal of the Academy of Marketing Science*, **15**(4), 1–8.

Henderson, B.D. (1973). The experience curve revisited: IV. The growth share matrix of the product portfolio. Boston: Boston Consulting Group.

Herremans, I.M. and Ryans, J.K. (1995). The case for better measurement and reporting of marketing performance. *Business Horizons*, **38**(5), 51–60.

Jacobson, R. (1988). Distinguishing among competing theories of the market share effect. *Journal of Marketing*, **52**(4), 68–80.

Jaworski, B.J. and Kohli, A.K. (1993). Market orientation: Antecedents and consequences. *Journal of Marketing*, **57**(3), 53–70.

Jaworski, B.J. and Kohli, A.K. (1996). Market orientation: Review, refinement, and roadmap. *Journal of Market-Focused Management*, **1**, 119–35.

Jones, T.O. and Sasser, E.W. (1995). Why satisfied customers defect. *Harvard Business Review*, **73**(6), 88–99.

Kaplan, R.S. and Norton, D.P. (1992). The balanced scorecard – Measures that drive performance. *Harvard Business Review*, **70**(1), 71–9.

Kaplan, R.S. and Norton, D.P. (1996). Using the balanced scorecard as a strategic management system. *Harvard Business Review*, **74**(1), 75–85.

Katsikeas, C.S. and Morgan, N. (1998). Assessing firms' export performance: A literature review and guidelines for future research. Working paper, Cardiff Business School, University of Wales, Cardiff.

Keller, K.L. (1993). Conceptualizing, measuring, and managing customer-based equity. *Journal of Marketing*, **57**(1), 1–22.

Keller, K.L. (1998). *Strategic Brand Management*, Upper Saddle River, NJ: Prentice-Hall.

Kohli, A.K. and Jaworski, B.J. (1990). Market orientation: The construct, research propositions, and managerial implications. *Journal of Marketing*, **54**(2), 1–18.

Kohli, A.K., Jaworski, B.J., and Kumar, A. (1993). MARKOR: A measure of market orientation. *Journal of Marketing Research*, **30** (November), 467–77.

Kotler, P., Gregor, W., and Rodgers, W. (1977). The marketing audit comes of age. *Sloan Management Review*, **18**(2), 25–43.

Kumar, N., Stern, L.W., and Achrol, R.S. (1992). Assessing reseller performance from the perspective of the supplier. *Journal of Marketing Research*, **29** (May), 238–53.

March, J.G. and Sutton, R.I. (1997). Organizational performance as a dependent variable. *Organization Science*, **8**(6), 698–706.

Marketing News Directory of Customer Satisfation Measurement Firms (1997). *Marketing News*, **31**(22).

Mavrinac, S. and Siesfeld, T. (1997). Measures that matter: An exploratory investigation of investors' information needs and value priorities. Working paper, Ivey School of Business, University of Western Ontario, London, ON, Canada.

Mehrotra, S. (1984). How to measure marketing productivity. *Journal of Advertising Research*, **24**(3), 9–15.

Meyer, M.W. (1998). Finding performance: The new discipline in management. In *Performance Measurement – Theory and Practice*, ed. A.D. Neely and D.B., Waggoner, Vol. I, pp. xiv–xxi. Cambridge University, Cambridge: Centre for Business Performance.

Miller, D. (1994). What happens after success: The perils of excellence. *Journal of Management Studies*, **31**(3), 325–58.

Narver, J.C. and Slater, S.F. (1990). The effect of market orientation on business profitability. *Journal of Marketing*, **54**(4), 20–35.

Narver, J.C. and Slater, S.F. (1994). Does competitive environment moderate the market orientation-performance relationship? *Journal of Marketing*, **58**(1), 46–55.

Narver, J. C. and Slater, S. F. (1998). Additional thoughts on the measurement of market orientation: A comment on Deshpande and Farley. *Journal of Market-Focused Management*, **2**(3), 233–6.

Peterson, R.A. and Wilson, W.R. (1992). Measuring customer satisfaction: Fact and artifact. *Journal of the Academy of Marketing Science*, **20**(1), 61–71.

Piercy, N. (1986). Marketing asset accounting: Scope and rationale. *European Journal of Marketing*, **20**(1), 5–15.

Piercy, N. (1997). *Market-Led Strategic Change*. Oxford: Butterworth-Heinemann.

Piercy, N. and Morgan, N. (1995). Customer satisfaction measurement and management: A processual analysis. *Journal of Marketing Management*, **11**, 817–34.

Reichheld, F.F. (1994). Loyalty and the renaissance of marketing. *Marketing Management*, **2**(4), 10–21.

Rothe, J.T., Harvey, M.G., and Jackson, C.E. (1997). The marketing audit: Five decades later. *Journal of Marketing Theory and Practice*, **5** (Summer), 1–16.

Selnes, F. (1993). An examination of the effect of product performance on brand reputation, satisfaction and loyalty. *European Journal of Marketing*, **27**(9), 19–35.

Sevin, C.H. (1965). *Marketing Productivity Analysis*. New York: McGraw-Hill.

Sheth, J.N. and Sisodia, R.S. (1995). Feeling the heat. *Marketing Management*, **4**(2), 8–23.

Simon, C.J. and Sullivan, M.W. (1993). The measurement and determinants of brand equity: A financial approach. *Marketing Science*, **12**(1), 28–52.

Spreng, R.A., MacKenzie, S.B., and Olshavsky, R.W. (1996). A reexamination of the determinants of customer satisfaction. *Journal of Marketing*, **60**(3), 15–32.

Srivastava, R.K., Shervani, T.A., and Fahey, L. (1998). Market-based assets and shareholder value: A framework for analysis. *Journal of Marketing*, **62**(1), 2–18.

Szymanski, D.M., Bharadwaj, S.G., and Varadarajan, P.R. (1993). An analysis of the market share-profitability relationship. *Journal of Marketing*, **57**(3), 1–18.

Teas, R.K. (1993). Expectations, performance evaluation, and consumers' perceptions of quality. *Journal of Marketing*, **57**(4), 18–34.

Teas, R.K. and Palan, K.M. (1997). The realms of scientific meaning framework for construct-
    ing theoretically meaningful nominal definitions of marketing concepts. *Journal of
    Marketing*, **61**(2), 52–67.

Twentieth Century Fund (1939). *Does Distribution Cost Too Much?* New York: The Twentieth
    Century Fund.

Walker, O.C. and Ruekert, R.W. (1987). Marketing's role in the implementation of business
    strategies: A critical review and conceptual framework. *Journal of Marketing*, **51**(3), 15–33.

Wrenn, B. (1997). The market orientation construct: Measurement and scaling issues. *Journal
    of Marketing Theory and Practice*, **5** (Summer), 31–54.

Wyner, G.A. (1996). Customer valuation: Linking behavior and economics. *Marketing
    Research*, **8**(2), 36–8.

Voss, G.B., Parasuraman, A., and Grewal, D. (1998). The roles of price, performance, and
    expectations in determining satisfaction in service exchanges. *Journal of Marketing*, **62**(4),
    46–61.

Yi, Y. (1990). A Critical Review of Customer Satisfaction. In *Review of Marketing 1990*, ed. V.A.
    Zeitham, pp. 68–123. Chicago IL: American Marketing Association.

3 Measuring performance: The operations perspective

Andy Neely and Rob Austin

Background

Interest in performance measurement continues unabated on both sides of the Atlantic. The latest data suggest that somewhere between 40 and 60 percent[1] of large US firms will have adopted the balanced scorecard by the end of 2000 (Frigo and Krumwiede, 1999). All of the major enterprise resource planning software vendors – SAP, PeopleSoft, Baan, and Oracle – are in the process of rolling out their balanced scorecard reporting packages. The UK government continues to release data in the form of performance league tables for a variety of public sector organizations, including schools, hospitals, universities, and police forces. In the eBusiness arena the demand for measures and measurement data is growing. Jamie Lerner, CTO and Chairman of Xuma, an internet start-up, illustrated the challenge eBusinesses face when speaking recently:

> At Christmas we [Xuma] were 50 people. Today [late March] we are 250 people. We are currently recruiting at a rate of 30 or 40 people a week . . . How do you manage an operation that is growing so rapidly and has to deal with customers 24 hours a day, 7 days a week, 365 days a year? How do you measure a software/web site feature's effectiveness, usefulness, value to customers? How do you measure the cost of a web site feature's development and maintenance? How do you measure capacity for an internet business? How do you measure cycle time in an internet business? How do you measure in an environment where time accounting has replaced cost accounting?

This last statement is a particularly important one – "how do you measure in an environment where time accounting has replaced cost accounting." The speed with which businesses are being forced to adapt and change in today's global market places is massive. Increasingly one of the ways that managers appear to be trying to make sense of the turmoil that faces them is through measurement data. There appears to be a perception among managers that "if

[1] The higher figure is the one currently being quoted by GartnerGroup, the US-based research consultancy.

only we could sort out the measures, then we would know what was happening inside our businesses and we could regain control over them and get back to an environment of relative stability." Of course, this is an unrealistic pipe dream, but it is a significant driving force behind management's desire to measure. In fact this desire to measure has become so strong that it is now leading to a new crisis in measurement.

In the early 1980s, influential authors, such as Kaplan (1983, 1984) from the accounting community and Miller and Vollmann (1985) from the operations management community, began to argue that the measures traditionally used by managers were inappropriate given the modern manufacturing environment. Changes in technology and working practices, for example, meant that assigning overheads on the basis of direct labour resulted in wildly erroneous product costs. Well-documented and widely publicised arguments, such as these, heralded recognition of the first measurement crisis – measurement myopia – that in essence stemmed from the fact that we were measuring the wrong things.

In response to these concerns numerous performance measurement frameworks, such as the balanced scorecard (Kaplan and Norton, 1996) and the performance prism (Neely and Adams, 2000), and alternative methods of measurement, such as activity-based costing (Cooper and Kaplan, 1997) and shareholder value analysis (Rappaport, 1998), were proposed. The widespread interest in, and rapid adoption of, these frameworks and methods of measurement resulted in the measurement revolution that Eccles (1991) predicted.

Today, however, a new measurement crisis – measurement madness – is looming. In the 1980s the problem was that the wrong things were being measured. Now the problem is that society is obsessed with measurement. The desire to measure and quantify has become overwhelming. Governments are introducing school league tables and hospitals waiting lists, which take no account of the different contexts within which schools and hospitals operate. International, national, and regional agencies are establishing quality and business excellence awards. Hence the plethora of Baldridge and EFQM (European Foundation for Quality Management) awards that are now being offered. Organizations are seeking to value their intellectual assets, their brands, their innovative potential, in addition to their operating efficiency, their economic profit, and the satisfaction of their employees, customers, and shareholders. Today the old adage "if you can't measure it, you can't manage it" has been taken to a new extreme and in many organizations the result is confusion. When there was a single over-riding indicator, such as profit or return on investment, it was relatively easy for managers to know what they were supposed to achieve, even if they did not know how to achieve it. In these days of multiple measures, all of which are assumed to be equally important, it is no longer clear to many people where the organization's priorities lie. It must be remembered that measurement is merely a means to an end. Measures provide data, which allow progress to be assessed. They do not, and never will, ensure that progress is made. The only way that progress can be made is if action, designed to improve performance, is taken once the measurements have been taken. Measurement data might provide insight into which actions should be taken, assuming the measures are good ones, but in today's society Albert Einstein's message that "not everything that counts can be counted, and not everything that can be counted counts" appears to have been forgotten.

Rather than add yet more confusion and complexity, there is a need to step back from recent developments and reflect upon where the field of performance measurement has been and where it is going. This contribution seeks to do just this, albeit in a very modest way by addressing just two questions. The first is "what do operations managers want from their measurement systems?" and the second is "how have these wants and needs changed over the years?" The main body of the contribution consists of four sections. The first three each take a different time frame, pre-1980, 1980–2000, and post 2000 and explore what operations managers want and need from their measurement systems. Within each of these sections the same structure is adopted. The section begins with a brief review of the business environment during the time period under study. The operations' issues for that time period are then presented. This allows the question – "what do operations managers want from their measurement systems?" to be addressed. Which in turn provides an opportunity to address the final two issues – "how did the operations management academic community react?" and "what was the impact of their research on practice?" The fourth and final section is different from the ones that precede it in that it is more speculative in nature and offers some views on the emerging research needs in the field of performance measurement from an operations management perspective.

The authors contend that this contribution makes three contributions. First it explicitly recognizes the changing nature of the measurement crisis. Second it provides one of the few structure reviews of performance measurement from an operations management perspective. Third it offers some new insights and thoughts into future directions for research.

The past: Pre-1980

In the period immediately following the second world war demand for manufactured goods outstripped supply in the vast majority of industries, with many countries effectively having to rebuild their manufacturing capacity. The dominant management paradigm appeared to be sales, rather than customer, led. Hence the focus was on making a narrow range of products cheaply and then selling them to relatively undemanding customers. Given this context, the role of the operations function became how to manufacture as efficiently as possible. Hence the question that operations managers wanted their measurement systems to help them answer was, "how efficient are we?"

The result was a stream of research on productivity measurement and management (Burgess, 1990; Kendrick, 1984; Sink, 1985). Some authors concentrated on contrasting different dimensions of productivity. Bicheno (1989), for example, explored the different ways in which productivity can be enhanced. Ruch (1982), asked how traditional measures of blue-collar productivity can be used in white-collar environments. A particularly significant stream of literature was that associated with the measurement of total factor productivity. The thesis underpinning this literature was that too often managers rely on partial measures of productivity – e.g., labor productivity. Several authors questioned the veracity of single dimensional measures of productivity on the grounds that they only provide a partial picture of firm performance (Craig and Harris, 1973; Mundel, 1987). In reality the productivity a firm achieves is a function of how efficiently it uses all of its inputs – labour, capital, technology, and energy – to produce outputs (Hayes and Clark, 1986).

While practitioners adopted some of this research, it became increasingly apparent that the operations management academic community had lost its way by the late 1970s. At that time several leading management schools had begun to question whether operations management was a core course and whether it merited a department in its own right. What saved operations management was the resurgence of the Japanese manufacturing industry and the highly vocal and influential papers written by authors, such as Hayes and Abernathy (1980), that argued that much of Japan's economic success was due to their operational efficiency and effectiveness.

The present: 1980s–2000

Throughout the early part of the 1980s there was considerable soul searching in the US and Europe. The question managers and academics were asking themselves was "what underpins the Japanese economic miracle?". Authors, such as Schonberger (1986) and Hall (1983), argued that the operations in Japanese firms were simply better managed. Books appeared that explained the Toyota Production System (Monden, 1996) and the importance of kaizen (Imai, 1986). The rising popularity of the quality gurus, such as Deming and Crosby, resulted in the widespread recognition that the operations function can have a significant impact on product quality (Deming, 1986; Crosby, 1972). As a direct result authors began to ask how can you measure the cost of quality (Crosby, 1972; Feigenbaum, 1961; Plunkett and Dale, 1988). As ever greater numbers of managers recognized the need to change their manufacturing operations and adopt modern manufacturing philosophies, operations management academics began to realize that the traditional measurement systems would have to change (Dixon, Nanni, and Vollmann, 1990).

At the same time Skinner's work on manufacturing strategy was gaining in popularity (Skinner, 1969). In both the US and UK, conferences devoted to the topic were held in the early 1980s. One of Skinner's core arguments was that operations managers had to focus and decide whether to compete on the basis of quality or time or cost or flexibility. Naturally enough, people then began asking for clarity about the definitions of these dimensions of manufacturing performance and suggestions as to how they could be measured. Hence the stream of literature associated with quality, time, cost, and flexibility (Garvin, 1987; Stalk, 1988; Gerwin, 1987; Slack, 1983).

Underpinning all of this activity was a growing recognition that operations had a strategic role to play in organizations. Suddenly operations managers were interested in understanding whether the operation they managed was achieving appropriate levels of performance. This question sparked a significant stream of research and literature associated with benchmarking. Camp (1989), who described how benchmarking had helped Xerox realize how much it had to improve, popularized the concept. Academics, such as Womack, Jones, and Roos (1990), and others picked up on this theme and began to search for more academically rigorous ways of comparing operational performance. Subsequently international comparative studies of operations performance have blossomed (Delbridge, Lowe, and Oliver, 1995; Hanson and Voss, 1995; New and Szwejczewski, 1995).

Despite all of the apparent activity, however, the impact on management practice of much of this research was limited. While the frameworks developed and the lessons learned have been integrated into teaching programmes around the world, it appears that many of the academic developments have lagged rather than led practice. Tools, techniques, and management philosophies, such as kanban, kaizen, benchmarking, and lean manufacturing, were developed by practitioners and then documented by academics. In the measurement field specifically, academics made contributions, but the impact of them on practice – with the notably exception of the balanced scorecard – was relatively limited.

The future: 2000 and beyond

In recent months the pace of change appears to have stepped up a gear. The week commencing 6 March 2000 was a fairly typical one given today's economic environment. On Monday the Bank of Scotland announced plans to extend their online banking services, "Whereonearth.com" was reported to be preparing for a £250 million flotation, and new survey data suggested that online shopping was taking off more rapidly through interactive television than the computer. On Tuesday NTL and Alta Vista announced that they were planning to offer free Internet access in the UK and Pearson and AOL unveiled plans to develop an online education network. On Wednesday a new generation of high-tech dot.coms, such as Freeserve, ousted nine brick and mortar businesses from the FTSE 100, including Thames Water, Scottish & Newcastle, and Hanson. On Thursday BT announced that it was going to reduce phone line rates for people accessing the Internet and Gordon Brown, the UK Chancellor, warned investors yet again that the dot.com bubble was unstable and that technology stocks were over-valued. While on Friday it emerged that a week before its floatation, the "lastminute.com" share offer was already oversubscribed by a factor of 10.

Businesses in the new economy are growing incredibly rapidly. From opening its virtual doors in July 1995, Amazon.com has moved from being a gleam in Jeff Bezos' eye to one of the world's largest bookstores. Now Amazon.com has decided that it wants to be the Wal-Mart of the Internet. By June 1999, the company had built a customer base consisting of more than 10 million people. But, during the 1999 financial year, the business made a loss of more than 300 million dollars. And yet still the investment community values Amazon.com at a staggering 21 200 million dollars, giving it a market capitalization that is more than 20 times that of its rivals Borders or Barnes and Noble.

In the more traditional brick and mortar sector, businesses are facing unprecedented pressure. New competitors are entering markets on almost a daily basis. Globalization and internationalization offer significant challenges. Partnerships and alliances are becoming increasingly important. As far as measurement is concerned operations managers still want to be able to establish whether their operation is performing efficiently and effectively in terms of quality, speed, dependability, flexibility, and cost. Today, however, they also want to be able to track the relationships upon which their operations are intimately dependent. As organizations continue to outsource non-core activities and continue to establish joint ventures and alliances, those with operational responsibility for ensuring that customers still receive great service from autonomous operations need information on inter- and intra-organizational performance.

A second significant development is in the way that operations managers are seeking, or should be seeking to use their measurement data. In the last few years of the twentieth century numerous operations adopted enterprise resource planning (ERP) systems, such as SAP, PeopleSoft, Oracle, and Baan. The systems provide operations managers with unparalleled access to data. In fact in many operations the problem is data overload. The ERP systems provide operations managers with the potential to access significant volumes of data and hence one of the skills that operations managers will have to develop is how to analyze and summarize key data, rather than track everything they are able to.

Thoughts for the future

It seems that the challenges for the academic community in terms of performance measurement have never been greater. Organizations the world over have adopted the balanced scorecard as a way improving their measurement systems. Yet even those who claim to have fully adopted the balanced scorecard still report that while it is an improvement on the measurement systems they had before, it is still barely adequate for their needs (Frigo and Krumwiede, 1999). Why is this? Well there are multiple reasons, but a significant one has to do with the pace of change in organizations. Take, for example, the dot.coms. In businesses that are doubling in size every few months and constantly changing their strategies the notion of a balanced scorecard and a monthly reporting system is an anathema. Managers in dot.coms would be more interested in a measurement system that provides them data like a newspaper provides news coverage. As new information becomes available the organization needs to process it, analyze it, and disseminate it. Gone are the days when managers are willing to wait until a couple of weeks after the month end for their performance reports. Today they want them online and up to date.

Within the operations function specifically there is still a tendency to measure those things that are easy to measure. As one senior operations manager commented to one of the authors recently – "we measure everything that walks and moves, but nothing that matters." Developing measures that really reflect what matters in the operation is crucial. Matching the measures to the organizations business processes and, particularly in service operations, to the moments of truth or customer touch-points is vital. Exploring how to use the data more fully is another area that is ripe for research. Too often managers in organizations are faced with spreadsheets full of numbers that are effectively meaningless. Nobody within the operation appears to understand why performance has improved, or got worse; nobody understands the root causes of good and/or bad performance; and all too frequently nobody has the necessary technical and managerial skills to complete the analysis necessary for the root causes to be identified.

Still within organizations the vast majority of measures are historical or backward looking. Within manufacturing operations we have been able to apply statistical process control to machining operations. Effectively statistical process control provides a means of predicting whether or not a process is going out of control. Could the same technology be applied to business processes? Can measurement data be used to identify when business processes are about to go out of control?

Overall the measurement research agenda is a full one. Increasingly it is becoming apparent that measurement is a multi-functional discipline. Academics specializing in operations management will naturally be interested in developing measures for operations and, while there will always be a need for functionally specific measures, there is also a need for cross-disciplinary work, especially that associated with the design, implementation, and use of measurement data. The specifics of what to measure may depend upon one's functional perspective, but the challenges associated with measurement are the same whether one is seeking to measure operational, marketing, or employee performance.

REFERENCES

Bicheno, J. (1989). Exploring productivity accounting for management and strategy in manufacturing and services. *International Journal of Operations and Production Management,* **9**(5), 56–68.

Burgess, T.F. (1990). A review of productivity. Work Study, January/February, pp. 6–9.

Camp, R.C. (1989). *Benchmarking – The Search for Industry Best Practices that Lead to Superior Performance.* Milwaukee, WI: ASQS Quality Press.

Cooper, R. and Kaplan, R.S. (1997). *Cost and Effect – Using Integrated Cost Systems to Drive Profitability and Performance.* Boston, MA: Harvard Business School Press.

Craig, C.E. and Harris, C.R. (1973). Total productivity measurement at the firm level. *Sloan Management Review,* **14**(3), 13–29.

Crosby, P.B. (1972). *Quality is Free.* New York: McGraw-Hill.

Delbridge, R. Lowe, J., and Oliver, N. (1995). The process of benchmarking: A study from the automotive industry. *International Journal of Operations & Production Management,* **15**(4), 50–62.

Deming, W.E. (1986). *Out of the Crisis.* Cambridge, HA: MIT.

Dixon, J.R., Nanni, A.J. and Vollmann, T.E. (1990). *The New Performance Challenge – Measuring Operations for World-Class Competition.* Homewood, IL: Dow Jones-Irwin.

Eccles, R.G. (1991). The performance measurement manifesto. *Harvard Business Review,* January–February, 131–7.

Feigenbaum, A.V. (1961). *Total Quality Control.* New York: McGraw Hill.

Frigo, M.L. and Krumwiede, K.R. (1999). Balanced scorecards: A rising trend in strategic performance measurement. *Journal of Strategic Performance Measurement,* **3**(1), 42–4.

Garvin, D.A. (1987). Competing on the eight dimensions of quality. *Harvard Business Review,* November–December, 101–09.

Gerwin, D. (1987). An agenda for research on the flexibility of manufacturing processes. *International Journal of Operations and Production Management,* **7**(1), 38–49.

Hall, R. (1983). *Zero Inventories.* Homewood, IL: Business One/Irwin.

Hanson, P. and Voss C. (1995). Benchmarking best practice in European manufacturing sites. *Business Process Engineering and Management Journal,* **1**(1), 60–74.

Hayes, R.H. and Abernathy, W.J. (1980). Managing our way to economic decline. *Harvard Business Review,* July–August, 67–77.

Hayes, R.H. and Clark, K.B. (1986). Why some factories are more productive than others. *Harvard Business Review,* September–October, 66–73.

Imai, M. (1986). *Kaizen: The Key to Japan's Competitive Success.* New York: McGraw Hill.

Kaplan, R. (1983). Measuring manufacturing performance – a new challenge for managerial accounting research. *The Accounting Review,* **58**(4), 686–705.

Kaplan, R.S. (1984). Yesterday's accounting undermines production. *Harvard Business Review,* **62**, 95–101.

Kaplan, R.S. and Norton, D. P. (1996). *The Balanced Scorecard – Translating Strategy into Action.* Boston, MA: Harvard Business School Press.

Kendrick, J.W. (1984). *Improving Company Productivity: Handbook with Case Studies.* Baltimore, MD: John Hopkins University Press.

Miller, J.G. and Vollmann, T.E. (1985). The hidden factory. *Harvard Business Review,* September–October, 142–50.

Monden, Y. (1996). *The Toyota Management System: Linking the Seven Key Functional Areas.* Cambridge, MA: Productivity Press.

Mundel, M. (1987). *Measuring Total Productivity of Manufacturing Organizations.* White Plains, NY: Unipub – Kraus International.

Neely, A.D. and Adams, C. (2000). Perspectives on performance: The performance prism. Centre for Business Performance.

New, C. and Szwejczewski, M. (1995). Performance measurement and the focussed factory: Empirical evidence. *International Journal of Operations & Production Management.* 15(4), 63–79.

Plunkett, J.J. and Dale, B.G. (1988). Quality costs: A critique of some economic cost of quality models. *International Journal of Production Research*, 26(11), 1713–26.

Rappaport, A. (1998). *Creating Shareholder Value: The New Standard for Business Performance.* New York: Free Press.

Ruch, W.A. (1982). The Measurement of white-collar productivity. *National Productivity Review*, Autumn, 22–8.

Schonberger, R.J. (1986). *World Class Manufacturing: The Lessons of Simplicity Applied.* New York: Free Press.

Sink, D.S. (1985). *Productivity Measurement – Planning, Measurement and Evaluation, Control and Improvement.* Chichester, John Wiley and Sons.

Skinner, W. (1969). Manufacturing – missing link in corporate strategy. *Harvard Business Review*, May-June, 136–45.

Slack, N. (1983). Flexibility as a manufacturing objective. *International Journal of Operations and Production Management*, 3(3), 4–13.

Stalk, G. (1988). Time – the next source of competitive advantage. *Harvard Business Review*, July–August, 41–51.

Womack, J.P., Jones, D.T., and Roos, D. (1990). *The Machine that Changed the World.* New York: Rawson Associates.

Finding performance: The new discipline in management

Marshall W. Meyer

Introduction

Performance is not an easy subject. There is clearly a need to study and rethink what is meant by the performance of the firm and how to measure it. Performance has become the mantra of the 1990s. Many firms claim to be running for performance and seek to measure their performance, improve performance, and compensate their people for performance. Yet, at the same time, there is widespread dissatisfaction with most performance measurement systems. Many firms, perhaps the majority, feel that they have not got it right. A 1995 article in *Chief Financial Officer* (CFO) begins, "According to a recent survey, 80 percent of large American companies want to change their performance measurement systems." The high level of dissatisfaction is sometimes attributed to the dearth of non-financial predictors of financial performance: "Yesterday's accounting results say nothing about the factors that actually help grow market share and profits – things like customer service innovation, R&D effectiveness, the percent of first-time quality, and employee development (Birchard, 1995)." At the same time, according to another article in *CFO*, controllers cite the burdens imposed by "newfangled performance measures," i.e., non-financial measures, as a key source of burnout *CFO* (Goff, 1995). Reports like these, though anecdotal, suggest that executives are seeking measures that their controllers have so far been reluctant to deliver, leading to frustration on both sides.

Somewhat better evidence on the quality of measures comes from several surveys conducted by the cost management group of the Institute of Management Accountants (IMA) beginning in 1992 (IMA, 1993, 1995, 1996). The coverage of the IMA surveys has increased over time. The 1992 survey covered 350 large US companies, but the 1996 survey included some 1300 companies ranging in size from approximately $1 million to more than $10 billion in sales – clearly, many more small firms than large firms are represented in the IMA data. Most of IMA's informants are accountants, controllers, comptrollers, and the like, although some are line officers. The bulk of the items in the IMA surveys asked companies what measures they now use and anticipate using in the future. In the 1992 survey, 50 percent of companies reported using non-financial measures, whereas 66 percent of companies used non-financial measures in 1996. However, in 1992, 1993, 1995, and 1996 – there was no 1994 survey – 90 percent or more of the companies indicated that even greater use of non-financial measures would be desirable. Beginning in 1995, the IMA also asked companies whether they were measuring economic value added and whether they intended to implement EVA at some future time. In 1995, 18 percent of companies were using EVA and another 27 percent were planning to use EVA. By 1996, 34 percent of companies actually used EVA and another 45 percent anticipated using EVA.

Given their preferences for greater use of non-financial measures and their plans to implement metrics like EVA, it is not surprising that measurement systems are changing more rapidly than even a few years ago. One of the key items in the IMA survey asked informants whether they had been involved in changing their company's performance measurement system. The proportion of managers responding affirmatively increased from 35 percent in 1992 to 56 percent in 1993, 64 percent in 1995, and 63 percent in 1996. (An item unique to the 1996 survey also asked managers to indicate whether they were under-taking "a major overhaul" of their current measures or replacing their entire performance measurement system. Sixty percent said they were.) What is sur-prising, however, is that many informants found that even the new measures did not adequately support the objectives of top management. The propor-tion of managers stating that their measurement system supported manage-ment objectives "less than adequately" or "poorly" rose unevenly in this period, moving from 35 percent in 1992 to 43 percent in 1993, 38 percent in 1995, and 43 percent in 1996. These changes are small and do not necessarily reflect a trend. But they suggest that, while people are changing their perfor-mance measures rapidly, they do not experience these changes as improve-ments.

In a world of perfect measurement, managers would be able to design optimal performance measurement systems. The measures chosen would meet the following requirements – note that I am not saying what the meas-ures would be, only what the measures would look like:

1 There would be relatively few measures to keep track of, perhaps as few as three financial measures and three non-financial measures. This is a matter of parsimony. If there are too many measures, cognitive limits will be exceeded and information will be lost.

2 The non-financial measures would predict subsequent financial performance, in other words, the non-financials would serve as leading performance indicators (and the financials as lagging indicators). Non-financials not demonstrated to be leading indicators would be sidelined unless, of course, they were tracked as matters of compliance, ethics, and security – "must-dos" for firms.

3 These measures would pervade the organization – the same measures would apply everywhere. Measures pervading the organization can be summed from the bottom to the top of the organization and decomposed downward, the latter giving managers drill-down capability. Measures pervading the organization, moreover, permit performance to be compared across units.

4 The measurement system would be stable. Measures would evolve slowly so as to maintain people's awareness of long-term goals and consistency in their behavior.

5 People would be compensated for performance on these measures, that is, for performance on both financial measures and the non-financial measures known to be leading indicators of financial results.

I wish I could recommend specific measures meeting these requirements. But I cannot. Such a measurement system, to the best of my knowledge, does not exist and probably will not exist. Here is why:

1 Firms are swamped with measures, and the problem of too many measures if anything is getting worse. It is commonplace for firms to have 50 to 60 top-level measures, both financial and non-financial. The longest list of top-level measures I have seen contains 117 measures – 17 financial measures, 17 customer measures, 19 measures of internal process, 35 measures of renewal and development, and 26 human resources measures.[1] Many firms, I am sure, have even more top-level measures.

2 Our ability to create and disseminate measures has outpaced, at least for now, our ability to separate the few non-financial measures containing information about future financial performance from the many that do not. Some non-financial measures, such as customer satisfaction properly measured, have been shown to predict financial performance (Anderson, Fornell, and Lehmann, 1994) but the jury is still out on most measures.

3 It is very difficult to find non-financial measures that both predict financial performance and pervade the organization. It is somewhat easier to find

---

[1] The full list of 117 measures is currently used by Skania, the Swedish financial services firm. See Edvinsson and Malone (1997).

financial measures that pervade the organization, but keep in mind that firms still struggle to drive measures of shareholder value from the top to the bottom of the organization.

4 Performance measures, non-financial measures especially, never stand still. With use they lose variance, sometimes rapidly, and hence the capacity to discriminate good from bad performance. This is the use-it-and-lose-it principle in performance measurement. The result is a continual shuffling of measures.

5 Compensating people for performance on multiple measures is extremely difficult. Paying people on a single measure creates enough dysfunctions, and paying them on many measures creates many more. The problem is combining multiple and often disparate measures into an overall evaluation of performance and hence compensation. If measures are combined formulaically, people will game the formula. If measures are combined subjectively, people will not understand the connection between measured performance and their compensation.

Here is the nub of my argument: the dissatisfaction people experience with current measures and their yearning for better measures can be traced to an underlying but unrecognized cause. Superficially, the problem is measurement, and the solution is better measures. The measurement problem arises because the performance of the firm is not entirely measurable. Firm performance is ultimately future cash flows – "cash flows still to come" – discounted to present value. Future cash flows cannot, by definition, be measured. What we can and do measure are past cash flows (financial performance), which can be used as possible predictors or proxies of future cash flows (share prices). All of these are imperfect measures, second-best measures in my terminology. The measurement problem is one of finding the best of these second-best measures, sometimes through analysis, sometimes through intuition. But I do not think measurement is the nub of problem. If measurement was the problem, then managers should be getting happier as their measures become more refined. Instead, they are getting more frustrated.

The more fundamental problem is that we are stuck with an archaic conception of the firm and where to look for performance. We think of firms mainly as black boxes. Investment flows into the box, activities take place inside but out of sight, products are made and sold to customers as results of these activities, and an income statement, balance sheet, and market valuation of the firm follow. Since financial results – the income statement, balance sheet, and market valuation – are reported for the firm as a whole or, internally, for large chunks of the firm called business units, we try to find measures describing the internal processes, products, and customers of the firm or large chunks of it. These aggregate measures conceal important sources of variation within the firm. The things a firm does well are lumped together with the things it does poorly. Critical information about performance is obscured.

To recover this information, to make the performance of the firm transparent, we must return to an elemental conception of the firm and what it does. Think of a firm as a bundle of activities, nothing more. These activities incur costs. These activities may also add value for the customer, although they may not. When activities add value for the customer, the customer supplies revenues to the firm. When activities do not add value, the customer holds on to his wallet. The elements of the firm, then, are activities, costs, customers (who decide which activities add value and which do not), and revenues. The problem for the firm is finding those activities that add value for the customer and generate revenues in excess of costs, extending those activities, and reducing or eliminating activities that incur only costs. Finding performance is the issue of this contribution. Finding the right performance measures is a trivial task, although actually measuring performance, as will be seen, is not.

How did I come to the conclusion that an elemental conception of the firm is needed, that the problem is finding the activities the firm performs to add value for the customer and to generate revenues in excess of costs rather than finding better firm-level performance measures? I came to this conclusion mainly by struggling with anomalies, things that did not make sense. A few of these anomalies bear mentioning. One anomaly was definitional. Look in the *Oxford English Dictionary* (*OED*) under performance as I did. You will find nothing about organizational performance. Performance is theatrical, mechanical, or psychological. Performance, according to the *OED*, is what people or machines do. It is a functioning, not an economic result.[2] Other anomalies were empirical. Performance measures for firms are generally uncorrelated – this has been known for years. This means that measurement is poor, raising the question of why firms pursuing performance would tolerate poor measurement, particularly when people's compensation depends on measured performance. Still other anomalies were in the response of the academic and business communities to my earlier work. Whenever I attacked existing performance measures, I was received warmly, but I was attacked whenever I suggested ways to improve current performance measures – with one exception. The exception occurred when I suggested that activity-based

---

[2] Readers are more likely to have access to the dictionary in Microsoft Bookshelf® than the *OED*. They will find roughly the same definitions of performance, and organizational performance is not mentioned.

costing (ABC) could be turned on its head to identify the drivers of revenues. This upending of ABC is called activity-based revenue or ABR below. Part of the appeal of ABR is its familiarity – it is, after all, based in ABC, an established technique – but part of the appeal of ABR lies in the way it reduces the firm to activities, and the costs, customers, and revenues associated with them. Reductionism is an established principle in science. Modern science reduces complex phenomena to simpler elements in order to aid understanding and to better control them. The message I heard was that it is now time to apply reductionist principles to the management of firms and the measurement of their performance in particular.

Modern performance measurement joins the dictionary definitions of performance and the prevailing definition of economic performance. The dictionary definition of performance, again, is the act of performing; what people, machines, or, for that matter, firms do. The economic definition of performance is future revenues discounted to present value. *Modern performance measurement searches for what firms do that generates revenues in excess of costs.* But, having bridged the dictionary and economic definitions of performance, modern performance measurement has gone awry because it remains firm-centric. Firm-centric measurement treats the firm as a single entity and attempts to measure both the financial and non-financial performance at the level of the firm. It starts, in other words, with the firm and its financial results, asks how the functioning of the firm affects these results, and then searches for the right measures of the functioning of the firm, that is, the right non-financial measures. This approach, I believe, is inherently flawed because the right non-financial measures are hard to find and are always in dispute – recall the unhappiness managers experience with their measures. Activity-centric performance measurement, by contrast, decomposes the firm into the activities it performs and then identifies the costs incurred and revenues generated by each of these activities. Activity costs can be measured directly, and the revenues generated by activities can be measured indirectly provided that the activities performed for each customer and the revenues contributed by each customer are known. The principle difference between the firm-centric and activity-centric performance measurement, then, lies in the unit that is assumed to perform, the firm versus the activity.[3]

---

[3] Some will argue that there is a market-centric view of performance as well because it is desirable to drive market-like measures into the firm. But I think not. The firm and the activity are *units on which performance is measured.* Financial markets value firms and such valuations may or not be useful indicators of the performance of the firm depending on their purpose.

The implications of this difference for the quality of performance measures are profound. Firm-centric performance measurement measures everything. It creates a panoply of non-financial measures that may or may not contain information about the performance of the firm. There is no way to know without conducting elaborate statistical tests, which as often as not are inconclusive. Activity-centric performance, by contrast, requires a inventory of the activities performed by a firm, measurement of the costs incurred and revenues generated by each of these activities, and maintenance of these measures. Creating an activity inventory, measuring costs and revenues associated with activities, and maintaining measures are daunting tasks, to be sure, but activity-centric performance measurement has the advantage of making the financial results of activities transparent. Activity-centric performance measurement thus avoids the problems created by a myriad of non-financial measures whose relevance to the bottom line is always in doubt.

My research on performance measures has identified some additional reasons why firm-centric performance measurement is so frustrating to managers. One source of frustration is that firm-centric measures never stand still. They are always in turmoil. A key source of this turmoil lies in a phenomenon I call the running down of performance measures. Almost all measures lose variance and hence the capacity to discriminate good from bad performance as they are used. This triggers an on-going search for new and different measures. Elsewhere, I illustrate running down, drawing on examples from major league baseball (specifically, batting averages), health care, nuclear power, commercial banking, mutual funds, and the J.D. Powers ratings of the quality of new cars (Meyer and Gupta, 1994). I also identify several causes of diminished variance in performance outcomes, among them positive learning (improvement), perverse learning or gaming (learning how to meet the measure without improving the performance that is sought), selection (replacing low performers with high performers), and suppression (withholding performance data when differences persist). While the causes of running down are different and often indistinguishable, the effects of running down are consistent, principally the on-going pursuit of new and different measures. There is, in other words, a use-it-and-lose-it principle in performance measurement: the longer a measure is used and the more intensely it is applied, the less information it yields and the more urgent it becomes to find new measures.

Another source of frustration with firm-centric measurement is that it makes it very difficult to compensate people for measured performance. Many businesses have tried to pay their people using a combination of financial and non-financial measures suggested by the "balanced scorecard." The Western region of a firm I call Global Financial Services (GFS) tried to compensate its people on both financial and non-financial measures from 1993 through 1996. GFS's initial approach to balanced compensation made use of a formula assigning explicit weights to various financial and non-financial measures. The intent was to place financial and non-financial performance on equal footings. But there were unanticipated consequences. People learned how to game the formula and earn substantial bonuses without delivering bottom-line results – they were writing their own bonus checks. In response, GFS's management attempted to restore balance by adding contingencies that made bonus payouts dependent on meeting certain financial and customer satisfaction hurdles. This complicated the bonus formula and made it very difficult to communicate. GFS then switched to a compensation system where financial and non-financial measures were weighted subjectively. Again, there were unanticipated consequences. Absent fixed weights, combining performance on different measures into an overall performance evaluation and a bonus payout was extremely time consuming. People were nonetheless dissatisfied with the compensation system because they could not understand how they were being paid and whether they were being paid on the right measures. (It turns out they were paid on the wrong non-financial measures.) Moreover, despite the rhetoric of balance, little balance between financial and non-financial measures remained after several quarters of trying to weight financial and non-financial measures subjectively. Instead, overall performance evaluations and compensation were increasingly determined by financial results, precisely the outcome GFS had sought to avoid (Ittner, Larcker, and Meyer, 1997).

Activity-centric performance measurement starts from activity-based costing. A cardinal principle of ABC is this: if products or services are made to specifications known to add value for the customer, then activities, and hence costs, that can be removed without compromising these specifications are unnecessary and should be removed. This principle is responsible for many of the productivity improvements that have occurred in manufacturing. I then ask the following question: can performance be improved in complex service settings where the specifications adding value for the customer are not known, or, more precisely, where the activities incurring costs cannot be easily separated from the specifications adding value? (Consider, for example, an airline journey where the relative contribution to customer value of the cabin attendant's smile, the quality of the peanuts, and an on-time arrival are not known.) Two studies I have conducted are germane to the problem. The first study compares a local competitor with Global Financial

Services' retail operations in an Asian city. The local competitor succeeds by setting rigid specifications for customer service – customers' preferences are known, and the service specifications are surrogates for revenue drivers – and then removing unnecessary costs relentlessly. GFS, however, cannot imitate the strategy of standardizing service and removing costs because it is a global firm whose customers have different requirements. The second study reports the results of GFS's search for analytical method to separate cost drivers from revenue drivers. The search originated in an ABC project in Latin America that nearly backfired because the cost-cutting recommendations made by the ABC team would have damaged the business if implemented. Rather than abandoning ABC, however, GFS transformed ABC into activity-based revenue or ABR, a tool capable of estimating the revenue consequences of customer transactions.

In the short space allowed for this contribution, I cannot fully describe the implementation of ABR, nor can I illustrate the underlying concepts with graphics given the space limitation of this contribution, but some of the basics can be sketched. First, transaction counters recorded in real time virtually all financial and non-financial customer transactions, including among the latter balance inquiries, requests for documents, and the like. The counters recorded virtually all transactions taking place between each customer and the GFS organization. Overall, more than 400 types of transactions were tracked for more than 100 000 customers. Second, activity-based costing was done throughout the GFS organization that was the subject of this study. Costs were identified at four levels: short-term variable, long-term variable, capacity, and fixed costs. The first three categories of costs accounted for about 65 per cent of the organization's total expenditures. The unit cost of each type of transaction was then computed based on the activities involved in the transaction initiated by the customer and the support transactions incident to it – note that there was no one-to-one correspondence of activities with transactions. Third, the revenues contributed by each customer were also recorded in real time. The three kinds of data available for each customer, then, were transaction frequencies by type, transaction costs, and revenues. These data were reported monthly. In principle, it is a fairly simple matter to estimate both the short- and long-term revenues attributable to each transaction. Since transaction costs are known, the short- and long-term profitability of each transaction can be estimated as well. (This implementation of ABR is really transaction-centric rather than activity-centric, but keep in mind that all transactions are supersets of activities.)

The implications of ABR for compensation of individual performance and the design of the firm are substantial. First, ABR drives individual accountability for results much deeper into the organization than firm-centric measurement. Some of the thorniest issues surrounding compensation disappear, although other issues remain. Second, as accountability is driven deeper into the organization, some of the classic dilemmas of organizational design recede in significance. Indeed, ABR renders individual accountability independent of organizational design. The result is that functional stovepipes that in the past have had to sacrifice accountability in order to achieve scale economies become more advantageous. The scale at which firms can operate effectively may be enhanced by ABR. ABR also blurs the distinction between the human resources and marketing functions because the two share data bases and methodologies – revenues at the activity (or transaction) level are estimated by modeling the revenue contributed by each customer as a function of the frequency of activities (or transactions) performed for that customer. ABR has substantial limitations of course. It is most useful when many products are supplied to many customers and the product specifications adding value for customers are not understood, in other words, in complex service firms engaged in mass customization. ABR adds little where product specifications exist and are known to add value for customers, for example, in mass production (such as, DRAMs, where the critical specifications are capacity, reliability, and speed). And ABR is not feasible where a wide range of products is supplied to a small group of customers, which would exhaust the degrees of freedom in revenue equations.

Considerable discipline is needed to implement activity-centric performance measurement and ABR in particular. The impetus for activity-centric performance measurement and ABR usually comes from experience with customers at both ends of the spectrum. Firms often find that their largest customers are among their most profitable and their least profitable customers – the largest customers can be highly profitable because of the volumes involved, but they can be highly unprofitable because they negotiate the best prices and then consume inordinate amounts of the firm's resources (Kaplan and Cooper, 1997). And firms seeking to grow by adding small customers must understand their costs and the relationship of revenues to costs for these customers or risk massive losses. The resistance to activity-centric performance measurement and ABR comes from accountants and financial controllers who find the approach unduly complex and imprecise, which, like any innovation, is true of its formative stages. My experience has been that this resistance can be overcome by asking one question: "What is the alternative once all the low-hanging fruit has been picked, once conventional cost control methods have been exhausted?" So far, no one has had an alternative.

A reprise: I began by echoing the complaints people have about performance measures. These complaints are deeply felt. New and more refined firm-centric measures will not relieve these complaints any better in the future than they have in the past. A solution to the problem, I believe, lies in adopting an elemental view of the firm and in shifting performance measurement from the firm to the activity (or, in the case cited above, the transaction). By shifting attention from the firm to the activity, by shifting from firm-centric to activity-centric measurement, and by implementing techniques like ABR, performance becomes what the firm does and performance measures describe the costs and revenues resulting from this performance. Measurement of this sort is not easy, but the quarreling about what to measure vanishes. The critics will object to my looking inside rather than outside the firm to find performance. They will say, "You have failed to consider that the performance of the firm is its return to shareholders." My reply will be straightforward. The performance of a firm is what it does. If the firm performs well and if the firm adds value to customers in excess of its costs and promises to continue to do so, then it will have performed well for its shareholders. Whether shareholders will profit from this performance is a somewhat different matter because the wealth of shareholders also depends on the vicissitudes of the market.

REFERENCES

Anderson, E.W., Fornell, C., and Lehmann, D.R. (1994). Customer satisfaction, market share, and profitability: Findings from Sweden. *Journal of Marketing*, **58**(3), 53–66.

Birchard, B. (1995). Making it count. *CFO: The Magazine for Senior Financial Executives*, **11**(10, October), 42.

Edvinsson, L. and Malone, M. (1997). *Intellectual Capital: The Proven Way to Establish Your Company's Real Value by Measuring Its Hidden Brainpower*. London: Piatkus.

Goff, John (1995). Controller burnout. *CFO: The Magazine for Senior Financial Executives*, **11**(9, September), 60.

Institute of Management Accountants (IMA), Cost Management Group (1993). *Cost Management Update*, **32** (October).

Institute of Management Accountants (IMA), Cost Management Group (1995). *Cost Management Update*, **49** (March).

Institute of Management Accountants (IMA), Cost Management Group (1996). *Cost Management Update*, **64** (June).

Itnner, C.D., Larcker, D.F., and Meyer (1997). Performance, compensation and the balanced scorecard, Whatten School, Working Paper.

Kaplan, R.S. and Cooper, R. (1997). *Cost and Effect: Using Integrated Cost Systems to Drive Profitability and Performance*, pp. 183–97. Boston: MA: Harvard Business School Press.

Meyer, M. and Gupta, S. (1994). The performance paradox. *Research in Organisational Behaviour*, **16**, 309–69.

Part II

Performance measurement – theoretical foundations

The second part of the book is concerned with some of the key theoretical and conceptual issues underpinning the field of performance measurement. Again a deliberately diverse set of contributions are presented, which between them draw on disciplines and theories as varied as control theory, agency theory, motivation theory, transaction cost economics, and contingency theory. The authors of these contributions explore issues that build upon those developed by Marshall Meyer – most notably the question of what is performance – and extend Meyer's analsyis, by also debating the behavioral implications of measurement and reward.

The first contribution comes from Professors Michel Lebas and Ken Euske, who ask explicitly, "what is performance?". Lebas and Euske describe performance as one of those "suitcase words (Bourguignon, 1995) in which everyone places the concepts that suit them, letting the context take care of the definition." They argue that this is one of the reasons why it is so difficult to develop theories in the field and suggest that performance should be equated with purposeful action taken today, designed to produce meaningful results tomorrow. Building upon this theme Lebas and Euske then develop nine propositions designed to illustrate how performance can best be defined and understood through causal models shared by organizational decision makers.

The second contribution explores the concept of performance from a different perspective, asking why do individuals and teams perform in situations where they would not be expected to. Austin and Gittell identify three basic premises that are taken for granted by most designers of measurement systems – performance should be clearly defined, performance should be accurately measured, and reward should be contingent upon performance. They then present a series of vignettes, which illustrate how high performance can result, even when these basic principles are contravened. This leads them to argue that there are two different forms of performance measurement. In the first, performance measures are used as part of a management control system that is tightly aligned with an extrinsic reward system. In the second, performance measures result in behavioral modification through ambiguity and intrinsic motivation.

The third contribution in this part builds upon the issues raised by Austin and Gittell and addresses the question, "does pay for performance really work?". In their contribution, Osterloh and Frey, review the literature and the results of a variety of field studies that explore whether intrinsic or extrinsic motivation is more powerful. They seek to develop a framework that allows practitioners to ensure that they achieve an appropriate balance of intrinsic and extrinsic methods of motivation. At the heart of their framework is the argument that "extrinsic motivation is sufficient when the work is routinized and performance is easy to measure, while intrinsic motivation is necessary when labor contracts are characterized by a high degree of incompleteness as well as ambiguity."

The final contribution in this part is provided by Professor Clive Emmanuel, in a piece that explores management's tolerance of dysfunctional behaviors. Emmanuel questionned 77 managers to gauge their response to a variety of seemingly dysfunctional behaviors that fell into one of six categories – smoothing, biasing, focusing, gaming, filtering, and illegal acts. He found a wide range of tolerance to dysfunctional behaviors, both within and between firms, and suggests that some of the reasons for this are "the superior's concern with his/her own well-being and the avoidance of embarrassment of threat." He also argues that one of the significant drivers of dysfunctional behavior was "apparent reliance on financial performance measures."

REFERENCE

Bourguignon, C. (1995). Pent-on défins la performance? *Revue Française de Comptabilité*, no 269, July–August.

5 A conceptual and operational delineation of performance

Michel Lebas and Ken Euske

Introduction

In this contribution the questions of what performance is and how to create it are addressed. A series of nine propositions that, taken together, provide an answer to the questions are developed.

After a brief overview of the reasons that led to this questioning and a review of the relevant literature that shows the extent of diversity of meanings, the authors develop step by step the process that leads to performance, showing it to be a social construct which results from the identification and the sharing of a causal model. That observation leads to the conclusion that performance is meaningful only within a decision-making context. The concept of performance is, therefore, specific to a given set of decision makers. Creating alignment between decision makers both inside and outside the firm is a prerequisite for performance to occur.

In the last sections of the contribution, the impact of responsibility assignment and of measurement on the operational definition of performance are shown. All in all the nine propositions form the basis on which performance can be defined, identified, measured, and managed.

Background

In the Fall of 1995, the French Conseil National de la Comptabilité[1] organized committees to revise the *1982 Plan Comptable Général*. As part of the revision of the whole text,[2] the charge of the Comptabilité de Gestion (Management

---

[1] The National Accounting Council is a government agency placed under the auspices of the French Ministry of Finance and Economics with the mission to define and interpret the national accounting code or *Plan Comptable Général*.

[2] The *Plan Comptable Général* defines the standardized universal chart of accounts that French firms must follow for both their fiscal and external reporting. Financial institutions have a specific version of this standardized and compulsory plan. It defines both the standardized organization of the accounting

Table 5.1 List of concepts

Fundamental concepts	Concepts pertaining to objectives or results	Concepts linked to resources
Unicity of accounting[a]	Decision making	Accounting hypotheses
Information versus data	Performance	Responsibility
Accounting quality		Simplification
		Security

Note:

[a] This concept refers to the fact that, despite the separation, which was reaffirmed in the *1982 Plan*, of financial and managerial accounting that became accepted in the mid thirties in France and made official as early as the 1947 *Plan Comptable* (Lebas, 1996), the same data are used, albeit differently, in both financial and managerial accounting processes. Given this common data base, the sometimes differing measures of value created can always be reconciled.

Accounting) Committee was to update the third part (Title III)) of the *Plan* that dealt with management accounting. Although the Title III is not compulsory, unlike the first two parts, it was felt that the field of management accounting had sufficiently evolved to deserve a radical update. The Committee, organized to represent all interested parties, is comprised of managers, academics, representatives of the accounting profession, and representatives of the Ministry of Finance (the supervisory body to the Conseil).

The work plan of the Management Accounting Committee, decided by its members and approved by the Conseil, had two parts: (1) to define the basic concepts that underlie management accounting and (2) to review the state of the art in managerial accounting practice. The Committee report was designed to have seven chapters. Chapter 1 was released in 1997. The remaining six chapters, still in progress in early 1999, offer a review of the state of the art in management accounting. The chapter 1 covered concepts in three categories as shown in table 5.1.

One of the authors was a major contributor to the discussion of the concept of performance. The contribution below is an elaboration on the ideas developed for that topic.

Footnote 2 (*cont.*)

system for any business enterprise and the presentation of its financial results and position (Standish, 1995). The published *Plan Comptable* is comprised of three parts (called Titles), the first two apply to financial accounting, with Title II focusing on a simplified version of the full chart of accounts for small businesses. To bring the text in conformance with European Union Directives and, when possible, with IASC standards, the French Ministry of Finance undertook a complete revision of the 1982 text in the mid nineties.

Performance

The word performance is widely used in all fields of management. In the management control area, terms such as performance management (Euske, Lebas, and McNair, 1993) measurement, evaluation, or appraisal (e.g. Bruns, 1992) are used. Despite the frequency of use of the word, its precise meaning is rarely explicitly defined by authors even when the main focus of the article or of the book is performance (e.g., Baird, 1986; Richard, 1989). Often, performance is identified or equated with effectiveness and efficiency (e.g., Neely, Gregory, and Platts, 1995; Corvellec, 1994). A publication of the French Ministry of Industry[3] equated performance with lean production, competitiveness, cost reduction, value and job creation, growth, and long-term survival of enterprises. In short, performance is one of those "suitcase words" (Bourguignon, 1995) in which everyone places the concepts that suit them, letting the context take care of the definition.

Using context to clarify the meaning may help create a basis for understanding and discussion, yet it may engender ambiguous definitions. Ambiguity can be beneficial. Differing interpretations of the same reality may generate interaction that spawns new and creative outcomes. However, differing interpretations of the same reality may also generate interaction that is counterproductive and wastes scarce resources. The role of management and the systems they design is to not waste resources but rather use the scarce resources to create value for the various stakeholders of the organization. If management is to induce performance directly or through their systems and minimize counterproductive behavior, they must know what performance is and what it implies.

A diversity of meanings of performance

A review of dictionaries (of both the French and the English language) shows a diversity of meanings for the term performance. It seems logical in the first place to list all these connotations as their sum might provide a usable definition of performance. Performance is:
- measurable by either a number or an expression that allows communication (e.g., performance in management is a multi-person concept);

[3] *Guide de la performance industrielle*, Ministère de l'Industrie, Délégation à l'Information et à la Communication, octobre 1993.

- to accomplish something with a specific intention (e.g., create value);
- the result of an action (the value created, however measured);
- the ability to accomplish or the potential for creating a result (e.g., customer satisfaction seen as a measure of the potential of the organization for future sales);
- the comparison of a result with some benchmark or reference selected – or imposed – either internally or externally;
- a surprising result compared to expectations;
- acting out, in psychology;
- a show, in the "performing arts," that includes both the acting or actions and the result of the actions as well as the observation of the performers by outsiders;
- a judgment by comparison (the difficulty here is to define who the "judge" is, and to know on which criteria the judgment will be formed).

While Baird (1986) states that performance is action oriented (i.e., it must be expressed by a verb) as opposed to a substantive or a noun that would refer to performance as an event, performance is referred to in most of the references as either an action (obtaining performance) or an event (a result) or both simultaneously. This list leads us to agree with Corvellec (1994, 1995) and Bourguignon (1995) in saying that performance refers simultaneously to the action, the result of the action, and to the success of the result compared to some benchmark. Viewing performance as a comparative judgment captures some of this complexity. If there is a judgment, a judge must be selected and criteria for the judgment need to exist.

The criteria for the judgement are likely to focus on results, since the purpose of management is to create a continuous flow of value. Therefore, it becomes important to create a definition that will focus managers on anticipation of performance. We take the position that performance is the sum of all processes that will lead managers to taking appropriate actions in the present that will create a *performing* organization in the future (i.e., one that is effective and efficient). In other words, we define performance as doing today what will lead to *measured* value outcome tomorrow.

To create something in the future a causal model is necessary, so that the process through which performance (future results) will be created can be identified and managed. Past performance (past results) alone is not necessarily a good predictor of future performance. Most everyone has illustrations of the lack of predictability of results, there are very few examples of predictable results.

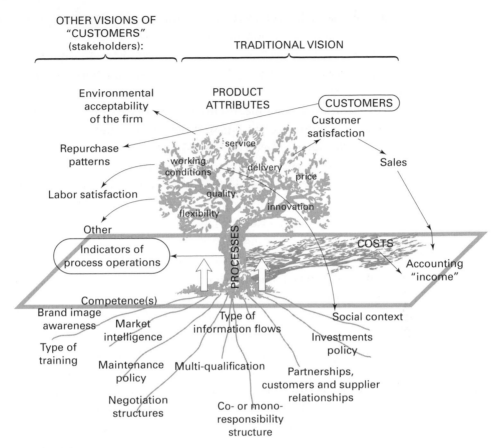

OTHER VISIONS OF "CUSTOMERS" (stakeholders):

TRADITIONAL VISION

Environmental acceptability of the firm

PRODUCT ATTRIBUTES

CUSTOMERS

Customer satisfaction

service

Repurchase patterns

working conditions

delivery

price

Sales

Labor satisfaction

quality

innovation

flexibility

Other

Indicators of process operations

PROCESSES

COSTS

Accounting "income"

Competence(s)

Brand image awareness

Market intelligence

Type of information flows

Social context

Type of training

Investments policy

Maintenance policy

Multi-qualification

Partnerships, customers and supplier relationships

Negotiation structures

Co- or mono-responsibility structure

Figure 5.1.   The performance tree.
Source: Adapted from Lebas, 1995.

Performance and the causal model

A causal model that links actions now to results in the future can take a variety of forms. Figure 5.1 illustrates an example of a generic 3 stage causal model:
- outcome (often reduced to output and results),
- processes, and
- foundations.

Each firm or organization will need to define uniquely the concepts that apply to its own situation. The very process of definition of the three components of the model is, in our view, an essential step in creating performance. Once the model is defined, each organization must select the appropriate indica-tors[4] to describe it and monitor its status.

This model is portrayed as a tree to illustrate how an organization goes through the process of creating performance. The analogy to a tree helps to capture process complexity and characteristics of growth and change.

In our illustration outcome, results, or outputs are divided into two broad categories: traditional conceptualizations and other conceptualizations. Accounting income shown on the right-hand side of figure 5.1 is an example of a traditional conceptualization of a result that might be held by an owner-manager or a stockholder. However, other results are valued by groups of stakeholders, such as the environmental acceptability of the organization, the contribution to the social welfare, labor, and social climate. Social climate is particularly important because it captures the continued acceptability of the organization to political, regulatory, and administrative powers that either implicitly or explicitly grant the organization its license to operate (Fligstein, 1990; RSA, 1995).

These results or outputs are consequences of the product attributes that con-stitute the fruit of the tree. These attributes are the elements of the product that the customer values. They include, of course, the traditional quartet: price, availability, service, and quality. They can include other elements, such as working conditions (e.g., buy union-made products or don't buy products made by child labor), innovation, and flexibility. The attributes are the basis for cus-tomer satisfaction but also of stakeholder satisfaction in general. The attributes are the result of business processes. These constitute the trunk of the perfor-mance tree. They have to be monitored so that they deliver what the stakeholders want within the constraints of the strategic intent of the organization.

Costs that loom quite large as descriptors of financial performance, both directly (cost minimization) or indirectly (earnings maximization), do not play a large role in our causal model; costs are the mere "shadow" of the pro-cesses and of the attributes created.[5] Costs are important but they are second-order variables in the understanding of the generation of results.

Continuing the tree analogy, the quality of the processes would be the rich-ness of the sap and its effective movement through the trunk and the branches.

---

[4] We deliberately prefer the word "indicator" to the more traditional one of "measure." A measure often implies precision. A measure is usually well defined and in similar circumstances its numerical value should be the same. An indicator may be less precise but meaningful. Indicators tend to allow for more timely and sensitive signals.

[5] Johnson (1990) used Plato's cave analogy to explain the concept. In the cave analogy, above the ground are objects and forms, such as customer satisfaction and activities, below the ground are artificial like-nesses and shadows, such as accounting information and costing models.

Further, the quality of processes rests in part on the nutrients in the soil. They are such elements as competence, awareness of brand value, maintenance policy, existing structures of negotiation, partnerships with both customers and suppliers, and the organizational responsibility structure. Concepts that are not normally captured in accounting and control systems. Why are these elements rarely measured by the accounting and control system? They are in the "soil" and do not normally catch the light that is needed to create the accounting "shadow." If they do catch the light (i.e., are "seen" by the accounting system), it is a sign that things are not going very well because it signifies that the tree has been uprooted.

Modeling the performance creation process as a tree offers an opportunity to visualize that outcome, results or outputs often do not happen in the same time frame as that of actions: the work in the soil, the choice of the type of tree, the care of the tree are actions that must be implemented long before any fruit can be seen, let alone harvested. Just as a tree takes several years to bear fruit, the consequences of the interaction with the environment (bad health of the workers or of the surrounding community due to hazardous chemicals) take time to materialize. Accounting data do not capture such lags. This illustration is consistent with the fact that results of an organization are multifaceted and must be described over a long period of time.

Performance is a complex concept. The complexity increases both the difficulty of defining the concept, and the likelihood that indicators of performance will at times be contradictory. The contradictions can be managed if one has a good understanding of the process that generates the various types of results; hence, the importance of the causal model as a means to understanding the organization and its interaction with its environment. However, once a model is adopted, performance, because we define it as the process as well as the future outcome, cannot be separated from the model. The model both defines and legitimates the performance (Fligstein, 1990). Performance is a social construct. The model creates the reality about what performance is.[6]

The causal model is elaborated by trial and error, critically using past data.

Proposition 1

Performance can only be expressed as a set of parameters or indicators that are complementary, and sometimes contradictory, that describe the process

---

[6] The view taken is this paper can be illustrated by a story told about the definition of a "penalty" in football (soccer) in which the first referee says "I blow my whistle when *there is* a penalty," the second one says "I blow my whistle *when I see* a penalty," while the third one declares "there is no penalty *until I blow my whistle.*"

through which the various types of outcome and results are achieved (Lebas, 1995; Kaplan and Norton, 1992).

Proposition 2

Understanding performance relies on the identification of a causal model that describes how actions today can influence results in the future. Performance is not a one-time event. Performance is dynamic. A performance measure is an instance in the continuous performance creation process. A performance measure is a leading indicator of performance only if the organization has acquired the knowledge and the mastery of its causal relationships and can reproduce this outcome or result in the future. We suggest that the term performance be reserved for the sum of all processes that lead to a potential or future sequence of outcomes and results.

Performance and decision making

Even with a common causal model, the description of performance – whether simple, complex, cardinal, ordinal, or literal – has no intrinsic value. The description becomes valuable if one or several individuals use it for decision-making purposes. If the description of performance has no possibility of impacting on the decision of the user, it has no value. However, each user can interpret the performance data as he or she pleases according to different time frames, objectives, intent, risk-avoidance attitudes, or perspectives (e.g., inside or outside the organization). This diversity of interpretation increases the complexity of providing a definition of performance.

A description of performance that would be correct from a fiduciary perspective (e.g., balance sheet) is not likely to satisfy a user who viewed the organization as an operating entity. Such a description would likely be even less meaningful to a stakeholder preoccupied by the impact of the organization on the social welfare in a community. Even though the decision context may be the same, users with differing time horizons or differing objectives are not likely to seek the same description of organizational performance.

Given a common causal model the perceived contradiction between the various views of performance may be related to a world view based on the concept of "or" implying a concept of exclusion (i.e., some may say the organization *either* is profitable *or* maintains employment). However, a view based on the concept of "and" implies a concept of inclusion. That is, the organization can be profitable *and* maintain employment. From an internal, operational point of view, the difference is between dissolving a conflict and living with a conflict (i.e., accepting the coexistence of multiple dimensions of the same concept). The manager is no longer faced with a dilemma. Rather, the manager has the challenge of taking a proactive position regarding the complexity of performance. One consequence of this view is that today some organizations see profit as a constraint, not a goal *per se.*

Proposition 3

Performance is defined by the user of the descriptive signals of performance. Performance, because it is a social construct, is a concept with no objective description. Each person defines it her or his own way.

Performance defined from inside or from outside the organization

Someone inside or outside the organization can develop a causal model to define performance. An internally defined model of causal relationships is likely to focus on the construction of the result through actions. An externally defined model more likely will focus on anticipating the possible actions the internal actors might select and estimate the probability of certain future results to be used in some other decision making-process.

The descriptors used in either case will not be the same. An outsider will look at general indicators based on some preconceived, and possibly statistically defined, relations, such as the ones found in financial analysis. The actual workings of the organization will remain a black box. It will, therefore, not be surprising that performance as seen by outsiders will lead to much debate, as each analyst will necessarily introduce his or her own bias to the inferences drawn from externally available signals about the activity of the organization.

An insider, on the contrary, will model action variables. While it is normal to have a diversity of views about performance as seen from the outside, the concept of performance as defined from the inside of the organization is more likely to have a unique, although many-faceted, definition, shared by all actors involved in its creation. If the members of an organization do not share the same view of performance, actions cannot be coordinated and resources may be wasted.

Proposition 4

Performance does not have the same meaning if the evaluator is inside or outside the organization. The operations of the organization remain a black box for the outsider while the insider operationalizes performance in cooperation with other internal actors.

Performance and responsibility

For reasons of effectiveness and because of limits on individual competence, each causal model is generally broken down into sub-models. The sub-models are either additive (a Taylor-based view, still prevalent in many organizations) or overlapping (views of the enterprise as a network of cross-functional processes and management of the "white space"[7] on the organization chart). Each sub-model defines a domain of responsibility (e.g., the manager, the responsibility center,[8] teams, the management systems, the product or service) and, conversely, each definition of responsibility implies a causal model.

For each of these domains of responsibility, there will be different descriptors of performance, and different uses for the signals describing it. All these descriptors will not necessarily be consistent with one another. Therefore, it is crucial to admit that performance does not have a unique operational definition in a organization. However, the dialogue that will take place to define the richness and the complexity of the concept will be a foundation for the management of performance (i.e. for the pro-active construction of performance).

Proposition 5

Performance is always connected or attached to a domain of responsibility. The different views of performance associated with the domains provide the basis for an understanding of the complexity and management of performance in the organization.

Performance and measurement

As Lord Kelvin said long ago, "if you cannot measure it, it does not exist." As we said, performance is multifaceted and encompasses elements describing both the results and the processes creating the results. However, the descriptors, the qualitative and quantitative measures, are mere surrogates of performance.

---

[7] The concept of "white space" is developed by Rumler and Brache (1990).

[8] It is generally understood that it is important to separate performance of an organizational sub-unit (generally a responsibility center) from that of the individual(s) in charge of the sub-unit. A manager may very well have good performance in an organizational sub-unit that does not perform well. For example, a manager may do a great job of closing down a loss-making branch or subsidiary.

They should not be mistaken for performance itself (Euske, 1983). Accounting definitions and measures of performance are but synthetic representations of decisions made previously by managers and that can be visualized as parts of the "performance tree" of figure 5.1. It is important for management accounting to identify, measure, and transmit data about these intermediate results, even though they may not be expressed in "accounting language." The management accounting process is a mechanism to provide legitimacy to what may be estimations or forecasts. These estimates and forecasts may be better descriptors of the process than accounting data.

Accounting data or quasi-accounting data are provided to the manager for his or her information. They need not be used if the causal model used does not require them. However, the causal model may not be permanently relevant and sometimes intuitions derived from the data will lead to an update of the causal model to reflect the rapidly evolving markets and technologies. Therefore, it may be important to add to the complexity of measures or indicators, by recognizing that there will be two types of signals: those assuming the model is still valid (efficiency and effectiveness, for example) and those allowing a verification of the continued relevance of the model.

Proposition 6

Performance exists only if outcome and results can be described or measured so that they can be communicated for someone to decide to do something within the shared model of causal relationships.

Proposition 7

The relevance of the causal model needs to be continuously validated both within and without the organization.

Proposition 8

Performance indicators or measures should not be confused with what they only partially describe.

Performance is only a relative term

Performance corresponds to a potential for value creation. That value is to be created over a period of time. Any causal model must, therefore, specify a time frame, in addition to decision parameters and a context. The context is comparative.

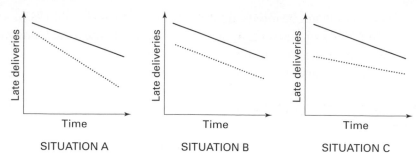

Figure 5.2.   Performance is only relative.

Performance measures and the underlying performance must be qualified as good or bad. No signal of performance is intrinsically either. There must always be a comparison to qualify the performance. If, for example, we consider that late deliveries are a parameter descriptive of an organization's performance, we cannot decide whether 10 percent of orders being five days late is good or bad. We cannot even decide whether a reduction in late orders from 10 percent to 5 percent is really an improvement or not. In order to interpret these data, one has to know (or surmise) what competitors or other users of similar processes do. Performance cannot be taken out of its comparative context as shown in figure 5.2. In this figure, the solid line indicates that over time an absolute reduction in the service rate, defined as the percent of late deliveries, is decreasing. From a continuous improvement perspective, the change is clearly an improvement. However, from another perspective the change in performance may not be a relative improvement. For instance, in the three situations described in figure 5.2 another organization using a similar or comparable process enjoyed a reduction in late deliveries shown by the dotted line. In situation A, the organization indicated by the solid line is losing ground relative to the other organization. In situation B, the relationship of the two organizations remains constant. Only in situation C is the gap between the two organizations narrowing. The concept of performance only has meaning as part of a comparison.

Proposition 9

Performance is a relative concept requiring judgment and interpretation. Performance is affecting a superior process or result relative to the referent. Choice of the referent is a significant decision with long-term consequences. The relatively superior position could be short or long term and over few or many indicators. Contradictions among the temporal measures and the other indicators are inevitable. Performance will again be in an interpretative context in which managers or users of information will decide on the key parameters of performance.

Performance can be managed

As mentioned above, measuring parameters descriptive of performance makes sense only if the data are to be used in making decisions. The decisions can relate to both strategic orientations and steering the organization in the implementation of the strategic intent. The decisions contribute jointly to the creation (i.e., the management) of performance.

In order to achieve performance, the causal model has to be defined in terms of leading indicators. Lagging indicators only provide history; leading indicators allow for the creation of the conditions for fostering performance. In order to maintain the validity of the leading indicators, the model must be continuously validated for its relevance. This validation must also be as "leading" as possible (i.e., incorporate the most current information pertaining to the parameters of the causal model).

Performance management requires that procedures be put in place that allow the evolution of the organization and of its management system in line with the evolution of its environment. Therefore, in order to manage performance one must:

- describe the value creation process in its context and time (propositions 1 and 2);
- share this model with all relevant actors (proposition 4);
- partition and allocate decision rights on the basis of this model (proposition 5);
- identify and select the descriptive indicators both for results and for steps to create the results (propositions 3 and 4);
- document these indicators through an appropriate information system (proposition 6);
- choose the reference for benchmarking and external validation (propositions 7, 8, and 9);
- evaluate the signals and messages coming from each indicator (proposition 8);
- identify, evaluate, and implement all actions likely to improve the likelihood that the result will be coherent with the strategic intent (propositions 7, 8, and 9).

Conclusion

Performance is not just something one observes and measures; it is the result of a deliberate construction. Performance is a relative concept defined in terms of some referent employing a complex set of time-based and causality-based indicators bearing on future realizations. Performance is about the capability of generating future results. The capability of generating future results can be described through a causal model. Each part of the model can in turn be subjected to an analysis.

Performance is meaningful only when used by a decision maker. It is specific to the individual's needs and interpretation. A domain of responsibility defines the parameters of performance that are relevant and, conversely, performance defines a domain of responsibility.

Finally, the specific meaning performance takes in a organization should be the result of extensive discussions between the various managers or decision makers of the organization. The goal of the discussions is to identify a coherent set of causal relationships and select a common set of indicators so that the coordination of all actors takes place and generates the value that, in the end, stakeholders define performance from their own point of view.

This definition of the performance creation process highlights the importance of creating alignment as a basic condition for an efficient use of resources and an effective trend towards the fulfillment of strategic intent.

Performance management is the process of creating alignment. Some of the best-known processes leading to such alignment are dialogue-based and de-emphasize local optimization focusing on the development of integrated business processes

Figure 5.1 showed the conceptual three-step approach and highlighted the fact that, unless foundations (positions, views, and beliefs) are well understood and managed, outcome and results can hardly be modified.

REFERENCES

Baird, L. (1986). *Managing Performance*. New York: John Wiley.

Bourguignon, C. (1995). Peut-on définir la performance? *Revue Française de Comptabilité*, n° 269, July–August.

Bruns, W. J. Jr. (ed.) (1992). *Performance Measurement, Evaluation and Incentives*. Boston, MA: Harvard Business School Press.

Corvellec, H. (1994). Performance: From one language into another or the mutations of a Notion. Paper presented at the 17th EAA Congress, Venezia, Italy.

Corvellec, H. (1995). *Stories of Achievements: Narrative Features of Organizational Performance*. Sweden: Lund University Press.

Euske, K.J. (1983). *Management Control: Planning, Control, Measurement, and Evaluation*. Reading, MA: Addison-Wesley.

Euske, K.J., Lebas, M.J. and McNair, C.J. (1993). Best practices in world class organizations. Consortium for Advanced Manufacturing-International, Arlington, Texas.

Fligstein, N. (1990). *The Transformation of Corporate Control*. Cambridge, MA: Harvard University Press.

Johnson, H.T. (1990). Beyond product costing, cost management systems meeting. CAM-I, 21–4 May.

Kaplan, R.S. and Norton, D.P. (1992). The balanced scorecard – measures that drive performance. *Harvard Business Review*, 70 (1, January–February), 1.

Lebas, M.J. (1995). Oui, il faut définir la performance. *Revue Française de Comptabilité*, n° 269, July–August.

Lebas, M.J. (1996). Management accounting practice in France. In *Management Accounting: European Perspectives*, ed. Al Bihmani. Oxford: Oxford University Press.

Neely, A., Gregory, M. and Platts, K. (1995). Performance measurement systems design. *International Journal of Operations and Production Management*, **15**(4), 80–116.

Richard, J. (1989). *Audit des performances*. Paris: La Villeguérin.

RSA (The Royal Society for the Encouragement of Arts, Manufacture and Commerce) (1995). *Tomorrow's Company*, London: RSA.

Rumler, G.A. and Brache A.P. (1990). *Improving Performance: How to Manage the White Space on the Organization Chart*. San Francisco, CA: Jossey-Bass.

Standish, P. (1995). Financial reporting in France. In *Comparative International Accounting*, ed. C. Nobes, and R. Parker, 4th edn. Hemel Hempstead, Prentice Hall International.

6 When it should not work but does: Anomalies of high performance

Rob Austin and Jody Hoffer Gittell

Introduction

One ostensible objective of research on performance measurement is to determine the characteristics of measurement systems that lead to high performance. To this end, descriptive theories of performance measurement hypothesize relationships between work contexts, the design of measurement systems, the aptitudes and behavior of workers, and the outcomes that result from the work. Normative theories specify principles of design for measurement systems intended to produce desirable outcomes.

Normative theories do not usually specifically assert that high performance results *only* from performance measurement systems constructed in accord with theory. But high performance achieved via means other than performance measurement should surely operate in a way that is *consistent* with the mechanisms inherent in these performance measurement theories. Furthermore, some theories in use, such as the one summarized by the widely accepted aphorism "What you can't measure, you can't manage," seem to imply that a performance measurement system designed according to certain basic principles is a prerequisite for high performance.

This contribution is simple in its layout and objectives. First, we identify a minimal set of principles for designing performance measurement systems that can be extracted from theories in a wide variety of academic disciplines and applied settings. We arrive at three principles that we believe would seem unobjectionable to most performance measurement proponents. Second, we present four vignettes that describe actual events from the airline industry in which the principles of performance measurement seem to be deliberately subverted in order to produce high performance. It is important to emphasize here that these are not merely examples of high performance arrived at via a different means than performance measurement. Rather, in these vignettes basic principles of performance measurement have been specifically subverted in order to improve performance. That there are exceptions to general theories is not remarkable. We suggest, however, that some of these exceptions challenge existing theories of performance measurement; and that broadening the theories to encompass phenomena such as those described in the vignettes suggest new options for the use of performance measurement to generate high performance.

Basic principles of performance measurement

Research in performance measurement spans fields as diverse as economics, industrial engineering, organizational theory, psychology, public policy, and statistics. Methodological approaches vary greatly. It is nearly impossible to survey the research exhaustively across these fields. We focus here on economics and organizational theory – fields that consider performance measurement issues quite directly – and we cite representative research rather than attempting to be exhaustive.

We have made efforts to derive a "lowest-common denominator" set of measurement principles. These are principles that, according to many theories, enhance performance. There are research findings that are not consistent with these principles and we do not claim that they are universal. Rather, we use them as theoretical "tripwires" that when violated indicate a need to look deeper for explanations.

These principles do have considerable "commonsense" appeal. They are consistent with many practical approaches to performance measurement. Our field research in software engineering and healthcare as well as in airlines leads us to believe that there is a great deal of commonality in the notions that underlie practical approaches to performance measurement. We venture that these very basic principles would seem so innocuous to most implementers of real measurement systems that they are often taken for granted.

Principle 1: Performance should be clearly defined

Performance should be clearly defined, if not in advance, then in terms of criteria that can be agreed after the fact, if not by a third party, then by the worker and manager.

This principle is an explicit part of many performance measurement systems. For example, the Software Engineering Institute explains the purpose of its Software Capability Evaluation process, which assigns a quantitative proficiency rating to software development organizations, in the following terms:

[One] objective is to provide a public process which is defined in advance and for which the contractors can prepare (Humphrey and Sweet, 1987).

Third-party verifiability and definition in advance are seen as desirable characteristics of such systems, not only because they are perceived to increase the fairness of a process, but also because they are associated with a lack of ambiguity in what constitutes performance. The assumption here is that if multiple people can observe an outcome and judge it relative to a pre-specified standard of performance, then agreements can be formed about what performance is and confidence is increased that high performance has been achieved. Such clear pre-definitions are actionable. Thus, clear definition of performance is associated with the effectiveness of a measurement system in producing desirable outcomes.

The ability to specify performance criteria *before* work is performed is an assumption in much of the economic literature on performance measurement. The mechanisms that underlie much of agency economics (e.g., Ross, 1973; Holmstrom, 1979; Jensen and Meckling, 1976; Holmstrom and Milgrom, 1991) depend on the formation of "contracts" which are agreements forged between the agent (worker) and principal (owner/manager) on how the benefits of production will be distributed to the worker, contingent on (often measured) outcomes. Within these theories, a clear pre-definition of what constitutes performance allows agency contracts to be enforced.

Institutional economists have explored the implications of the inability to specify performance *ex ante*. Williamson (e.g., 1975) suggests that difficulties in pre-defining performance are a source of incompleteness in contracts that explain in part the use of organizations rather than markets to coordinate production. An economics literature on property rights (e.g., Hart and Moore, 1989) discusses how such difficulties manifest themselves in ownership arrangements, arguing that the structure of ownership might change where there are difficulties in reaching agreement on what constitutes performance.

A significant literature within agency economics addresses the possibility of "subjective contracts" that do not require up-front agreements about performance (e.g., Baker, Jensen, and Murphy, 1988; Baker, Gibbons, and Murphy, 1994). "Specifying the correct objective measure of employee performance is often impossible . . . The principal knows, in general terms, what he wants the agent to do, but the range of possible actions that the agent can take, and the range of possible outcomes, is enormous" (Baker, Jensen, and Murphy, 1988). Subjective or relational contracts can be used in place of more formal ones "based on outcomes that are observed by only the contracting parties *ex post*, and also on outcomes that are prohibitively costly to specify *ex ante*. A relational contract thus allows the parties to utilize their detailed knowledge of their specific situation and to adapt to new information as it becomes available" (Baker, Gibbons, and Murphy, forthcoming). Even though performance is not third-party verifiable, parties to subjective contracts are dissuaded from reneging by the possibility of reprisals in future interactions between principal and agent. The expectation of repeated interaction is therefore a requirement for subjective contracting.

As Baker, Gibbons, and Murphy (1994) note, engaging in work without a clear *ex ante* definition of performance seems to require *trust*. Also, though performance need not be defined *ex ante* for subjective contracts, the principal and agent must agree on a characterization of performance *ex post*.

The difficulty of defining performance *ex ante* was addressed in organization theory several decades earlier. In reaction to the dominant bureaucratic model (e.g., Weber, 1890; Taylor, 1911; Barnard, 1938), which relied heavily on the pre-specification of performance, the neo-Weberians explored its dysfunctional effects. Defining performance *ex ante* reduces conflict in the organization, they argued, but it also increases the rigidity of behavior (Merton, 1936; Gouldner, 1954). Employees work in accordance with pre-specified performance rather than seeking to do the right thing under the circumstances that arise. Performance is therefore poorer, the greater the pre-specification of performance. Gouldner (1954) suggested that organizations often respond to this decline in performance by substituting close supervision in place of pre-defined performance. But close supervision results in workplace conflict, he argued, motivating a return to *ex ante* performance specifications. The negative cycle is repeated.

Selznick (1949) explored delegation as an alternative to specifying performance *ex ante*, but noted that delegation has its own pitfalls. Given authority to manage their own performance, units or individuals tend to develop commitment to goals that may not be conducive to meeting overall organizational goals, a problem that motivated later economic agency theories to insist on *ex ante* definitions of performance.

Cohen, March, and Olsen (1972) present a "garbage can" model of organizational activity which assumes ambiguity in the pre-work definition of performance. They too suggest an alternative to defining performance *ex ante*. "Although organizations can often be viewed conveniently as vehicles for solving well-defined problems . . . they also provide sets of procedures through which participants arrive at an interpretation of what they are doing and what they have done while in the process of doing it" (p. 2). Contrary to traditional organizational theory, both the problems to be solved and the desired solutions to them can be defined in the context of doing the work rather than prior to doing the work.

Principle 2: Performance should be accurately measured

As work is performed, performance should be measured in a way that conveys the maximum amount of information possible, so that it can be used to determine the degree to which performance has been achieved.

This principle seems so obvious to most practitioners that it is often merely assumed rather than stated; but it does manifest itself in discussions of what should be measured. For example, Grady and Caswell (1987) suggest that measurement related to the production of software should begin by establishing a wish list of quantities that might be measured, then reducing that set to a handful of quantities that can be measured accurately (and inexpensively). Another reason practitioners value accuracy in measurement is that they often aim to use measurement information more broadly, as an input to decision making and to promote organizational learning. The importance of accuracy of information in decision-making inputs and for learning is obvious.

A common analogy is drawn between models of engineering control theory and organizational performance measurement. Engineering control models use differential equations to describe and predict the behavior of physical systems that use measured feedback to adjust themselves. When these models are applied they produce systems that have self-correcting capabilities that also seem very desirable in organizational contexts. One simple example of an engineering control application is the thermostat commonly used for temperature control. The Software Productivity Consortium uses the thermostat analogy as the basis for its performance measurement system.

An example of a closed loop feedback control system is a thermostatically controlled heating system. The thermostat is set to a certain "set point" temperature which is the input goal . . . the heat output is continuously compared to the set point goal . . . The thermostat will turn the heater on for a temperature lower than the set point and off otherwise. Uncertainty can exist in the system in establishing the set point according to uncertain temperature requirements. Also, the temperature-measuring device may be inaccurate. However, the system's operation can be improved by ascertaining the temperature requirements and servicing the thermometer.

The closed loop feedback control model represents the software process . . . as a "black box" system with interest focused on the input and outputs at the interfaces of the system. Process and product goals are established . . . the process is initiated . . . measurements are collected . . . and compared to measurement goals. The goals correspond to the set point inputs and the measurements correspond to the outputs of the feedback control system . . . the differences between the goal and the measurement is the process variance that becomes the driver of process correction (1992).

This analogy suggests that measurement accuracy is an essential element of a performance measurement system, so essential that the measurement device itself requires regular servicing to ensure accurate measurements. Without accurate measurement, performance can exhibit undesirable behaviors such as accelerating away from the desired standard. This example also reiterates the importance of principle 1: lack of agreement about desired performance must be remedied for the system to operate effectively. The thermostat analogy can be detected (and is often quite explicit) behind many performance measurement systems found in practice.

Measurement accuracy clearly plays a role in the construction of verifiable contracts in economic models. This literature has dealt extensively with the consequences of inaccurate signals in the form of statistical imprecision and bias (e.g., Banker and Datar, 1989). Inaccuracy in measurement is typically predicted to diminish performance in these models. There are, however, notable exceptions. Meyer and Vickers (1997) claim that measurement serves the purpose of assessing the capability of the agent, and that therefore inaccurate (i.e., statistically noisy) measures make the agent work harder to convey information about how capable he is. Inaccurate measures therefore are expected to generate higher performance. Narayanan and Davila (1998) consider tradeoffs between the use of measurement information for performance evaluation and its use for belief revision (e.g., for learning about the effectiveness of a process or machine). They demonstrate that conveying information about evaluation can lead to agent manipulation that makes the information less useful for organizational learning.

Organizational theorists have also argued for the importance of the ability to measure performance accurately. Thompson (1967) predicts that organizations will choose between measures of inputs and measures of outputs based on what can be measured with greater accuracy. Ouchi (1979) predicts the accuracy with which measurement can be accomplished is a primary determinant of the mode of control that will be adopted in an organizational setting. Theorists of quality management have emphasized the importance of detailed measurement for the purposes of improving performance.

However, one of the chief theorists of quality management, W. Edwards Deming, warned that measurement is potentially one of the most harmful things an organization can do with respect to improving performance over time (1986). The value of the information contained in a measure must be counterbalanced against the fear of reprisal. Because of that fear, people will systematically subvert the measurement system, causing a decline in the accuracy of the measures and hence undermining their usefulness. Edmondson (1996) demonstrates negative effects of fears associated with performance measurement, particularly negative effects on the sharing of information. This dysfunction suggests the possibility that a better understanding of performance may in fact result from *less* precise measurements, in particular from measurements that lack the diagnostic power to assign outcomes to individual actors. Thus more ambiguity in measurements themselves, as well as in the initial definition of performance, may well enhance performance.

Principle 3: Rewards should be contingent on measured performance

There should be a clear linkage between desirable performance and rewards such that desirable performance by the worker leads to rewards for the worker; the fact of this linkage, if not the precise relationship, should be known by both worker and manager before work commences.

Many practitioner systems are consistent with this principle as it is the basis for pay-for-performance systems that have become increasingly popular in recent years (Tully, 1993). Clearly, this principle relies on the first two in that pay-for-performance requires clear definition and accurate measurement of performance.

The economic agency literature explicitly examines how pay should be made contingent on performance. There are a wide variety of models addressing a great diversity of issues – for example, whether compensation might be deferred to encourage workers to remain with a given employer (e.g., Lazear, 1986), or whether workers might be overpaid ("efficiency wages") to make the prospect of losing the job less attractive and therefore motivate higher effort (e.g. Shapiro and Stiglitz, 1984). Others have addressed the issue of whether performance pay should be associated with group or individual performance (e.g., Wageman and Baker, 1997). Piece rates have been found to improve performance (e.g., Lazear, 1996), although, as Prendergast (1999) notes, most of these empirical findings have addressed jobs that were quite simple. The economics literature also suggests that firms with clearer linkage between rewards and performance should attract the better workers (Lazear, 1986). In all of these models, there is a vital contingency between measured performance and resulting payments to agents. Without the enticement of payments, agents are expected to perform at a nominal level if at all.

Some economists have noted the potential for dysfunctional behaviors resulting from pay-for-performance (Baker, Jensen, and Murphy, 1988; Baker, 1992). Still, performance rewards are present even in the models of subjective contracts (Baker, Gibbons, and Murphy, 1994). Although there is no third-party recourse, there are punishments that can be inflicted if principal or agent refuse to live up to the terms of the contract, and rewards that can be granted if the parties do honor the contract.

Organizational theorists have also supported making pay contingent on performance. Taylor (1911) introduced pay for performance as part of his proposal to rationalize the workplace through industrial engineering. March and Simon (1958) characterized the organizational literature as supporting the view that "the greater the dependence of monetary reward on performance, the more favorable are the consequences perceived as resulting from a decision to increase production" (p. 82). Rewards work particularly well when performance can be clearly defined *ex ante*, they stipulate, suggesting that the effectiveness of principle 3 depends upon effective implementation of principle 1.

Some organizational theorists, however, have noted the dysfunctional effects of linking rewards and punishments with measurement (Ridgway, 1956; Blau, 1963; Stake, 1971). Consistent with these concerns, there is a substantial literature that suggests the wisdom of relying on intrinsic rather than extrinsic motivation to accomplish some tasks (see, for example, McGregor, 1960; Ouchi, 1981; Frey, 1993). McGregor argued that "the typical incentive plan is of limited effectiveness as a method of control if the purpose is to motivate human beings to direct their efforts toward organizational objectives" (p. 10). People are motivated more effectively through intrinsic than through extrinsic means, he hypothesized.

Reliance on intrinsic motivation calls for affecting the preferences of workers so that those preferences are more aligned with the objectives of the organization, rather than simply attempting to control worker behavior (Barnard, 1938). Reliance on intrinsic motivation also calls for the organization to shape some of its own goals to be more consistent with worker preferences, in what McGregor calls the "selective adaptation" to employee preferences. This approach is a departure from traditional organizational and economic theories, which have tended to treat underlying worker preferences as exogenous, rather than as shaped by participation in the organization.

Proposals to use intrinsic motivation in organizations have raised the question of whether intrinsic motivation can co-exist with performance measurement systems based on extrinsic motivators like rewards. McGregor (1960), Frey (1993), and others suggest that intrinsic motivation may be "crowded out" by extrinsic rewards. McGregor (1960) argues that even a well-managed incentive plan "creates attitudes which are the opposite of those desired [including] indifference to the importance of collaboration with other parts of the organization (except for collusive efforts to defeat the incentive plan)" (p. 9). Prendergast (1999) argues, however, that conclusive empirical evidence of this phenomenon is sparse.

Some have emphasized that the linkage between measurement and rewards often arises regardless of the intentions of the system designers. Even in the absence of explicit rewards attached to measurement, the fear of reprisal from measurements serves in effect as a negative reward (Deming, 1986). Fear of reprisal in turn leads to the hiding of information and efforts to subvert the measurement system.

Summary

Although the principles we list are not universal, we suggest that they do nevertheless retain appeal, especially in practical settings. Where exceptions to the principles have been identified in research, existing theory has tended to focus on specific exceptions one at a time, and to incrementally adjust existing models to accommodate exceptions in isolation. Moreover, exceptions have often been characterized as detrimental influences on performance, such that we can not do as well as we would be able to if the principles could be held in force. Especially in practice, the prevalent view seems to be that these principles should be aimed for, that conditions conducive to them should be constructed, and that they should be adhered to when the conditions can be constructed. Furthermore, it seems a common assessment that the principles are in fact realizable in most situations.

In this contribution, we describe vignettes in which the principles are seemingly violated not only to add to the prevalent sense that existing frameworks need to be further elaborated, but also to explore whether the exceptions, considered collectively, might suggest ways of enhancing performance according to a different model. That is, conditions in which the principles can be met, whether naturally occurring or constructed, may not be the only or best way to achieve high performance in most organizational settings. Rather, high performance may occur via a model that is not consistent with these principles.

Performance measurement in the airline industry[1]

Standard practice for tracking the cause of departure delays in the airline industry is to assign each delay to the party that caused it. Delays that are caused by gate agents (e.g., failure to check in all customers on time) are

---

[1] These observations are taken from a nine site, four airline study of the departure process that focused on the effects of formal organizational practices on coordination among front-line employees, and on performance outcomes (see Gittell, 2000a, 2000b).

assigned to customer service. Delays that are caused by the baggage handlers (e.g., failure to load all bags on time) are assigned to baggage. Delays that are caused by flight attendants (e.g., failure to get all passengers seated on time) are assigned to in-flight. Delays that are caused by cabin cleaners (e.g., failure to get the aircraft cleaned on time) are assigned to cabin cleaning, and so on.

The purpose of this system is to accurately assign accountability for delays, in order to evaluate the performance of individual employees and their managers, to motivate better performance, and to improve the departure process over time. According to one manager:

> It helps a lot just to keep score. People are naturally competitive. They absolutely need to know the score. Once they know, they will do something about it. Every delay comes to my attention and gets a full investigation . . . The last thing most of them want is the spotlight on them.

A customer service supervisor at another airline explained:

> The supervisor has to track down the cause of the delay. With a delay, we'll first talk to the customer service agent and the lead and ask what kind of problems were there. Was it the captain, the flight attendant, the control center, cleaning, catering, a disabled passenger? Any of these would be [someone else's] delay. They should know what time the cleaners got off. If it was a catering delay, it would be charged to catering or to the flight attendants if they counted wrong.

Field managers were evaluated by headquarters along a clearly defined set of performance dimensions, including departure delays. In several companies, headquarters allocated to each field manager a number of acceptable delays, mishandled bags, and customer complaints. Any number greater than the quota was unacceptable. The intent of the system was to focus managerial attention, to motivate good performance, and to create a basis for evaluating managers over time.

This system has obvious similarities to the engineering control model described earlier. Feedback provided by measurement is perceived as a way in which the organization self-corrects and improves. The system is predicated on the three principles outlined above: pre-specification of what constitutes good performance; the assumption that measurements will be accurate enough to serve as inputs to decision making and improvement efforts; and linkage of performance to rewards (winning the "competition") and punishments (having the "spotlight" on you). It is important to note that, through these features, the three principles are *designed* into this system.

Evidence of dysfunction in airline performance measurement

There was evidence of dysfunctional behaviors associated with the airline on-time departures system. Some indicators of this dysfunction are listed below.

1 Lack of alignment between pre-specified delay codes and actual events (which were more various than anticipated) caused a proliferation of delay types and also mis-coding of delays. "We have delay codes for when the Pope visits, or if there are beetles in the cockpit," said a field manager only half in jest, "but sometimes a problem occurs and we have no code for it . . . So we tag it on the last group off the plane."

2 At some stations, employees reported that delays were coded to weather and air traffic control whenever possible, to shift the onus to outside parties.

3 There was often a failure to focus on the actual goals of the departure process. According to a supervisor, "If you ask anyone here, what's the last thing you think of when there's a problem, I bet your bottom dollar it's the customer. And these are guys who bust their butts everyday. But they're thinking "how do I keep my ass out of the sling'."

4 Execution of the delay tracking system consumed considerable resources that might have been better spent. One customer service employee observed, "Here . . . the ultimate goal is not the customers. It's the report card." The attitude was, "If they are taking a delay at least it's not mine, so you would sort of forget about it. You spend so much time filling out delay forms and fighting over a delay – just think what we could be doing." A similar sentiment was expressed at another airline, "There is so much internal debate and reports and meetings. This is time that we could be focusing on the passengers." Rather than focusing on the process itself, managers tended to focus on meeting their numbers to avoid punishment. One manager complained about being "harassed on a daily basis . . . Headquarters has a performance analysis department that is looking at my MAPS [minimal acceptable performance standards] every day, analyzing the station's performance. Failure to meet MAPS is perceived to result in punitive action."

5 Working relationships between groups suffered as well. "There was always a lot of finger-pointing," according to a ramp manager at one airline. "Barriers between groups – it all comes down to the delay coding system," said a station manager at another airline.

6 Managers were willing to do what was necessary to meet their performance goals, even if it meant doing things that were not in the company's best

interests, in their judgment. "The field manager is judged on the numbers and not on how he got them," said the manager of human resources. "He could have used a club for all it matters to his rewards." The employee-relations manager concurred, "All that matters is the numbers – how you achieve them is secondary. This is part of the culture of fear." According to a field manager, "It is scary to delegate, especially here, where there is a very strong culture toward accountability. This is fine, but the penalties that go along with that accountability make people afraid to take risks."

7 Managers transmitted to the front-line workers the pressures they perceived from headquarters. As a result, employees were well aware of their managers' performance evaluation system, and how it affected them. "Here you only care about delays," said a customer service agent. "Otherwise the little report card won't look good that week. The ultimate goal is not the customers, it's the report card."

These dysfunctional behaviors appeared to be linked to the measurement system, which in turn was based on the three principles outlined above. The following vignettes suggest ways that performance in this setting was enhanced by deliberately subverting these principles.

Vignettes: Anomalous high performance

Vignette 1: "I don't know how I'm measured" (violation of principle 1)

The airline with the industry's fewest delays, mishandled bags and customer complaints – the best performer in aggregate – is deliberately vague about the basis for managerial evaluation. When asked, field managers were vague about how their own performance was assessed. "I don't know," was one typical response, given with a laugh. "I'll hear about it if I'm not doing a good job." "It is watched but there is no fear factor," said another. "Everybody here is a self-motivator." Some other observations from employees at this high-performance airline:

"I know what the relationship [between headquarters and the station] is usually like, because I worked at [another airline] for 20 years," according to another field manager at this airline. "It's usually an entrenched bureaucracy between the station manager and the headquarters. It's nothing like that here."

"Each station is like an entrepreneur," said his assistant manager. "We do what we think is right and talk directly to our executive vice presidents and [the CEO]. They are just a phone call away. If they question something we did today, they will call tomorrow."

Field managers at this airline expressed a comfort with the relationship with headquarters that contrasted dramatically with the resentment expressed by field managers at other airlines. They described a dialogue with their superiors, and a flow of information that was focused on identifying problems and finding solutions.

Discussion of vignette 1

The high performance of this organization seems anomalous in light of principle 1, which calls for clear definition of performance. The fact that employees do not know how they are evaluated suggests that there are no objective performance contracts. But both the organizational and economic literatures have acknowledged that dysfunctional behavior can result from specifying performance *ex ante*. Dysfunctional behaviors, such as those described at other airlines, occur when measures are not true or complete measures of performance – measures do not fully specify the performance that is desired in part because desired performance is not fully known *ex ante*.

Given the apparent dysfunction induced by the measurement systems of airlines that are not high performers, the ambiguity in the definition of performance at the high-performing airline might be seen as a defense against dysfunction. Evaluation criteria are left ambiguous because the criteria on which a contract could be agreed are not adequate. Being more specific about performance, then, would lead to managers focusing on certain measures to the detriment of overall performance – just as was described above by employees at lower-performing airlines.

It is possible that performance at this organization results from delegating control to the station-level instead of pre-specifying performance. As Selznick (1949) and Simon (e.g., 1991) point out, delegation is an option when performance is difficult to pre-specify. This allows criteria for decision making to be specified at the level of the organizational unit at the time of action rather than in advance. The statement that "each station is like an entrepreneur" seems consistent with this view.

However, this is not a story about a hands-off relationship. The evidence presented here suggests that managerial performance at this airline is evaluated *ex post*, in the context of multiple factors that could not have been specified in advance. One manager points out that performance is watched. Another says, "I'll hear about it if I'm not doing a good job." Yet another says if headquarters "questions something we did today, they will call tomorrow." There is a notion of performance as defined by headquarters, but like field managers themselves, they do not know it until they see it and hear about it in detail. These factors could only be analyzed *ex post*, through frank discussion of specific scenarios and specific decisions that were made. Thus, high performance at this airline seems consistent with the use of subjective contracts.

Reliance by this high-performing airline on ambiguous measures appeared to require trust, as predicted by Baker, Gibbons, and Murphy (1994). It required trust by field managers that headquarters was motivated more by a desire to coach and develop, than to judge and punish. It required trust by headquarters that field managers were motivated by a desire to do the right thing, whatever that turned out to be in a particular context. The vignette gives some indication that this trust was indeed present on both sides: "There is no fear factor. Everyone here is a self-motivator." But perhaps trust was inspired by the ambiguity of the measurement system itself. Field managers could trust headquarters because the measurement system removed fear from the relationship. Headquarters could trust field managers because they were "self-motivators," driven by intrinsic motivation (McGregor, 1960; Ouchi, 1979).

Hence, it seems that the first principle of performance measurement – that performance should be clearly defined – can be detrimental to performance in situations that might be of considerable prevalence, and that its systematic violation can be conducive to high performance.

Vignette 2: "Team delay" (violation of principle 2)

Management at this high-performing airline had also addressed dysfunctional behaviors among front-line employees. These behaviors, known as finger-pointing and covering-your-butt, were described by employees in several airlines as common in the industry. This organization's solution was to introduce a new delay code called a "team delay," as an alternative to the more detailed performance measures that were traditionally used. "We've had a team delay for a couple of years now," said a top manager. "We had too many angry disagreements about whose fault it was." According to another:

> "The team delay is used to point out problems between two or three different employee groups in working together. We used to do it – if people were still on the jetway at departure time, it was a station delay. If people were on-board at departure time, it was a flight crew delay. But now if you see everybody working as a team, and it's a team problem, you call it a team delay. It's been a very positive thing."
>
> "We could have more delay categories," said the head of operations, "but we just end up chasing our tail."

The team delay became the single most-used delay category for station-controllable delays. Within this airline, the team delay was regarded as an innovation that partly explained why this airline had the best on-time performance in the industry.

Discussion of vignette 2

Consider what is being described in this vignette: a company institutes a performance measurement system, one that is conventionally used in its industry. It then intentionally subverts the same performance measurement system by providing a blanket category – the team delay – that can be used to code delays where there is controversy about who caused the delay. Measurement information is apparently lost. Measurement has become less accurate, less revealing of the underlying phenomena. Principle 2 seems violated. But, interestingly, performance seems to have improved.

The earlier accounts of the dysfunctional effects of the performance measurement system at relatively low-performing airlines make clear the rationale behind a team delay. The team delay solved many of the problems of dysfunctional performance measurement. It eliminated reasons for devoting resourcefulness to managing numbers rather than actual performance. Delays occurred less frequently because people were focused on getting the plane out rather than trying to avoid being "tagged."

But the team delay clearly resulted in a loss of measurement information for the organization. When the team delay was used to code a delay, the measurement system did not capture detailed diagnostic information regarding the causes of that delay. The team delay was sometimes used when a more specific coding was possible. Workers realized that the job of getting the airplane out in a difficult situation was made easier when there was tacit agreement that any delay would be coded as a team delay. Hence, sometimes the team delay reflected not collective responsibility for a delay but rather the perceived difficulty of a situation before any delay occurred. Faced with a difficult situation, early commitment to a team delay made all parties more willing to join in problem solving to avoid the delay even when the delay subsequently occurred anyway. In approving the team delay, the airline was implicitly approving these behaviors. This performance-enhancing solution was in effect a company-sanctioned loss of measurement information.

It is not at all clear, however, that there was a *net* loss of information due to the use of team delays. By allowing the less-precise reporting of station delays, the company in reality *improved* the flow of information and avoided unproductive conflict. People who were not worried about how measurements would reflect on them personally were more willing to discuss the causes of delays. People were therefore better able to learn from previous mistakes. Information exchange was voluntary and unimpeded by the efforts to manage appearances that were rampant at other airlines.

All of the theoretical frameworks we know of have at least some difficulty explaining why a company would install an information system, then subvert it to improve performance and communication, all the while continuing to maintain the system. As has been mentioned, there are economic models that suggest that dysfunction might result from accurate measurement. Narayanan and Davila (1998) find that firms will delegate or set up multiple measurement systems when an agent can manipulate measurements that can be used for both evaluation and for belief revision (e.g., learning). But this vignette seems not to provide a pure example of either possible solution. As we will discuss later, creating a performance measurement system and then "removing its teeth" may be a gesture intended to communicate a message to workers.

Vignette 3: "I'll take this delay" (violation of principle 2)

Tom Dag, a safety coordinator for another airline, created his own personal solution to the problems created by performance measurement. It was well-known at his airline, he explained, that delays were often tagged on the last party still touching the aircraft when the delay occurred. As a result, he explained, people would hold back from helping when a delay seemed imminent, to avoid being tagged. The result, too often, was that an imminent delay became an actual delay. This aggravated him.

> Nobody wants to be responsible for a delay. It's a cover-your-butt situation. Personally I say put the delay on my tab. I'll do what I can do. It's my way of jesting with them. They come and help when I do this, because they know I don't care about a delay. So they don't have to worry about it being their delay. They come out of the woodwork to help.

Dag was willing to have the delay attributed to him, regardless of the actual cause, but the result was to prevent delays that were occurring simply as a result of people trying to avoid being tagged with a delay.

Discussion of vignette 3

As in vignette 2, Dag's solution to the problems created by performance measurement resulted in a loss of information to the organization. The two situations are in many ways similar, and both appear to violate principle 2. Vignette 3, however, is arguably more difficult to explain. Dag's "creative" approach to delay coding was not sanctioned by the company. In fact, it was probably a punishable behavior, had it been known at high enough levels in the organizations. In addition, he was more likely to be tagged than he would have been had he behaved as others did – that is, pulling back when a delay seemed imminent.

There are several theoretical incongruities in this situation. The company has instituted a measurement system that seems to reduce performance. An employee has taken on significant risks that others are not willing to take to defuse dysfunction and to improve aggregate performance, not to maximize his own well-being. In a game-theoretic frame, it appears that Dag is choosing a dominated, or irrational strategy. Although the apparent presence of anomalous cooperation means economic models lack explanatory power for this vignette, this kind of behavior is often observed in social situations. Psychologists (e.g., Dawes, 1991) have noted that a variety of social factors cause individuals to choose irrational behavior, including verbal communication, promising, and group identity.

Non-sanctioned behaviors that seek to *neutralize* the effects of a dysfunctional measurement system by reducing the accuracy of its measurements could be quite prevalent in organizations. It is interesting to consider the effects such behaviors might have on attempts to empirically verify the effectiveness of measurement systems.

Vignette 4: "I know you'll do your best" (violation of principle 3)[2]

Ted Derwa, an executive with a major US auto company, was running late trying to catch a flight to Frankfurt. He was sure that he would make it to the plane on time, but he was worried about his luggage. His whirlwind schedule would take him and a group of fellow executives to a different city every day for two weeks; if his bags did not get on the plane, they might never catch up with him. He solved this problem in a novel way.

Standing on the airport sidewalk, he removed a $20 from his wallet and handed to a nearby baggage handler. "Those are my bags," said Derwa, pointing. "They need to be on the 7:35 for Frankfurt." Immediately the baggage handler began to protest. He tried to hand back the $20. There were several reasons what Derwa was asking of him was impossible, he explained.

---

[2] This vignette is not taken from the same field study as the other three. Rather, it is a recounting of a story told within a company that is the former employer of one of this paper's authors. Although it surely classifies as organizational "lore" and is part of the "legend" of a widely admired manager, it is represented as fact within this company; parts of the story were corroborated by other "witnesses" within the company.

Derwa held up a hand, stopping the baggage handler from talking and said: "Look, to be honest, I don't really expect my luggage to get on that flight. But I want you to know, you do seem to me like the kind of person who could do it, if it is possible. So I'd like you to keep the twenty and give it your best shot. If it doesn't work out, I'll understand completely." Then Derwa turned and, without looking back, walked into the terminal, leaving the $20 with the baggage handler and his luggage on the sidewalk.

A few minutes later, Derwa boarded the flight. Within minutes, the plane pulled away from the gate. There was no way Derwa's bags had made it to the plane (he had barely made it himself). But, as the plane reached the taxiway, suddenly it lurched to a stop. Looking out through a window, Derwa saw a vehicle speeding toward the plane. In the driver's seat a man spoke urgently into a hand-held radio. Seated beside him, in the passenger seat, was the baggage handler. Piled in the back of the cart were Derwa's bags. The bags were loaded on to the plane. The small group of executives literally applauded the exceptional service.

Discussion of vignette 4

This vignette raises numerous questions that are relevant to performance measurement issues. Consider:

1 The level of performance exhibited by the baggage handler, with respect to the task defined by Derwa, was exceptionally high.
2 The "rational" action for the baggage handler in this situation was to pocket the $20 and slide the bags on to the luggage belt to be discovered later. There were no imaginable adverse consequences for this act. In choosing instead to take heroic action to get the bags on the plane, the baggage handler probably forwent tips (possibly totaling more than $20) and maybe even risked reprimand for going outside of procedures.
3 There was no conditional linkage between the reward of $20 and performance of the task. There was no "carrot" and no "stick."

The biggest question here with respect to common frameworks of measurement performance is "Why did this work at all?" The answer, it seems likely, has to do with the baggage handler's image of himself. Derwa, with his unconditional gift of $20 and with his brief words, was making an investment in the baggage handler. The fact that it was unconditional made the investment all the more impressive. It communicated a message that said, "Whether or not you succeed this particular time, faced with this particular set of difficulties, I believe you are a person who can succeed and who is worthy of trust and investment." So honored by Derwa, the baggage handler wanted to deserve the honor, in his own evaluation of himself. Given this honored status, the baggage handler performed to retain it in his own reckoning.

Although the apparent mechanism at work in this vignette will seem at first familiar – many have experienced being motivated by a desire to retain approval – the behaviors herein are anomalous in the context of almost any theoretical framework. It is tempting to access organization theories on intrinsic motivation or commitment. But even within the context of those literatures, the events in this vignette remain remarkable in that the baggage handler's fervor for performance came about so quickly, based on so little interaction between himself and Derwa. Derwa and the baggage handler were strangers, and remained so after their brief interaction. Rapid development of commitment to a "cause" has been demonstrated in other social science contexts. In a set of experiments performance by Dawes, Orbell, and van de Kragt (1988), people exhibited seemingly irrational cooperative behaviors for which they paid personal penalties when they were told that they were a group that was competing against another group. Fifteen minutes before the experiment, none of the participants had ever met, and they had in common only that they had all randomly selected the same colored chip from a gym bag. But commitment formation is not a part of most theories of performance measurement.

Some additional "data" that might be added to this discussion: Derwa was known for this style of management, in which he would place confidence in his employees and act in their interests in a way that was not contingent on outcomes. In this way, he consistently produced strong performance.

Alternative models of performance measurement

How is it that some organizations consistently achieve high performance without relying on the three traditional principles of measurement? In other words, what is the alternative to the traditional model of performance measurement? We hypothesize that what we have referred to as "anomalous high performance" holds within it the promise of systematically achieving high performance. To see how this might operate, we take a closer look at the principles and the vignettes, to identify what common threads run through them. The vignettes, although some of them are explainable within existing theory, reveal a possible alternative model when viewed collectively.

Taken collectively, the principles imply a system of performance that might be described as "closed loop." That is, in accordance with the engineering control analogy to which we have alluded, actual behavior is compared to desired behavior (whether defined before or after performance) in a way that is designed to provide at least the opportunity to correct behavior via rewards and punishments. The control mechanism is systemic and external to agents.

The common thread in the vignettes, however, is that in each the closed loop is intentionally opened and the opportunity for sanctions is foregone. Making aspects of the measurement environment ambiguous for performance measurement purposes opens the loop. The effect is to make some party to the joint effort vulnerable to opportunistic behavior by the other. By making performance evaluation ambiguous, the high-performance airline's management makes itself vulnerable to opportunistic behavior by workers. The team delay operates similarly. Dag's scheme for reducing delay involves making himself vulnerable to reprisals. And Derwa quite clearly sets himself up for the loss of $20 without commensurate benefit. Interestingly, high performance seems to follow when one party acts to make her/himself vulnerable to opportunistic behavior by others who are also involved.

We hypothesize that high levels of performance in organizations result when one party to a joint effort, whether an individual or management collectively, acts unilaterally and explicitly to make her/himself vulnerable to opportunistic behavior by others. This behavior, when it works (and we suspect it does not always), aligns preferences and enhances intrinsic motivation of the other party.

The act of inserting ambiguity into a performance measurement situation, of opening the performance measurement loop, is a gesture. The gesture is impressive precisely because it exposes the party making the gesture to the potential for opportunism. It contains the implicit message that the gesturing party thinks so highly of the other parties to the effort that it believes the other parties will not take advantage. Placed in this situation, interestingly, people tend to react by also not behaving in a self-interested manner. In fact, the reaction is often to align preferences and enhance motivations of all parties.

This phenomenon is familiar in human experience and often equated to notions of *heroism*. Acts are made more heroic by the degree to which they exhibit selflessness – that is, by the degree to which they *lack* of the type of behavior that forms the basis for much performance measurement theory. Further, selfless heroism appears to be contagious in the sense that observing a heroic act makes one more likely to behave in similar fashion. Selfless collective action inspired by one party's selfless individual action is a cultural idiom that exhibits itself in inspirational stories and behavioral ideals.

There is a tendency to think of this behavior as exceptional and not reliable in a systematic way. We hypothesize that this may not be the case. There was little that was obviously exceptional about the baggage handler's situation in observe this instance of organizational "heroism" will become aligned with those of the organization. Workers will have no reason to manipulate measures because they are not threatening; rather, they will choose instead to volunteer information relevant to the objectives of the organization. Intrinsic motivation will be enhanced. Some workers might free ride; if they do, there will be performance loss from this source.

We suggest that organizations choose between these meta-models of performance, sometimes without full awareness of the choice. The compliance-based model creates a self-fulfilling prophecy. It leads to manipulation of measures that then appear to move in the way expected by managers. Extrinsic rewards lead to extrinsically motivated behavior and to an expectation that desirable behavior will be extrinsically rewarded. The implicit assumption that people will not behave "heroically" in the long run is rendered true by the apparent approval of non-heroic behavior as designed into the performance measurement system. The popularity of pay-for-performance and other compliance-based techniques may be due in part to this self-fulfilling prophecy. Furthermore, heroic behavior (e.g., Dag's "I'll take this delay") and the general lack of external validation of the effectiveness of real systems, may lead to false conclusions about the effectiveness of compliance-based techniques.

The ambiguity-based model, by contrast, makes use of the contagious nature of selfless behavior to achieve high levels of performance and to avoid dysfunction. We hypothesize that actions that improve performance via the creation of ambiguity and vulnerability often occur in organizations, overtly in some (e.g., the high-performing airline) but covertly in others (Dag's airline). Moreover, we suggest that organizations can make systematic use of this model and that doing so increases the probability that parties within the organization will behave "heroically." Just as the compliance-based model conveys an expectation that behavior will be opportunistic, the ambiguity-based model conveys and expectation that it will not be. Worker preferences are endogenous and influenced by the implicit assumptions about tendencies toward opportunism in the design of performance measurement systems. To make this last point in a more dramatic way: we are what we make of ourselves, and our performance measurement systems are one powerful way through which we make ourselves.

It seems likely to us that the ambiguity-based model does work within the broad limits of organizational systems intended to insure the organization against major risks of worker misbehavior (e.g., embezzlement, theft). These systems tend to involve measurement, but are not performance measurement systems per se. Rather, they are "boundary systems" (Simons, 1996), organizational alarms that detect egregious examples of opportunistic behavior.

Conclusions

Economic and organization theories have both traditionally supported the three principles of performance measurement put forth in this contribution. Both literatures have more recently suggested weaknesses in these principles, though organization theorists in most cases pointed out these weaknesses earlier than did economists. Both fields have subsequently explored these weaknesses and in so doing have suggested pieces of an alternative model of performance measurement.

Building upon this previous work and our four vignettes, we have suggested two alternative meta-models of performance measurement. One is based on compliance and evokes extrinsic effort, resulting in goal displacement, distortion of information, and declining performance, as well as stronger commitment to the compliance-based approach. The other is based on ambiguity and evokes intrinsic effort, resulting in focus on real goals, enhanced information, and higher performance, as well as stronger commitment to the ambiguity-based approach.

The ambiguity-based model of performance measurement bears resemblance to the high commitment model of organizations introduced by Walton (1980) and further elaborated by Walton and Hackman (1986). Like our model, the high-commitment model relies on intrinsic rather than extrinsic motivation. As in our model, managers in the high-commitment model evoke intrinsic motivation by voluntarily relinquishing efforts to control. Our model differs however in focusing on the role of performance measurement.

We acknowledge that we have not come near to a full description of the ambiguity-based model. Also, it is impossible to reach conclusive answers through reasoning from anecdotal information. But we maintain that there is something very interesting that asserts itself in these vignettes, and, whatever that is, it deserves more mainstream attention. Moreover, the continued acceptance of the ideal expressed in the three principles of performance measurement seems misplaced.

BIBLIOGRAPHY AND REFERENCES

Austin, Robert (1996). *Measuring and Managing Performance in Organizations*. New York: Dorset House Publishing.
Baker, George. P. (1992). Incentive contracts and performance measurement. *Journal of Political Economy*, 100(3), 598–614.

norms is often indispensable. These values or norms may be undermined or even destroyed by offering monetary incentives.

Our basic message is that focusing on money as an incentive scheme with complex tasks causes problems. Complex tasks are a typical feature of knowledge-intensive companies which today comprise the most rapidly growing segment of the economy. In contrast variable pay for performance (e.g. via piece rates) is adequate only for simple jobs. For complex tasks monetary rewards are no substitute for good management. Relying solely on money is too simple to motivate people in complex jobs. Successful management consists in wisely choosing among the many different possibilities to evoke interest in the work i.e., raising intrinsic motivation. This can be achieved by establishing personal relationships within the firm, strengthening participation, and securing procedural justice. All serve to communicate to the employees recognition and appreciation of their work.

We first clarify the underlying concepts of extrinsic and intrinsic motivation. On the basis of theoretical and empirical evidence the following section demonstrates that intrinsic and extrinsic motivation are not additive. Rather, there is a systematic dynamic relationship between the two, called "crowding effects." In particular, monetary compensation can crowd out the intrinsic motivation to work for one's own sake. In the following section we discuss when and why intrinsic motivation is needed. However, as argued in the next section, intrinsic motivation sometimes has disadvantages for the organization. Hence an important task of management is to produce the right mixture of motivations. The contribution concludes that the current fad for variable pay for performance is ill-founded.

Intrinsic and extrinsic motivation

Extrinsic motivation obtains when employees are able to satisfy their needs indirectly, most importantly through monetary compensation. Money as such does not provide direct utility but serves to acquire desired goods and services (de Charms, 1968; Deci, 1975; an extensive survey is given in Heckhausen 1991, chapter 15). Extrinsically motivated coordination in firms is achieved by linking employees' monetary motives to the goals of the firm. The ideal incentive system is strict pay-for-performance.

In contrast, motivation is *intrinsic* if an activity is undertaken for one's immediate satisfaction. Intrinsic motivation "is valued for its own sake and appears to be self sustained" (Calder and Staw, 1975, p. 599; Deci, 1975; Deci and Ryan, 1980). Intrinsic motivation can be directed to the activity's flow (Csikszentmihalyi, 1975), to a self-defined goal, such as, for example, climbing a mountain (Loewenstein, 1999) or to the obligations of personal and social identities (March, 1999, p. 377). The ideal incentive system consists in the work content itself, which must be satisfying and fulfilling for the employees. It follows that "if you want people motivated to do a good job, give them a good job to do" (Herzberg, as quoted by Kohn, 1993, p. 49).

Intrinsic motivation is emphasized by the behavioral approach of the organization. This approach has a long tradition in motivation-based organization theory (Argyris, 1964; Likert, 1961; McGregor, 1960). More recent examples are the critics of transaction cost theory (e.g., Ghoshal and Moran, 1996; Donaldson, 1995; Pfeffer, 1997) as well as the literature on psychological contracts (e.g., Morrison and Robinson, 1997; Rousseau, 1995). They emphasize intrinsic motivation and identification with the firm's strategic goals, shared purposes and the fulfillment of norms for its own sake.

Intrinsic motivation is dealt with by only a few authors in economics; examples are trust (Arrow, 1974), sentiments (Akerlof and Yellen, 1986; Frank, 1992), firm loyalty (Baker, Jensen, and Murphy, 1988), managerial incentives (Güth, 1995), and implicit contracts or norms (Akerlof, 1982). Some economists admit the existence of intrinsic motivation but leave it aside because it is difficult to analyze and control (e.g., Williamson, 1985). Even if the assumption of opportunism is an "extreme caricature" (Milgrom and Roberts, 1992, p. 42), it is taken to be prudent to consider a worst case scenario when designing institutional structures (Williamson, 1996; see also Brennan and Buchanan, 1985 for the case of the constitution), i.e., dealing only with extrinsic motivation. Transactions cost theory goes a step further by assuming that individuals are opportunistic and seek self-interest with guile. Opportunism is a strong form of extrinsic motivation when individuals are not constrained by any rules. The same assumption is made by the principal agent theory as is clearly visible in the recent comprehensive surveys by Gibbons (1998) and Prendergast (1999).

To analyze intrinsic and extrinsic motivation in isolation is normally warranted and corresponds to a useful division of labor between psychology (focusing on intrinsic motivation) and economics (focusing on extrinsic incentives) as long as they do not depend on each other. But this dependence has been shown to exist in a large number of careful experiments undertaken by Deci and his group (see Deci, 1971, 1975; Deci and Ryan, 1980, 1985; Deci and Flaste, 1995). This evidence was largely ignored by scholars in organization theory as well as in human resource management (exceptions are

Ghoshal and Moran, 1996; Pfeffer, 1995a, p. 51, 1995b). The following section considers this relationship.

Motivation crowding-out effects

For a long time it has been taken as a matter of course that *extrinsic* motivation raises performance. It seemed to be a well-established result in the psychological (see, e.g., Eisenberger and Cameron, 1996) as well as in the managerial literature (see, e.g., Blinder, 1990; Lawler III, 1990) that positive reinforcement of a particular action increases the future probability of that action. Mechanisms of instrumental and classical conditioning lead to the *(relative) price effect* which is fundamental for economics (see Becker, 1976; Stigler and Becker, 1977; Frey 1992). The opportunity cost of unrewarded behavior is raised.

However, rewards crowd out intrinsic motivation under particular conditions. The most important conditions are, firstly, that the task is considered to be interesting (i.e. there must be an intrinsic motivation in the first place) and, secondly, that the reward is perceived to be controlling by the recipient. This effect has been called the "hidden costs of reward" (Lepper and Greene, 1978) or "the corruption effect of extrinsic motivation" (Deci, 1975). Frey (1997) has introduced it as the "crowding-out theory" into microeconomics. Extensive surveys are given in Lepper and Greene (1978) Pittman and Heller (1987), and Lane (1991). Kohn (1993) and Deci and Flaste (1995) provide popular applications.

The effect may be illustrated with an experience many parents have with their children. Consider children who are initially enthusiastic about a task. When they are promised a reward for fulfilling the task they lose part of their interest. Parents who try to motivate their children with rewards to do their homework may be successful in the short run. However, in the long run the children do their homework *only* if they receive a monetary reward. The crowding-out effect has set in. In the worst case, the children are prepared to do *any* housework, such as cutting the lawn, only if they are paid.

Such experiences hold not only for children but can be generalized. In particular it also applies to variable pay for performance or bonuses. As a consequence, such reward systems usually, but not always, make employees lose interest in the immediate goal (such as serving the customers) and lower their performance. These insights are corroborated by theoretical arguments as well as experimental and field studies.

Theoretical background

The crowding-out effect is based on *cognitive evaluation theory* (Deci, 1975; Deci and Ryan, 1985) and on *psychological contract theory* (Schein, 1965; Rousseau and McLean Parks, 1993).

According to *cognitive evaluation theory* intrinsic motivation is substituted by an external intervention which is perceived as a restriction to act autonomously. The locus of control shifts from inside to outside the person (Rotter, 1966). The person in question no longer feels responsible but rather attributes responsibility to the person undertaking the outside intervention. This shift in the locus of control does not always take place. Each external intervention, e.g., a reward, has two aspects, a controlling and an informing one. The controlling aspect strengthens perceived external control and the feeling of being stressed from the outside. The informing aspect influences one's perceived competence and strengthens the feeling of internal control. Depending on which aspect is prominent, intrinsic motivation is reduced or raised (see, e.g., the experiments in Enzle and Anderson 1993). An underminig effect on intrinsic motivation called crowding out is complemented by a positive effect on intrinsic motivation called crowding in. If a task is at the same time extrinsically and intrinsically motivated, the more devalued the attribution of a self-determined action is, the more strongly the individuals believe themselves to be subject to outside control (Kruglanski, 1975).

The crowding-out effect is stronger with material than with symbolic rewards. It is also larger with expected than with unexpected rewards. When the problems at issue are complicated, the negative relationship between reward and performance is stronger than when the problems are simple (Heckhausen, 1991, chapter 15). In all these cases, it is required that the behavior was initially perceived to be interesting and therefore intrinsically rewarding (see Calder and Staw, 1975).

According to the *theory of psychological contracts*, each contract includes an extrinsically motivated (transactional) aspect as well as a relational aspect, directed towards a reciprocal appreciation of intrinsic motivation. If the relational part of the contract is breached, the reciprocal good faith is put into question. Empirical evidence shows (Robinson, Kraatz, and Rousseau, 1994) that the parties to the contract then perceive the employment arrangement to be transformed into a purely transactional contract. For example, when the superior acknowledges an employee's extraordinary effort with a symbolic gift (such as a bunch of flowers), the intrinsic motivation of the employee tends to be raised because he feels that his intrinsic motivation is appreciated. But if the employee feels that the superior's gesture only serves in an instrumental purpose his intrinsic motivation is impaired. The bunch of flowers is perceived to be controlling. The relationship is interpreted to be transactional.

The reciprocal appreciation of motives also explains why commands normally crowd out intrinsic motivation more than the use of prices. Commands do not take into account the motives of the recipients, while the price system leaves the choice open as to whether one cares to receive the reward or not.

An important part of psychological contracts involves perceptions of fairness. Fairness includes both outcome as well as procedural justice. *Outcome justice* includes, firstly, that employees evaluate their salary not in absolute terms but relative to their co-workers (see the equity theory by Adams, 1963). Secondly, the contract between employer and employee is seen as a gift relationship based on norms of reciprocity. If the perceived reciprocity is violated, employees reduce their voluntarily offered supernormal performance (Akerlof, 1982; for experimental evidence see Fehr, Gächter, and Kirchsteiger, 1997). *Procedural justice* means that people are prepared to accept substantial differences in wages if the process of their determination is perceived to follow transparent and fair rules (Kim and Mauborgne, 1991, 1998; Tyler, 1990).

Empirical evidence

There is such a large number of *laboratory experiments* on crowding out that a more comprehensive view is needed. Fortunately the experimental evidence has been the subject of several meta-analytical studies. Wiersma (1992) looks at 20 studies covering 1971–90; and Tang and Hall (1995) at 50 studies from 1972 to 92. These meta-analyses support the crowding-out theory. This view was challenged by Eisenberger and Cameron (1996) who, on the basis of their own meta-analysis covering studies published in the period 1971–91, concluded that the undermining effect is largely "a myth." However, Deci, Koestner, and Ryan (1999) in a very extensive study were able to show that these conclusions are unwarranted. This most recent meta-analysis includes all the studies considered by Eisenberger and Cameron as well as several studies which appeared since then. The 68 experiments reported in 59 articles span the period 1971–97, and refer to 97 experimental effects. It turns out that tangible rewards, a subset of which is pay for performance, undermine intrinsic motivation for interesting tasks (i.e., tasks for which the experimental subjects show an intrinsic interest) in a highly significant and very reliable way. Thus there can be no doubt that the crowd-ing-out effect exists and is a robust phenomenon of significant size under the conditions identified.

In real-life situations we have to look at the net outcome, composed of the relative price effect as well as the crowding-out effect. This holds because the effect of intrinsic motivation cannot always be neatly separated from extrinsic incentives. When someone is fond of communication with customers for fun, it is always possible to find a corresponding external motive, such as selling better. Therefore it is important to consider *field studies* which take into account the net effect of the relative price and crowding-out effects. There exist several such studies:

1 A real-life case for the crowding-out effect is provided by blood donations, as argued by Titmuss (1970). Paying donors for giving blood undermines the intrinsic motivation to do so. Though it is difficult to isolate the many different influences on blood supply, in countries where most of the blood is supplied gratis, paying for blood is likely to reduce total supply (Upton, 1973).

2 A field study refers to the so-called NIMBY (Not In My BackYard)-syndrome (Frey and Oberholzer-Gee, 1997). In a community located in central Switzerland, in a carefully designed survey more than half the respondents (50.8 percent) agreed to have a nuclear waste repository built in their commune. When compensation in monetary terms was offered, the level of acceptance dropped to 24.8 percent.

3 An econometric study of 116 managers in medium-sized Dutch firms shows that the number of hours worked in the company decreased with the intensity of personal control effected by the superiors (Barkema, 1995).

4 A large-scale study conducted over 3,860 family businesses finds that performance pay is ineffective because it violates a psychological contract, directed on higher-order goals, such as affiliation and recognition (Buchholtz, Schulze, and Dino, 1996).

5 Austin (1996) shows, on the basis of interviews with eight experts, that performance measurement is highly contraproductive for complex and ambiguous tasks in computer software development.

To summarize, both theoretical considerations as well as empirical evidence from laboratory and field research strongly suggest that external interventions crowd-out intrinsic motivation under the conditions specified. In particular, piece rates, bonuses and other forms of variable pay for performance undermine employees' work ethics, especially in complex jobs where intrinsic motivation is important and rewards are used in a controlling way. The crowding-out effect thus provides a possible explanation for the overwhelm-ing empirical evidence that there is no significant connection between pay and performance, except for simple jobs (Gibbons, 1998; Prendergast, 1999). Even for piece-rates applicable to simple jobs the "literature on incentive plans is full of vivid descriptions of the counterproductive behaviors that piece-rate incentive plans produce" (Lawler III, 1990, p. 58). The same holds for mana-gerial compensation (for a survey see Barkema and Gomez-Mejia, 1998), a fact which is even admitted by the proponents of principal agent theory (e.g., Güth, 1995; Jensen and Murphy, 1990).

In the following section we discuss in a more detailed way when and why intrinsic motivation is needed.

Why intrinsic motivation is needed

Intrinsic motivation is required whenever extrinsic rewards in the form of pay for performance lead to undesired consequences:

1 Intrinsic motivation is needed for tasks that require creativity; in contrast, extrinsically motivated persons tend to produce stereotyped repetition of what already works (see Schwartz, 1990; Amabile, 1996, 1998). In addition, experimental research shows that the speed of learning and the conceptual understanding are reduced when people are monitored. The pressure of sanctions leads to lower levels of learning, and the work is performed in a more superficial way than with intrinsically motivated employees (Deci and Flaste, 1995, p. 47).

2 Intrinsic motivation helps to overcome the so-called multiple task problem (Holmstrom and Milgrom, 1991; Prendergast, 1999). This applies to cases where contracts cannot completely specify all relevant aspects of employee behavior and its desired outcome. Moreover, it is often not clear to the prin-cipals which goals are to be set. Financial goals cannot always be broken down into operational goals for employees. This problem has led to the recent success of the balanced scorecard concept (Kaplan and Norton, 1996). As a result, contracts offering incentives to reach given goals can give rise to dysfunctional behavioral responses. Agents focus only on the rewarded aspects of the job and disregard the unrewarded ones. Neither do they have sufficient incentives to reflect on the adequacy of the goals they should achieve for the overall success of the firm. Multiple task problems are the subject of incomplete contracts, which are characteristic of employ-ment contracts (e.g., Simon, 1951; Williamson, 1975). Empirical evidence

suggests that the outcome of incomplete contracts will not normally be evaluated by variable pay-for-performance, but that firms rely considerably on intrinsic motivation (Austin, 1996).

3   The transfer of tacit knowledge requires intrinsic motivation. Tacit knowledge cannot be expressed in writing or symbols. In contrast, explicit knowledge can be coded, is easily transferable and multipliable and can be stored in books or diskettes. The distinction entails important consequences with respect to the transfer of knowledge and the kind of motivation required. The transfer of tacit knowledge cannot be measured directly. Hence, when several persons contribute their tacit knowledge, joint output is not attributable to a particular person. In the absence of intrinsic motivation, employees would tend to free ride (Osterloh and Frey, 2000).

Disadvantages of intrinsic motivation

Intrinsic motivation should serve to support a firm's goals. It thus is not a goal in itself. Sometimes a specific intrinsic motivation is disadvantageous, for example surfing the internet for private pleasure during work hours. Consequently, the managers must compare the benefits and costs related to motivating employees intrinsically and extrinsically. Though intrinsic motivation is indispensable, it nevertheless sometimes has disadvantages.

1   Changing intrinsic motivation is more difficult and the outcome more uncertain than relying on extrinsic motivation or carrots and sticks. This is the reason why economists as well as managers traditionally prefer a reward and command policy (Argyris, 1998).

2   Intrinsic motivation can have an undesirable content. As history shows, some of the most terrible crimes committed have been at least partly intrinsically motivated. Envy, vengeance, and the desire to dominate are not less intrinsically motivated than altruism, conscientiousness, and love. All of them contribute to immediate satisfaction rather than to achieving externally set goals.

3   Extrinsic motivation enables behavior to become more flexible. The motivation of volunteers in a not-for-profit organization, for instance, depends strongly on how it differs compared to the organizational goal. A profit-oriented firm in contrast does not have to be so much concerned about the personal values of its employees as long as it pays them well and the costs of supervision are low.

The art of producing the right motivation

Motivation is not a goal by itself but should serve to support a firm's goals. Enterprises are not interested in producing *some* kind of intrinsic motivation with their employees, say the joy of stamp collecting. Rather, they must be motivated to perform in a *coordinated* and *goal-oriented* way. For this purpose, the managers must compare the benefits and costs related to motivating employees intrinsically and extrinsically. Further research is needed to spell out more precisely the conditions for the right balance between intrinsic and extrinsic motivation. Nevertheless, several systematic determinants can be identified to help to manage the kinds of motivation required within firms.

Extrinsic motivation is sufficient when the work is routinized and the performance is easy to measure. This condition obtains for simple jobs. In such cases empirical evidence shows that the price effect increases performance. An example is given by Lazear (1996). He finds that in a large autoglass company, productivity increases of between 20 percent to 36 percent of output were reached when the firm switched from paying hourly wages to piece-rates.

This is a striking example showing that extrinsic motivation may result in considerable efficiency gains in a situation where the persons affected by the external intervention have little or no intrinsic motivation.

Intrinsic motivation is a necessary production factor in the firm when labor contracts are characterized by a high degree of incompleteness as well as ambiguity. In contrast to pure market contracts, labor contracts typically include incompleteness to a high degree (Simon, 1951; Hodgson, 1998). In well-defined situations this incompleteness can be outweighed by commands, and the opportunity costs of unwarranted behavior can be raised. However, if the description of the tasks to be fulfilled is incomplete *and* ill-defined, intrinsic motivation, i.e., interest in the task itself, is the only way to avoid shirking. According to the theories of cognitive evaluation and psychological contracts mentioned above the following factors favor a higher level of intrinsic motivation:

Personal relationships and communication. A large number of experiments show that communication strongly raises the intrinsic motivation to cooperate (originally, Dawes, van de Kragt, and Orbell, 1988, more recently, Frey and Bohnet, 1995). Even if no communication takes place but persons can identify each other, cooperation is increased (Bohnet and Frey, 1999a, 1999b). Personal relationships are a precondition for relational psychological contracts (Rousseau, 1995).

Participation. The larger the possibilities to co-determine, the more the employees engage themselves in mutually set goals and adopt them as their own. Participation thus raises self-determination. Mutually agreed goals – in contrast to exogenously imposed goals – strengthen intrinsic motivation because the employees are informed about their capacity to perform. As experiments show, this effect only takes place when the agreements about the goals primarily serve as self-control and self-obligation. In contrast, perceived external control inhibits creativity while pursuing goals (see Schwartz, 1990).

Interest in the activity. Employees are more motivated to work when they are aware of the results of their input, when they are responsible for the outcome, and when they consider their work to be meaningful (Hackman and Oldham, 1980). Clearly, self-determination is supported.

According to the crowding-out theory discussed above, the following factors determine how strongly intrinsic motivation is undermined:

1 *Contingency of reward on performance.* The closer the dependence of a reward on the required performance, the more strongly intrinsic motivation is crowded-out. This holds provided the perceived controlling effect of rewards is stronger than the perceived informing effect. In that situation, employees feel their self-determination to be curtailed. This is an argument in favor of time-based compensation and against strict forms of pay-for-performance in situations characterized by high intrinsic motivation.

2 *Commands.* A command restricts the perceived self-determination of the persons affected more strongly than would a corresponding reward. This distinction between the effect of commands and rewards on motivation has been disregarded in traditional economic theory. The recent research on behavioral anomalies reveals that opportunity costs, in our case not receiving a reward, are systematically less valued than direct costs of the same size, in our case the punishment following from not obeying commands (e.g., Dawes, 1988; Thaler, 1992).

3 *Violation of justice.* Agents who feel unjustly paid reduce their intrinsic motivation. A large number of empirical studies show that people judge the fairness of their pay relative to other persons. "It is more critical how their pay compares to the pay of others than what they make in absolute dollars

and cents" (Lawler III, 1990, p. 24). This corresponds to the above-mentioned fairness considerations.

These factors influencing the level of intrinsic motivation obtaining in the firm demonstrate that managing motivation cannot be achieved solely by monetary rewards. Money alone causes serious problems for motivating employees.

Concluding remarks

Our main message is: Monetary reward is no effective substitute for well-managed human resources. Monetary incentives are entangled in an extensive web of psychological contracts, cognitive self-evaluation, and fairness considerations. In our contribution we have shown the traps into which management may fall when applying variable pay for performance.

We have systematically disentangled the complicated web of motivations characterizing the relationships in firms. It is only for simple jobs that variable pay for performance is applicable and useful. Performance is easy to measure and can be attributed to the particular employee. Moreover, such jobs are typically undertaken for monetary reasons only. But today such jobs are increasingly losing importance as the competitive advantage of firms depends on knowledge and organizational learning. These attributes are by their very nature difficult to meter. Because they are demanding and offer a high degree of self-determination, these activities both enable and necessitate employees intrinsically motivated for the firm's goals. In such positions, variable pay for performance as sole motivator crowds out intrinsic motivation.

This does not mean that monetary rewards are unimportant. To avoid the crowding-out effect they must take into account various aspects. Compensation should be based on an overall evaluation of employees. This may include bonuses or gain sharing, as long as procedural fairness and perceived justice relative to co-workers are observed. In any case, to strengthen intrinsic motivation, monetary rewards must be embedded in detailed feedback discussions. This feedback should not concentrate solely on outcome criteria but should express the appreciation of the employee's intrinsic motivation. Such feedback supports relational psychological contracts and reciprocal trust. Employees then feel informed about their competence and their contribution to the firm's goals. In contrast to the current fad, variable pay used as the only tool of handling performance underestimates the complexity of human motivation.

REFERENCES

Adams, J.S. (1963). Towards an understanding of inequity. *Journal of Abnormal and Social Psychology*, **67**, 422–36.

Akerlof, G.A. (1982). Labor contracts as partial gift exchange. *Quarterly Journal of Economics*, **84**, 488–500.

Akerlof, G.A. and Yellen, J.L. (1986). *Efficiency Wage Models and the Labor Market.* Cambridge: Cambridge University Press.

Amabile, T.M. (1996). *Creativity in Context: Update to the Social Psychology of Creativity.* Boulder, CO: Westview Press.

Amabile, T.M. (1998). How to kill creativity. *Harvard Business Review.* September–October, 77–87.

Argyris, C. (1964). *Integrating the Individual and the Organization.* New York: John Wiley.

Argyris, C. (1998). Empowerment: The emperor's new clothes. *Harvard Business Review*, May–June, 98–105.

Arrow, K.J. (1974). *The Limits of Organizations.* New York: Norton.

Austin, R.D. (1996). *Measuring and Managing Performance in Organizations.* New York: Dorset House Publishing.

Baker, G.P., Jensen, M.C., and Murphy, K.J. (1988). Compensation and incentives: Practice versus theory. *Journal of Finance,* **43**, 593–616.

Barkema, H.G. (1995). Do job executives work harder when they are monitored? *Kyklos*, 48, 19–42.

Barkema, H.G. and Gomez-Mejia, L.R. (1998). Managerial compensation and firm performance. A general research framework. *Academy of Management Journal*, **41**, 135–45.

Becker, G.S. (1976). *The Economic Approach to Human Behavior.* Chicago, CO: Chicago University Press.

Blinder, A.S. (ed.) (1990). *Paying for Productivity. A Look at the Evidence.* Washington D.C: Brookings.

Bohnet, I. and Frey, B.S. (1999a). The sound of silence in prisoner's dilemma and dictator games. *Journal of Economic Behaviour and Organization*, **38**, 43–57.

Bohnet, I. and Frey B.S. (1999b). Social distance and other-regarding behavior in dictator games: Comment. *The American Economic Review*, **89**(1), 335–9.

Brennan, G. and Buchanan, J.M. (1985). *The Reason of Rules: Constitutional Political Economy.* Cambridge: Cambridge University Press.

Buchholtz, A.K., Schulze, W.S. and Dino, R.N. (1996). Breaking the psychological contract: A social exchange theory perspective of performance-based managerial pay. Working Paper University of Connecticut, School of Business Administration.

Calder, B.J. and Staw, B.M. (1975). The self-perception of intrinsic and extrinsic motivation. *Journal of Personality and Social Psychology*, **31**, 599–605.

Csikszentmihalyi, M. (1975). *Beyond Boredom and Anxiety.* San Francisco, CA: Jossey-Bass.

Dawes, R.M. (1988). *Rational Choice in an Uncertain World.* San Diego and New York: Harcourt, Brace, Yovanovich.

Dawes, R.M., van de Kragt, A.J.C. and Orbell, J.M. (1988). Not me or thee but we: The importance of group identity in eliciting cooperation in dilemma situations – experimental manipulations. *Acta Psychologica*, **68**, 83–97.

DeCharms, R. (1968). *Personal Causation: The Internal Affective Determinants of Behavior.* New York: Academic Press.

Deci, E.L. (1971). Effects of externally mediated rewards on intrinsic motivation. *Journal of Personality and Social Psychology,* **18**, 105–15.

Deci, E.L. (1975). *Intrinsic Motivation.* New York: Plenum Press.

Deci, E.L. and Flaste, R. (1995). *Why We Do What We Do: The Dynamics of Personal Autonomy.* New York: Putnam.

Deci, E.L. and Ryan, R.M. (1980). The empirical exploration of intrinsic motivational processes. *Advances in Experimental Social Psychology,* **10**, 39–80.

Deci, E.L. and Ryan, R.M. (1985). *Intrinsic Motivation and Self-Determination in Human Behavior.* New York: Plenum Press.

Deci, E.L., Koestner, R. and Ryan, R.M. (1999). A meta-analytic review of experiments examining the effects of extrinsic rewards on intrinsic motivation. *Psychological Bulletin,* **125**, 627–68

Donaldson, L. (1995). *American Anti-Management Theories of Organization: A Critique of Paradigm Proliferation.* Cambridge: Cambridge University Press.

Eisenberger, R. and Cameron, J. (1996). Detrimental effects of reward: Reality or myth?" *American Psychologist,* **51**, 1153–66.

Enzle, M.E. and Anderson, S. (1993). Surveillant intentions and intrinsic motivation. *Journal of Psychology and Social Psychology,* **30**, 257–66.

Fehr, E., Gächter, S. and Kirchsteiger, G. (1997). Reciprocity as a contract enforcement device. Experimental evidence. *Econometrica,* **65**, 833–60.

Frank, R.H. (1992). Melting sociology and economics: James Coleman´s foundations of social theory. *Journal of Economic Literature,* **30**, 147–70.

Frey, B.S. (1992). *Economics as a Science of Human Behaviour.* Boston, MA and Dordrecht: Kluwer.

Frey, B.S. (1997). *Not Just for the Money: An Economic Theory of Personal Motivation.* Cheltenham, UK and Brookfield, US: Edward Elgar.

Frey, B.S. and Bohnet, I. (1995). Institutions affect fairness: Experimental investigations. *Journal of Institutional and Theoretical Economics,* **151**(2), 286–303.

Frey, B.S. and Oberholzer-Gee, F. (1997). The cost of price incentives: An empirical analysis of motivation crowding-out. *American Economic Review,* **87** (September), 746–55.

Ghoshal, S. and Moran, P. (1996). Bad for practice: A critique of the transaction cost theory. *Academy of Management Review,* **21**(1), 13–47.

Gibbons, R. (1998). Incentives in organizations. *The Journal of Economic Perspectives,* **12** (Fall), 115–50.

Güth, W. (1995). Shirking versus managerial incentives of chief executive officers (CEOs): A note on a possible misunderstanding of principal-agency theory. *Journal of Institutional and Theoretical Economics,* **151**(4), 693–8.

Hackman, R.J. and Oldham, G.R. (1980). *Work Redesign.* Reading, MA: Addison-Wesley.

Heckhausen, H. (1991). *Motivation and Action.* New York, Berlin and Heidelberg: Springer.

Hodgson, G.M. (1998). Competence and contract in the theory of the firm. *Journal of Economic Behavior and Organization,* **35**, 179–201.

Holmström, B. and Milgrom, P. (1991). Multitask principal-agent analyses: Incentive contracts, asset ownership and job design. *Journal of Law, Economics and Organization* (Special Issue), **7**, 24–52.

Jensen, M.C. and Murphy, K.J. (1990). Performance pay and top-management incentives. *Journal of Political Economy*, **98**, 225–64.

Kaplan, R.S. and Norton, D.P. (1996). *Translating Strategy into Action – The Balanced Scorecard*. Boston, MA: Harvard Business School Press.

Kim, W.C. and Mauborgne, R.A. (1991). Implementing global strategies: The role of procedural justice. *Strategic Management Journal*, **12**, 125–43.

Kim, W.C. and Mauborgne, R. (1998). Procedural justice, strategic decision making, and the knowledge economy. *Strategic Management Journal*, **19**, 323–38.

Kohn, A. (1993). *Punished by Reward. The Trouble with Gold Stars, Incentive Plans, A´s, Praise, and Other Bribes*. Boston, MA: Houghton Mifflin.

Kruglanski, A.W. (1975). The endogenous-exogenous partition in attribution theory. *Psychological Review*, **82**, 387–406.

Lane, R.E. (1991). *The Market Experience*. Cambridge: Cambridge University Press.

Lawler, E.E. III (1990). *Strategic Pay*. San Francisco, CA: Jossey-Bass.

Lazear, E.P. (1996). Performance pay and productivity. NBER Working Paper 5672.

Lepper, M.R. and Greene, D. (eds.) (1978). *The Hidden Costs of Reward: New Perspectives on the Psychology of Human Motivation*. Hillsdale, NY: Erlbaum.

Likert, R. (1961). *The New Patterns Of Management*. New York: McGraw-Hill.

Loewenstein, G. (1999). Because it is there: The challenge of mountaineering . . . for utility theory. *Kyklos*, **52**, 315–430.

March, J.M. (1999). *The Pursuit of Organizational Intelligence*. Malden, MA and Oxford: Blackwell.

McGregor, D. (1960). *The Human Side of Enterprise*. New York: McGraw-Hill.

Milgrom, P.R. and Roberts, J. (1992). *Economics, Organization and Management*. Englewood Cliffs, NJ: Prentice Hall.

Morrison, E.W. and Robinson, S.L. (1997). When employees feel betrayed: A model of how psychological contract violation develops. *Academy of Management Review*, **22**(1), 226–56.

Osterloh, M. and Frey, B.S. (2000). Motivation, knowledge transfer and organizational forms. *Organization Science*, **11**(5), 538–50.

Pfeffer, J. (1995a). Competitive advantage through people. Boston, MA: Harvard Business School Press.

Pfeffer, J. (1995b). Incentives in organizations: The importance of social relations. In *Organization theory. From Chester Barnard to the Present and Beyond*, ed O.E. Williamson. New York and Oxford: Oxford University Press.

Pfeffer, J. (1997). *New Directions for Organization Theory*. New York and Oxford: Oxford University Press.

Pittman, T.S. and Heller, J.F. (1987). Social Motivation. *Annual Review of Psychology*, **38**, 461–89.

Prendergast, C. (1999). The provision of incentives in firms. *Journal of Economic Literature*, **37**, 7–63.

Robinson, S.L., Kraatz, M.S., and Rousseau, D.M. (1994). Changing obligations and the psychological contract: A longitudinal study. *Academy of Management Journal*, **37**(1), 137–52.

Rotter, J.B. (1966). Generalized expectancies for internal versus external control of reinforcement. *Psychological Monographs*, **80**(1), 1–28.

Rousseau, D.M. (1995). *Psychological Contracts in Organizations: Understanding Written and Unwritten Agreements*. Thousand Oaks, London and New Dehli: Sage Publications.

Rousseau, D.M. and McLean Parks, J. (1993). The contracts of individuals and organizations. *Research in Organizational Behavior*, **15**, 1–43.

Schein, E. (1965). *Organization Psychology*. Englewood Cliffs, N.J: Prentice-Hall.

Schwartz, B. (1990). The creation and destruction of value. *American Psychologist*, **45**, 7–15.

Simon, H.A. (1951). A formal theory of the employment relationship. *Econometrica*, **19**, 293–305.

Stigler, G.J. and Becker, G.S. (1977). De gustibus non est disputandum. *American Economic Review*, **67** (March), 76–90.

Tang, S.H. and Hall, V.C. (1995). The overjustification effect: A meta-analysis. *Applied Cognitive Psychology*, **9**, 365–404.

Thaler, R.H. (1992). *The Winner's Curse. Paradoxes and Anomalies of Economic Life*. New York: Free Press.

Titmuss, R.M (1970). *The Gift Relationship*. London: Allen & Unwin.

Tyler, T.R. (1990). *Why People Obey the Law*. New Haven, CT: Yale University Press.

Upton, W. (1973). Altruism, attribution and intrinsic motivation in the recruitment of blood donors. *Selected Readings on Donor Motivation and Recruitment*, vol. III, ed. by American Red Cross.

Wiersma, U.J. (1992). The effects of extrinsic rewards on intrinsic motivation: A meta-analysis. *Journal of Occupational and Organizational Psychology*, **65**, 101–14.

Williamson, O.E. (1975). *Markets and Hierarchies: Analysis and Antitrust Implications: A Study in the Economics of Internal Organization*. New York: Free Press.

Williamson, O.E. (1985). *The Economic Institutions of Capitalism. Firms, Markets, Relational Contradicting*. New York: Free Press.

Williamson, O.E. (1996), Economic organization: The case for candor. *Academy of Management Review*, **21**, 48–57.

8 Superior managers tolerance to dysfunctional behavior: A test

Clive Emmanuel

Introduction

The advent of corporate governance has rejuvenated interest in the effectiveness of systems and procedures by which enterprises and their managements are held accountable. The design of management control systems therefore becomes of increasing interest to an enlarged audience of stakeholders. As a consequence, the managerial behavior induced by control systems has resulted in public debate. The troubles at Baring Brothers, the Shell Transport forward contract fiasco, and others can be interpreted at a micro-behavioral level (Macintosh, 1994) as rational, legitimate responses to the systems employed in these companies. A more traditional interpretation indicates dysfunctional behavior.

Beginning with the premise that all human beings wish to show themselves in the most favorable light, it is inevitable that providers of information will attempt to manipulate reports to suit their own purposes (Prakesh and Rappoport, 1977). "Earnings management" is one critical and controversial area where manipulation can occur. Reported income may not reflect true economic achievement, but instead an apparent and misleading signal which is nevertheless consistent with the message the superior wants to hear (Merchant and Rockness, 1994). The means of managing earnings is informed in this research by six broad categories of dysfunctional behavior (Birnberg, Turpolec, and Young, 1983), namely smoothing, biasing, focusing, gaming, filtering, and "illegal acts." A scenario for each category was presented to managers who responded on a scale of 1–5 as to the acceptability of a subordinate manager's action (Bruns and Merchant, 1990). The main research enquiry is to discover whether a consensus emerges as to the acceptability or otherwise of subordinate actions. The corollary is an examination of the tolerance levels different managers display to dysfunctional behavior.

The helpful comments of Kenneth Merchant, Norman Macintosh, Lokman Mia, and Bob Scapens are gratefully acknowledged as are the views of the participants at research workshops at Canberra and Deakin Universities on earlier drafts.

Consistent with Birnberg, Turpolec, and Young (1983), a further analysis by category of dysfunctional behavior is reported to test the claim that superior manager ability to analyze and verify data, conditions the category of behavior used. For this analysis, the responses of 50 managers in a large UK company (Company A) are analyzed.

Prior to the data being collected, pilot testing of the scenarios had been conducted with a sample of 16 finance staff in a different UK company (company B) and with a small sample of finance directors and controllers in a variety of multinationals (MNEs) based in the UK. These provide the basis by which to compare superior tolerance between functional roles, hierarchical positions, and corporate enterprises. The findings suggest that no clear consensus exists for any category of dysfunctional behavior. The differing levels of tolerance are not explained by functional role, hierarchical position, nor company.

A summary of the literature is reviewed in the next section outlining the persistence of dysfunctional behavior and the judgments available to superior managers. Then the research method and findings are reported. Discussion of findings, particularly in comparison with Merchant and Rockness (1994), occupies the next section followed by the implications for future research and, finally, the conclusions.

Literature review

The budgetary control literature has identified the impact of budgets on managerial behavior for several decades (Argyris, 1952). Further investigation into the motivational effect of budgets (Hofstede, 1968) and into participation during the budget development process (Schiff and Lewin, 1970) documented the potential dysfunctional effects of budgets. With a focus on the style of evaluation, Hopwood (1972) and Swieringa and Moncur (1972) indicated a relationship with differing degrees of manipulation of accounting reports. Otley's apparently confounding findings (1980) led to the search for contingent variables and a growing awareness that budgetary control, of necessity, should be examined in an organizational context (Waterhouse and Tiessen, 1978).

One of the significant developments relates to empirical investigations of the direct effects of components of control systems. Kren and Liao (1988), Birnberg, Shields, and Young (1990), Young and Lewis (1995), Shields and Shields (1998), amongst others, have examined the effect of budget participation, standard tightness, and performance-based incentives on job-related satisfaction, stress, attitude, motivation, and performance. The emphasis of these studies is firmly placed on the manager's attitude to participation in target setting, with an implicit assumption that consequent performance is accurately recorded and can be relied upon. Superior managers are assumed capable of detecting dysfunctional behavior and will take the necessary corrective action. This, in turn, assumes that all superior managers share a similar level of tolerance or intolerance to the questionable actions of subordinate managers.

These studies which may be described collectively as investigations of the reliance placed on accounting performance measures (RAPM) therefore concentrate on the "front-end" of the control process. The relationship between superior and subordinate managers as to the level of accuracy in reporting actual performance which is acceptable is less well explored.

Superior manager concern with the subordinate's ability to achieve short-term performance levels may explain the tendency to manipulate reports (Merchant, 1990). One interpretation of a Merchant and Manzoni (1989) study, where profit center managers achieved their budget targets 80–90 percent of the time, is that managers collude. Superiors and subordinates develop defensive routines which avoid threat and embarrassment (Argyris, 1990). The adoption of achievable budgets minimizes the potential for embarrassment or threat. Superior managers may be willing to accept manipulation of accounting reports to ensure their own well-being. Subordinate managers become aware of superior manager tolerance over time and feel it is appropriate to indulge in dysfunctional behavior. Otley and Berry (1994) illustrate the systematic and persistent distortion of information to superiors by subordinates in the NCB case. Interestingly, the dysfunctional behavior appears to be permitted by headquarter management, a comment echoed in Merchant (1990) which suggests that the unintended control system side effects may even be encouraged by top management.

Whilst this review of dysfunctional behavior and superior–subordinate interaction could be classed as illustrative of a Baudrillard simulacrum (Macintosh, 1996), of a need to explore the corporate cultural web (Johnson, 1987) or to examine the cognitive psychological characteristics of managers (Dermer, 1973), a more mundane path is chosen here. Is there a consensus regarding the acceptability of dysfunctional behavior? If there is not, then earnings management in different segments of the same enterprise or between enterprises suggests reported income is a less than adequate reflection of economic performance and potentially an unreliable comparative measure.

Six broad categories of dysfunctional behavior are suggested by Birnberg, Turpolec, and Young (1983):

- smoothing – the manipulation of performance indicators especially between time periods;
- biasing – the effectiveness of participation in budget setting and the relationship with corporate strategy;
- focusing – the emphasis on individual unit performance relative to corporate;
- gaming – the conflict-resolving procedures required to overcome problems of interdependence;
- filtering – the level of surrogation in reports provided to superiors;
- illegal acts – the pressure to meet targets in the short term.

It is argued that these six forms of dysfunctional behavior may be used to cover up or disguise failures or to avoid threats or embarrassment. That is, they may form part of the human defensive mechanism when faced with the pressure to achieve financial targets. However, their use may increase the potential of threat or embarrassment if the subordinate manager's actions are detected. But detection is only part of the problem.

There is some limited evidence (Hopper, 1985) that suggests divisional accountants are more concerned with compliance with internal reporting conventions than with the substance of accurate recordings. Understandably, as a member of the divisional management team, the accountant may come under peer pressure not to report manipulated data, in order to avoid isolation and the danger of being ostracized within the divisional work place.

Likewise, there is the distinct possibility that superior managers may display varying degrees of consent when manipulation by subordinates becomes apparent. This implied permission may vary between superior managers but, once a subordinate becomes aware that certain dysfunctional acts are acceptable, they may continue until the superior moves on. Therefore detection of manipulation may be of secondary importance relative to the reaction of the superior managers. If superior managers within the same company display varying degrees of consent to the same forms of dysfunctional behavior, how accurate or reliable are the internal reports of different divisions, segments, or units of the business? Can they be relied upon for comparative purposes when resource distribution questions concerning capital budgets or internal managerial performance are being assessed? These appear to be non-trivial implications concerning the incidence and implied permission of superior managers to condone dysfunctional behavior.

The scope for agreement on acceptable and unacceptable dysfunctional behavior should be most pronounced within a single enterprise. Whatever corporate mores, accounting manuals, and training schemes exist, all managers who have been employed for a substantial time should be aware of them. In addition, managers who undertake the same or similar functions are more likely to present a consensus regarding the six categories of dysfunctional behavior. For these reasons, the responses of 50 managers from a single UK company are concentrated on for this part of the research study.

The same data are employed to test the contention that different categories of dysfunctional behavior will be employed when superiors enjoy differing capabilities to analyze and verify data (Birnberg, Turpolec, and Young, 1983). When superiors are able to verify subordinate's information at low cost but encounter difficulties analyzing the data, subordinates may indulge in filtering and focusing to argue the merits of their cases and to appear in a favorable light. When the superiors are less able to verify the data but can analyze effectively, that is, ask the right questions of subordinates, it is suggested that biasing, gaming, smoothing, and illegal acts are the prevalent categories of dysfunctional behavior. A test of information-related behavior of superior managers may therefore contribute to a contingency theory which distinguishes the use of different categories of manipulation by subordinate managers.

Consistent with Merchant and Rockness (1994), corporate climate and professional norms are recognized as two potentially important factors which may link tolerance to dysfunctional behavior. Additional data from a UK company and from a sample of MNEs are introduced. More significantly, the hierarchical position of managers in the original UK company (company A) is used to discover whether superior and subordinate managers display consistent levels of tolerance to dysfunctional behavior.

Research method

Taking the six categories of dysfunctional behavior from Birnberg, Turpolec, and Young (1983), a scenario for each was developed (appendix A). The intention of each short scenario was to describe a potentially questionable action by a hypothetical subordinate manager. Each respondent was requested to judge each scenario as the superior manager and to indicate (a) what action they would take and (b) what action should be taken. The introduction of the normative form of questioning was an attempt to discover whether the respondents were aware of corporate rules, conventions, or culture, with which they may not agree personally. All tests revealed no significant differences between the normative and positive forms (chi-square, Kolmogorov–Smirnov, Students-t), and the positive responses are reported here.

There was a pilot study undertaken with 30 part-time MBA students, all of whom had at least two years work experience. This was administered as part of a taught course and was intended to test the realism, clarity of expression, and jargon of each scenario. Participants were asked to evaluate each scenario on a scale developed by Bruns and Merchant (1990) consistent with prior studies, such as Karnes *et al.* (1989) and Flory *et al.* (1992). This 1–5 scale was as follows:

1 Ethical practice: "An acceptable action."
2 Questionable practice: "I would not say anything to the manager but it makes me uneasy."
3 Minor infraction: "The manager needs to be warned not to do it again."
4 Serious infraction: "The manager should be seriously reprimanded."
5 Totally unethical: "The manager should be fired."

After providing their judgments and tabulating the scores, the participants took part in an open discussion concerning the reality of the scenarios, ambiguities, jargon, and whether any of the instances related to their own experiences. Minor modifications to the gaming and filtering scenarios were suggested and adopted. Refreshingly, the realism of the scenarios was generally accepted and several participants offered similar experiences of potentially dysfunctional behavior. Unlike Bruns and Merchant (1990), Merchant (1990), and Merchant and Rockness (1994), a conscious decision to exclude quantitative and financial data was made. The open discussion revealed that the inclusion of such data might have influenced some respondents. However, the influence would not have been uniform because materiality varied with the respondents' current positions and employment. Other participants felt that the principles were more important regardless of monetary value. This debate was repeated at the next two deliveries of the scenarios. On balance, it was felt that inclusion of financial data could adversely affect consensus and, thus, were excluded.

The modified scenarios were next presented to a self-selected sample of 16 members of the finance function in a very large UK company, Company B, who were attending a programme on multi-divisional accounting control issues. At that time, there was an expectation in this enterprise that further adoption of the multi-divisional structure was a fore-runner to privatization. Again the judgments on the scenarios was followed by an open discussion. The same procedure was conducted with a sample of financial directors and controllers of MNEs shortly afterwards.

Given the relatively small size of the groups and their non-random selection, access to the subsidiary of a large UK company, company A, in the plant and equipment leasing industry was pursued. With the assistance of the subsidiary

CEO, 68 questionnaires were sent to depot managers and regional directors with a stamped addressed envelope for onward mailing to the researcher. Overall, 79 percent of those contacted responded of which four questionnaires were incomplete, which gave 50 as the sample size. All six regional directors replied and 44 of the total population of 62 depot managers.

The scenarios formed the largest section of the questionnaire. In addition to demographic details, such as length of service, respondents were invited to give their views on which performance indicators were used, how frequently evaluation occurred, the importance of achieving targets with respect to reward schemes, and whether managerial and unit performance were distinguished. These questions were included to place the judgments surrounding the scenarios in context. At the time when the data were collected (January 1995), the company and the subsidiary were reporting improved financial results. Some rationalization had occurred in previous years, 1992–3, but there was general optimism that strategic direction was appropriate and advantages, especially for the plant and equipment leasing subsidiary, would result from any upturn in the UK economy.

In summary then, a research framework based on six categories of dysfunctional behavior was adopted using a research instrument, that is, scenarios, similar to previous studies (Merchant and Rockness, 1994). Table 8.1 indicates the respondents by enterprise and/or role. The results of the questionnaire responses to the scenarios are reported next with additional information obtained from open discussions and other sections of the questionnaire.

Results

In total, 77 respondents judged each category of dysfunctional behavior in the scenarios (see table 8.1 for a classification of respondents). Table 8.2 presents mean scores and standard deviations for the respondents in company A. The main intention is to discover whether a consensus emerges as to the acceptability or otherwise of subordinate actions. A priori, this consensus might be expected when experienced managers in the same or similar functions in a single enterprise are examined.

The results relate to the positively worded question, "what action would you take as the superior manager." No statistically significant difference is found when the normative question, "what actions ought to be taken", responses are analyzed. This implied that each manager believed their judgment to be consistent with the prevailing corporate mores or culture. An

Table 8.1 Classification of respondents

	Company A	Company B	MNEs
General managers	50	–	–
Finance staff	–	16	11
Total	50	16	11

Table 8.2 Judgments by company A managers

Scenario	Mean	Standard deviation	Range
1	2.88	1.07	1–5
2	2.00	0.98	1–4
3	3.42	1.09	1–5
4	2.65	1.11	1–4
5	2.36	1.23	1–5
6	3.32	1.12	1–5

Note:
The Kolmogorov–Smirnov one sample test revealed minimum statistically significant differences of 0.05 for each scenario when applied in two sequences. Chi square applied to all scenarios indicated statistically significant differences at 0.01.

alternative explanation is that the respondents were unaware of any corporate held ethical views.

For each scenario, there is a lack of agreement on the acceptability of the actions taken by the subordinate manager. The wide range of responses and high-standard deviations for all scenarios indicate that the respondents did not agree in their judgments. No consensus is revealed and this implies that different managers have varying tolerance to dysfunctional behavior. On average, the respondents had over five years experience in their current managerial positions and within the enterprise: 95 percent expressed the view that the scenarios were realistic and 56 percent indicated that they had first-hand experience of similar situations. Company A also had a detailed accounting manual and encouraged line managers to attend in-house training courses. Against this background, the range of judgment on what is regarded as dysfunctional behavior is disquieting.

With the same data, the Birnberg, Turpolec, and Young (1983) contention that different categories of dysfunctional behavior are displayed when superior management has varying ability to analyze and verify the data is examined.

Table 8.3 The association between category of dysfunctional behavior and superior management ability to analyze and verify data

Superior management ability to	Hypothesized category of dysfunctional behavior	Mean	Standard deviation	t-statistic
(a) Analyze data low	Filtering Focusing	2.89	1.28	
(b) Verify data low	Biasing Smoothing Gaming Illegal acts	2.53	1.19	2.273[a]

Note:
[a] Statistically significant at 0.05%.

Firstly filtering and focusing are hypothesized to be prevalent when superior managers have difficulty in analyzing the data provided by subordinates. Secondly, when superiors are less able to verify the data, biasing, smoothing, gaming, and illegal acts are expected to be experienced. Table 8.3 outlines the results of the test.

The results therefore appear to confirm the hypothesized association, that ability to analyze and verify data by superior management relates to different categories of dysfunctional behavior. However, further tests of the data (see appendix B) reveal statistically significant differences at 0.01 between filtering and focusing, biasing and illegal acts, biasing and gaming, gaming and illegal acts, smoothing and biasing. These results tend to confound the contention that categories of dysfunctional behavior cluster or group together when superior management ability to analyze and verify data varies.

One obvious limitation is that some of the scenarios fail to reflect the category of dysfunctional behavior satisfactorily. The scenarios were developed from the illustrations provided by Birnberg, Turpolec, and Young (1983) but in that their main interest concerned resource allocation and the capital budgeting process. Further refinement of the scenarios may provide a more satisfactory test.

The range of judgments for this sample of managers does appear to vary. On the scale of 1–5, for filtering the judgments follow the sequence 18, 9, 11, 11, 1. That is, 36 percent believed the subordinate's action acceptable, 46 percent thought it unacceptable, and 18 percent were not sure. Similarly, for biasing, the sequence of responses over the 1–5 scale indicated 19, 17, 9, 5, 0 or that 38 percent thought the action acceptable, 28 percent unacceptable and

Table 8.4 Judgments across companies, functional roles and hierarchical position

Sample	Mean	Standard deviation	t-Statistic
Between company			
A ($n=50$)	2.71	1.215	A vs B $=2.02$
B ($n=16$)	2.99	1.17	
A ($n=50$)	2.71	1.215	A vs MNE $=0.296$
MNE ($n=11$)	2.76	1.4	
B ($n=16$)	2.99	1.17	B vs. MNE $=1.14$
MNE ($n=11$)	2.76	1.4	
Between function			
Finance ($n=27$)	2.9	1.23	Finance vs Manager $=1.605$
Manager ($n=50$)	2.71	1.215	
Between hierarchical position in company A			
Depot managers ($n=44$)	2.75	1.21	Depot managers vs regional directors $=0.2304$
Regional directors ($n=6$)	2.7	1.22	

34 percent were not sure. Whereas for focusing, 8 percent thought the action acceptable, 78 percent unacceptable, and 14 percent were not sure, the sequence being 4, 7, 8, 26, 5. The level of tolerance for each category of dysfunctional behavior for this sample of managers does not appear to display a clustering pattern as hypothesized.

By introducing the prior pilot tests, company B and the MNEs, it is possible to evaluate whether judgments varied across respondent populations, between functional roles, and hierarchical position. Table 8.4 indicates the results.

Of these tests, only the between-company A and B finding approaches statistical significance at 0.05. It may be argued that finance staff are more conservative in their judgments than managers (means 2.9 and 2.71 respectively). This finding contradicts Merchant and Rockness (1994) who also found an across-company difference, which is largely absent in this study.

The comparison of regional director and depot manager judgments in company A reveals similar ranges of varying tolerance to the dysfunctional behavior scenarios. This, in one sense, is surprising as the depot managers judgments in response to the other sections of the questionnaire revealed that:
- attaining the six monthly financial target was very important (84 percent), important (16 percent);

- rewards in the form of cash bonus are associated with attainment (100 percent);
- penalties for non-attainment exist, such as headquarter involvement, loss of self-esteem (73 percent);
- targets were set at regional director level without participation (64 percent).

These features of the overall performance measurement system suggest a style of evaluation which approximates budget constraint. There was some evidence to substantiate this in that 46 percent of depot managers believed their performance was evaluated monthly with the remainder indicating a more frequent evaluation. The managers were clear that financial measures were the most important element of their evaluation: very few indicated that quantitative and qualitative indicators complemented the financial measures. But there was some doubt whether actual profit compared with budget or actual profit compared with the same six month period for last year was the key measure. Regional directors stated that both were equally important.

Within company A, the judgments of managers occupying different hierarchical positions appear remarkably similar, yet the style of evaluation would suggest high job tension with a need to produce results in line with performance targets. This may suggest that less than totally truthful responses were obtained and that an alternative methodology should be tried. Conversely, there is no consensus amongst depot managers and their judgments cannot be distinguished from those of the regional directors. The different levels of tolerance shown under the present research method do not therefore seem to be clearly associated with the style of evaluation employed and other characteristics of the performance measurement system.

Discussion and limitations

A primary aim of this study was to gauge the judgments of managers to potential dysfunctional behavior by subordinates. The attempt to assess levels of tolerance to six categories of behavior was undertaken using a scale employed by Merchant (1990). Whilst the scenarios are not directly comparable with previous studies, it is worthwhile comparing the results of this study with those of Merchant and Rockness (1994) who collected data from American managers.

In respect of managers perceptions of acceptable actions taken by subordinates, both studies reveal a wide range of judgments. Both American and

British managers appear to have different levels of tolerance as to what constitutes dysfunctional behavior. Whilst the US study revealed some between company and between functional role differences, there are no similar patterns in the UK. Both studies found that hierarchical position did not affect the consensus (or lack of consensus). Superior managers in practice display a range of tolerance levels to dysfunctional behavior which is also shown by subordinate managers.

The current study in addition attempted to test the Birnberg, Turpolec, and Young (1983) hypothesis that superior manager ability to analyze and verify data is associated with different categories of dysfunctional behavior. When focusing and filtering behaviors are compared with all others, there is some evidence to merit examining the association further. However, close comparison of individual categories of dysfunctional behavior revealed statistically significant patterns and no evidence of clustering.

With the additional description of the performance measurement system, which operated in company A, the opportunity arose to place the managerial responses in context. Classifying the style of evaluation of depot managers as budget constrained may suggest that their judgments on dysfunctional behavior tend to be more relaxed than harsh. That is, their first-hand experience may lead to a consensus on the acceptability of the dysfunctional behavior scenarios. There is no evidence of this and an alternative method of data collection or research methodology may be required to overcome the problem, if indeed one exists.

Other limitations of this study concern the scenario descriptions and their ability to reflect specific categories of dysfunctional behavior. Provision of greater contextual detail may have elicited different judgments from respondents. Exclusion of financial data was an intentional attempt to avoid confusion over materiality and principled or ethical judgments. This contrasts with the Merchant and Rockness (1994) approach. Additionally, collecting data on other aspects of the performance measurement system under which respondents currently operate may enhance interpretation of the judgments given. In this sensitive area, it is difficult to recommend the case study approach as a feasible alternative.

The data are limited to three research sites, two of which were opportunistically sampled, that is, the respondents and researcher came together for a related but different purpose. Possible extensions to include more managers in different functional roles and hierarchical positions could prove useful. Similarly, the views of external auditors and regulators could provide alternative perspectives. The most rewarding insights are likely to emerge from investigation in a single enterprise, or a series of enterprises. If consensus is to be found, it may reside at certain functional levels in an enterprise where top management follows and communicates certain judgment criteria.

Implications

The absence of consensus as to the level of accuracy in reporting actual performance which is acceptable carries implications for several measurement issues. At one level, there is the interaction with the style of evaluation adopted by the superior managers. It is unclear whether a budget constrained, profit conscious, or non-accounting style (Hopwood, 1972) is preferable for adoption by all superior managers in the same company. The short-term emphasis of the budget-constrained style may cause the subordinate's dysfunctional actions. If the same style is used to evaluate the superior, why not show tolerance when the performance target is, as a result, achieved? Reporting the dysfunctional behavior may mean the superior's performance is adversely affected.

Taking a longer-term perspective of the financial performance as suggested, under the profit-conscious style, may institutionalize a level of tolerance by the superior. For example, "smoothing" the accounting record over successive time periods may be acceptable under this style as long as they are not systematic and recurring. Likewise, the non-accounting style of evaluation reduces the emphasis superiors need to place on financial records of performance, enabling greater tolerance to be exercised when manipulation is uncovered. The need for subordinates to bias, focus, game, or enter into illegal acts is thereby diminished. The style of evaluation may therefore legitimize the level of tolerance exercised by the superior.

A related issue is whether a consistent level of tolerance can be regarded as appropriate for a single company, a level of managers, or even one superior manager. The latter is not addressed by the empirical study but it is possible that differing degrees of tolerance to the manipulation of financial reports are essential when subordinates face distinct, dynamic situations with varying degrees of uncertainty. Less tolerance is shown for the subordinate undertaking repetitive, programmed tasks than for those making novel decisions in uncertain situations. Organizational culture, or social or peer controls may impose a degree of conformity on the behaviors which are deemed acceptable or may, alternatively, encourage diversity.

At a more specific level relevant to the RAPM literature, the acknowledgment of different degrees of tolerance to the accurate reporting of actual performance may help explain job-related tension. A relationship between budget emphasis, participation, task uncertainty, and job-related tension was found by Brownell and Hirst (1986) and Shields, Deng, and Kato (1998) but not by Lau, Low, and Eggleton (1995). A number of explanations for the inconsistency, including the national cultures of the participants, appear reasonable but, additionally, the tolerance of superior managers to the accurate reporting of actual performance seems worthy of consideration. Tolerance may intervene in the relationship between job-related tension and performance. Job-related tension may be significantly reduced when subordinates learn that a superior tolerates a certain degree of dysfunctional behavior. Alternatively, a superior who demands absolute accuracy in the reporting of actual performance may substantially increase job-related tension.

In this last respect, the model of RAPM may be extended to emphasize the consequence of the controls (tolerance, style of evaluation) rather than the antecedents (uncertainty, participation). Future research in this area may usefully incorporate the tolerance of superior managers to explain the interrelated effects of the control process.

Conclusions

The study, in conjuction with earlier studies (Bruns and Merchant, 1990; Merchant and Rockness, 1994) suggests there is a wide range of tolerance to dysfunctional behavior. This result is not diminished by examining responses from single enterprises or even single functional roles in a particular enterprise. When faced with the same scenario different managers interpret the seriousness of the subordinate's action differently.

The explanation of these differing levels of tolerance is complicated. Bound up in the judgment of dysfunctional behavior is likely to be the superior's concern with his/her own well-being and the avoidance of embarrassment or threat. Apparent reliance on financial performance measures encourages subordinates to indulge in dysfunctional behavior to attain targets. Superiors tolerate the subordinate actions as they are dependent on their own need to avoid embarrassment and threat. Perception by subordinates of the level of tolerance shown by superiors provides guidelines of future acceptable actions and thereby weakens the superior's ability to question or investigate. Hence, the circularity of implicit tolerance enables perennial dysfunctional behavior to occur. The acceptability of manipulations may

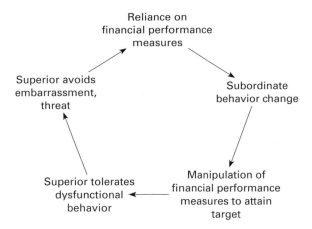

Figure 8.1. Non-neutrality impact of over-reliance on financial performance measures.

only be broken by specific corporate policies, for example to prevent fraud or by the replacement of a superior with different values and tolerance levels. The non-neutrality long established with an over-reliance on financial performance measures may therefore extend to superior tolerance which implicitly reinforces subordinate dysfunctional behavior (Figure 8.1).

As Argyris (1990) argues the defensive mechanisms to avoid embarrassment and threat are merely symptoms of the problem. The levels of tolerance and range of judgments superiors displayed in this study are just one way in which the charade of accountability by means of financial performance attainment is allowed to perpetuate. However, the approach is unlikely to lead to learning organizations or adventurous target setting or innovative management.

In a perverse way, the current emphasis on corporate governance and internal control procedures may promote flexible tolerance. External financial statement users and possibly top management within the enterprise would be unaware of the actions described in the scenarios and the superior management judgments exercised. Transparency is confined by information asymmetry and inertia. Why investigate if the results are more or less as expected? By exercising judgment on dysfunctional behavior in a flexible manner, internal investigation may be avoided or deemed superfluous. The real danger however is that financial reports for parts of the enterprise may reflect more the differing judgments of superiors to dysfunctional behavior than economic viability. Perpetuation by promotion of the flexibly tolerant suggests financial performance measure reliability for internal and external users becomes increasingly questionable.

Appendix A

Situation	Example
Smoothing	A divisional/subsidiary/unit manager realizes that he needs a strong performance in the last quarter of the year to reach his budget target. By gaining the agreement of a sub-contractor to delay the billing date for work already performed, the target is achieved.
Biasing	Recognizing that her performance is evaluated by her ability to meet an annual revenue target, the marketing manager successfully negotiates a reduced sales budget. This she regards as an insurance against the environmental uncertainty she faces.
Focusing	A subsidiary manager is evaluated each year by the rate of growth in sales revenue, rate of return on investment on a comparison of actual and budgeted and this year's actual against the previous year. In addition, non-financial measures of training performance, meeting orders on time and customer complaints are part of the evaluation. With weeks to the year end, the manager improves the actual return on investment by selling a piece of equipment now. The sale will, however, adversely affect the subsidiary's ability to meet orders in the future.
Gaming	A capital investment project is being developed at the subsidiary level. One version of the project would improve the current ROI in the next two years substantially. The second version of the project maintains the current ROI but gives a significantly higher net present value over the project's entire life than version 1. The manager proposes to pursue the first version.
Filtering	When negotiating a transfer price with a sister subsidiary, the supplying subsidiary manager has the opportunity to divulge the average costs of manufacture at different production levels or to give the detailed fixed and variable costs breakdown for each production level. He decides not to give the detailed breakdown. Each subsidiary manager is held responsible for profit.
Illegal acts	For a construction subsidiary, group policy states that all contracts should be broken down to identify their constituent parts. The site inspector discovers that man-hours are being recorded inaccurately against specific parts of the job. In total, the hours are accurate and have been worked but they are being mis-recorded in order that the planned and actual hours for individual parts of the contract are consistent with the annual budget. The subsidiary site manager knows and is responsible for the practice.

Appendix B The association between individual category of dysfunctional behavior and superior management ability to analyze and verify data

Superior management ability to	Individual category of dysfunctional behavior	Mean	Standard deviation	t-statistic
(a) Analyze data is low	Filtering	2.36	1.23	Filtering vs focusing = 4.56 **
	focusing	3.42	1.09	
(b) Verify data is low	Biasing	2.00	0.98	Biasing vs illegal acts = 6.27 **
	illegal acts	3.32	1.12	
	Biasing	2.00	0.98	Biasing vs gaming = 3.104 **
	gaming	2.65	1.11	
	Illegal acts	3.32	1.12	Illegal acts vs gaming = 3.0045 **
	gaming	2.65	1.11	
	Smoothing	2.88	1.07	Smoothing vs biasing = 4.288 **
	biasing	2.00	0.98	
	Smoothing	2.88	1.07	Smoothing vs illegal acts = 2.009*
	illegal acts	3.32	1.12	
	Smoothing	2.88	1.07	Smoothing vs gaming = 1.055
	gaming	2.65	1.11	

Notes:
** statistically significant at 0.01.
* statistically significant at 0.05.

REFERENCES

Argyris, C. (1952). The impact of budgets on people. Controllership Foundation.

Argyris, C. (1990). The dilemma of implementing controls: The case of managerial accounting. *Accounting. Organizations and Society*, 15(6), 503–11.

Birnberg, J., Shields, M. and Young S.M. (1990). The case for multiple methods in empirical management accounting research. *Journal of Management Accounting Research*, 2, 33–66.

Birnberg, J., Turpolec, L. and Young, S.M. (1983). The Organizational Context of Accounting. *Accounting, Organizations and Society*, 8, 111–30.

Brownell, P. and Hirst, M.K. (1986). Reliance on accounting information, budgetory participation and task uncertainty: Tests of a three-way interaction. *Journal of Accounting Research*, 24(2), 241–9

Bruns, W.J., Jr. and Merchant, K.A. (1990). The dangerous morality of managing earnings. *Management Accounting*, 72(2, August), 22–5.

Dermer, J. (1973). Cognitive characteristics and the perceived importance of information. *The Accounting Review*, **48**(3), 511–19

Flory, S.M., Phillips, T.J., Reidenback, R.E., and Robin, D.P. (1992). A multidemensional analysis of selected ethical issues in accounting. *The Accounting Review*, **67**(2, April), 284–302.

Hofstede, G.H. (1968). *The Game of Budget Control*. London: Tavistock.

Hopper, T. (1985). Role conflicts of management accountants and their position within organizational structures. *Accounting, Organizations and Society*, **5**, 401–12.

Hopwood, A.G. (1972). An empirical study of the role of accounting data in performance evaluation. Empirical Research in Accounting. Supplement to *Journal of Accounting Research*, **10**, 156–82.

Johnson, G. (1987). *Strategic Change in the Management Process*, Oxford: Blackwell.

Karnes, A., Sterner, J., Welker, R., and Wu, F. (1989). A bicultural study of independent auditors' perceptions of unethical business practices. *International Journal of Accounting*, **24**(1). 29–41.

Kren, L. and Liao, W. (1988). The role of accounting information in the control of organizations: A review of the evidence. *Journal of Accounting Literature*, **7**, 280–309

Lau, C., Low, L.C., and Eggleton, R.C. (1995). The impact of reliance on accounting performance measures on job related tension and managerial performance: additional evidence. *Accounting, Organizations and Society*, **20**(5), 359–81

Macintosh, N. (1994). Human relations and budgeting systems. *Readings in Accounting for Management Control*, London: Chapman & Hall, 215–31.

Macintosh, N. (1996). Postmodernity – Baudrillard: Simulacrum, hyperreality and implosion. *Wards Trust Research Seminar Series*, October, 44.

Merchant, K. (1990). The effects of financial controls on data manipulation and management myopia. *Accounting, Organizations and Society*, **15**,(4), 297–313.

Merchant, K. and Manzoni, J.-F. (1989). The achievability of profit center budget targets: A field study. *The Accounting Review*, **64**, 539–58.

Merchant, K. and Rockness, J. (1994). The ethics of managing earnings: An empirical investigation. *Journal of Accounting and Public Policy*, **13**, 79–94.

Otley, D.T. (1980). The contingency theory of management accounting: Achievement and prognosis. *Accounting, Organizations and Society*, pp. 413–28.

Otley, D.T. and Berry, A. (1994). Case study research in management accounting and control. *Management Accounting Research*, **5**(1), 45–65

Prakash, P. and Rappoport, A. (1977). Information inductance and its significance for accounting. *Accounting, Organizations and Society*, pp. 29–38

Schiff, M. and Lewin, A.Y. (1970). The impact of people on budgets. *The Accounting Review*, April, 259–68.

Shields, M., Deng, F.J., and Kato, Y. (1998). The design and effects of control systems. Presented at the International Management Control Association conference at the University of Reading, UK.

Shields, J. and Shields, M. (1998). Antecedents of participative budgeting. *Accounting, Organizations and Society*, **23**, 49–76.

Swieringa, R.J. and Moncur, R.H. (1972). The relationship between managers' budget oriented behavior and selected attitude, position, size and performance measures. Empirical

Research in Accounting: Selected Studies, Supplement to *Journal of Accounting Research*, 10, 194–209.

Waterhouse, J.H. and Tiessen, P. (1978) A contingency framework for management accounting systems research. *Accounting, Organizations and Society*, pp. 65–76.

Young, S.M. and Lewis, B. (1995). Experimental incentive contracting research in management accounting. In *Judgement and Decision Making Research in Accounting and Auditing*, ed. R. Ashton and A.A. Ashton, Cambridge: Cambridge University Press.

Part III

Performance measurement – frameworks and methodologies

The third part of the book explores some of the frameworks and methodologies associated with performance measurement. While there is considerable interest in the balanced scorecard, there are of course numerous other measurement frameworks and methodologies, each with their own strengths and weaknesses. The first contribution in this section, from Kennerley and Neely, reviews some of these other measurement frameworks and then proposes an alternative framework – the performance prism. Kennerley and Neely argue that the strength of the performance prism lies in the fact that it unifies existing measurement frameworks and builds upon their individual strengths. The balanced scorecard, for example, is strong in that it argues for a balanced set of measures, but weak in that it omits some extremely important stakeholder perspectives – that is employees and suppliers. Similarly, activity-based costing is strong in that explicitly recognizes the importance of activities and processes, but weak in that it does not link these processes back to strategies or stakeholders. The performance prism addresses these, and other issues, by providing an integrated framework with which to view organizational performance.

The second contribution in this part argues the case for focusing on the critical few performance indicators. Murray and Richardson present case study evidence that illustrates how recent developments in performance measurement have resulted in confusion in organizations. In the past managers were asked to focus on optimizing single dimensions of performance. Today they are expected to manage multiple performance indicators, often presented in the form of balanced scorecards. The result is confusion, steming from a lack of organizational clarity about priorities. There are two ways in which this issue can be addressed. One is to make explicit the links between the various dimensions of performance through success maps or cause-and-effect diagrams. The second is to focus on fewer measures. Hence Murray and Richardson's assertion that executives should seek to establish the critical few measures for their organizations.

The third contribution in this part draws on research carried out at Strathclyde University that set out to establish how the efficiency and effectiveness of an organisation's performance measurement system could be audited. No matter which measurement framework a management team decides to adopt, no matter how

143

focused they are on the critical few, there is still a need for managers to step back and review the efficiency and effectiveness of their measurement systems. Of course this immediately raises the question – what does a good measurement system consist of? – and it is this question that the Strathclyde research team set out to answer. In their contribution, Bititci *et al.* argue that Stafford Beer's Viable Systems Model can be used as the basis of a measurement audit framework. They derive a theoretical structure for an idealized measurement system and then illustrate how this can be used in practice to critically appraise a variety of organization's measurement systems.

The fourth and final contribution in this part deals directly with the issue of why measurement initiatives succeed and fail. Even when managers adopt valid performance measurement frameworks, even when they undergo a rigorous process and identify the right measures to focus on, even when the result is a good measurement system, practitioners still find it difficult to implement their measurement system. The aim of Bourne and Neely's contribution is to explore why this is the case. Bourne and Neely present the results of a three-year study in why measurement systems succeed and fail and propose a framework that can be used to assess the likelihood of successful implementation.

9 Performance measurement frameworks: A review

Mike Kennerley and Andy Neely

Introduction

It has been widely reported that there has been a revolution in performance measurement in the last 20 years. The enormous interest in measurement has manifested itself in practitioner conferences and publications as well as in academic research (Neely, 1998).

Research indicates that organizations using balanced performance measurement systems as the basis for management perform better than those that do not (Lingle and Schiemann, 1996). For this benefit to be realized, it is necessary for organizations to implement an effective performance measurement system that "enables informed decisions to be made and actions to be taken because it quantifies the efficiency and effectiveness of past actions through acquisition, collation, sorting, analysis, interpretation, and dissemination of appropriate data" (Neely, 1998, pp. 5–6). This definition is important as it indicates that a performance measurement system has a number of constituent parts:

- individual measures that quantify the efficiency and effectiveness of actions;
- a set of measures that combine to assess the performance of an organization as a whole;
- a supporting infrastructure that enables data to be acquired, collated, sorted, analyzed, interpreted, and disseminated.

For the full benefit of measurement to be exploited it is important for organizations to maximize the appropriateness and effectiveness of measurement activity at each of these levels. This contribution is concerned with the second of these points, that is how an organization identifies a set of measures that

The authors are grateful to the Engineering and Physical Sciences Research Council (EPSRC) for the award of research grant number GR/K88637, to carry out the research reported in this contribution. The research reported in this contribution has been undertaken in close collaboration with Accenture.

reflects the performance it is trying to achieve. Numerous processes have been proposed that organizations should follow in order to design and implement performance measurement systems (Bourne *et al.*, 2000; Neely *et al.*, 1996). Many frameworks have been proposed that support these processes. The objective of such frameworks is to help organizations to define a set of measures that reflects their objectives and assesses their performance appropriately.

This contribution will review existing performance measurement frameworks and identify the key characteristics that they exhibit which help organizations to identify and define an appropriate set of performance measures. The contribution presents a performance measurement framework, developed by the authors, that seeks to reflect the characteristics and address the shortcomings of existing frameworks.

Existing performance measurement frameworks

For many years frameworks have been used by organizations to define the measures that they should use to assess their performance. From early in the twentieth century, DuPont used a pyramid of financial ratios, which linked a wide range of financial ratios to return on investment. The pyramid of financial ratios had an explicit hierarchical structure, linking measures at different organizational levels.

Following their review of the evolution of management accounting systems, Thomas Johnson and Robert Kaplan highlighted many of the deficiencies in the way in which management accounting information is used to manage businesses (Johnson and Kaplan, 1987). They highlighted the failure of financial performance measures to reflect changes in the competitive circumstances and strategies of modern organizations. These deficiencies indicate shortcomings in the DuPont pyramid. Its cost focus provides a historical view, giving little indication of future performance and encouraging short termism (Bruns, 1998).

The subsequent revolution in performance measurement, prompted organizations to implement non-financial measures that appropriately reflect their objectives as well as financial measures that indicate the bottom line result. Although General Electric first implemented a balanced set of performance measures in the 1950s (Bruns, 1998), it was the enormous growth in interest in performance measurement in the 1980s and 1990s that brought widespread acceptance of the need for organizations to take a balanced approach to measurement. This interest led to a plethora of measurement frameworks designed to help organizations implement a balanced set of measures.

Keegan, Eiler, and Jones (1989) proposed a performance measurement matrix reflecting the need for balanced measurement. It categorizes measures as being "cost" or "non cost," and "external" or "internal," reflecting the need for greater balance of measures across these dimensions. This is a simple framework and, whilst it does not reflect all of the attributes of measures that are increasingly considered necessary, the matrix should be able to accommodate any measure of performance (Neely *et al.*, 1995). This allows an organization to plot its measures and identify where there is a need to adjust measurement focus.

The SMART (Strategic Measurement and Reporting Technique) pyramid developed by Wang Laboratories (Lynch and Cross, 1991) also supports the need to include internally and externally focused measures of performance. It adds the notion of cascading measures down the organization so that measures at department and work-center level reflect the corporate vision as well as internal and external business unit objectives.

Following their study of performance measurement in service industries, Fitzgerald *et al.* (1991) proposed a framework classifying measures into two basic types. Those that relate to results (competitiveness, financial performance) and those that focus on the determinants of those results (quality, flexibility, resource utilization, and innovation). This reflects the concept of causality, indicating that results obtained are a function of past business performance in relation to specific determinants. This demonstrates the need to identify drivers of performance in order to achieve the desired performance outcomes.

Brown (1996) developed the concept of linking measures through cause and effect relationships further. In his Macro Process Model of the Organization, he shows clear links between five stages in a business process and the measures of their performance. These stages are defined as inputs, processing system, outputs, outcomes, and goals respectively. The model demonstrates how inputs to the organization affect the performance of processing systems and ultimately the top-level objectives of the organization (goals). Brown argues that each stage is the driver of the performance of the next.

The most popular of the performance measurement frameworks has been the balanced scorecard proposed by Kaplan and Norton (1992 and 1996a). The balanced scorecard identifies and integrates four different ways of looking at performance (financial, customer, internal business, and innovation and learning perspectives). The authors identify the need to ensure that financial performance, the drivers of it (customer and internal operational performance), and the drivers of on-going improvement and future performance, are given equal weighting. The balanced scorecard reflects many of the attributes of other measurement frameworks but more explicitly links measurement to the organization's strategy. The authors claim that it should be possible to deduce an organization's strategy by reviewing the measures on its balanced scorecard.

Kaplan and Norton argue that the full potential of the balanced scorecard will only be realized if an organization links its measures clearly, identifying the drivers of performance (Kaplan and Norton, 1996b). Conceptually, this use of the scorecard is similar to the use of the Tableau de Bord (Epstein and Manzoni, 1997). Developed in France in the early twentieth century the Tableau de Bord establishes a hierarchy of interrelated measures and cascading measures to different organizational levels, forcing functions and divisions of an organization to position themselves in the context of the company's overall strategy.

Despite its widespread use, numerous authors have identified shortcomings of the balanced scorecard. It does not consider a number of features of earlier frameworks that could be used to enhance the framework. The absence of a competitiveness dimension, as included in Fitzgerald's *et al.*'s (1991) results and determinants framework, is noted by Neely *et al.* (1995). Others emphasize the importance of measurement of the human resources perspective/employees satisfaction, supplier performance, product/service quality, and environmental/community perspective (Maisel, 1992; Ewing and Lundahl, 1996; Lingle and Schiemann, 1996; Brown, 1996). Failure of the balanced scorecard to consider these dimensions limits its comprehensiveness, because not all measures can be included, as is the case with the performance measurement matrix for example. A further criticism of the balanced scorecard is that it does not reflect different dimensions of performance as the SMART pyramid and results and determinants model do. Neither the customer nor internal perspective are defined in terms of the dimensions of performance that determine success, such as the generic strategic objectives of quality, cost, delivery (speed and reliability), and flexibility.

Although not designed as performance measurement frameworks, the European Foundation for Quality Management's (EFQM) Business Excellence Model and its US equivalent the Malcolm Baldrige Quality Award take a broader view of performance, addressing many of the areas of performance not considered by the balanced scorecard. The Business Excellence

Model is a broad management model that explicitly highlights the enablers of performance improvement and indicates result areas that should be measured. However it is a subjective self-assessment too rather than an objective measurement framework and the categories for measurement are very broad. Whilst the results areas are readily measurable, some of the enablers are not (Neely and Adams, 2001).

Characteristics of performance measurement frameworks

The performance measurement frameworks discussed in the previous section display a number of key characteristics that help an organization to identify an appropriate set of measures to assess their performance:

1 The work of Kaplan and Norton (1992) and Keegan, Eiler, and Jones (1989) emphasize the fact that the set of measures used by an organization has to **provide a "balanced" picture of the business**. The set of measures should reflect financial and non-financial measures, internal and external measures, and efficiency and effectiveness measures.

2 The populated framework of measures should provide a **succinct overview of the organization's performance**. For example, the simplicity and intuitive logic of the balanced scorecard has been a major contributor to its widespread adoption, as it is easily understood by users and applied to their organization.

3 Each framework demonstrates the need for organizations to implement a set of performance measures that are **multi-dimensional**. This reflects the need to measure all the areas of performance that are important to the organization's success. However there is no consensus over what the dimensions of performance are. The EFQM model provides the broadest indication of dimensions of performance to be measured.

4 The Performance Measurement Matrix (PMM) provides **comprehensiveness**. It is possible to map all possible measures of an organization's performance on to the framework and identify where there are omissions or where there is a need for greater focus. However, the PMM provides little indication of the different dimensions of performance that should be measured.

5 The Tableau de Bord, along with the work of Bititci *et al.* (1998), explicitly demonstrates the fact that performance measures should be **integrated both across the organization's functions and through its hierarchy**, encouraging congruence of goals and actions.

6 The Tableau de Bord and the work of Fitzgerald *et al.* (1991) explicitly, and the balanced scorecard and performance pyramid implicitly, explain how **results are a function of determinates**. This demonstrates the need to measure results and the drivers of them so that the performance measurement system can provide data for monitoring past performance and planning future performance. This demonstrates the way in which measures contribute to an organization's planning (feed forward) and control (feedback) system (Ballantine and Brignall, 1994).

As well as defining a similar set of "core" criteria, in their review of performance measurement frameworks, Ballantine and Brignall (1994) identify the need for a set of performance measures to reflect what they refer to as "noncore elements" of performance measurement systems. This indicates the need for the performance measures implemented to be consistent with management techniques and improvement initiatives that exist within the organization, such as benchmarking, activity-based costing management, total quality management, and business process redesign. There are also other measurement frameworks and methodologies, such as shareholder value added or cost of quality which have been developed to focus on the measurement of a specific performance issue (Neely and Adams, 2001). A comprehensive and multi-dimensional measurement system should encompass these measurement techniques.

So far the contribution has presented the key attributes of existing performance measurement frameworks that enable them to help organizations identify the set of performance measures that appropriately reflect their performance and objectives. Its clear from the discussion that each of the frameworks presented in the literature falls short of satisfying the previously discussed criteria in a number of areas. The remainder of the contribution presents a multi-faceted framework, the Performance Prism, which attempts to address the shortcomings of the frameworks that are currently available, whilst satisfying the key criteria identified.

The Performance Prism

According to Teddy Wivel, senior partner in the Danish arm of Ernst and Young "It will not be possible to create shareholder value without creating stakeholder value" (Crowe, 1999). Since Freeman's (1984) work there has been considerable attention paid to the stakeholder approach to management of organizations. In the Tomorrow's Company report, the RSA suggested that competitive success in the future will increasingly depend on taking an inclusive approach to management, reflecting the need for consideration of the requirements of all stakeholders to be central to performance measurement and management activities (RSA, 1995).

To reflect the growing importance of satisfying stakeholder requirements, the Performance Prism adopts a stakeholder centric view of performance measurement. For many organizations shareholders will remain the most important stakeholder. Consideration must be given, however, to other important stakeholder groups, such as other investors, customers, employees, and suppliers, all of which are incorporated into the balanced scorecard or variants of it.

In addition to these stakeholders, the Prism also considers a group of stakeholders of growing power and significance in the current business environment: regulators and pressure groups. A key consideration for many organizations is the satisfaction of regulatory and legal communities. Regulators of the recently privatized utilities in the UK have particularly significant influence, including the power to impose price restrictions, to insist on investment in operations, or even to revoke an organization's licence to operate if performance does not meet its requirements. Regulators are not confined to recently privatized industries however. There are a variety of regulatory and legislative bodies seeking to prevent organizations from exploiting their competitive position, exploiting their employees, or damaging the environment for example. Regulators often provide a voice for stakeholders that do not have a collective voice, whilst pressure groups often express collective opinions and can have a significant influence on the operations of an organization. Within the Prism regulators and communities consider those stakeholders and the overall impact of the organizations operations on society as considered in the Business Excellence model.

Having identified the key stakeholders of the organization and defined their requirements, it is necessary to consider whether the organization has the strategies in place to deliver stakeholder satisfaction. The need to implement measures that reflect and communicate an organization's strategies has been a consistent message in much of the recent literature on performance measurement. There is recognition of the need to communicate strategy, check that it is achieved, and challenge whether it is correct (Neely, 1998)

Roth (1993) gathered empirical data showing a correlation between business unit viability, competitive capabilities, and business process performance. This demonstrates the need for the third and fourth facets of the Performance Prism: measurement of the processes required to deliver objectives and the capabilities required to support and enhance these processes. None of the existing measurement frameworks addresses and aligns each of these issues.

The fifth and final facet returns to consideration of stakeholders, which lie at the heart of the Prism. Whilst the first facet is concerned with delivery of stakeholder satisfaction, the final facet reflects the need for organizations to maximize the contribution that stakeholders make to support its operations. For example, satisfaction of customer requirements is a key objective for most businesses, however there is a growing appreciation of the need to focus on the contribution of loyalty and profitability from customers in return.

The five distinct but linked perspectives of performance identified prompt the following questions for organizations to address when defining a set of performance measures:

- *Stakeholder satisfaction* – who are our key stakeholders and what do they want and need?
- *Strategies* – what strategies do we have to put in place to satisfy the wants and needs of these key stakeholders?
- *Processes* – what critical processes do we need to operate and enhance these processes?
- *Capabilities* – what capabilities do we need to operate and enhance these processes?
- *Stakeholder contribution* – what contributions do we require from our stakeholders if we are to maintain and develop these capabilities?

Answering these questions demonstrates the creation of stakeholder value as demonstrated in figure 9.1. This clearly demonstrates the way in which the Prism framework explains that an organization's **results** (stakeholder satisfaction) **are a function of determinants** (the other prism facets). Whilst discussion of the Prism has focused on top–down deployment of strategy, explicit inclusion of capabilities ensures its consistency with the resource-based view of the firm, where strategies emerge from an organization's capabilities being designed to achieve specific goals.

Answering the questions at an organizational level also provides a **succinct overview of the organization's performance,** similar to the way in which the balanced scorecard does. However, considerable additional levels of detail that have been developed for each of the facets ensure that the framework is **comprehensive**, enabling all measures to be mapped on to it so that gaps in measurement can be identified. Consideration of each of the Prism facets ensures that the framework can be used at any organizational level, **integrated both across the organization's functions and through its hierarchy**. The authors

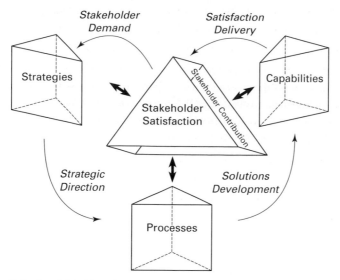

Figure 9.1.   Delivering stakeholder value.

consider the framework to be **multi-dimensional** reflecting all of the areas of performance that influence the performance of an organization. This enables a balanced picture of the business to be provided, highlighting external (stakeholder) and internal (strategy, process and capability) measures, as well as enabling financial and non-financial measures and measures of efficiency and effectiveness throughout the organization.

These attributes of the performance prism have enabled the authors to develop a comprehensive catalogue containing over 200 performance measures that are applicable to all parts of an organization. The catalogue is designed to be used as a reference guide by people seeking information on how they might measure specific dimensions of performance.

Conclusion

Many performance measurement frameworks have been developed to help organizations design a set of performance measures that appropriately assess their success. These frameworks assist organizations in a number of different ways, each having its strengths and weaknesses. The performance prism developed by the authors is a multi-faceted framework that builds on the strengths and addresses many of the weaknesses of existing frameworks.

REFERENCES

Ballantine, J. and Brignall, S. (1994). A taxonomy of performance measurement frameworks. Warwick Business School Research Paper, Warwick.

Bititci, U.S., Carrie, A.S., Turner, T., and Lutz, S. (1998). Integrated performance measurement systems: Implementation case studies. In *Strategic Management of the Manufacturing Value Chain: Proceedings of the International Conference of the Manufacturing Value Chain*, ed. U.S. Bititci, and A.S. Carrie, Troon, August, pp. 179–84.

Bourne, M., Mills, J., Wilcox, M., Neely, A., and Platts, K. (2000). Designing, implementing and updating performance measurement systems. *International Journal of Operations and Production Management*, **20**(7), 754–71.

Brown, M.G. (1996). *Keeping score: Using the Right Metrics to Drive World-Class Performance.* New York: Quality Resources.

Bruns, W. (1998). Profit as a performance measure: Powerful concept, insufficient measure. Performance Measurement – Theory and Practice: The First International Conference on Performance Measurement, 14–17 July, Cambridge.

Crowe, R. (1999). Winning with integrity. *The Guardian*, 27 November.

Epstein, M.J. and Manzoni, J.F. (1997). The balanced scorecard and tableau de Bord: Translating strategy into action. *Management Accounting* (US) **79**(2), 28–36.

Ewing, P. and Lundahl, L. (1996). The balanced scorecard at ABB Sweden – the EVITA Project. The International Workshop on Cost Management, 27–9, June, Venice, Italy.

Fitzgerald, L., Johnston, R., Brignall, T.J., Silvestro, R., and Voss, C. (1991). *Performance Measurement in Service Businesses.* The Chartered Institute of Management Accountants, London.

Freeman, R.E. (1984). *Strategic Management: A Stakeholder Approach.* Boston, MA: Pitman.

Johnson, H.T. and Kaplan, R.S. (1987). *Relevance Lost – The Rise and Fall of Management Accounting.* Boston, MA: Harvard Business School Press.

Kaplan, R.S. and Norton, D.P. (1992). The balanced scorecard – measures that drive performance. *Harvard Business Review*, **70** (1, January/February), 71–9.

Kaplan, R.S. and Norton, D.P. (1996a). *The Balanced Scorecard – Translating Strategy into Action.* Boston, MA: Harvard Business School Press.

Kaplan, R.S. and Norton, D.P. (1996b). Linking the balanced scorecard to strategy. *California Management Review*, **39**(1), 53–79.

Keegan, D.P., Eiler, R.G., and Jones, C.R. (1989). Are your performance measures obsolete? *Management Accounting* (US), **70** (12, June), 45–50.

Lingle, J.H. and Schiemann, W.A. (1996). From balanced scorecard to strategy gauge. Is measurement worth it? *Management Review*, March, 56–62

Lynch, R.L. and Cross, K.F. (1991). *Measure Up – The Essential Guide to Measuring Business Performance.* London: Mandarin.

Maisel, L.S. (1992). Performance measurement: The balanced scorecard approach. *Journal of Cost Management*, Summer, 47–52.

Neely, A.D. (1998). *Performance Measurement: Why, What and How.* London: Economist Books.

Neely, A.D. and Adams, C.A. (2001). The Performance Prism perspective. *Journal of Cost Management*, **15**(1), 7–15.

Neely, A.D., Gregory, M., and Platts, K. (1995). Performance measurement system design – a literature review and research agenda. *International Journal of Operations and Production Management*, **15**(4), 80–116.

Neely, A.D., Mills, J.F., Gregory, M.J., Richards, A.H., Platts, K.W., and Bourne, M.C.S. (1996). *Getting the Measure of Your Business.* London: Findlay Publications.

Roth, A.V. (1993). Performance measurement in services. In *Advances in Service Marketing and Management*, ed. D. Bowen. Greenwich, CT: JAI Press.

RSA (1995). Tomorrow's company: The role of business in a changing world. Royal Society of Arts, Manufacturers and Commerce, London.

10 The critical few: First among equals as parameters of strategic effectiveness

Elspeth Murray and Peter Richardson

The importance of defining the critical few

In today's complex and rapidly changing business environment, a strategic plan is an executive team's blueprint for changing the organization and growth. The process undertaken to develop that plan provides executives and other stakeholders with the opportunity to periodically re-think the business in a creative manner. In doing so, they can develop a shared understanding of what will be critical for future success, as well as enhance their knowledge of the business and its possible future environment. In our experience, if during this process executives are forced to make hard choices about what is critical, and focus future strategy around a limited (3–5) set of initiatives with associated specific, measurable objectives, *the critical few*, implementation effectiveness will be significantly improved, and organizational performance will be enhanced.

In this chapter, we provide the results of a research study which makes the case, previously only supported anecdotally, that building shared understanding among the executive team, of the *critical few* corporate initiatives, has a positive impact on strategic planning effectiveness, and hence on organizational performance. In describing our study more fully, this introductory section is followed by a discussion of the practical challenges in creating a shared understanding of the *critical few*. We then outline the process we have found useful for overcoming these challenges, enabling the definition of a highly focused strategic agenda – something we believe can be done for any organization, no matter how large or small. The chapter concludes with a discussion of our research approach, the research findings, and the implications of these findings for corporations and the executives who lead them.

The challenge of creating shared understanding and focus

In practice, executives in many organizations facing complex challenges appear to experience difficulty in reducing the possible set of strategic initiatives and related objectives to a *critical few*. While this can happen for many reasons, a common one is the inability of the executive team to differentiate among initiatives that are truly make-or-break, i.e. *the critical few*, and those that are merely important. As a consequence, the organization often ends up with a strategic plan that contains multiple, and often conflicting, initiatives, objectives, strategies, and action plans. In our research, we have found that in many organizations a strategic plan may encompass ten or 12 major initiatives and associated objectives, upwards of 50 strategies and hundreds of action items. In addition, organizations today are tracking and measuring an increasing number of strategic and operational performance parameters, many of which are derived from the numerous initiatives contained in the strategic plan. It is not unusual for a corporation to monitor upwards of 20 financial, market, operational, and other strategic indicators. The result of all of this is a marked lack of focus among executives and managers as to which of these are critical in a given strategic time period. The result is often a lack of alignment in their activities.

Such realities of strategic planning should not be surprising. From the early work of March and Simon (1958), there has been a recognition of the cognitive limits on rationality. We believe that complex plans of the type just described, are for the most part beyond the capability of most executive teams to implement effectively, especially when in today's lean organizations much of their time necessarily goes into simply running the business. In organizations with strategic plans that contain an over abundance of initiatives, we find little sense of shared priority among members of the executive team. In fact, everyone selects their own two or three priority initiatives from among the larger array, resulting not only in a lack of alignment among key organization units, but also in resources that are spread too thinly across a broad array of initiatives. The end result is too often lengthy implementation times, loss of momentum, and an overall inability to implement the strategic plan.

This failure of strategic planning to create focus and achieve results is reflected in the findings from executives we have surveyed who were participants in Executive Programs at Queen's University in Kingston, Ontario. Typically between 60 and 80 percent of respondents to these surveys express strong dissatisfaction with the strategic planning processes in their organizations. The principal reasons cited for these concerns include plans that lack focus, failure to implement strategy effectively, and failure to follow-up and to demand accountability.

Recently, the notion of a *balanced scorecard* has been advanced as a means of focusing and tracking strategy implementation (Kaplan and Norton, 1996). This approach proposes a balanced set of four principal measurement dimensions for strategy (customer, financial, internal, and learning) and a set of associated measures cascaded hierarchically throughout the firm. As described by the authors, the approach should center around a limited set of key measures. However, in practice, our recent surveys indicate that corporations are establishing scorecards with many measures, in some instances in excess of 100, leading to conflict and confusion rather than alignment and clarity. One executive interviewed recently typified the views of many as follows:

> Our corporate *balanced scorecard* has resulted in my department and myself having over 20, unprioritized measures that we have to attempt to track and achieve. There is no possible way I can attain them all, and I'm not clear about which are critical.

In order to better understand the relationship between focus on the *critical few* and strategic planning effectiveness, we interviewed members of more than 20 executive teams. Our initial interviews revealed that lack of focus on the *critical few* initiatives was a widespread phenomenon in our sample. We found that in a typical executive team of 12 individuals, there may be as many as 15, or even 25 initiatives identified in total when each individual is asked the question: "What are the three most important initiatives for the organization, which, if nothing else were addressed, must be dealt with over the next strategic time period?" In smaller teams of five or six individuals, the same question produced a list of between ten and 12 "top three" initiatives. This lack of a shared sense of what is critical for their business points to a marked failure with many strategic planning processes.

This failure stands in marked contrast to a number of instances related to us by senior executives in firms that appeared to achieve success because they attained a high degree of focus and shared understanding around critical issues. For example, a senior technology executive with one of North America's leading innovative corporations related how a major business had been revitalized by focusing one of the company's major product development laboratories around a single product initiative – *nothing else* – for a period of 18 months. Another executive related how his corporation had reduced unit costs by 30 percent, and increased quality at the same time, by focusing exclusively on two initiatives across the entire organization. These, and similar anecdotes seemed to indicate that the effectiveness of the deployment of strategic plans depends significantly on the level of shared understanding, and subsequent degree of focus achieved by the process.

This chapter is based on the findings from a research study, inspired by these examples, evaluating the effectiveness of strategic planning relative to the definition of focus. It is our contention that sustained organizational performance, by any measure, is achieved through the use of an effective strategic planning process – not the static, numbers-driven processes of old that Mintzberg so roundly denounces in *The Rise and Fall of Strategic Planning* (Mintzberg, 1994), but the type of learning process that De Geus (1988) champions. It is also our contention that the failure of many strategic planning processes, and by extension the lack of organizational performance, is a result of the inability of the process, as implemented, to create focus among those executives charged with developing strategy, on the few challenges and opportunities that are critical to the future viability and success of the organization.

The importance of shared understanding to executive teams

There is an accumulating body of knowledge in the strategic management area centered around top executives and their effects on organizations. The roots of this work can be traced to Barnard (1938), followed by Learned, Christensen, and Andrews (1961) and Andrews (1971), and built upon most recently by Hambrick and Mason (1984) who maintain that "the performance of an organization is ultimately a reflection of its top managers."

Research in this field has found numerous significant relationships between executive characteristics and organizational outcomes, such as strategic choices and performance (see Finkelstein and Hambrick, 1995, for an excellent review). In consequence of the diversity of experiences and values that executives possess, it is reasonable to infer that, unless in strategy making there is a well defined process to bring executives to a clear focus, there will be a considerable divergence of opinion on what is critical in the future. As Hambrick (1989) notes:

> In the face of the complex, multitudinous, and ambiguous information that typifies the top management task, no two strategists will identify the same array of options for the firm. They will rarely prefer the same options. If by remote chance, they were to pick the same major options, they almost certainly would not implement them identically.

Lawrence and Lorsch (1967) and Galbraith (1977) suggest that integration of diverse perspectives can be achieved through a hierarchy of integrative mechanisms and structures. They remain silent, however, as to how these mechanisms and structures "work their magic." In examining Lawrence and Lorsch's original work more closely, it is possible that these mechanisms and structures work because they create, facilitate, and direct the kinds of understandings among the differentiated functions that lead to integration at a different level, an interpretive one. Integration of diverse perspectives might not be so much the result of a structure, but rather an outcome of a process where shared understanding is created. In short, shared understanding results in integration, and integration leads in turn to organizational performance.

If shared understanding is a necessary antecedent condition for organizational performance, the next logical question is, shared understanding of what? Clearly, recent events have proved that it is insufficient merely to have a shared understanding of some future vision for the organization. In the last decade, extensive corporate visioning exercises have resulted in many wonderful declarative statements by executive teams, but then little in terms of realization of those visions. It appears to be relatively easy to create *intellectual commitment* to an inspirational future state, but far more difficult to create a realistic *operational commitment*. As such there is a growing body of evidence that suggests that shared understanding is necessary across a broader array of organizational functions and processes.

Dougherty(1992), in her work on product innovation and its relationship to shared understanding, suggests that "innovation requires *collective action*, or efforts to create **shared understandings** from disparate perspectives." Dougherty conceives of this shared understanding as consisting of three different dimensions:
- what people see when they look into the future, including issues that are most uncertain;
- what people consider to be the critical aspects of the product development process; and
- how people understand the development task itself.

Murray's (1998) research into the development of shared understanding between information systems and line executives confirmed four distinct categories as relevant in that particular research context:
- vision for information technology;
- critical investments necessary for achieving that vision (i.e., doing the right things);
- key activities in managing those investments (i.e., doing things right); and
- measures of performance.

With respect to strategy making in organizations, it seems reasonable to infer that the following dimensions might be conceived of as key elements of shared understanding:
- what executives see as the vision for the organization;
- what they consider to be the key objectives and strategies for achieving that vision;

- what they understand the actions to be that are required to execute the strategies; and
- how they measure progress towards, and ultimate achievement of the vision.

Murray's (1998) research also found that shared understanding around a vision for information technology (IT) did not by itself lead to firms successfully deploying of IT within the organization. It was a shared understanding of *critical* investments and the *key* activities or actions on major projects that were most strongly linked to success in deploying IT strategies.

How, then, do executive teams create the necessary level of shared understanding? In our view, this is the role played by an effective strategic planning process. To accomplish this end, strategic planning has to be considered an ongoing and dynamic process, rather than a one-time annual event, and also has to be a creative, learning activity. The process, while creating a vision for the organization, must also establish a focused agenda of key initiatives that serve to guide and prioritize implementation activities. Specific, measurable outcomes and appropriate accountabilities ensure that implementation progress is tracked and allocated.

Based on the evident dissatisfaction with strategic planning expressed by many executives, our research sought to establish whether in fact a strategic planning process which results in a high degree of shared understanding by the *critical few*, results in an increase in strategic planning effectiveness. We do not explore the link to overall corporate financial performance in this contribution, but instead our focus is on the effectiveness of strategy implementation – achieving the intended outcomes in a desired time frame, and a high degree of satisfaction of executives with the planning process.

Methodology

In order to examine the relationship between shared understanding of the *critical few* and performance of strategic planning, we examined data collected over a three-year period, 1995–7, from a sample of 20 companies. Our sample included companies from Australia, Canada, and Chile, from businesses as diverse as mining, software development, equipment manufacture, and chemicals. Revenues for these companies ranged from $5 million to $2 billion annually, with a mean of $200 million and median of $100 million. As shown in table 10.1, the number of individuals in the executive teams of these companies ranged from five to 15, with a mean of ten. Five of the companies were subsidiaries of larger multinational corporations, but had considerable autonomy with respect to the structure and format of their strategic planning process.

Table 10.1 Research results

Company	Industry	Revenues ($M)	Executive team size	Prior formal process	Prior degree of satisfaction	Number of "top 3" challenges	Number of broad categories	Final number of key objectives	Rate of progress		Level of satisfaction with progress (1 yr)
									3 mths	1 year	
Travelco	Insurance	$100	11	Yes	Moderate	21	8	4	High	N/A	N/A
Indequipco	Equipment Manufacturing	$110	10	Yes	Low	16	6	4	Low	High	High
Medco	Health and Safety	$40	8	Yes	Low	18	6	3	High	High	High
Chemco	Chemicals Distribution	$130	14	Yes	Low	23	9	4	High	High	High
Finco	Financial Services	$980	12	Yes	Moderate	7	6	3	Low	High	High
Softco	Software Applications	$5	6	Yes	Low	11	5	4	High	High	High
Chilminco	Mining	$ –	6	Yes	Low	12	7	3	High	High	High
Logico	Logistics	$75	12	Yes	Low	15	7	5	High	High	High
Ausminco	Mining	$2500	15	Yes	Very Low	21	8	4	Moderate	Moderate	Moderate
Canminco	Mining	$1300	12	No	N/A	17	6	3	High	Low	Low
Zinco	Metals	$1800	10	Yes	Low	14	6	3	Low	High	High
Goldco	Gold	$80	9	No	N/A	12	7	4	Moderate	High	High
Printco	Publishing	$10	8	Yes	Low	15	6	4	Moderate	N/A	N/A

Company	Industry	Col1	Col2	Col3	Col4	Col5	Col6	Col7	Col8	Col9	Col10
Indco	Precision Manufacturing	$115	16	Yes	Low	14	7	4	High	High	High
Peopleco	Welfare Services	$200	10	Yes	Low	12	7	5	High	Moderate	Moderate
Moveco	Relocation	$70	8	No	N/A	14	6	4	High	High	High
Forequipco	Equipment Manufacturing	$95	14	Yes	Low	22	8	4	High	Moderate	N/A
Gasco	Gas Distribution	$40	7	Yes	Low	11	5	5	Low	Low	Low
Creditco	Financial Services	$40	15	Yes	Moderate	20	6	3	High	High	High
Lumberco	Forestry	$170	15	Yes	Very Low	18	7	4	Moderate	High	Moderate

Data were collected at several critical points during the continuing strategic planning process in each company, and were obtained primarily through a series of interviews with executives involved in these activities. As with any clinical study, detailed records were also kept of all group discussions conducted during the process. Relevant documents, such as past strategic plans, were also examined to corroborate interview data.

The strategic planning process each organization followed typically consisted of four distinct phases related to strategy development, followed by a continuing deployment process. The strategy development phases consisted of the following activities: individual pre-work, group size-up, detailed analysis, and, finally, strategic plan development. Data were collected prior to the start of the process as well as during each of the four phases. A complete description of this process is contained in Murray and Richardson (1998).

Prior to the start of the process, we interviewed executives individually and asked them to provide us with their views on the industry, the business, and the overall key issues facing the organization. We also asked for information about the effectiveness of the company's current strategic planning process. Following these interviews, executives were assigned a pre-work program, designed to further elicit their *individual* views on the company's future business environment, its existing strategy and capabilities, and between three and five critical "make-or-break" strategic issues facing the company.

This individual work was followed by a *group* size-up discussion among the executive team. This discussion was focused on developing a *shared* view of the company's future business environment, its existing strategy and capabilities, and so forth, leading to the identification and agreement on a maximum of five critical *make-or-break* strategic issues. Often, the initial list of *make-or-break* issues resulting from the activity included as many as 12 or 15 possible areas of concern. This initial list was then focused and consolidated to a *critical few* of three or four through a process which produced a *shared understanding* among the group of why these particular issues were truly "make-or-break."

Following this second phase, the participants then undertook a series of studies and reviews of each of these issues for a period of between four and six weeks. These studies were primarily carried out by task forces set up to confirm that the identified *critical few* were indeed the "right" ones and also to obtain additional information required before final agreement could occur. In the fourth phase, these issues were thoroughly reviewed via a series of briefings on task-force findings and subsequent discussions. Numerous opportunities were provided for participants to challenge the identified *critical few* before agreement was finalized. At the end of these briefings, however, the outcome was a final list of no more than five critical issues.

Following this agreement, discussions were held aimed at deriving an initial statement of corporate strategy which included a vision/mission, key objectives and strategies, as well as a three-month tactical deployment plan (that is action plans and associated goals) complete with specific accountabilities and time frames, all of which were linked back to the *critical few*. Part of the discussion around action plans was devoted to developing a shared understanding of the barriers and obstacles to effective deployment. In this discussion, we found that it was critical to have a process to elicit from the team the "undiscussables" – implementation challenges that the group felt extremely uncomfortable in discussing, yet which needed to be acknowledged and understood prior to execution. A communication plan for the strategy, together with a framework for periodic review was also developed.

Successful strategy implementation is by no means guaranteed even when the *critical few* have been identified. Other key requirements for effective strategy deployment include clear, specific objectives and associated performance measures, even for initiatives which, like employee satisfaction, executives may initially perceive to be intangibles. In addition, clear accountabilities and rigorous periodic reviews are also necessary. Commitment and buy-in from a broad cross-section of employees and stakeholders is also important in the implementation phase.

We view the development of shared understanding and knowledge as a continuing, dynamic process, an aspect of these concepts that has so far been largely ignored in the literature. It is not enough to create shared understanding once. As events unfold and more information is obtained, we believe that frequent periodic reviews and the associated action-planning activities are important elements of maintaining shared understanding.

In the process we have described, subsequent periodic reviews were conducted and executives were asked to review progress on the *critical few* strategic agenda items, brief each other on developments that either had taken place or were expected in the near future, and develop the next wave of action plans. This process contributed to a dynamic maintenance of the executive team's shared understanding and focus on *critical* business issues.

Throughout this process, the researchers acted as the facilitators of the executive teams' discussions and work processes. There is little doubt that we, as with most action researchers, did have some input into the substantive aspect of the team's discussions, as well as ensuring minority opinions were heard and discussed. However, the determination of the *critical few* issues was left entirely to the members of the executive team. Our relationship with the executives we studied provided us with invaluable access to their meetings, and permitted trust and confidence to develop between ourselves and the executive team that allowed for candor and openness in expressing opinions on the strategic planning process.

Performance of the strategic planning process was measured objectively in this study via the achievement of the identified strategic objectives in the anticipated time frames. A more subjective measure of performance was also obtained by asking executives involved in the process for their views on the overall success of the process as compared to their previous experience with strategic planning processes where the *critical few* methodology was not employed.

The impact of focus on strategic planning effectiveness

In the companies we studied, 17 had prior experience with formal strategic planning processes. In three of the companies, the process had been informal, but executives in these companies now believed that a more formal process was necessary. At the outset of our involvement, executives in 14 of the 17 firms reported frustration with the lack of impact of their existing strategic planning activity. Three of the remaining firms had no formal strategic planning process in place at the outset of our study, and two others possessed a strategic planning process which their executives believed to have been quite effective.

As was discussed during our overview of the strategic planning processes that the companies employed prior to the start of the planning process, we found a high degree of divergence among most of the executive teams with respect to their views on the top three *critical* issues facing their firms over the next strategic time horizon. The ratio of "top 3" issues to executives ranged from a low of 1:1 to a high of 2.25:1. In short, although there had been a formal strategic planning process in place in most of these firms, it appeared not to have created either a shared understanding or focus on what was critical for the business. Even when the specific topics mentioned by each executive were grouped under broad headings, such as "sales," "customer service," "distribution," or "human resources," no major consolidation was observed. While the number of items listed was reduced through the use of broad headings (by approximately 50 percent in each case), we still found at the outset of the process a range of between five and nine "top 3" issues.

Establishing a true shared understanding of key issues was challenging in most of the organizations involved in this study. Executives were initially satisfied with a high-level, general definition of an issue. For example, "our employees" are often identified either as a strength or weakness. However, for a true shared understanding to develop, the planning team had to develop a much more specific definition of the challenge or opportunity before real strategic insight could be gained. For example, a statement such as, "the dedication and expertise of our technical employees is a key strength of the company, but the productivity and culture of our sales-force is a major weakness," is much more likely to develop real shared insight and understanding than simply referring to "our employees."

Similarly, corporate executives were often prepared to accept objectives that were either not really ends or aims, but rather more process related ("our *objective* is to develop a communications plan"), or statements of intent that could not be measured ("our *objective* is to enhance communications with our customers"). Useful shared understanding only developed after executives were specific about what they wanted to achieve and how they would measure these achievements. The debate that ensued to reach agreement on these subjects was often challenging and vigorous, revealing significant differences among the participants in the discussion, even on subjects where they believed that they had prior agreement. However, by using the process we have described, one in which there are free and open discussions of tough issues, executives in our research samples were able to formulate a strategic plan that encompassed a maximum of five *critical* issues within its vision and mission. The following vignettes provide concrete examples of how the *critical few* came to be identified in two of our sample companies.

Case example: Medco

Medco is a government agency with a national occupational health and safety mandate, facing an increasingly competitive environment. At the time of our initial contact, Medco's customers were becoming increasingly dissatisfied with the level of service received, its business mandate was unfocused, and its future status as a government agency was uncertain. In spite of these threats, strategy implementation was ineffective and the required major changes to the organization's strategy were not occurring. Initial interviews revealed a wide variance in what members of the executive team felt were the critical issues facing the organization. Previous attempts to develop and implement a strategic plan for the organization had been unsuccessful, as there had been little follow-through on the broad strategic agendas that had resulted from the strategic planning process.

Following the four-phase strategic planning process outlined previously, the executive team was able to define a five-year vision for the organization which they believed to be challenging, yet realistic, and which if attained would meet the expectations of their key stakeholder groups. Through a series of discussions, supplemented with appropriate analytical tools, they were able to reduce their future strategic agenda to three critical issues, each with its associated objective and measure: focus the business by divesting non-core activities, dramatically improve the level of customer service, and reduce overall units cost by 15 percent. These three initiatives were not arrived at without a considerable amount of heated discussion and disagreement, but at the end of the day, with only one exception, the team agreed that this strategic agenda was the organization's key to survival. The one executive who could not agree to this agenda left the organization shortly afterwards.

While the organization was required by the Federal Government to monitor its performance via other items (not part of the new strategic agenda), its focus for the next 18 months revolved around the three critical issues identified in the strategic planning process. The executive team met every three months to review achievements, assess the current strategic situation, and develop specific action plans for strategy deployment during the next 90 days. The executives involved all agreed that these continuing reviews were critical to the maintenance and indeed deepening of their shared understanding in several respects: how to operate effectively in a business-like way within a government environment; the requirements for future success in their own line of business; and how to implement strategy effectively. After 18 months, the critical three initiatives had all been carried through successfully, and strategic planning was perceived as a critical organization process contributing to its success. This was in direct contrast to the failure of the previous strategic planning process, one in which the resulting plan was a broad, unfocused array of "things to be done."

Case example: Moveco

In 1991, Moveco was the fourth largest household mover in Canada, carrying out its business through approximately 200 independent agents. Its President had ambitions to be the number one household mover in the country, but found it hard to differentiate his company in an industry which had been commoditized, and where product improvements could be rapidly matched by competitors. In a strategic planning session early in the year, executives identified the creation of a strong alignment between the van line and it agents as a potential differentiating feature, one which competitors may find hard to replicate. In the fall of that year, the company initiated a strategic planning process that not only involved its executives, but also 100 of its most important agents.

Most of the van line's agents were relatively small, entrepreneurial businesses with owner/managers with little formal business education. Over an initial four-day session, these individuals were introduced to the concepts of strategic planning in the context of their own industry, and asked to carry out all the elements of strategy development described in this contribution.

During the process, many agents were heard to comment on the insight and understanding they were gaining into their own industry. The agents' independent size up of the industry and the van line almost exactly mirrored that of the van line's executive team. The agents developed a strategic agenda of five critical issues, four of which were the same as those identified by the executive team. At the end of the planning process, the executive team and the agents emerged with a shared understanding of how to take their van line to first place in the industry, an agenda of four critical issues, and an initial set of action plans for deployment.

Over the next five years, the executives and the agents together developed and implemented a focused set of critical initiatives, and in doing so achieved market leadership in that industry. During that period, the company did not lose one agent to a competitor. Throughout this period, the company and its agents focused on no more than four major strategic initiatives at any one time. While implementation was problematic in the first year, once the company and its agents started to develop a deeper shared understanding of the critical issues, joint strategic plan deployment became increasingly effective as resources were focused around this limited set of initiatives, and progress was carefully monitored. One of the most telling outcomes of the effectiveness of the approach was the number of agents who subsequently adopted the process in their own business.

Because of our continuing association with the companies involved in the study, we were able to track the progress of strategy implementation and the level of executive satisfaction with the process. In most firms, the rate of progress on strategy implementation improved. In these firms, executives reported that the increased focus and improved critical mass allocated to major initiatives, as well as the follow-up and maintenance around the shared understanding of the *critical few* initiatives, had all contributed to these outcomes.

Executives in most of the companies reported that they were satisfied with the outcome of the process. Table 10.1 shows that in most firms, after one year, the reported level of satisfaction among executives was high for both the strategic planning process and the effectiveness of implementation. Executives commented that the process itself created greater clarity about purpose and direction and provided a periodic forum in which differences could be aired and a renewed sense of alignment established. In all the companies with a high level of satisfaction around implementation, sustained achievement of critical objectives, as well as the implementation of a high percentage of action plans was reported. In a number of these companies, the process has now been in place for up to five years, and executives continue to report a high level of satisfaction with the outcomes.

Improved progress and satisfaction were not observed in all companies. In several firms, the rate of progress did not improve, and satisfaction levels remained low. Interviews indicated that in these firms, while the *critical few* had been defined, a continuing focus on them was not maintained. Executives in these companies reported that a discipline of periodic reviews had not been established, and accountabilities were not enforced. In one company, Forequipco, while its executives had developed a focused strategy and were maintaining the review process, poorer- than-expected short-term results due to local market conditions caused its foreign parent to intervene, resulting in a loss of focus and momentum, and, ultimately, the sale of the business.

The strategic importance of the *critical few*

The experience of companies that participated in our research demonstrates that using strategic planning as a process to build a shared understanding around the *critical few* issues for an organization is key to successful implementation of the strategic plan implementation, and thus is key to organizational performance. Results from the executive surveys we have conducted, combined with a substantial amount of anecdotal evidence, suggests that it is still not generally understood by many senior executives that a strategic planning process that results in the identification of a broad array "strategic" issues is less likely to be effective than one which results in a more focused set of critical issues. Linked to this, are the concomitant challenges that are posed with the performance measures that result from the inclusion of a broad array of initiatives in a strategic plan. It is possible that an overabundance of "strategic" initiatives and associated performance measures actually reduces alignment across the organization, diffuses focus, and, as one executive faced with an overwhelming array of performance measures noted, results in "scorecard paralysis."

It is our position in this chapter, and the research study we have described supports this, that a strategic planning process, such as the one which we have described, will be most effective if it:

- provides a periodic opportunity to creatively re-think the business and the organization;
- creates a shared understanding of the *critical few* strategic issues; and
- defines a clear, limited set of associated objectives, strategies, and measures.

Given the relatively limited time available in the hectic schedule of most executives and managers for strategic matters, the executives agreed that a focused strategic agenda, and one that allowed for each major initiative to be well resourced, was the approach most likely to result in tangible, timely achievements.

While it is important at the start of any strategic planning process to take a broad perspective encompassing the firm's macro-environment, industry, and markets, it is important throughout, to challenge the executive team to make choices about what is critical. In doing so, it is possible for executives charged with crafting organization strategy, to develop a shared understanding of four key elements of organizational strategy, none of which alone are sufficient to drive strategic planning effectiveness:

1 a vision for the organization;
2 what people consider to be the *critical few* issues in achieving that vision;
3 what people understand the key objectives (ends) and strategies (means) to be that are required to address the issues; and
4 specific measures of progress towards and ultimate achievement of the vision.

The experience of the companies in our sample also demonstrates that frequent strategy reviews, usually quarterly, are important not only as an opportunity for reviewing progress, but also because of the contribution that they make to deepening and enriching the shared understanding of the executive team about the organization's business and environment.

At this meeting, a typical agenda, focused around the *critical few* usually addresses the following questions:

1 What have we achieved in the past three months on these issues?
2 What, if anything, has changed in our environment and business that affects our strategic agenda?
3 What do we wish to achieve on our strategic agenda during the next quarter?
4 What few key action items are required to move us forwards?

In too many strategic planning activities, there is not enough mental toughness, political will, or shared understanding achieved to reduce the strategic agenda to a realistic and manageable *critical few*. As previously discussed, Hambrick (1989) suggests that it is difficult for strategists to identify the same array of options for the firm, and even more difficult for them to agree on implementation approaches. Unless the right process is employed, strategic planning becomes a *list*-making activity – long lists of opportunities, capabilities, and things to do, with no real sense of priority. Our research demonstrates that in using the right strategic planning process, this need not be the case. The strategic planning process we have described provides the framework for assisting executive teams in their task of defining, addressing, and monitoring the *critical few*. Achieving agreement on these issues is not always an easy task, but one that our research has indicated is instrumental in improving the odds of successful strategy implementation, and thus in improving organizational performance.

REFERENCES

Andrews, K.R. (1971). *The Concept of Corporate Strategy*. Homewood, IL: Irwin.

Barnard, C.I. (1938). *The Functions of the Executive*. Cambridge, MA: Harvard University Press.

De Geus, Arie P. (1988). Planning as Learning. *Harvard Business Review*, March–April, 70–4.

Dougherty, D. (1992). Interpretive barriers to successful product innovation in large firms. *Organization Science*, 3, 179–202.

Finkelstein, S. and Hambrick, D.C. (1995). The effects of ownership structure on conditions at the top: The case of CEO pay raises. *Strategic Management Journal*, 16, 175–94.

Galbraith, J. (1997). *Organization Design*. Reading: Addison-Wesley.

Hambrick, D.C. (1987). Top management teams: Key to strategic success. *California Management Review*, 30, 88–108.

Hambrick, D.C. (1989). Guest editor's introduction: Putting top managers back in the strategy picture. *Strategic Management* 10 (Special Issue), 5–15.

Hambrick, D.C. and Mason, P.A. (1984). Upper echelons: The organization as a reflection of its top managers. *Academy of Management Review*, 9, 193–206.

Kaplan, Robert S. and Norton, David P. (1996). *The Balanced Scorecard*. Boston, MA: Harvard School of Business Administration Press.

Lawrence, P. and Lorsch, J. (1967). *Organization and Environment*. Boston, MA: Harvard School of Business Administration Press.

Learned, E.P., Christensen, C.R., and Andrews, K.R. (1961). *Problems of general management-business policy*. Homewood, IL: Irwin.

March, J.G. and Simon, H.A. (1958). *Organizations*. New York: John Wiley & Sons.

Mintzberg, H. (1994). *The Rise and Fall of Strategic Planning*. Toronto: Free Press.

Murray, E. (1998). Bridging two solitudes: An examination of shared understanding between information systems and line executives. Unpublished Doctoral Dissertation, University of Western Ontario, London, Ontario.

Murray, E. and Richardson, P. (1998). Strategy as action. Working Paper 98–07, Queen's School of Business, Queen's University, Kingston, Ontario.

11 Integrated performance measurement systems: Structure and dynamics

Umit Bititci, Allan Carrie, and Trevor Turner

Introduction

The objective of this chapter is to provide an insight in to the background research, development, and practical application of the Integrated Performance Measurement Systems (IPMS) Reference Model and the associated audit method. The research described was conducted by a multi-disciplinary team based at the Centre for Strategic Manufacturing, University of Strathclyde. The research was funded through EPSRC and industry.

The point of departure for this work was that:

1 There are various performance measurement systems models, frameworks, and methodologies available – such as SMART (Cross and Lynch, 1988–9), Performance Measurement Questionnaire (Dixon, Nanni, and Vollmann, 1990), Performance Measurement for World Class Manufacture (Maskell, 1989), Performance Criteria System (Globerson, 1985), Cambridge Performance Measurement Design Process (Neely, Gregory, and Platts, 1995; Neely et al., 1996) and Balanced Scorecards (Kaplan and Norton, 1992 and 1996).

2 Other fields, such as Quality Management and Environmental Management, have *auditable* reference models and standards that describe the structure and content of a robust management system, i.e. ISO9000, QS9000, and ISO14000.

3 However, an *auditable* reference model, which describes the structure and constituent parts of a robust, integrated, efficient, and effective performance measurement system, was not available (Bititci, Carrie, and McDevitt, 1996).

The overall aim of the work was to establish whether an auditable reference model for IPMS could be developed. The more specific objectives included:

• to research and model the hierarchical structure and relationships between performance measures.

- to research and develop a reference model for comparison and benchmarking of integrated performance measurement systems;
- to provide a workbook and computer-based analysis tool to assist companies in auditing their performance measurement systems;
- to illustrate the methods developed using industrial case studies.

The research adopted a seven-stage research methodology. These stages were as follows:

- thorough analysis of the subject area to review all relevant academic work and industrial practices in order to establish a research baseline;
- develop a requirements specification for an integrated performance measurement system and associated reference models;
- conduct a critical review of existing models and approaches;
- research, evaluate, and identify frameworks to represent the reference model;
- develop an auditable reference model;
- validate the reference model through audits in collaborating organizations;
- develop and validate a formal audit method.

The work resulted in the development of a reference model for IPMS and an associated audit tool which have been used by the researchers to audit the performance measurement systems of over 30 organizations.

This work concluded that an auditable reference model for IPMS can be established and that the reference model developed provided valuable insights into the deficiencies of the performance measurement systems employed by various organizations through the audit process. The audits conducted also provided valuable insights into various aspects of performance measurement systems which are discussed in greater detail in this chapter.

Background

Analysis of the field

An in-depth analysis of the subject area was conducted, which consisted of a detailed academic literature review as well as workshops with industrial collaborators and discussions with other industrial colleagues and contacts. The objective of this analysis was to establish:

- what performance measures are used for, and
- what an integrated performance measurement system should do.

The academic literature review included over 260 publications covering a broad range of disciplines. This survey uncovered numerous concepts and principles relating to performance measurement. Many of these either addressed a particular aspect of performance measurement or they provided empirical evidence to support good or bad practices with respect to performance measurement. Very few publications provided a complete and structured view for an integrated performance measurement system. Those works, which provided a near-complete view of a performance measurement system, have been already identified in the previous section (i.e. introduction).

The industry-based research included in-depth study of collaborators performance measurement systems (i.e. ICI, Grand Metropolitan plc, and Clyde Blowers plc), as well as companies which were considered to be "good practitioners," such as Hewlett Packard, Texas Instruments, DuPont, TNT, Rank Xerox, etc.).

Requirements specification

Based on the key messages from the literature, as well as a review of good and bad industrial practices, answers to the two questions above were deduced. These were then validated and amended following various industrial workshops and seminars facilitated by organizations, such as Scottish JIT Club, Scottish Enterprise, Strategic Planning Society, Institute of Management Consultants, and Institute of Operations Management.

The final answers to the questions posed at the beginning of this section may be summarized as follows:

Performance measures were required for the following purposes:
- to monitor and control;
- to drive improvement;
- to maximize the effectiveness of the improvement effort;
- to achieve alignment with organizational goals and objectives;
- to reward and discipline (to a lesser extent).

An integrated performance measurement system should:
- reflect stakeholders requirements to maximize stakeholder satisfaction;
- reflect external/competitive position of an organization;
- focus on the competitive criteria of the organizations markets in order to facilitate strategies and actions to improve the competitive position of the organization;
- provide an input to strategy development;
- deploy strategic objectives through a logical path to business processes to ensure that strategy, actions, and measures are aligned;

- differentiate between control and improvement measures;
- focus on critical areas of the business to maximize the effect of the improvement effort;
- be expressed in a locally meaningful terminology to encourage understanding and maximize ownership;
- facilitate resource bargaining to ensure the provision of necessary resources to processes and activities critical to overall performance;
- facilitate intelligent and logical performance planning based on constraint management;
- promote proactive management by focusing on leading measures to facilitate a more proactive management style;
- accommodate both quantitative and qualitative measures;
- measure organizational capability and learning where appropriate;
- ensure that measures are used at correct levels;
- promote understanding of the causal relationships between various measures;
- facilitate simple reporting – demonstrating trends where possible;
- be dynamic and change in response to the changes in the internal and external environment of the organization;

Critical review of existing models

Each one of the models identified earlier in this introduction to this chapter was compared against the requirements summarized above. This study revealed that *none of the existing models or approaches completely addresses the requirements identified.*

The IPMS reference model

At the outset of the research the basic specification for the reference model was discussed and agreed between the industrial collaborators and the researchers. It was agreed that the objectives of the documented reference model would be to explain the structure and content of an integrated performance measurement system.

1 Make the reference model auditable by documenting it in a format compatible with other auditable business models, such as the European Model for Business Excellence, ISO9000, QS9000, and ISO14000.

2 Integrate other business and financial models into the basic framework of the reference model in order to provide guidance in interpreting the reference model by referring to the appropriate models and approaches in the requirement statements.

3 Make the reference model useful for both the designing of new and for auditing of existing performance measurement systems.

The challenge here was that research to this point resulted merely in a list of requirements which to a certain extent describe the contents of an IPMS but without a structure thus making it almost impossible to audit and integrate with other models in a clear and precise fashion. The research then progressed to identify an appropriate structure, which could serve as a framework upon which a complete reference model could be built.

Reference model: development

At the outset of the research it was stated that the Viable Systems Model (VSM) (Beer, 1979, 1981, 1985) might provide the appropriate framework to accommodate a reference model. In order to examine the VSM and other systems frameworks and methods available it proved useful to adopt the total systems intervention theory (Flood and Jackson, 1991).

Having examined the available approaches in some detail, VSM together with the CIM-OSA Business Process Architecture (ESPRIT Consortium AMICE, 1991, Maull, Childe, and Bennet, 1994) and policy deployment (Bechtell, 1995) proved to provide the most appropriate framework for the reference model. Table 11.1 demonstrates how these approaches fulfil the reference model requirements.

The following points outline the particular reasons for selecting VSM:

1 VSM reflects the hierarchical nature of an organization through its recursion feature.

2 Performance measurement system is an information system. VSM incorporates the information system, which links and integrates other systems within an organization.

3 VSM incorporates the interaction between an organization and its external environment.

4 VSM is more readily recognizable as a model of a manufacturing enterprise.

5 VSM provides a complete model of an organization as it exists naturally, which is independent of its physical organizational structure.

6 VSM differentiates between management and operations (at various levels) of an organization, whilst providing a number of mechanisms to integrate management and operations.

7 Business units and business processes exist naturally in all organizations, although they are not necessarily formally recognized by the management.

8 Business units and business processes are viable systems at different levels of recursion in the viable systems model of an organization.

Reference model: Structure

In summary the fundamental structure of the reference model was built upon:
- systems concepts;
- The viable systems model;
- CIM-OSA business process architecture;
- Concepts of policy deployment.

These models and concepts are reflected within the structure of the reference model. The reference model considers an organization at four levels based on the recursion concept within the VSM theory. These four levels are:
- the business – recursion 1;
- the business units – recursion 2;
- the business processes – recursion 3;
- the activities – recursion 4.

The business level represents the entire organization which exists for a purpose. To fulfil this purpose *the business operates a number of business units*, each servicing a market which has particular requirements. In this context a business unit is defined as the portion of the organization which serves a particular market segment with particular competitive requirements. In order to service this demand *each business unit operates a number of operating processes, which are supported by a number of support processes*. Finally *each business process operates a series of activities* to fulfil its purpose.

These four levels may be physical or logical. The term "logical" means that the organization does not need to be physically organized to have the four levels. In the experience of the researchers in all businesses these four levels do exist, but they are not always recognized by the management.

The CIM-OSA business process architecture, illustrated in figure 11.1, provides guidance on the nature of managing, operating and support business processes. The business process level of the reference model includes operating and support processes as related, but separate viable systems. However the

Table 11.1 PMS Requirements v VSM and CIM-OSA Business Process Architecture

Requirements	VSM	CIM-OSA	Policy deployment
Reflects stakeholders requirements	System 5 – Stakeholders of a business set the ultimate direction of that business. In order to remain viable the business must recognize the requirements of its stakeholders.	Reflects relationships between different types of processes	Deploys stakeholders requirements throughout the hierarchy
Reflects external/competitive pos.	System 4 – External monitor		
Focus on competitive criteria	System 4 – External monitor		
Differentiates between control and improvement measures	Amplification and attenuation loops		
Facilitates strategy development	System 4 – External monitor and System 3 – objective setting and monitoring		
Deploys strategic objectives	System 3 – Objective setting and monitoring Amplification and Transduction	Defines a logical deployment path	Deploys strategic objectives throughout the hierarchy
Objectives deployed to business processes and activities	Amplification and transduction through levels of recursion to systems 1 which are business processes	Defines a logical deployment path and identifies standard business processes	Deploys objectives to business processes and activities
Focuses on critical areas of the business	Recursion and amplification	Assists in defining priorities	Simplifies recognition of criticality
Expressed in a locally meaningful terminology	Transduction		Facilitates transduction
Facilitates resource bargaining	Resource bargaining	Specifically between operating and support processes	Facilitates resource bargaining
Facilitates performance planning	Normative planning		Facilitates performance planning

Focuses on leading measures as well as lagging measures		Assists in the development of leading and lagging measures	
Accommodates both quantitative and qualitative measures		Assists in the development of qualitative measures	
Measures organizational capability and learning where appropriate			
Uses measures at correct levels	Recursion		Facilitates use of measures at correct levels
Promotes understanding of the relationships between measures	Partially addressed through recursion, transduction and amplification	Assists in defining the relationships between processes	Facilitates understanding of the hierarchical relationships
Facilitates simple reporting – demonstrating trends		Develops a reporting structure	Simplifies the reporting structure

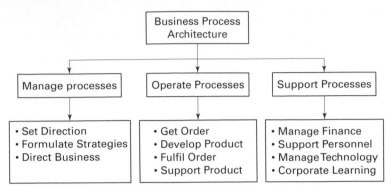

Figure 11.1.   The CIM-OSA Business Process Achitecture.

management processes are treated as part of the structure within each business unit which manages the operating and support processes.

Elements at each level

Again based on the five systems of the VSM, the reference model at each of its four levels considers four elements. These are:

* stakeholders requirements – system 5;
* external monitor – system 4;
* objectives – system 3;
* performance measures – system 2.

System 1 is represented by the next level, e.g at the business level the business units would be systems 1, at the business unit level the business processes would be system 1, and so on.

The reference model requires that, at each level of the business, the organization:

* *sets direction* (system 5) by recognizing and understanding the requirements of its *stakeholders*;
* *monitors its external environment* (system 4), with respect to the stakeholders requirements, against competitors and world class performance to identify the development needs of the business;
* *Sets and deploys internal objectives* (system 3) based on the implications and criticality of the development gaps together with appropriate targets and time scales;
* *Coordinates* (system 2) its sub-systems (system 1) by monitoring, reviewing, and reporting on these objectives through *performance measures* reports.

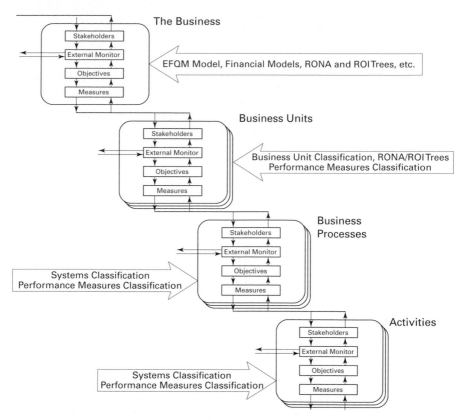

Figure 11.2. Reference model for integrated performance measurements systems.

Figure 11.2 illustrates the final structure of the reference model. Additionally, a number of references and concepts are provided which may be used for guidance at each stage.

Within each level of the reference model one could clearly identify three systems, which relate to performance measurement. These are:

- *the external control system*, which monitors critical parameters with respect to the external environment (VSM system 4);
- *improvement and alignment system*, which deploys the improvement objectives, and negotiates priorities, targets and resources through the critical parts of the business ensuring alignment (VSM system 3);
- *the internal control system*, which monitors and coordinates lower-level systems and that includes the algedonic signal (i.e. warning / early warning signal) that provides the active monitors (VSM system 2).

Reference model: Principles

There are a number of fundamental principles integrated within the reference model, which the reader should be aware of in order to understand the logic of the model. These principles are inherent within the models that were used to build the reference model. This is reflected in table 11.1. The objective of this section is to explain these principles to the reader in an explicit and simple way.

Management control

Deployment is a key requirement from an effective performance measurement system. Through deployment two objectives are fulfilled, namely alignment and improvement. In order to facilitate deployment it is important to establish a management and control structure. Within VSM this management and control structure is clearly specified. VSM views each level of the organizational structure as consisting of two elements:
- a management element (i.e. systems 2, 3, 4, and 5), and
- an operational element (system 1).

This convention enables the separation of the "management element" from the "operational element." This feature repeats itself through the four levels of the reference model. The following statements will help to clarify this principle.

1 The business represents the management element and the business units represent the operational elements of this business.

2 Each business unit has its own management element and its own operational elements. The business processes inherent within a business unit represent the operational elements of that business unit.

3 Similarly, each business process has its own management element and its own operational elements. The activities inherent within each business process represent the operational element of that business process.

Deployment

Again continuing through the management and control structure within VSM, as the reference model progresses downward through the four levels the higher level becomes a stakeholder of the lower level. In addition, other stakeholders may be added, as appropriate at each level. Therefore, the management element at each level deploys its objectives to its operational levels. That is:

1 The business deploys its objectives and targets at the business unit level.
2 Each business unit deploys its local objectives at the business process level.
3 Similarly, each business process deploys its local objectives at the Activity level.

Criticality

Deployment as explained above is not universal. In other words not all the objectives of the higher level should necessarily be deployed to lower levels. For example, a business with an objective to maximize return on investment may achieve this objective by increasing sales and/or by reducing costs. If this business operated two business units, one a with a mature product in a mature market place and the other with a young product in a growing marketplace, the costs reduction and increase sales objectives would be deployed respectively rather than universally. This principle is based on the policy deployment theory where the potential impact, contribution, or return is assessed and objectives are deployed to those parts which have a critical impact or contribution.

Transduction

This is a key feature of deployment and is a feature inherent within VSM and policy deployment. As the objectives are deployed from one level to the next, they are expressed in locally meaningful and unambiguous terminology.

Resource bargaining

This is a feature that is strongly emphasized within VSM and is reflected within certain applications of policy deployment. It is the term applied to the action of negotiation between two levels of the model. This is also a key feature of deployment. It relates to the need to ensure that deployed local objectives are realistic and achievable and that operations have the necessary resources to achieve the objectives and targets.

Normative planning

The principle of normative planning by Beer (Beer, 1979) relates to target setting and performance improvement planning. It is linked strongly to deployment and resource bargaining. Normative planning suggests that in setting the objectives due consideration should be given to recognizing the following three performance levels:
- actuality, i.e. the actual performance;
- capability, i.e. the maximum performance achievable under current constraints;
- potentiality, i.e., the performance achievable providing all constraints are removed.

When deploying objectives from one level to the next, attention should be paid to targets set. If the target set is within the potentiality range then appropriate resources should be made available to remove specified constraints.

Active monitoring

Most performance measures relating to objectives tend to be reactive, i.e., they measure performance after the event. To promote an agile and proactive management style it is important that the reactive performance measures associated with the objectives are supported/accompanied by a number of active performance measures.

For example, "percent customer satisfaction" is a reactive measure of the order fulfilment process. A factor which influences customer satisfaction may be partnership agreements, thus "number of partnership agreements in place" may be a good active measure to adopt.

Again, as in other principles, active monitoring can exists at all levels. In the example quoted above, where "percent customer satisfaction" was a reactive measure of the order fulfilment process, it can easily be classified as an active measure for sales which itself may be classified as a reactive measure at the business unit level.

The experience of the research team is that the concept of active monitoring makes managers think about the causal relationships between measures.

UNCERTAINTY / COMPLEXITY	HIGH	LOW
HIGH	• Aerospace • Shipbuilding • Major Construction • Etc. FITNESS FOR PURPOSE KEY Competence: Product Design and Development	• Cosmetics • Textiles • Food and Drink • Etc. TIMELINESS KEY Competence: Time to Market
LOW	• Automotive • White Goods • Conventional Machine Tools • Etc. VALUE FOR MONEY KEY Competence: Supply Flexibility	• Simple Components • Paper • Commodity Tools • Glass • Etc. PRICE KEY Competence: Manufacturing Productivity and Logistics

Figure 11.3. Business classification model.

Classification

Business units can be classified according to the complexity and uncertainty of their operating environment. This classification provides guidelines on the most appropriate type of performance measure.

Figure 11.3 illustrates this classification for business units. This is a classification system used by the DTI's Factory of the Future Project, which was conducted as part of a European Programme (DTI, 1996; Kehoe and Little, 1997).

As illustrated in figure 11.3 this classification model allocates business units into four sectors and for each sector specifies the performance criteria associated with that sector (e.g., fitness for purpose, timeliness, value for money, and price) as well as the key competencies required.

The audit process

An audit method has been developed, which allows assessment of the integrity of an organization's performance measurement system against the reference model. The audit method examines:

- the level of conformity with the structure of the reference model;
- appropriateness of the performance measures used;
- appropriateness of the targets and objectives set.
  Typically an audit identifies issues such as:
- absence of performance measures critical to the strategic objectives;
- use of surplus and meaningless performance measures;
- wrong emphasis on measures;
- lack of deployment of measures due to absence of criticality, transduction, and resource bargaining;
- confusion between control and improvement measures;
- absence of a logical system for performance planning.

The audit experiences gained by the researchers together with the experiences of the participating companies have been used to develop the first draft of a formal audit workbook. It has been found that a software-based workbook, although greatly simplifying the analysis stage throughout the audit process, also obscures the logic of the reference model during the audit process. The structure of the audit process is illustrated in figure 11.4.

IPMS audit: case studies

In this section three case studies are presented to illustrate the practical use of the IPMS reference model and the associated audit method. The following audit structure was used in all three cases:

1 First audit action was to give the management team a presentation on the reference model, the audit process and the objectives of the audit.

2 Immediately following the presentation the logical structure (i.e. scope of business, definition of business units, and business processes) of the business was defined through a workshop in conjunction with the management team.

3 Interviews were arranged with various managers and their staff to collect data regarding the business as well as each business unit, business process, and critical activities. The audit workbook together with the reference model was used extensively for this purpose.

4 Where possible objective evidence on plans, objectives, competitive studies/comparisons, and performance measures were collected.

5 During the interviews the audit team spent some time structuring, sanitizing, and clarifying the information provided.

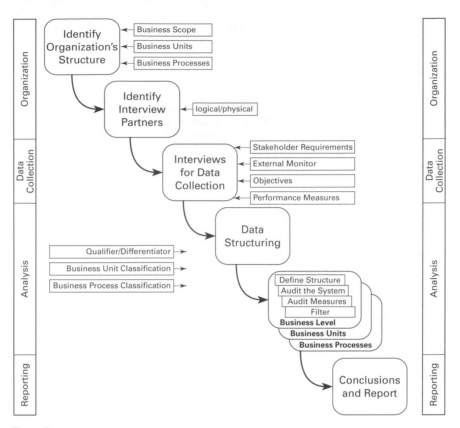

Figure 11.4.   The audit process.

6   On completion of all the information, the audit team conducted an analysis of the information provided using the audit workbook which led to development of key conclusions.

7   The findings of the audit were presented back to the management team for discussion and decision on possible actions.

In all cases two people completed an audit within a one-week time scale. Actions 1 and 2 were completed within the first half day of the audit. The remainder of the time was spent on data collection and analysis. Another half a day was allocated for the feedback presentation to allow discussion and agreement on future actions.

Case Study 1 – S. Distribution Limited (SDL)

SDL is a cost center within the S. Corporation, which specializes in the configuration of the companies' products to customer specification before delivery.

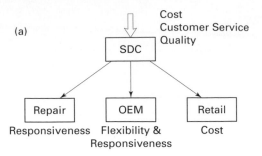

(a)

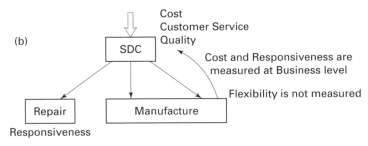

(b)

Figure 11.5.   (a) Logical structure of SDC; (b) Physical structure of SDC.

Its customers can be broadly categorized as original equipment manufacturers (OEMs) – such as Sun, Compaq, Digital, Dell, Apple, etc. – and distributors who in turn supply the high street retail outlets and specialists shops. In addition "S. Distribution" has a service and repair center which offers rapid repair and replacement service to its customer and end-user base.

The researchers were invited to SDL to conduct a performance measurement system audit against the Integrated Performance Measurement System Reference Model Version 2.3. The audit results can be summarized as follows.

1 The company's logical and physical structure is represented in figure 11.5. Here it can be seen that, although logically there are three business units, the company treats the OEM and the retail business units as a single business.

2 In general terms all stakeholder requirements were understood at all levels.

3 There was a general absence of an external monitor with the exception of the areas which are monitored through the key customers quarterly business reviews. This lack of visibility could compromise the company's competitive position in the long term.

4 The objectives set at each level reflected most of the stakeholder's requirements, however there were some critical gaps with respect to competitive requirements of some of the retail and repair business units.

5 The company did not differentiate between control and improvement measures. This led to a certain amount of confusion within the business.

6 The business unit objectives, although clearly understood, were measured at the business level. This was because the company did not differentiate between the two logical business units (i.e., OEM and retail). Consequently, the company did not have a clear understanding of the level of responsiveness they were achieving at a given cost.

7 The business and business unit objectives were relatively well deployed to the core business processes (i.e., the order fulfilment processes) with the exception of flexibility.

8 Flexibility was identified as a key order winning criteria for the OEM business unit. However, there was no evidence of a performance measure, which measured the flexibility of the OEM business unit or the OEM order fulfilment process.

9 The stakeholder and core business process requirements were not deployed at all to the support processes, such as engineering support and people capability management. There was no evidence of a practical resource bargaining process based on objective performance measures, relating to the support processes and their stakeholders' requirements.

10 The performance reports did not include targets (except in some cases) and time scales, which suggests that these measures are for control purposes rather than improvement.

11 There was no evidence of active measures being used against each one of the performance measures relating to objectives. However, there is an improvement planning system in place in the form of action plans, which loosely relate to the business objectives.

12 Although the company had detailed improvement plans, there were no measures which monitored the company's progress and achievement of milestone targets.

13 There was no evidence of an agenda to review the relevance of the performance measures.

As a result of this IPMS audit the company has made the following changes to its performance measurement systems to overcome the gaps identified:

- introduced a balanced set of measures at business unit level for each business unit;
- introduced measures of flexibility at activity levels;
- changed the planning systems to manage the OEM and retail jobs separately;

- implemented an organizational change – one manager is now responsible for both order fulfilment and engineering support;
- introduce measures to link core and support processes;
- introduce a system of resource bargaining and performance planning for the support processes.

Case Study 2 – D. S. Limited (DSL)

DSL is a major textile manufacturer. Its main operations consist of design, manufacture, sale, and distribution of gents and ladies garments, such as jackets, trousers, and skirts. An IPMS audit against reference model v.2.4 was conducted during January 1998, results of which may be summarized as follows.

1 Logically DSL comprises of two business units. The contract business unit and the signature business unit. Physically the company recognized the two different business units and clearly differentiated between the competitive criteria associated with each business unit.

2 In general terms DSL was aware of its stakeholders and their requirements, but failed to recognize society as a key stakeholder.

3 There was no formal external monitor which monitored DSL's performance with respect to its competitors. However, the senior management team demonstrated a good understanding of the company's financial performance with respect to its key competitors.

4 In most areas the objectives failed to reflect the stakeholders' requirements completely and directly.

5 The majority of the objectives were not associated with targets and time scales.

6 Critical performance measures were missing against a large number of key objectives.

7 The performance of key business processes was not measured consciously, e.g., product development process.

8 There was no differentiation between control and improvement measures.

9 Majority of measures focused on cost and there was no balanced set of measures which focused on business units or processes.

As a result of this audit, DSL included the re-design of its performance measurement system as a key objective into its BPR programme.

Case study 3 – B. Manufacturing Limited (BML)

BML is a cost center of a major pharmaceuticals and cosmetics manufacturer. Its main operation is the packaging of the cosmetics to the final product. In support of its packaging operations it also manufactures some of the cosmetics. An IPMS audit, conducted during October 1997, revealed the following.

1 BML is comprised of three business units.
2 Stakeholders requirements were fully recognized.
3 Although there was an awareness of competitive position it was not fully quantified.
4 The main objectives related to cost, quality, and delivery.
5 Flexibility, although an important requirement, was not stated as an objective.
6 The "new product realization" process was considered to be the most critical process but had no measures for the critical requirements of flexibility and responsiveness.
7 There was a range of measures, which related to business activities, but these appeared random and did not clearly relate to business process or business unit objectives.
8 In general there was no differentiation between improvement and control measures.

As a result of this audit the company made the following changes to its performance measurement systems to overcome the gaps identified:

- put an action in place to fully quantify the competitive position of the BML with its competitors. As BML was one of several manufacturing units within the parent group which are in effect in competition with each other, the management team felt that it would be relatively simple to ascertain their competitive position in a quantitative manner;
- commissioned a project to investigate what was meant by flexibility and how BML could best measure flexibility;
- introduced a more balanced set of measures at the new product introduction process level, balancing cost, responsiveness, flexibility, and quality;
- reorganized their performance measures in a meaningful structure, reflecting the causal relationships between measures, and within this structure clearly distinguished between control and improvement measures by color coding these.

Audit findings

The research team conducted audits with over 30 organizations. The range of organizations audited included:

- pharmaceutical manufacturing,
- explosives manufacturing,

- bottling and packaging,
- textiles manufacturing,
- utility providers (e.g., water, electricity),
- electronics manufacturing,
- construction,
- engineering consultancy,
- Public sector organization.

The collective experience from these audits resulted in a number of findings that are categorized below as organization-related findings and reference-model-related findings.

Company-related findings

1 All organizations have a performance measurement system of some form, that may be formal or informal, structured or unstructured.
2 Most managers do not recognize performance measurement as a system until they are prompted.
3 Very few organizations can demonstrate an understanding of the cause and effect relationships between the performance measures used.
4 Most organizations have a static performance measurement system, and any changes in priorities and emphasis in response to changes in the external or internal environment of the organization are deployed through informal channels, which often conflict with static, formalized, or semi-formalized, performance measurement systems. This has a negative effect on the integrity of the performance measurement system as well as on the agility and responsiveness of the organization.
5 The main barriers, to an organizations ability to adopt a more dynamic approach to performance measurement systems, can be summarized as follows:
   - lack of a structured framework;
   - absence of a flexible platform which allows organizations to effectively and efficiently manage the dynamics of their performance measurement systems;
   - inability to quantify the relationships between performance measures within a system.
6 Some organizations do not recognize their business units and some organizations have incorrectly defined business units.
7 Most organizations do not realize that business processes are specific to business units.

8   Very few organizations consciously manage business processes, but some unconsciously measure the output of their business processes.

9   Most organizations do not recognize the internal customer–supplier relationship between core and support processes; thus this interface is generally poorly managed.

10 Resource bargaining and performance planning is often unfocused in most organizations, and particularly between operate and support processes.

11 Most organizations do not differentiate between improvement and control measures. In most cases the need for differentiation is not understood. Once prompted most managers agree with the need to differentiate.

12 The concept of active monitoring is not widely understood, and it is not used consciously in most companies.

13 Some organizations have too many performance measures – i.e. more than required.

14 Most organizations have performance measures which do not relate to objectives

Reference-model-related findings

1   Most managers were able to understand the content of the reference model after attending the initial briefing session.

2   The reference model represents a dynamic system. Its external monitoring feature requires organizations to assess their position with respect to stakeholders' requirements. This in turn allows them to respond to changes in the internal and external environment of the organization by adjusting or changing their strategies, objectives, priorities, and targets to achieve maximum stakeholder satisfaction.

3   In collecting data on performance measures used in a company it is difficult to relate a performance measure to a logical part of the business. That is at what level should an existing performance measure belong to: business, business unit, or process. The facilitator's experience becomes valuable during this part of the audit process.

4   Assessment of the deployment process remains the most subjective part of the audit process and therefore is the most facilitator dependent area.

5   The audit also identifies possible redundant and surplus measures.

6   Auditors require group facilitation skills to communicate effectively with the business teams during the audit process.

Conclusions

The reference model for integrated performance measurement systems presented in this contribution is based on a collection of academic works and industrial best practices. A number of existing models and concepts have been used to provide a framework which facilitates the integration of various models, concepts, and practices into a single reference model.

The reference model has been documented in a form to make the academic theories and concepts transparent to the user. The reference model is presented as a simple series of requirements, which are easily understood without any specialist knowledge.

The reference model has been used in over 30 organizations. In all cases the application of the reference model and the IPMS audit identified gaps in the organization's existing performance measurement systems. In all cases the senior management in the organization decided to take action to rectify the identified gaps.

The final conclusion of this research is that an auditable reference model could be developed for performance measurement systems with considerable benefit to industrial users and that the reference model developed as part of the work described in this chapter is valid.

Performance measurement systems should be dynamic and they should change and adapt with the changing internal and external environment. There is little evidence of recognition of this need for dynamic systems within the practitioners and there is little theory and technology to facilitate creation of truly dynamic performance measurement systems. Dynamics of performance measurement systems should be an area of focus for future research.

BIBLIOGRAPHY AND REFERENCES

Bechtell, M. L. (1995). The management compass: steering the corporation using Hoshin Planning. Ama Management Briefing.

Beer S. (1979). *The Heart of the Enterprise.* Chichester: Wiley.

Beer S. (1981). *Brain of the Firm.* Chichester: Wiley.

Beer S. (1985). Diagnosing the System for Organizations. Chichester: Wiley.

Bititci, U.S. and Carrie, A.S. (1998). Integrated performance measurement systems: structures and relationships. EPSRC Research Grant Final Report (GR/K 48174), Engineering and Physical Sciences Research Council, Swindon, UK.

Bititci, U.S., Carrie, A.S., and McDevitt, L. (1996). Performance measurement: A business process view. IFIP WG 5.7 Workshop on Modelling Techniques, Business Processes and Benchmarking, April, Bordeaux, France.

Cross, K.F. and Lynch, R.L. (1998–1989). The SMART way to define and sustain success, *National Productivity Review*, **9**(1), 23–33.

Dixon, J.R., Nanni, A.J. and Vollmann, T.E. (1990). The New Performance Challenge: Measuring Operations for World Class Competition. Irwin Homewood, IL: Dow Jones.

DTI (1996). Factory of the future, DTI, London.

ESPRIT Consortium AMICE (1991). Integrated manufacturing: A challenge for the 1990s, *International Journal of Computing and Control Engineering*, May.

Flood, R.L. and Jackson, M.C. (1991). *Creative Problem Solving: Total Systems Intervention*, John Wiley.

Gelders, L., Mannaerts, P., and Maes, P. (1993). Manufacturing strategy and performance indicators. Proceedings of IEPM'93.

Ginzberg, M.J. (1980). An organizational contingencies view of accounting and information systems implementation. *Accounting Organization & Society*, **5**(4).

Globerson, S. (1985). Issues in developing a performance criteria system for an organization. *International Journal of Production Research*, **23**(4), 639–46.

Kaplan, R.S. and Norton, D.P. (1992). The balanced scorecard: Measures that drive performance. *Harvard Business Review*, January–February, 71–9.

Kaplan, R.S. and Norton, D.P. (1996). *Translating strategy into action: The balanced scorecard*. Boston, MA: Harvard Business School Press.

Kehoe, D.F. and Little, D. (1997). Integrated Performance Measurement Systems, EPSRC Research Grant Report, January.

Maskell, B. (1989). Performance measures of world class manufacturing, *Management Accounting*, May, 32–3.

Maull R., Childe, S. and Bennet, J. (1994). Frameworks for understanding BPR, IJOPM no.12.

Neely, A., Gregory, M. and Platts, K. (1995). Performance measurement system design: a literature review and research agenda, *International Journal of Operations and Performance Management*, **15**(4), 80–116.

Neely, A., Mills, J., Gregory, M., Richards, H., Platts, K., and Bourne, M. (1996). Getting the measure of your business. Manufacturing Engineering Group, Mill Lane, University of Cambridge.

Russell, R. (1992). The role of Performance Measurement in Manufacturing Excellence, BPICS Conference.

12 Why measurement initiatives succeed and fail: The impact of parent company initiatives

Mike Bourne and Andy Neely

Introduction

Currently, there is considerable interest in performance measurement, and, within the growing literature on the subject, an influential section has focused on promoting performance measurement (e.g., Eccles, 1991; Simons, 1995; Kaplan and Norton, 1996). However, less attention has been paid to the problems or difficulties associated with implementing a balanced performance measurement system.

Traditional performance measures, developed from costing and accounting systems, have been heavily criticized in the literature for encouraging short termism (Banks and Wheelwright, 1979; Hayes and Garvin, 1982), lacking strategic focus (Skinner, 1974), encouraging local optimization (Hall, 1983; Fry and Cox, 1989), encouraging minimization of variance rather than continuous improvement (Johnson and Kaplan, 1987; Lynch and Cross, 1991), and not being externally focused (Kaplan and Norton, 1992). But judging from the reaction of practitioners attending our industrial workshops, the problems with traditional accounting based measures are now much more widely recognized than they were two to three years ago.

In an attempt to overcome these and other criticisms, performance measurement frameworks have been developed which provide a more balanced view between internal and external focus (Keegan, Eiler, and Jones, 1989), between levels in the organization (Cross and Lynch, 1988–9), between results and their determinants (Fitzgerald *et al.*, 1991), between the four perspectives of the balanced scorecard (Kaplan and Norton, 1992), and the multiple stakeholder perspectives of the performance prism (Neely and Adams, 2000). In

This contribution was produced during the research project – Manufacturing Strategy and Performance Measurement – which was sponsored by the CDP section of EPSRC under grant numbers GR/H21470 and GR/K53086.

particular, the balanced scorecard is being widely promoted, through articles (Kaplan and Norton, 1993), books (Kaplan and Norton, 1996; Olve, Roy, and Wetler, 1999) and conferences (e.g., Norton, 1997).

Within this growing literature, one subset focuses on the management processes for designing balanced performance measurement systems. These management processes have been developed from the literature (Wisner and Fawcett, 1991), through consultancy experience (Sink, 1986; Eccles and Pyburn, 1992; Kaplan and Norton 1993; Vitale, Mavrinac, and Hauser, 1994; Kaplan and Norton, 1996; Kaydos, 1998), and through action research (Bitton, 1990; Dixon, Nanni, and Vollmann, 1990; Neely *et al.*, 1996). However, this activity has not been matched by research into the implementation and embedding of the resulting performance measurement system.

Researchers have identified difficulties with implementation (Meekings, 1995; Kaplan and Norton, 1996) and longer-term problems with the use of performance measures (Townley and Cooper, 1998; Meyer and Gupta, 1994), but, Lewy and Du Mee (1998) excepted, there have been no published comparative longitudinal studies of successful and unsuccessful performance measurement system implementations.

Our research into the design and implementation of performance measurement systems using the Neely *et al.* (1996) process revealed that half of the initial six companies who set out to undertake the process did not implement the performance measures (Bourne *et al.*, 1999). This finding led to further research into the reasons why there was successful implementation in some companies and not in others, with a further six case studies being undertaken during the last quarters of 1998 and 1999.

This contribution begins by briefly summarizing the findings from the initial six cases before describing the main cases in more detail.

Initial case studies

The six initial case studies all started in the first quarter of 1996 as part of on-going testing of the Neely *et al.* (1996) process for the design and implementation of performance measurement systems. Four academic researchers acted as process facilitators in the case companies. The case companies were all individual business units, some stand-alone companies and others subsidiaries of larger groups (see Table 12.1 which provides background detail about the case study sites and identifies how far they progressed through the first five parts of the performance measurement system design set out in

Table 12.1 Summary of initial cases

Company	A	B	C	D	E	F
Ownership	Subsidiary of UK Plc	Subsidiary of large US corporation	Subsidiary of large Japanese corporation	Venture capital backed	Privately owned	Subsidiary of private group
Business	Control Instruments	Group central European machine shop	Components manufacturer and supplier	Manufacturers of leak detection equipment	Manufacturers of pumps and turbines	Manufacturers of seals and compression packings
Senior team participating in process	MD, Prod. Dir. & Com. Dir. & Tech. Dir. part 1 only	Group Manuf. Manager, Site GM, & 6 Local Managers	2 Directors & 4 Managers	MD & 4 Managers	MD & 4 Directors	Site Director, 4 BU GMs, & 11 Managers
Progress						
Part 1 Groups established	Yes	Yes	Yes	Yes	Yes	Yes
Part 2 Objectives agreed	Yes	Yes	Yes	Yes	Yes	Yes
Part 3 Measures designed	No	Yes	Yes	Yes	Yes	Yes
Part 4 Measures agreed	No	Yes	Yes	Yes	Yes	Yes
Part 5 Measures implemented	No	No	No	Yes	Yes	Yes

Table 12.2 Summary of main cases

Company	W	X	Y	Z1	Z2	Z3
Ownership	Subsidiary of UK Plc	Subsidiary of Singaporean corporation	Subsidiary of UK plc	UK division of US corporation	UK division of US corporation	UK division of US corporation
Business	Control instruments	Producer of high tech. thin films	Aerospace, part manufacturer and repairer	Manufacturers of materials	Manufacturers of materials	Manufacturers of materials
Senior team participating in process	MD, 2 Market MDs, Ops. Dir., Quality and HR Managers	Ops. Manager and 4 Functional Managers	MD, 3 Directors & 8 Managers	Div. Chairman GM & 2 Managers	Div. Chairman GM & 1 Manager	Div. Chairman GM & 3 Managers
Progress						
Part 1 Groups established	Yes	Yes	Yes	Yes	Yes	Yes
Part 2 Objectives agreed	Yes	Yes	Yes	Yes	Yes	Yes
Part 3 Measures designed	No	Yes	Yes	Yes	Yes	Yes
Part 4 Measures agreed	No	No	Yes	Yes	Incomplete	Yes
Part 5 Measures implemented	No	No	Yes	No	No	Yes

Neely *et al.*, 1996). The specific objective of this phase of the research was to investigate how the process might be tailored for different circumstances and how the performance measures become embedded in the management of the business.

The research was based on an "action research intervention" but used a structured methodology (see Bourne *et al.*, 1999) which adopted Yin's (1994) framework for case study research with the design of data collection instruments informed by the work of Pettigrew, Whipp, and Rosenfield (1989) and Platts (1994). Data were therefore collected on organizational context, the intervention process, and the performance measurement content, with process data collection focusing on Platt's (1994) 4 Ps (point of entry, project management, procedure, and participation).

Of these six companies, three took the vast majority of the measures developed during the design process and implemented them. The other three implemented none at all.

Analysis of the case studies revealed that there were three significant factors influencing the progress of the performance measurement interventions (Bourne et al., 1999). Firstly, IT infrastructure was found to have a major influence on the implementation of the measures, but the cases did not explain why some companies overcame this difficulty and others did not. Secondly, some of the measurement projects were overtaken by other events, but why the management allowed this to happen was not fully explained. Thirdly, the fact that the companies not continuing were all subsidiaries of larger groups was an unexpected result and merited further investigation. It was, therefore, decided to conduct a further series of six case studies designed to investigate these other influences on management commitment to the project and these are described below.

The second phase case studies

Selection of cases

The second set of cases was selected to match broadly the initial cases, drawing on a wide range of manufacturing companies employing fewer than 500 people. The final selection was partly influenced by two opportunities which arose. First, one of the case companies which failed to complete the process during the initial phase of the research expressed interest in being taken through the process for a second time. In the intervening period, the organization had changed with the merger of two business units into a single entity, and only one of the directors had been involved in the initial process. This provided an opportunity to study the application of the process twice in virtually the same organization and it was considered that the benefits of doing this outweighed the loss of range in selecting the case companies.

Second, another organization approached the researchers with a request to take three divisions through the performance measurement design process. The three divisions had operated as independent profit centers since in 1992. Although based on the same site, they served different markets having different facilities and only sharing central services, such as laboratory services, engineering, and research and development. The decision to include these three divisions was influenced by the fact that the companies came from an industry not previously represented and by the opportunity the cases provided for cross-case comparison within the same organization. This was seen as being more beneficial than the loss of variety resulting from taking three cases from the same organization.

Methodology

Besides collecting background data on the organizational context, the application of the process and the resulting content of the strategy and performance measures developed, semi-structured interviews were conducted before and after the process. These interviews focused on the demands being placed on the individual managers and directors directly involved in the performance measurement project.

Each manager (or director) was asked to identify all their current improvement projects. They were then asked to rank these in order of importance, estimate the effort required to complete the projects, and estimate their total effort available. In this way, it would be possible to gauge:

• what priority the performance measurement project had within the context of all the other development projects;
• whether this priority changed in the period between the interviews before and after the performance measurement intervention;
• whether the individual managers had the resources (in terms of their own effort) available to undertake the project.

The answer to these questions could then be used to investigate the reasons for the changes in priority and how these changes influenced the design and implementation of the performance measures. The six cases and the results of this analysis are now described in turn.

Case W

The management team in company W failed to complete the performance measurement design process for reasons unrelated to the parent company. The management team was relatively newly formed and there was disagreement between the members over the benefit of undertaking the project. This conflict resulted in most of the senior management team not participating in the workshops and undermining the quality of debate, and the project did not progress further.

Case X

The performance measurement project was overtaken by other events in case X, but the semi-structured interviews provided greater insights into how this occurred.

Before the intervention, the senior management team all shared a small number of interlinked improvement projects. The performance measurement project had the lowest priority but the management team believed they had sufficient resources (effort) available to complete the project. However, part way through the series of workshops the parent company restructured the senior management team. This resulted in key members taking on considerably more responsibility for the day-to-day operation of the business and significantly reducing the effort available for improvement projects. As a result, the higher priority projects were completed whilst the performance measurement was discontinued through lack of resources. In this way, the parent company intervention caused the performance measurement project to stall.

Cases Z1 and Z2

Both these organizations were divisions of a larger US-based material manufacturer.

The projects in both these divisions failed when the parent company reorganized, merging Z1 and Z2 with other divisions to create a completely new divisional structure. This undermined the whole rationale behind the performance measurement project. As the parent company director responsible for coordinating the performance measurement project stated:

> Its pointless continuing to develop performance measures for a division which won't exist after Christmas.

Consequently in these two cases, the parent company restructuring directly stopped the continuation of the performance measurement initiative.

The successful cases

Even in the two successful cases, parent company initiatives had an impact on the implementation of the performance measures.

In case Z3, this division was not included in the merging of the other divisions, and as a result the business strategy and resulting performance measures were unaffected. However, the restructuring did have an impact on the service functions shared by all the divisions requiring a series of changes to integrate the new structure. This created new high priority projects and a reduction in the priority of the performance measurement projects for five of the six members of the senior measurement team. In this case, there was sufficient resources available to continue the performance measurement initiative, but, if circumstance had been different, the project might well have been overtaken.

In case Y, the company changed ownership just as the performance measurement project was beginning. The new owners had very specific expectations of the future financial performance they required from their new subsidiary (expressed in terms of aggressive targets for return on sales and return on assets). However, apart from these financial targets, the parent company was prepared to allow company Y to manage its own business. During the performance measurement system design workshops, the managing director communicated these targets to the rest of the management team and they were incorporated into the performance measures being developed, but as the targets were purely financial, the team was free to continue to develop their own strategy and appropriate performance measures. However, during implementation, the performance measurement project had to compete for resources with new initiatives resulting from the parent company's financial strategy. These new projects reduced the priority of the performance measurement project for six of the 11 members of the senior management team. Consequently, implementation was not stopped, but progressed more slowly.

Discussion and conclusions

The initial six cases suggested that there was something different about implementing a performance measurement system in a subsidiary company which reduced the chances of success. As can be seen from the six main cases, parent company initiatives have a significant impact on the performance measurement interventions. In the six main cases, four failed to implement the performance measures designed during the intervention. Out of these four failed attempts, three were as a direct result of parent company initiatives undermining the performance measurement system implementation. Even in the latter two cases, where performance measures were implemented, changes initiated at parent company level had an impact. The only difference in these two cases, was that the impact did not undermine the process or divert sufficient resources to stop the project.

The results also suggest that parent company interventions can be categorized into two types:

1 Fundamental strategic changes – these are changes which go to the heart of the rationale behind undertaking the performance measurement process and from which the process cannot recover. Restructuring the divisions was one such initiative observed here. The restructuring renders the performance measures being developed invalid destroying the purpose of the project. Other fundamental changes which might fall into this category include changes in strategy decided at the parent company level and imposed on the subsidiary, or the parent company requesting regular returns of a wide range of financial and non-financial measures unrelated to those developed during the performance measurement project.

2 Changes in strategic focus – these are changes in priority or resource availability, both having a very similar effect. A change in priority may result in resources being redirected to other higher priority projects, creating the same result as resources being depleted. In case X, the project was overtaken when resources were removed by the parent company restructuring the management team. In case Y the new focus on financial performance in itself did not undermine the rationale behind the performance measurement process. It did however divert resources. Similarly, the fundamental business of Z1 was not changed by the divisional restructuring, but the resulting reorganization at a lower level took resources. Focus changes can therefore be viewed as changes, which the performance measurement intervention may survive depending on the resource context, provided the changes are limited purely to focus and do not undermine the rationale of the project.

The conclusion reached here is that, despite the best endeavours of any local management team or process facilitator, some parent company initiatives will significantly influence the success or failure of performance measurement interventions in subsidiary companies. These are not always foreseen at the local management level and therefore cannot be planned for in advance. It may be suggested that greater communication between the subsidiary and parent company might allow local managers earlier knowledge of parent company initiatives, but, as the three main cases which failed through parent company intervention show, many of these changes have to remain confidential up to the point at which the decision is made.

REFERENCES

Banks, R.L. and Wheelwright, S.C. (1979). Operations versus strategy – trading tomorrow for today. *Harvard Business Review*, May–June, 112–20.

Bitton, M. (1990). Méthode de conception et d'implantation de systèmes de measure de performances pour organizations industrielles. Thèse d' automatique, Université de Bordeaux I.

Bourne, M.C.S., Mills, J.F., Bicheno J., Hamblin, D.J., Wilcox, M., Neely, A.D., and Platts, K.W. (1999). Performance measurement system design: Testing a process approach in manufacturing companies. *International Journal of Business Performance Measurement*, **1**(2), 154–70.

Cross, K.F. and Lynch, R.L. (1988/89). The SMART way to sustain and define success. *National Productivity Review*, **8**(1), 23–33.

Dixon, J.R., Nanni, A.J., and Vollmann, T.E. (1990). *The New Performance Challenge: Measuring Operations for World-Class Competition.* Irwin, Homewood, IL: Business One Irwin.

Eccles, R.G. (1991). The performance measurement manifesto. *Harvard Business Review*, January–February, 131–7.

Eccles, R.G. and Pyburn, P.J. (1992). Creating a comprehensive system to measure performance. *Management Accounting* [US], October, 41–4.

Fitzgerald, L., Johnston, R., Brignall T.J., Silvestro, R., and Voss, C. (1991). Performance measurement in service businesses. CIMA, London. The Chartered Institute of Management Accountants, London.

Fry, T.D. and Cox, J.F. (1989). Manufacturing performance: Local versus global measures. *Production and Inventory Management Journal*, **30**(2), 52–6.

Hall, R.W. (1983). Zero inventories. Irwin, Homewood, IL: Dow, Jones.

Hayes, R.H. and Garvin, D.A. (1982). Managing as if tomorrow mattered. *Harvard Business Review*, May–June, 70–9.

Johnson, H.T. and Kaplan, R.S. (1987). Relevance Lost: *The Rise and Fall of Management Accounting.* Boston, MA: Harvard Business School Press.

Kaplan, R.S. and Norton, D.P. (1992). The balanced scorecard – measures that drive performance. *Harvard Business Review*, January–February, 71–9.

Kaplan, R.S. and Norton, D.P. (1993). Putting the balanced scorecard to work. *Harvard Business Review*, September–October, 134–47.

Kaplan, R.S. and Norton, D.P. (1996). *The Balanced Scorecard – Translating Strategy into Action*, Boston, MA: Harvard Business School Press.

Kaydos, W. (1998). *Operational Performance Measurement – Increasing Total Productivity.* Boca Raton, London, New York, Washington, DC: St Lucie Press.

Keegan, D.P., Eiler, R.G., and Jones, C.R. (1989). Are your performance measures obsolete? *Management Accounting*, June, 45–50.

Lewy, C. and Du Mee (1998). The ten commandments of balanced scorecard implementation. *Management Control and Accounting*, April.

Lynch, R.L. and Cross, K.F. (1991). *Measure Up – The Essential Guide to Measuring Business Performance*. London: Mandarin.

Meekings, A. (1995). Unlocking the potential of performance measurement: A guide to practical implementation. *Public Money and Management*, October–December, 1–8.

Meyer, M.W. and Gupta, V. (1994). The performance paradox. In *Research in Organizational Behavior*, ed. B. M. Staw and L.L. Cummings, Vol. 16, pp. 309–69. Greenwich CT: JAI Press.

Neely, A.D. and Adams, C.A. (2000). Perspectives on performance: the performance prism. Centre for Business Performance, Cranfield School of Management.

Neely, A.D., Mills, J.F., Gregory, M.J., Richards, A.H., Platts, K.W., and Bourne, M.C.S. (1996). *Getting the Measure of Your Business*. London: Findlay.

Norton, D.P. (1997). The balanced scorecard. Business Performance Measurement Business Intelligence Conference, London.

Olve, N., Roy, J., and Wetler, M. (1999). *Performance Drivers: A Practical Guide to Using the Balanced Scorecard*. Chichester: John Wiley.

Pettigrew, A., Whipp, R., and Rosenfield, R. (1989). Competitiveness and the management of strategic change processes. In *the Competitiveness of European Industry: Country Policies and Company Strategies*, ed. A. Francis and P.K.M. Tharakan, London: Routledge.

Platts, K.W. (1994). Characteristics of methodologies for manufacturing strategy formulation. *Computer Integrated Manufacturing Systems*, 7(2), 93–9.

Simons, R. (1995). Control in an age of empowerment. *Harvard Business Review*, March–April, 80–8.

Sink, P.E. (1986). Performance and productivity measurement: the art of developing creative score boards. *Industrial Engineer*, January, 86–90.

Skinner, W. (1974). The decline, fall and renewal of manufacturing. *Industrial Engineering*, October, 32–8.

Townley, B. and Cooper, D. (1998). Performance measures: rationalization and resistance. *Performance Measurement – Theory and Practice*, July, Cambridge.

Vitale, M.R., Mavrinac, S.C., and Hauser, M. (1994). New process/financial scorecard: A strategic performance measurement system. *Planning Review*, July–August, 12–16 and 44.

Wisner, J.D. and Fawcett, S.E. (1991). Link firm strategy to operating decisions through performance measurement. *Production and Inventory Management Journal*, 3, 5–11.

Yin, R.K. (1994). *Case Study Research, Design and Methods*, 2nd edn. Thousand Oaks: Sage Publications.

Part IV

Performance measurement – practical applications

The first three parts of the book have concentrated largely on measurement theory, although many of the authors have drawn on their practical experiences and research studies. The fourth part sees a change in tone and focuses exclusively on measurement in practice.

The first contribution, from Mayle, Hinton, Francis, and Holloway, addresses the seemingly simple question – what really goes on in the name of benchmarking? This contribution is based on research data gathered from some 700 firms. The aim of Mayle *et al.* studies has been to elicit information on benchmarking approaches and practices. Not surprisingly they found widespread interest in benchmarking, across a wide variety of industrial sectors and sizes of organization. They also found no universal understanding of the term benchmarking, with some firms using benchmarking to gather ideas (idea benchmarking), while others use it to gather performance data (indicator benchmarking).

The second contribution in this part is again based on survey data, but this time concentrates on marketing performance measurement. Ambler and Kokkinaki present the results of a study designed to establish how marketing effectiveness is measured. They contrast academic theory with actual practice, by pointing out that the academic community assumes that the most important marketing metrics are sales and sales growth, market share, profit contribution, and customer preference, while their data suggest that board members pay far more attention to traditional financial measures of marketing performance. In fact measures, such as competitive position, consumer behavior, and innovativeness, appear to receive relatively little board attention.

The third contribution in this part presents an in-depth case study of a large restaurant chain. Over a four-year period the case company continually sought to improve its measurement systems, yet failed to do so. In spite of this the case company, which competed in a highly turbulent environment, was able to grow profitability and increase market share during the same time period. These contrasts result in the authors, Ahrens and Chapman, asking why the company is successful, when it has a measurement system that is perceived to be ineffective. At the heart of Ahrens and

Chapman's thesis is the assertion that actually the changes the head office were seeking to make to the measurement system were inappropriate. Head office appeared to want a more detailed measurement system that would allow it to take more control over the delivery of service in the local operations. The local operations, however, recognized that they had to tailor the service they were delivering to their clients depending upon the situation and circumstances. Hence to have a tightly coupled and closely pre-scribed measurement system would have been wrong for the organization given the market in which it competes.

The fourth contribution in the section moves out of the private and into the public sector. Ogata and Goodkey describe the Albertan government's experience of perfor-mance measurement and contrast it with the approaches taken by the Oregon, Minnesota, and Florida municipal authorities. In addition to providing a rich descrip-tion of these various approaches, Ogata and Goodkey identify four performance measurement system design principles – political leadership, citizen feedback, an explicit strategic plan, and an integrating/coordinating mechanism.

13 What really goes on in the name of benchmarking?

David Mayle, Matthew Hinton, Graham Francis,
and Jacky Holloway

Introduction

Best-practice benchmarking is today taken to describe a process whereby organizations pursue enhanced performance by learning from the successful practices of others. Comparisons may be made with other parts of the same organization, with competitors, or with organizations operating in different spheres whose business processes are nevertheless deemed to be in some way relevant. By implication at least, the lessons learned are implemented and the cycle continues anew.

The purpose of this chapter is to shed some light on the rather broad range of activities that are often subsumed under the umbrella term of benchmarking. The authors' original interest in the topic stems from a conviction that benchmarking offers rather more than the mere establishment of performance "league tables." Although we fully accept the value of these as a means of ascertaining comparative performance levels, and hence directing attention towards areas or processes which are seen, in relative terms, to be under-performing, our conviction remains that true benchmarking entails rather more. Specifically, the network of contacts generated by the activity represents a treasure-trove of good (if not necessarily best) practice, much of which could be adopted by the organization in some shape or form. It has been argued that benchmarking can only be about catching up; if good practice were to be copied slavishly then this would undoubtedly be the case, but a more general receptivity to good ideas, and the willingness to try them out in some new context, is arguably a major ingredient for innovation (see, e.g., Drucker, 1985; Peters, 1989; Zairi, 1996a).

The authors wish to acknowledge the assistance of the Chartered Institute of Management Accountants (CIMA) for their funding of much of the work on which this report is based.

What is benchmarking?

Notwithstanding these convictions about underlying cultural themes the practice of benchmarking, in the West at least, arguably emerged from the Xerox Corporation in the late 1980s (Jacobson and Hillkirk, 1986; Camp, 1989; Zairi, 1996b). Since then it has become one of the more popular of management fashions, with every airport lounge bookstall offering at least one treatise extolling its virtues and proffering advice on how to "do" it. Like so many management fashions, however, actual implementation seems to come in all shapes and sizes, with a huge variety of activities being carried out under a benchmarking umbrella. The problem would appear to be that, in spite of the best efforts of academics, practising managers do not always read the more formal management texts, and even those that do will often vary whatever methodology is on offer to suit local conditions. They may even claim to have been "doing" benchmarking for many years, albeit under other names, such as "inter-firm comparison."

Method and general characteristics

In order to investigate the current state of benchmarking practice, the authors initially sent out a series of postal questionnaires to potential benchmarkers in the UK. It was important to gather current data about the nature and extent of benchmarking activity from organizations of all sizes and from a wide cross-section of industry sectors and geographic areas. This also facilitated the identification of organizations for follow-on case studies. With this in mind, the initial target audience was drawn from members of the Chartered Institute of Management Accountants (559 responses out of 5000), and students and past-students of an Open University Business School MBA elective course, Performance Measurement and Evaluation (174 out of 690). The most immediately visible results from this first questionnaire were the influence of size and sector as correlates of claimed benchmarking activity (see tables 13.1–13.2).

As can be seen, benchmarking begins to look like a big company phenomenon, with its incidence reflecting both increasing size and subsidiarity (local organization being part of some wider enterprise).

Given the recent political emphasis on league tables, the higher than average level of activity in the old "public" sector (government, education, health, and

Table 13.1 Effect of organizational size and subsidiarity

Size	Number not part of a larger group	Benchmarking?		Number part of a larger group	Benchmarking?	
<25	96	14	(15%)	16	3	(19%)
26–99	66	16	(24%)	48	17	(35%)
100–250	45	14	(31%)	88	43	(49%)
251–999	55	24	(44%)	99	60	(61%)
>1000	77	51	(66%)	124	100	(81%)

Table 13.2 Benchmarking activity by sector

Description	Total number	Number claiming to be benchmarking	
Government	55	32	(58%)
Education	37	23	(62%)
Health	52	36	(69%)
Manufacturing and construction	269	135	(50%)
Financial services	57	19	(33%)
Services and retailing	189	68	(36%)
Utilities	18	14	(78%)
Other	49	19	(39%)
Total	726	346	(48%)

the utilities) is hardly surprising, but the low levels found in more overtly competitive areas, such as financial services or services and retailing, was more unexpected (for a fuller description of these findings, see Holloway, *et al.*, 1999).

Of the initial respondents, just over 45 percent were prepared to participate further in the project; as a result, the 200 active benchmarkers amongst them have now been subjected to a further questionnaire aimed, amongst other things, at exploring their experience of the process of benchmarking in greater detail. From the 200 copies of this second questionnaire, 97 were returned. On the basis of these latter responses, selected organizations were visited to provide a source of richer, more qualitative information. These case studies were chosen to reflect a wide range of benchmarking activity and levels of experience.

Findings and discussion

For the purposes of this contribution, we shall be concentrating on four substantive but related questions:

1 To what extent is benchmarking just concerned with establishing a position in some league table of performance, and to what extent does it function as a process to aid environmental scanning with a view to revealing, and somehow importing, best practice?

2 To what extent does benchmarking fit with other management frameworks?

3 How useful are third party agencies in facilitating benchmarking activity?

4 Is the experience of benchmarking subject to any universal set of stages and is this evidence for some form of maturity curve?

Indicators or ideas?

The distinction between *results benchmarking* and *process benchmarking* (Trosa and Williams, 1996) is an important one, but we would suggest that the terms chosen are less than helpful in emphasizing the crucial difference: is the activity to do with collecting indicators or is it concerned with collecting ideas? This dimension can be caricatured as a "League table" mentality versus a "creative swiping" mentality. Peters (1989) provides a passionate advocacy of creative swiping as a means of competitive advantage. We would suggest that the terms indicator-benchmarking and idea-benchmarking offer a more explicit distinction.

Those of the "league table" persuasion are often involved in benchmarking at the behest of someone else. Health, education, the newly privatized utilities, all are required to publish performance against some pre-determined criteria so that this information can be collected, collated, and published. Without in any way denying the public's right to have access to such information, the only spur to improvement may often be the knowledge that "someone else is doing it better." Although this is of itself a valid benefit, especially where complacency is suspected in the host organization, we would argue that the contacts established in "face-to-face benchmarking" (i.e., as opposed to the pooling of performance indicators via some third-party agency) offer far greater potential for the discovery and exploitation of "good practice."

Large divisionalized organizations are interested not just in the relative performance of their various outposts, but also presumably in promulgating best

Table 13.3 Indicators or ideas?

To determine place in league table	22
To focus on areas for improvement	37
In order to set targets	21
As a framework for improvement	11
As a source of new ideas	3
Other	3
(Total)	(97)

practice wherever it may be found. In this sense, any explicit ownership of the process of idea-transfer will represent a real step away from simple indicator benchmarking. Since earlier work has suggested that the occurrence of benchmarking correlates strongly with both size of organization and subsidiarity (see above), this category represents a significant subset (Holloway *et al.*, 1997).

The "creative swiping" camp is more interested in useful ideas than in performance indicators *per se*, and is always on the look out for good practice of whatever sort. These organizations need to know not just how well others are doing, but how they are doing so well. Indeed several of our more ideas-oriented benchmarkers seem to have almost left behind the formal comparison of indicators. They typically exhibit an open, outward-looking culture, often feature key individuals with previous experience in a different sector, and generally seem to have overcome the NIH syndrome (not-invented-here syndrome), welcoming good ideas wherever they originate.

To pursue this line of investigation, our second questionnaire sought to ascertain where on this spectrum organizations felt themselves to be. Answers to the question: "Which one of the following *best* describes your organization's experience of benchmarking?" are tabulated in table 13.3.

On the basis of this result, it would seem that the indicator dimension dominates. The first three options are all concerned with position in some league table, if not as an end in itself then at least in the sense of establishing what areas are "under-performing" (and by how much) relative to some emergent norm. Since the fourth option is at best neutral on this dimension, we found only three organizations who saw benchmarking primarily in terms of a route to new ideas.

Alongside the very explicit question reported in table 13.3, the questionnaire also invited respondents to locate their organization's experience of

Table 13.4 Improvement versus measurement

Improvement	1	2	3	4	5	6	7	Measurement
	8	21	17	10	13	20	6	
	«	46	»		«	39	»	

Table 13.5 Similar or dissimilar partners?

Similar	1	2	3	4	5	6	7	Dissimilar
	24	28	16	13	7	6	1	
	«	68	»		«	14	»	

benchmarking on a series of seven-point Likert scales, one of which ran from "more to do with process improvement" to "more to do with measurement." This result is tabulated in table 13.4.

Although this might be interpreted as painting a more balanced picture, we believe the responses to be entirely consistent, interpreting the enhanced improvement dimension as indicative of the context and/or motivation of the exercise (the "focus" and "target-setting" categories from table 13.3). It is perhaps more revealing that 39 of the 95 responses were quite unashamedly "more to do with measurement." If measurement is all they are seeking, benchmarking is likely to achieve their goals.

This issue is further illuminated by the responses to another Likert scale, this time enquiring whether respondents were "using mainly similar or dissimilar partners." These results are presented as table 13.5.

As can be seen, very few of our sample were engaged in benchmarking with dissimilar partners. This has implications for the earlier debate: in the commercial sectors at least, similar organizations are likely to be in some sense your competitors. Under such circumstances the exchange of performance indicators is a perfectly reciprocal arrangement – "you show me yours and I'll show you mine." The exchange of *ideas* however is much more likely to be inhibited by considerations of commercial advantage. Given the increasingly competitive nature of the old public sector, this phenomenon appears to be spreading to these organizations too.

We would argue, therefore, that these two dimensions are inextricably linked. An emphasis on indicators drives benchmarkers towards issues of comparability which argues (initially at least) for similar partners. Similar

Table 13.6 Concurrent activities (From 97 respondents)

Activity-based costing	27
Business process engineering	30
Investors in people	46
Total quality management	36
Quality management systems	57
None of these	10
Other (specified)	18

partners are more likely to exist in a competitive relationship and hence will be more ready to pool indicators than to share ideas.

If indicator benchmarking is then about auditing the past and ideas benchmarking about scoping the present, what can benchmarking offer to engineer the future?

Co-existence of benchmarking with other approaches

There seems to be little guidance in the published literature regarding a well-developed implementation phase within benchmarking. Indeed, although the latest volume from one of the field's acknowledged gurus is subtitled "Finding and Implementing Best Practices", in the 159 pages devoted to describing the process, implementation merits only a brief mention in the final paragraph (Camp, 1995).

Apart from the already mentioned size and subsidiarity effects, there is also evidence to suggest that the adoption of benchmarking is generally indicative of a willingness to embrace current management thinking, as witnessed by the co-existence of several other approaches to performance improvement such as total quality management, business process re-engineering, investors in people and activity based costing (see also Elnathan, Lin, and Young, 1996). We would hypothesize that this effect helps to camouflage the observed poverty of the implementation phase in so much of the benchmarking literature. Our second questionnaire asked specifically about this issue: "Have you employed any of the following methodologies to help drive your improvement activity? (please tick any that apply)." Responses to the five activities offered are tabulated as table 13.6.

The cynical might observe from these results that benchmarkers will try anything. Indeed subtracting the ten organizations that checked "none of these" and distributing the 214 activities among the remainder leads to a mean score of nearly two-and-a-half each. Benchmarkers are evidently not averse to trying out different methodologies. The original rationale for enquiring about this aspect was to identify whether benchmarking could be characterized as another management fad to be tried out by those organizations who are keen on such things. Thus far we have only qualified support for that hypothesis, but the inability of benchmarking (or at least indicator benchmarking) to implement changes to close the gaps that it has identified is emerging as an alternative possibility.

The use of third parties: Clubs and networks

The number of benchmarking clubs and networks in the UK continues to increase. This raises the question as to why do organizations turn to a third party to facilitate benchmarking and to what degree are such interventions really useful? The sort of clubs and networks which exist include:

- the large and relatively impersonal Best Practice Club (primarily a "clearing house" offering contact details, access to an electronic database and survey service, and some courses and company visits);
- regional networks and services offered by Chambers of Commerce, TECs and Business Links;
- sector-specific groups in, for example, the NHS and civil service.

Some consultants also offer a "dating agency" service, bringing together several client organizations or undertaking to collect and disseminate comparative data (usually of the "league table" variety) between a group of similar organizations. Universities and colleges also host various forms of networks, particularly in the manufacturing sector and often linked to research projects or post-experience courses.

All of these forms of networking were mentioned in our surveys and cases studies. However, even when we include respondents who mentioned using a consultant to facilitate their benchmarking work, less than 10 percent of the organizations stated that they used such services either as a route to meeting partners or as a source of information about benchmarking processes or outputs. Our findings are very similar to those reported by Partnership Sourcing (1997) with relatively low levels of participation particularly among smaller firms, while some large companies were members of several associations or networks (as was the case in our Royal Mail case study). This low participation is not completely a cause for regret, since some of the feedback from our research suggests that clubs often provide disappointing results. However, some organizations stressed the value of having access to a selection of managers with similar interests in benchmarking from whom they could make their own contacts – the "club" being a means to an end. Sub-groups often form within the clubs to undertake activities, the larger entity simply having brought them together. This can make it difficult for new members to feel welcome or gain support. However, using clubs and networks to find partners can certainly be more effective than "cold calling."

Where there is relatively little direct contact between members we may find the criticism that benchmarking information collected through a club cannot be validated. Where the main activity involves informal meetings and sharing of stories about benchmarking experiences, the evidence provided gains weight through the physical presence of its originator. Before one shares details about processes which may raise sensitivities or reveal weaknesses, it is far easier to develop the necessary trust through personal contacts than through surveys and reports. The experiences of our interviewees at Babergh District Council and food producers A.H. Worth bear this out.

The Business Link is a major national network aimed particularly at assisting small enterprises, and a core service offered is assisted self-assessment against the Business Excellence Model framework. Our findings suggest that where this is the main offering, managers feel it does not meet their needs very well as they may not be in a position to use the model yet. Often they approach Business Link as complete beginners in performance improvement and need much more basic advice; they may particularly benefit from being introduced to other organizations but this does not always happen. The particularly low take-up from small organizations suggests that there is ample scope for new initiatives, such as Business Link, to have an impact, but only if they can establish what their potential customers want and need.

To move beyond the league table focus, a number of sectors are developing their own networks. There have been several benchmarking clubs within the NHS for some time, and the Civil Service College is currently developing a new club, building on an existing, more informal, database. Successful clubs may also cross sectoral boundaries and reflect strong local organizational efforts. The North-East Benchmarking Club in Newcastle has been running for five years and involves two local councils, hospital trusts and GPs, two theatres, and a large group of SMEs. Their activities include seminars and small group meetings where generic process benchmarking is fostered. This is seen as valuable, particularly for organizations that are wary of working with competitors.

Some industries also seem intrinsically suited to sharing information. The funfair industry is one example where potential rivals talk to one another and exchange information (Graham, 1998). A similar situation can be found in airline maintenance. Our research with a leading UK charter airline shows that what such organizations have in common is the need to avoid accidents and bad publicity, as the public may regard them all in the same light when something goes wrong. Benchmarking can work to the collective advantage of the industry, which transcends, in some senses, individual competitive advantage.

Our surveys show that there is a lot of enthusiasm for clubs and networks where people meet in an informal context, rather than the impersonal large-scale databases. There was scepticism about the quality of data from such services and a realization that little is understood about the business processes which give rise to such data. This may be seen as reflecting the move from indicator to ideas benchmarking, discussed previously.

Several of the non-benchmarkers interviewed were at a loss as to where to turn to get started with benchmarking. Participation in an appropriate network or club could provide a useful starting point and provide much needed expertise. The benefits of using clubs and drawing on experience are echoed in the reports of the winner (Employment Service) and runner-up (BT UK Access Network) in the 1997 European Best Practice Benchmarking Award (Benchmarking Centre, 1997). Whilst our findings highlight several limitations with clubs and networks, it is perhaps important to see them as a useful way for beginners to get started with benchmarking and for existing benchmarkers to progress their thinking. The next section discusses ways in which this may take place.

Towards a maturity curve?

Our work so far seems to suggest the existence of some form of maturity curve. Organizations that persevere with benchmarking would appear to move from simple comparisons of easily measured discrete activities using similar or even internal partners, to comparing more complex processes with dissimilar and/or external partners.

Although not originally conceived as a maturity curve *per se*, the most widely cited typology that would seem to describe this phenomenon is due to Camp (1995, p. 16):

Internal   A comparison among similar operations within one's own organization.

Competitive   A comparison to the best of the direct competitors.

Functional   A comparison of methods to companies with similar processes in the same function outside one's industry.

Generic process   A comparison of work processes to others who have innovative, exemplar work processes.

Table 13.7 Location on Camp's typology

Internal	21
Competitive	37
Functional	29
Generic	10

Certainly internal benchmarking would appear to be a natural starting point for large divisionalized organizations, and competitive is a logical next step (or a starting point for those smaller companies that do investigate benchmarking), but the jump to functional is arguably a qualitatively different transition. True generic benchmarking requires a particularly imaginative leap in order to be able to exploit good practice in what might be, at least superficially, a radically different situation. Nevertheless, as part of the second questionnaire, we asked our active benchmarkers which of these best described the nature of their benchmarking activity (the definitions were provided alongside each of the terms, table 13.7).

As can be seen, the respondents arrayed themselves along the continuum in such a way as to offer tentative support to some sort of progression through stages hypothesis, but the results needed amplification and so became part of our schedule for both face-to-face and telephone interviews. This meant that we were able to explore some of the longitudinal developments taking place.

Within the organizations that formed part of our in-depth case studies, the relative importance given to indicators and to ideas varied both between organizations and over time within organizations. In most cases there was some sort of transition away from focusing on the "easy to measure output variables" towards "understanding the underlying processes that cause the outputs." Where there are statutory requirements to report performance in terms of quantitative performance indicators (e.g., the old public sector), adopting an indicator-driven approach was a natural place to start. Unfortunately the more one concentrates on indicators, the greater become the problems of comparability and data quality

In an attempt to address the problems of comparability in the indicators, many of our case-study organizations deliberately set out to conceptualize their activities as more generic processes, thereby broadening the range of potential benchmarking partners. Such process-orientation has the additional benefit of involving partners who might not regard each other as direct competitors, thereby enabling an interchange of ideas as well as just indicators. A recent example of this involves a Dallas-based airline who were trying to improve their 40 minute refuelling time for their aircraft. As the airline was already an industry leader for this type of activity, they decided to look across industry. By adopting practices from the fastest refuellers in the world, Formula 1 motor racing, the airline can now refuel its aircraft in just 12 minutes (Murdoch, 1997).

Inevitably one has to conclude that, although many organizations involved in this project appear to have travelled along a "maturity curve" from relatively uncontentious internal benchmarking to more challenging and innovative generic approaches, there is no guarantee that this sort of journey will take place or be effective in all organizations.

So what facilitates this journey? Evidence from our case studies suggests that benchmarking is frequently started by "product" champions (as was the case at A. H. Worth, Britannia Airways, Warwick Ambulance Service). These are people who have learnt about benchmarking from a range of sources, most notably practitioner-oriented literature, networking, sometimes more academic literature, and reflections on their own practice. A further characteristic is that they are able to be authoritative when promoting benchmarking to colleagues. However, champions can only take benchmarking so far. If it is to be developed in terms of scope and generic ideas it is clear that a culture of sharing learning throughout the organization has to evolve. At Royal Mail, for example, a database has been developed so that staff can learn from the benchmarking practices of their colleagues rather than reinvent the wheel. Likewise, at a leading semiconductor manufacturer, performance improvements of all types are promoted through the interaction of cross-functional and cross-factory teams. To further speed up the exchange of good practice an intranet is being developed which will provide a portfolio of knowledge that can be drawn on by any member of staff.

Based upon our experience so far, we are increasingly attracted to a rather different model to illustrate the types of benchmarking activity, a familiar 2×2 matrix shown as figure 13.1.

Each of the four quadrants involves a qualitatively different type of activity. Benchmarking for *specific indicators* is probably the most familiar, embracing the league table approach already discussed. Benchmarking for *specific ideas* is attempting to emulate best practice in a chosen field by importing methods and processes from successful partners (and, yes, it probably is capable of no more than "catching up"). Benchmarking for *generic indicators* involves a shift of perspective. We are now operating at the level of the entire organization but still considering the metrics rather than the processes. The attraction here is

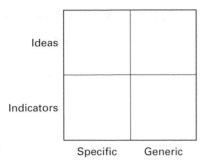

Figure 13.1.   A benchmarking matrix.

that there is little risk of parochiality, target performance may be radically different from local norms, and the magnitude of the gap may now demand radical, rather than incremental change. Finally we have *generic ideas* benchmarking. Good practice is good practice; not only can it be admired, there is always a chance that it could be adapted to good advantage.

The 11 case studies we have conducted offer differing pictures of maturity than that of the linear model suggested by Camp (1995). Indeed, they suggest that organizations follow different pathways through the matrix (in table 13.1). Furthermore, it is by no means a certainty that the right conditions will exist to stimulate benchmarking's progression. Indeed, in the particular case of a rolled-aluminium manufacturer, benchmarking activity started at the specific indicators stage. As continuing benefits are still being found through this activity, there is little stimulus to move benchmarking on, for the foreseeable future at least.

Concluding remarks

This contribution has outlined the levels of benchmarking activity as well as the size and nature of the organizations involved. However, this hides the wealth of knowledge that is to be gained from understanding the ways and means by which benchmarking takes place.

We have seen how a focus on indicators provides the initial framework for much benchmarking activity. This may take place informally or be supported by a benchmarking club or network. This focus leads benchmarkers to consider issues of comparability and, as a consequence, to look for similar partners, which introduces a competitive dimension. In terms of a maturity curve then, it would appear from our case studies that issues of comparability tend to push organizations from just dealing with *indicators* towards greater consideration of *ideas*, whilst issues of competition generate a pressure from the *specific* to the more *generic*. This taxonomy provides a useful framework for exploring how different forms of benchmarking are translated into real performance improvements.

REFERENCES

Benchmarking Centre (1997). *The European Best Practice Benchmarking Award 1997, Winning and Runner-up Reports.* Gerrards Cross: The Benchmarking Centre Ltd.

Camp, R.C. (1989). *Benchmarking. The Search for Industry Best Practices that Lead to Superior Performance.* Wisconsin: ASQC Quality Press.

Camp, R.C. (1995). *Business Process Benchmarking: Finding and Implementing Best Practice*s. Wisconsin: ASQC Quality Press.

Drucker, P.F. (1985). *Innovation and Entrepreneurship*, pp. 202–7. Oxford: Butterworth Heinemann.

Elnathan, D., Lin, T.W., and Young, S.M. (1996). Benchmarking and management accounting: a framework for research. *Journal of Management Accounting Research*, **8**, 37–54.

Graham, A. (1998). Welcome to the pleasure beach. *Radio Times*, 7–13 February, 21–2

Holloway, J.A., Hinton, C.M., Francis, G.A.J., and Mayle, D.T. (1999). Identifying best practice in benchmarking. Chartered Institute of Management Accountants, London.

Holloway, J.A., Hinton, C.M., Mayle, D.T., and Francis, G.A.J. (1997). Why benchmark?: Understanding the process of best practice benchmarking. Proceedings of the Business Process Track at the British Academy of Management Conference, pp. 271–91.

Jacobson, G. and Hillkirk, J. (1986). *Xerox, American Samurai.* New York: Macmillan.

Murdoch, A. (1997). Lateral benchmarking or what formula one taught an airline. *Management Today*, November, 64–67.

Partnership Sourcing (1997). *Benchmarking the Supply Chain. First Cycle of Surveys.* London: Partnership Sourcing Ltd.

Peters, T. (1989). *Thriving on Chaos*, pp. 228–36. London: Pan Books.

Trosa, S. and Williams, S. (1996). Benchmarking in public sector performance management. Performance Measurement in Government, OECD Occasional Papers No. 9.

Zairi, M. (1996a). *Benchmarking for Best Practice: Continuous Learning through Sustainable Innovation.* Oxford: Butterworth-Heinemann.

Zairi, M. (1996b). *Effective Benchmarking: Learning from the Best.* London: Chapman and Hall.

Measuring marketing performance: Which way is up?

Tim Ambler and Flora Kokkinaki

Introduction

Recent years have witnessed a renewed emphasis on delivering superior-quality products and services to customers. As cost cutting and downsizing produce diminishing returns, the corporate spotlight has returned to marketing to encourage growth in businesses. Effective marketing can be defined as success in winning and retaining customer preference and thereby achieving the firm's long-term goals. Putting customers at the heart of every business activity is claimed to be key to sustained competitiveness (Kotler, 1997).

Marketing has to be broadly defined as being *both* the whole company's activities designed to satisfy customers and achieve its own objectives thereby ("pan-company marketing") *and* the activities of the functional marketing department (see Webster, 1992). Marketers believe that the marketing paradigm is best for business compared to alternative orientations, such as those towards production or shareholders. But how well is that perception pursued?

Improving product and service quality and satisfying evolving customer needs and expectations requires on-going tracking and responsiveness to changing marketplace needs. Successful marketing requires monitoring of the effectiveness of marketing activities. Allocating resources to marketing, based on past effectiveness and the benchmarked experience of others, can significantly enhance performance. Better measurement leads to better marketing. What gets measured gets attention, particularly when rewards are tied to those measures (Eccles, 1991). The firm's orientation and objectives, how they measure progress towards those objectives, and the impact of measurement on performance are all likely to influence performance.

This study explores how marketing effectiveness is measured. We report how UK firms, in a variety of business sectors, assess marketing performance and whether measurement practice is related to firm characteristics (e.g., size, sector). Firms are not wholly satisfied with their current marketing measurement systems and the improvements sought provide insights into how measurement is changing. In addition, we examine the relations between measurement practice, performance and firm's orientation.

After developing hypotheses, we outline the methodology before discussing results. The final section outlines the limitations and draws conclusions.

Developing the hypotheses

Market share and profitability are the most common marketing performance indicators (Day, 1990; Green, Barclay, and Ryans, 1995). Day (1984) suggests that "the essence of a business strategy is an integrated set of actions in the pursuit of a competitive advantage," thus placing the emphasis on market share. Green, Barclay, and Ryans (1995) define performance as the degree of market success attained by a product at market maturity or the point at which product boundaries change. Other measures of performance include revenue, sales volume, ROI, ROS, customer satisfaction, customer loyalty, purchase intent, and perceived quality.

In a review of the operationalizations of marketing performance employed in the academic literature, Ambler and Kokkinaki (1997) found sales and sales growth to be the dominant (47 percent) measures of success followed by market share (36 percent), profit contribution, and customer preference/purchase intent (23 percent each).

The situation in practice, however, seems to be different. Marketing seems to have relatively little influence in many UK boardrooms with low representation and respect. The evidence for the low impact of *market* metrics is largely anecdotal (e.g., Kaplan and Norton (1992) discussions about the implementation of their balanced scorecard) but with some trade surveys (e.g., IPA/KPMG, 1997). Although senior executives have recognized the need for more comprehensive measurement systems and a range of non-financial indicators are routinely tracked, financial measures are still to be given priority in determining strategy, promotions, bonuses, and other rewards (Eccles, 1991). Most boards routinely consider management accounts at each meeting but only occasionally, or so we expect, consider marketing performance. This is not just a matter of frequency as it may well also imply importance. Hence, we expect to find that *internal financial performance measures are seen by management as more important in assessing marketing performance than market place measures* (H1).

The topic of market orientation is closely related to the "marketing concept" (Drucker, 1954). Market orientation refers to the generation and dissemination of and responsiveness to market intelligence pertaining to current and future needs of customers (Kohli, Jaworski, and Kumar, 1993). In other words, marketing-oriented companies are customer driven. Narver and Slater (1990) view market orientation as a uni-dimensional construct consisting of different behavioral components and decision criteria.

An alternative is to see winning customers and beating competitors as distinct, albeit linked, constructs. We use "customer orientation" to refer to "the sufficient understanding of one's target buyers to be able to create superior value for them continuously" (Narver and Slater, 1990, p. 21). "Competitor orientation" reflects the understanding of "the short-term strengths and weaknesses and long-term capabilities and strategies of both the key current and the key potential competitors" (Narver and Slater, 1990, pp. 21–2). Thus a firm may be preoccupied by building customer preference or by out-performing competitors or some mix of the two. A customer orientation may be reflected, for example, in close attention given to measures of customer satisfaction. Competitor orientation may be shown by primary attention being given to market share.

Market orientation has been found to drive, or at least to correlate with, success (Narver and Slater, 1990; Meehan, 1997; Slater and Narver, 1994). Consistent with these findings we expect *both customer and competitor orientations to be positively associated with performance* (H2).

The firm's orientation is reflected in its behavior (see Narver and Slater, 1990; Slater and Narver, 1994) and therefore in how it operationalizes its success. For example, if the objective is to create customer value, customer-based measures should be a crucial indicator of success. We therefore expect *customer and competitor orientation to influence measurement practice, i.e., to determine the frequency with which customer and competitor measures are collected and the weight attached to such measures, when firm characteristics (e.g., size, sector) are controlled* (H3).

Performance, explicitly or implicitly, is compared against benchmarks. Planning has been linked to successful performance in strategy (Fredrickson and Mitchell, 1984; Pearce, Robbins, and Robinson, 1987; Shrader, Taylor, and Dalton, 1984) and marketing (Lysonski and Pecotich, 1992; but see Mintzberg, 1994). Swartz *et al.* (1996), in a study on UK financial services, found no *general* association of planning with overall success. However, they found particular connections leading to the conclusion that firms tend to achieve subjective, their own specific goals, as distinct from objective universal goals. We therefore expect to find that *plans are the dominant benchmark used by firms for assessing marketing performance* (H4).

In recent years, it has become clear to most companies that intangible assets are instrumental in helping them achieve their success. In the past, one may have dismissed the intangible assets as immaterial in comparison to the tangible. Today, however, less than a third of the value of Wall Street quoted companies is explained by tangible assets (Standard and Poor, 1996). Brand equity (Aaker, 1991, 1996) reflects the long-term effects of marketing. Brand equity stems from the confidence that consumers place in one brand relative to its competitors. This confidence translates into consumers' loyalty and their willingness to pay a premium price for the brand. Building brand equity therefore provides firms with a competitive advantage that includes the opportunity for successful extensions, resilience against competitors' promotional pressures, and creation of barriers to competitive entry (Farquhar, 1990). In a Marketing Science Institute paper, Srivastava and Shocker (1991) provided an authoritative definition of brand equity: "a set of associations and behaviours on the part of a brand's customers, channel members and parent corporation that permits the brand to earn greater volume or greater margins than it could without the brand name and that gives a strong, sustainable and differential advantage." In aggregate, therefore, brand equity is the name for the firm's marketing asset. This is distinct from the financial valuation or any other single measure of the marketing asset.

The significance of the marketing asset, which is here called brand equity, for assessing marketing performance is not widely appreciated. Sales and profitability in any particular period benefit from marketing activities in prior periods. At the same time, future periods will gain from marketing activities, e.g., advertising, now. We believe this to be a crucial issue since the application of marketing resources in any period will also pay back in future periods. Some quantification of the *change* in the marketing asset, e.g., brand equity, is therefore essential if performance results are to be attributed to resources used. In other words, for any period:

Marketing performance = sales − costs + the increase in brand equity.

Thus marketing performance cannot be assessed without considering what change in the marketing asset has taken place between the beginning and end of the period under review. Nevertheless this concept of the marketing asset, whether it is called brand equity or reputation or any other name, is relatively new, and we would not expect it to have been widely adopted yet in practice.

Table 14.1 Respondents by business size and sector (qualitative study)

(# employees)	Retail	Consumer goods	Consumer services	B2B goods	B2B services	Other	Total
Small (<110)					1	1	2
Medium (<500)					2		2
Large (>500)	2	15	13	4	6		40
Total	2	15	13	4	9	1	44

Accordingly, we do not expect high levels of formal measurement of the marketing asset (H5).

Methodology

After six pilot interviews with chief executives and senior marketers, we conducted formal interviews in a qualitative study. On the basis of the findings of this study, a survey instrument was constructed for a subsequent quantitative, large-scale study. The sample of the qualitative study was similar to that of the survey, in terms of business sector. However, we interviewed executives in larger organizations because they were expected to represent best practice and to use more elaborate measurement processes.

Qualitative study

Forty-four in-depth interviews were conducted with marketing and finance executives from 24 British firms, representing all the main business sectors, to discuss their marketing assessment practices. The sample consisted of both marketing and finance managers in order not to restrict the perspective to the marketing department alone. Table 14.1 presents a description of this sample. An interview guide was used to structure the discussions. The issues addressed included: the type of measures collected, the level of review of these measures (e.g. marketing department, Board), the assessment of the marketing asset, planning and benchmarking, practitioners' satisfaction with their measurement processes and their views on measurement aspects that call for improvement, and firm orientation. Information on firm characteristics, such as size and sector, was also obtained.

Table 14.2 Respondents by business size and sector (survey)

(# employees)	Retail	Consumer goods	Consumer services	B2B goods	B2B services	Other	Total
Small (<110)	8	7	14	6	44	32	111
Medium (<500)	8	13	6	7	21	12	67
Large (>500)	51	111	38	30	38	77	345
Missing values							8
Total	67	131	58	43	103	121	531

Survey

On the basis of the findings of the qualitative study, a survey instrument was developed (self-administered questionnaire, see appendix). The questionnaire was sent to 1,014 marketing and 1,180 finance senior executives, recruited through their professional bodies (i.e., the Marketing Council, the Marketing Society, the Institute of Chartered Accounts of England and Wales). A total of 531 questionnaires were returned (367 from marketers and 164 from finance officers, response rate 36 percent and 14 percent, respectively). These were in line with the general 10–40 percent range found in the literature. The higher level of marketing responses was due to linking distribution with applications for seminars.

We did not employ formal non-response bias evaluation but the different waves of marketer data collection showed no significant differences. The arrangement with the Institute of Chartered Accountants of England and Wales did not allow reminder or follow up but comparing early and late returns (Armstrong and Overton, 1977) gave no cause for concern. The two sub-samples did not differ substantially in terms of the distribution of firm size, and business sector, with the exception of the consumer goods sector which was slightly over-represented in the marketers group (see table 14.2). Comparing the different data sources (i.e., the different professional bodies through which respondents were recruited) also showed no substantial differences either in terms of firm characteristics or in terms of performance and market orientation. The responses of the marketing and finance sub-samples, in respect to measurement practices, provided some significant differences, reported in the following section, but not in terms of the crucial variables of performance and customer and competitor orientation.

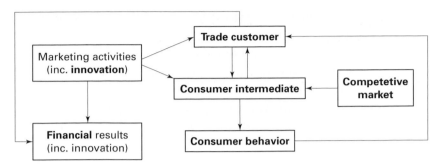

Figure 14.1.   Model of performance measures.

On the basis of the qualitative research, performance measures were classified into six categories:

- financial, e.g., sales volume/turnover, profit contribution, ROC;
- competitive market (i.e., those relative to a competitor or the whole market), e.g., market share, share of voice, relative price, share of promotions;
- consumer behavior, e.g., penetration/number of users/consumers, user/consumer loyalty, user gains/losses/churn;
- consumer intermediate being thoughts and feelings, e.g., awareness, attitudes, satisfaction, commitment, buying intentions, perceived quality;
- direct trade customer, e.g., distribution/availability, customer profitability, satisfaction, service quality; and
- innovation, e.g., number of new products/services, revenue generated from new products/services as a percentage of sales.

These labels are not entirely exclusive since some of the other categories have financial, e.g., customer profitability, characteristics. We retained them for ease of communication however, as UK practitioners refer to those emanating from the conventional profit and loss accounts as "financial" whereas other data, expressed in currency or not, are perceived as market analysis. Figure 14.1 provides a conceptual model of these relationships.

Figure 14.1 shows firms and their competitors influencing trade customers through push strategies (sales and promotion) as well as creating consumer pull through advertising and consumer promotions. What is in consumers' heads (intermediate), together with distribution and trade customer activities, drives consumer behavior which in turn feeds back to trade customer activity. Since firms do not sell directly to consumers, in this model, the achievement of the firm's goals is driven by trade customer responsiveness. In the survey, those respondent firms who did sell directly to consumers (e.g., retailers and financial services) omitted the trade customer section of the questionnaire.

Respondents were asked to indicate the importance attached to the different categories of measures by top management on a seven-point scale ranging from very important (7) to very unimportant (1). They were also asked to report how regularly data are collected for each measure category by ticking one of the following: "never," "rarely/*ad hoc*," "regularly yearly/quarterly," "monthly or more." In certain cases, and to allow for more detailed analyzes, these responses were coded as 1, 2, 3, and 4, respectively, and were treated as a continuous variable. Although the distances between the points of the scale are not necessarily equal, they can be perceived as a proximal measure of how frequently data are collected, with "never" indicating the lowest and "monthly of more" the highest frequency. Respondents were also asked to indicate the benchmark against which each measure category is compared (previous year, marketing/business plan, total category data, specific competitors, other units in the group). It should be noted that responses, in all the above cases, concerned measure categories (indicated with a number of examples in the questionnaire) and not specific measures, although they were encouraged to add measures not covered by the categories. Respondents were also asked whether they have a term for the main intangible asset(s) built by the firm's marketing efforts and whether this asset(s) is (are) formally (financial valuation and/ or other measures) and regularly (never (1) to monthly or more (7)) tracked. Customer and competitor orientation were measured with eight seven-point Likert type scales drawn from Narver and Slater (1990). For example, respondents were asked to indicate their degree of agreement with the following statements: "Top management regularly discusses competitors' strategies," "Our business objectives are driven by our commitment to serving customer needs" (strongly agree (7) /strongly disagree (1)). Separate single indices of customer and competitor orientation were computed as the mean of responses to these items (Cronbach's alpha = 0.81 and 0.69, respectively).[1]

Performance was operationalized as the mean of responses to two five-point scales asking participants to indicate how their competitors view them (strong leader (7) /laggard (1)) and to rate their success in comparison to the average in the sector (excellent (7) /poor (1), alpha = 0.52). Despite its low reliability, this item was retained as separate analyses for each individual

---

[1] The low Cronbach's alpha for competitor orientation items is close to that reported by Narver and Slater in their original implementation of the scale (0.71) (Narver and Slater, 1990).

Table 14.3 Key measures employed for assessing marketing performance (interview data)

	Marketers ($n=26$)	Finance ($n=18$)
Finance/shareholder	71	48
Consumer/end-user	50	17
Campaign effectiveness	17	3
Competitor (share)	19	13
Immediate trade customer	9	2
Product performance and logistics	9	6
Employee attitudes	2	1
Econometric models	2	–
Total	179	90

measure of performance yielded substantively similar patterns of results. Note that these measures are based on respondents' judgments and not independent assessments. However, it has been shown that subjective measures are strongly correlated with independent, objective assessments (Dess and Robinson, 1984; Venkatraman and Ramanujam, 1987).

Empirical findings

Table 14.3 indicates the number of key measures employed by firms to assess their marketing performance. Responses were obtained through an open-ended item and were then categorized. As can be seen in the table, financial measures were the most frequently mentioned, especially by the finance respondents. That provides some support for our assumption that financial measures dominate performance assessment. More robust evidence is provided by the survey data (table 14.4). Although a somewhat different classification system was used, financial measures are seen by top management as significantly more important than all other categories, providing support for H1. While the differences between customer and competitiveness measures are fairly small, it is interesting that consumer behavior rates are so low.

Further, our results indicate that practitioners are not fully satisfied with their marketing performance measurement systems (mean $= 4.06$). However, finance officers are more satisfied than marketers, probably because the focus is mainly on financial figures (4.02 vs. 3.9, $t(510) = -2.24$, $p < 0.05$). The areas

Table 14.4 Mean importance attached to performance measures by top management (survey data)

	Mean	t	df	Sig. t
Financial	6.51			
Competitive market	5.42	−16.78	523	0.000
Consumer (end user) behavior	5.38	−15.60	522	0.000
Consumer (end user) intermediate	5.42	−15.60	515	0.000
Direct (trade) customer	5.53	−14.90	499	0.000
Innovativeness	5.04	20.13	524	0.000

Note:
t-tests refer to the comparisons between financial measures and each of the other categories.

Table 14.5 Areas where improvement is sought (interview data)

Specifics (more detail) on campaign, launch and promotions performance
Speed and regularity of data which was now considered too slow and *ad hoc*
Predictiveness and modeling
More financial data (mostly from our finance respondents)
Better customer information.

where improvement is sought are shown as table 14.5, in declining frequency of mention.

A few respondents felt they already had too many data and needed no more. This last point is important. Our preliminary conclusion is that marketing performance is already assessed against plenty of measures but they are excessively weighted to internal financial figures and customer and competitor indicators are underweighted.

Irrespective of who reviews the data, financial measures are again more frequently collected than any other category (table 14.6). It is worth noting that in 33.5 percent of the cases consumer intermediate measures are collected only rarely/*ad hoc*. Innovation, which some see as the lifeblood of marketing, rates lowest of all and innovation measures are the least regularly collected. That may partly be due to the difficulty of quantifying the amount of a firm's innovation. Assessing its quality at the time is even more difficult even though, looking back, a single major breakthrough may dwarf all other marketing activities. To allow for further analyses responses were quantified on a 1 (never) to 4 scale (monthly or more). Firm size was found to have an effect on

Table 14.6 Regularity of data collection (valid percent, survey data)

	Monthly or more	Yearly/ quarterly	Rarely/ *ad hoc*	Never
Financial	**74.9**	16.6	6.9	1.5
Competitive market	36.2	**39.9**	21.1	2.7
Consumer (end user) behavior	23.0	**45.9**	26.9	4.2
Consumer (end user) intermediate	17.5	**43.5**	33.5	5.5
Direct (trade) customer	25.1	**42.0**	27.7	5.2
Innovativeness	10.3	**34.7**	40.9	14.1

frequency of data collection. With the exception of innovativeness, firm size was a significant predictor of frequency in all other categories. *Beta* weights ranged between 0.11 and 0.38, indicating that larger firms tend to be more thorough in the frequency of their data collection. Similarly, the business sector was found to have a significant effect on frequency of data collection, except in the case of innovativeness (F values ranged between 16.82, in the case of competitor measures, to 4.06, in the case of financial measures). Closer inspection of mean frequency per business sector, however, indicated no major differences across sectors. On average, irrespective of measure category, consumer goods and retail firms tend to collect data more frequently than other sectors ($F(5, 512) = 11.81$, $p < 0.000$).

Regularity is thus underscoring the primacy given to financial measures. About one-third of firms collect competitive data monthly and one quarter or less do so for the other market measures. The modal frequency for market measures is between quarterly and yearly.

Our results provide only partial support for marketing/business plan being the dominant benchmark against which performance is assessed (H4). As can be seen in table 14.7, plan is the most frequent benchmark of financial and innovativeness measures in those cases where such measures are used. However, in the case of competitive market measures, as one would expect, the dominant benchmark is the specific competitor, whereas consumer and direct customer measures are more frequently compared with previous year results.

A series of regression analyses were also performed to determine whether customer and competitor orientation have an effect on the practice of performance assessment. Tables 14.8 and 14.9 suggest that customer orientation

Table 14.7 Frequency of benchmarks used (valid percent, for those cases where this kind of measure is used)

Measures	Previous year	Marketing/ business plan	Total category data	Specific competitor(s)	Other units in the group
Financial	80.4	85.1	17.5	23.0	22.0
Competitive market	51.4	51.0	35.8	55.7	6.6
Consumer behavior	47.1	42.0	27.1	31.6	6.4
Consumer intermediate	36.7	30.3	22.0	27.7	5.1
Direct (trade) customer	40.3	37.7	17.3	22.8	7.3
Innovativeness	21.3	33.7	10.9	20.7	6.6

Table 14.8 Regression of "measures collected" on customer and competitor orientation (after partialling out the effect of firm size and sector)

	Customer orientation			Competitor orientation		
	beta	T	Sig. t	beta	t	Sig. t
Financial measures	0.05	1.37	0.171	0.06	1.57	0.115
Competitive market measures	0.12	3.03	0.003	0.24	6.11	0.000
Consumer behavior	0.20	4.74	0.000	0.14	3.19	0.001
Consumer intermediate	0.24	5.34	0.000	0.09	2.11	0.035
Direct (trade customer)	0.16	3.58	0.000	0.06	1.40	0.162
Innovativeness	0.25	5.80	0.000	0.12	2.85	0.005

Table 14.9 Regression of "importance attached by top management" on customer and competitor orientation (after partialling out the effect of firm size and sector)

	Customer orientation			Competitor orientation		
	beta	T	Sig. t	beta	t	Sig. t
Financial measures	0.11	2.67	0.008	0.07	1.67	0.094
Competitive market measures	0.16	3.81	0.000	0.28	7.08	0.000
Consumer behavior	0.31	7.50	0.000	0.25	6.03	0.000
Consumer intermediate	0.33	8.10	0.000	0.21	4.91	0.000
Direct (trade customer)	0.25	5.72	0.000	0.16	3.62	0.000
Innovativeness	0.24	5.62	0.000	0.18	4.27	0.000

tends to be associated with the frequency of collection and importance of consumer and direct customer-based and innovativeness measures, more so than competitor orientation, which is associated with the frequency of collection and importance of competitor-based measures. Furthermore, orientation does not seem to have an effect on financial measures. These findings provide partial support for H3.

Customer and competitor orientation were found to be correlated significantly with business success ($r = 0.25$, $p < 0.05$ and $r = 0.14$, $p < 0.05$, respectively). In order to determine whether orientation can predict business success, success was regressed separately on customer and competitor orientation after the effect of business size and sector had been partialled out. Both factors were found to be significant predictors of success, although the weight of customer orientation was stronger than that of competitor orientation ($beta = 0.26$, $t = 6.11$, $p < 0.001$ vs. $beta = 0.14$, $t = 3.26$, $p < 0.001$), providing support for H2.

In respect to understanding and measuring the intangible marketing asset, in 62.2 percent of the cases some term is used in the company to describe the concept. The most common terms used are brand equity (32.5 percent of those who use a term), reputation (19.6 percent), brand value (8.2 percent), and brand health (6.9 percent). However, in 146 (36.7 percent) of the *cases where any term is used*, the marketing asset is never valued financially, and in 231 cases (51.4 percent) it is not assessed in any other way, e.g., through customer/consumer-based measures. In 40 percent of the cases brand equity is assessed yearly or more frequently. Also, other measures of brand equity are formally collected in only 25 percent of the cases. Thus brand equity is the most popular term for the marketing asset but the marketing asset, by whatever name, does not receive the attention it should have if marketing performance is to be formally assessed. This supports H5.

Taking these findings as a whole, it would seem that the overall assessment of marketing performance is patchy at best:

1 The primary focus is on financial measures which are also in the plan and seen more often (mostly monthly).
2 Market measures are modally seen between quarterly and yearly.
3 Performance is not usually adjusted for the change in the marketing asset.

And yet market orientation does matter. Both customer and competitor orientation were associated with performance and, as one might expect, with the relevant measures. One cannot conclude that companies will improve their performance simply by reviewing market measures at their monthly board meetings. However, there is a consistency in these findings which companies may wish to note. It supports the original marketing concept that firms achieve their own objectives through first achieving their customers' objectives.

We have not distinguished here between immediate customer and end user orientation partly because the literature has only just begun to distinguish competitor from customer orientation. In crude terms, one only has to worry about the competition when one's brands are weak. Owners of strong brands can afford to ignore competitors but even they cannot afford to ignore the *measurement* of brand strength since they need to know when to deal with customers uniquely and when to respond to competitive threats.

This exploratory research confirms, to a limited extent, the greater importance of customer over competitive orientation but both are needed according, as noted above, to the circumstances.

Conclusions

Shaw and Mazur (1997) suggest other executives' dissatisfaction with marketing is due to out-sourcing measurement which is seen as a support role. "Marketing executives themselves have shown a marked reluctance to take on "support' roles, preferring the glamour of big-budget advertising over developing corporate marketing measures" (p. 1); and: "Marketing is rarely involved in measurement development, and consequently the finance department is left alone to do the job as best it can" (p. 4). Yet marketers are right to put the achievement of results before measurement. Making the runs matters more than adding them up. Nevertheless, marketers are responsible for ensuring that performance is properly evaluated. Unless they organize the evaluations in line with their own marketing philosophy, they can expect to be judged harshly by other managers using other criteria. Furthermore their credibility, and the credibility of marketing as a whole, will be eroded.

From the evidence we have seen thus far, marketers need to be clearer about what they are trying to achieve, and improve their presentation of their performance toward meeting those objectives. That *performance* itself should be better is a singularly unhelpful truism but that is not our point. There is some way to go in improving *clarity* both within functional marketing and between marketers and other managers. Pan-company marketing can only be achieved by a shared understanding of marketing. Clearer internal measures and communications may well then lead to improving performance itself.

Specifically, market measures should be included in annual plans and reviewed with the same frequency as financial measures at board level. Shaw and Mazur (1997) and IPA/KPMG (1997) are just indicative of the widespread view that marketers are not fully accountable. Marketers themselves may be hesitant in providing more clarity as it may cramp freedom of manoeuvre and marketing demands flexibility. In the long run, however, this flexibility will be curtailed unless pan-company marketing becomes reality, i.e., their colleagues know the game and know the score.

Similarly, their brand equities are many firms' most valuable assets. The board needs to understand how those assets are growing. Without that information, overall marketing performance is impossible to judge. The significance of brand equity has been widely recognized throughout the 1990s but, our findings suggest that it has not yet been fully adopted by firms in their routine measurement systems.

Future research

Although our findings provide some indications related to current practice in performance measurement and support the importance of customer and competitor orientation as determinants of success, they are limited in several aspects. The most important limitation concerns the use of self-reported measures of variables. Although secondary measures have been shown to be valid indicators of underlying constructs (e.g., Dess and Robinson, 1984; Venkatraman and Ramanujam, 1987), further research, preferably employing primary data, is necessary. Also, additional research is necessary to enable practitioners to distinguish between the effects of pan-company marketing and individual components of the marketing mix, i.e., the effectiveness of specific marketing initiatives.

Appendix

The Marketing Society initiated the Metrics project: please help us now by completing and returning this brief survey TODAY to any Conference staff member. If that is impossible, please use the reply paid envelope enclosed.

Please complete it on behalf of YOUR FIRM as a whole, <u>or</u> whichever part of the firm (i.e. BUSINESS UNIT) you identify most closely with. Some firms, e.g. charities, may need to adjust the wording to fit your activity. The form, which is anonymous and therefore confidential, applies to all. A spare form is enclosed for your own use.

If used at all, what is the highest level of <u>routine</u> review of this metric in your firm? (the top board is the one which answers to external shareholders or the equivalent Category/Metric ▼	Importance for assessing the overall marketing performance of your firm/unit? Definition/comment ▼	**HIGHEST LEVEL** 0 don't know 1 **not used** 2 junior marketing 3 top marketer 4 unit board 5 intermediate board 6 top board	**IMPORTANCE** 0 don't know 1 not at all important 2 somewhat important 3 fairly important 4 important 5 very important
CONSUMER/END USER THOUGHTS AND FEELINGS		Please enter 0–6: ↓	Please enter 0–5: ↓
1 **Awareness**	Prompted, unprompted or total		
2 **Salience**	Prominence, stand-out		
3 **Perceived quality/esteem**	How highly rated		
4 **Consumer satisfaction**	Confirmation of end user expectations		
5 **Relevance to consumer**	"My kind of brand"		
6 **Image/personality/identity**	Strength of brand individuality		
7 **(Perceived) differentation**	How distinct from other brands		
8 **Commitment/purchase intent**	Expressed likelihood of buying		
9 **Other attitudes, e.g. liking**	Other cognitive/emotional indicators		
10 **Brand/product knowledge**	Experience with product attributes		
END USER BEHAVIOUR		**HIGHEST LEVEL**	**IMPORTANCE**
11 **Total number of consumers**			
12 **Number of new consumers**	Purchased this year, not last		
13 **Loyalty/retention**	e.g. % buying this year and last		
14 **Price sensitivity/elasticity**	Any measure of volume sensitivity		
15 **Purchasing on promotion**	Share of volume sold on promotion		
16 **# products per consumer**	The width of range end user buys		
17 **# leads generated/inquiries**	Number of new prospects		
18 **Conversions (leads to sales)**	Prospects to sales conversions (%)		
19 **# consumer complaints**	Level of end user dissatisfaction		

	TRADE CUSTOMER		HIGHEST LEVEL	IMPORTANCE
20	**Distribution/availability**	e.g. number of stores in stock (weighted)		
21	**Customer satisfaction**	Direct customer acceptability, e.g. service		
22	**# customer complaints**	Direct customer dissatisfaction		
	RELATIVE TO COMPETITOR		HIGHEST LEVEL	IMPORTANCE
23	**Market share**	% SOM Volume &/or Value		
24	**Relative price**	e.g. SOM Value/SOM Volume		
25	**Loyalty (share)**	Share of category requirements		
26	**Penetration**	% of total who buy brand in period		
27	**Relative customer satisfaction**	e.g. satisfaction vs. Competitor		
28	**Relative perceived quality**	Perceived quality as % leader		
29	**Share of voice**	Brand advertising as % category		
	INNOVATION		HIGHEST LEVEL	IMPORTANCE
30	**# of new products in period**	New product launches		
31	**Revenue of new products**	Turnover, sales as share of total (%)		
32	**Margin of new products**	Gross profit as share of total (%)		
	FINANCIAL		HIGHEST LEVEL	IMPORTANCE
33	**Sales**	Value (turnover) and/or volume		
34	**% discount**	Allowances as % of sales		
35	**Gross margins**	Gross profit as % sales turnover		
36	**Marketing spend**	e.g. ads, PR, promotions		
37	**Profit/Profitability**	Contribution, trading, or before tax		
38	**Shareholder value/EVA/ROI**	The true financial bottom line		
	OTHER *(Please add any key measures we have missed)*		HIGHEST LEVEL	IMPORTANCE
39				
40				
41				
42				

And finally just a few questions about your firm/business unit for categorisation purposes

43   What sector is your firm/business unit in? *(If you are in several: tick the most appropriate one).*
Retail ☐   Consumer goods ☐   Consumer services ☐   Business-to-business goods ☐
Business-to-business services ☐   Other ☐   *Please state* _____

44   What is the structure of your whole organisational group?
1 unit (no separate marketing) ☐   1 unit with marketing department ☐   Subsidiaries with 1 parent board ☐
More complex (i.e. with intermediate boards) ☐

45   How many employees in your whole organisational group?
Less than 50 ☐   50–250 ☐   250–500 ☐   500–1000 ☐   1000–5000 ☐   More than 5000 ☐

46   How long has your firm (business unit) been in the sort of business it is now?
Less than 1 year ☐   1–5 years ☐   5–15 years ☐   15–50 years ☐   More than 50 years ☐

47   What is your role in the firm?

Finance ☐   Marketing manager ☐   Marketing services agency ☐   Other consultant ☐   Other ☐

48   Please rate your firm's overall marketing performance over the past year *(circle the appropriate number)*.

Excellent	good	average	poor	very poor	don't know
5	4	3	2	1	0

49   Please rate your firm's overall performance *relative* to its major competitors over the past year.

Much better	slightly better	similar	slightly worse	much worse	don't know
5	4	3	2	1	0

50   Please rate your firm's <u>profit</u> performance compared with <u>plan</u> *(leave blank if no formal plan)*.

Much better	slightly better	similar	slightly worse	much worse	don't know
5	4	3	2	1	0

51   Please rate your firm's annual <u>sales</u> performance compared with <u>prior year</u>.

Much better	slightly better	similar	slightly worse	much worse	don't know
5	4	3	2	1	0

Please now return this to a conference staffer or Flora Kokkinaki, London Business School, Sussex Place, NW1 4SA

REFERENCES

Aaker, D.A. (1991). *Managing Brand Equity.* New York: Free Press.

Aaker, D.A. (1996). *Building Strong Brands.* New York: Free Press.

Ambler, T. and Kokkinaki, F. (1997). Measures of marketing success. *Journal of Marketing Management*, **13**, 665–78.

Armstrong, J.S. and Overton, T.S. (1977). Estimating nonresponse bias in mail surveys. *Journal of Marketing Research*, **14** (August), 396–402.

Day, G.S. (1984). *Strategic Market Planning.* St. Paul, MN: West Publishing.

Day, G.S. (1990). *Market Driven Strategy: Processes for Creating Value.* New York: Free Press.

Dess, G.G. and Robinson, R.B. Jr (1984). Measuring organizational performance in the absence of objective measures: The case of the privately held firm and conglomerate business unit. *Strategic Management Journal*, **5**, 265–73.

Drucker, P. (1954). *The Practice of Management.* New York: Harper and Row.

Eccles, R.G. (1991). The Performance Measurement Manifesto. *Harvard Business Review*, January–February, 131–7.

Farquhar, P.H. (1990). Managing brand equity. *Journal of Advertising Research*, **30**, RC7–RC12.

Fredrickson, J.W. and Mitchell, R.T. (1984). Strategic decision processes: Comprehensiveness and performance in an industry with an unstable environment. *Academy of Management Journal*, **27**, 399–423.

Green, D.H., Barclay, D.W., and Ryans, A. (1995). Entry strategy and long-term performance: Conceptualization and empirical examination. *Journal of Marketing*, **59**(4), 1–16.

IPA/KPMG (1997). *Survey of Marketing Influence in the Boardroom*. London: IPA.

Kaplan, Robert S. and Norton, David P. (1992). The balanced scorecard – measures that drive performance. *Harvard Business Review*, **70** (January–February), 71–9.

Kohli, J., Jaworski, B. and Kumar, A. (1993). MARKOR: A measure of market orientation. *Journal of Marketing Research*, **30**, 467–77.

Kotler, P. (1997). *Marketing management: Analysis, planning implementation and control*, 9th edn., Englewood Cliffs, NJ: Prentice Hall.

Lysonski, S. and Pecotich, A. (1992). Strategic marketing planning, environmental uncertainty and performance. *International Journal of Research in Marketing*, **9**(3), 247–55.

Meehan, S.A. (1997). Market orientation: Values, behaviours and performance. Unpublished Ph.D. thesis, University of London.

Mintzberg, H. (1994). *The Rise and Fall of Strategic Planning*. Hemel Hempstead: Prentice Hall.

Narver, J.C. and Slater, S.F. (1990). The effect of a market orientation on business profitability. *Journal of Marketing*, **54**, 20–35.

Pearce, J.A.II, Robbins, K.D., and Robinson R.B. Jr (1987). The impact of grand strategy and planning formality on financial performance. *Strategic Management Journal*, **8**, 125–34.

Shaw, R. and Mazur, L. (1997). Marketing accountability: Improving business performance. *Financial Times*, London: Retail and Consumer Publishing.

Shrader, C., Taylor, L., and Dalton, D.R. (1984). Strategic planning and organizational performance: A critical appraisal. *Journal of Management*, **10**(2), 149–71.

Slater, S.F. and Narver J.C. (1994). Market orientation, customer value, and superior performance. *Business Horizons* (March–April), 22–28.

Srivastava, R.K. and Shocker, A.D. (1991). Brand equity: A perspective on its meaning and measurement. Working Paper No. 91–124, Marketing Science Institute, Cambridge, MA.

Standard and Poor (1996). *The Outlook*. Special Issue, **68**(2), New York: McGraw-Hill.

Swartz, G.S., Hardie, B., Grayson, K., and Ambler, T. (1996). Value for money? The relationships between marketing expenditure and business performance in the UK: Financial services industry. The Chartered Institute of Marketing, Maidenhead.

Venkatraman, N. and Ramanujam, V. (1987). Measurement of business economic performance: An examination of method convergence. *Journal of Management*, **13**, 109–22.

Webster, F.E. Jr (1992). The changing role of marketing in the corporation. *Journal of Marketing*, **56** (October), 1–17.

15 Loosely coupled performance measurement systems

Thomas Ahrens and Chris Chapman

Introduction

This chapter reports on the loosely coupled performance measurement practices of a high-performing restaurant chain. Over a period of four years we observed a series of initiatives aimed at "tightening up" the performance measurement systems of the case company. Yet none of these initiatives resolved the desire for what the finance director towards the end of the research period called "unambiguous performance information." Head office managers of all grades continued to demand performance measurement systems that allowed more comprehensive and detailed control over the operational decisions of restaurant managers. Whilst it was easy to see in principle how such systems could have been implemented, successive working parties did not impose them. This was not for lack of market competition, and it did not result in lower performance. Indeed, managers felt competitive pressures intensified during the research period and still managed to both increase market share and profitability of the case company. What we were faced with was a high-performing company in a competitive industry that espoused to rectify the flaws of its performance measurement system, yet did not. We think that this case holds a lesson for those who are interested in performance measurement system implementation, because it combines high performance with a handling of performance measurement issues that would seem to violate an implicit cornerstone of much of the performance measurement literature. We hypothesize that managers' "failure" to address the obvious shortcomings of their performance measurement systems may have been related to the management style that enabled the company to perform so remarkably well. Our analysis of this particular organization suggests the benefits of a certain degree of loose coupling in performance measurement due to the particular characteristics of its business processes.

Two context dimensions of performance measurement systems

Before analyzing those processes in detail, we should explain how loose coupling might benefit performance measurement. By loose coupling we mean that specific metrics are only loosely connected with specific managerial responses. This is not the same as bad management. In the case company the link between specific performance metrics and overall restaurant evaluation was ambiguous, but the operational hierarchy was in no doubt about the performance of individual restaurants. Specific sets of metrics informed operational management's definite views on a particular restaurant. But for a different restaurant, or at a different point in time, the same measures might well inform a different evaluation and give rise to different responsive actions. This made sense because of the complexities involved in delivering the product. In a full-service restaurant chain standardizing the food is only part of the task. Management also needs to provide an appropriate atmosphere. This is a logistical question of managing the waiting staff, but also of managing the social environment, a task that requires judgment and tact.

Performance measurement in the case company was therefore quite different from that in a fast food restaurant chain. In fast food restaurants there is no need to manage waiting staff or the social environment. Restaurant management concentrates on following the centrally optimized rules for assembling standard dishes. Specifications for all operations are detailed and unambiguous (e.g., Leidner, 1993; Love, 1987; Reiler, 1991, chapter 5; Wyckoff and Sasser, 1978, especially tables 6.3 and 6.4). In his study of large fast food chain restaurants in the USA, Bradach (1997) found that performance evaluation was based on adherence to standards. Head office concerns about violations of brand standards by restaurant managers were so great that profit was not used to evaluate them.

Those examples from the restaurant industry suggest that we might usefully distinguish between two dimensions of context in which performance measurement is practised. One dimension is the link between performance metrics and operational responses. This dimension addresses the *use of performance measurement*. After a measurement is taken, what is the appropriate action to follow? Here we distinguish between tightly specified (or programmed) and loosely specified responses. In the former case the purpose of the performance measurement system would be to trigger specific responses by particular readings of

		Use of performance measurement: Looseness of the metric-operational response link	
		LOW	HIGH
Local customization of product delivery	LOW	1. Programmed standardization (commodity) e.g. fast food restaurant chain	2. Individual standardization (poor administration) Pathological category
	HIGH	3. Programmed customization (mass-customization) e.g., financial services	4. Individual customization (tailored product) e.g., full service restaurant

Figure 15.1.   Two context dimensions of performance measurement systems.

performance metrics. For example, a budget overrun for waiting staff would be met with a simple response: stopping overtime.

In contrast, if the performance measurement system was operated in a more loosely coupled fashion, local restaurant managers would be given more freedom to evaluate and justify their budget overrun for waiting staff. They could, for example, explain it as part of their strategy to attract better waiting staff, because they operate in an affluent area where it is difficult to attract local waiting staff for the chain-wide hourly wage. Or they might explain it as part of a strategy to offer exceptional waiting service to the local clientele enticing them to purchase high-margin menu items, such as starters and desserts. The key to a successful operation of loosely coupled performance measurement is the autonomy of local restaurant management allowing them to vary the parameters of input factors in a way that improves overall financial performance.

The appropriateness of tight or loose coupling depends on who knows best how to handle operations. If the product delivery is standardized, a central office can prescribe operations unambiguously. This is the case in many fast food restaurant chains where local autonomy is minimal. If, however, product delivery is not wholly standardized, then operations are designed to vary product delivery according to customers' wishes. The second context dimension on which our two examples from the restaurant industry differ is therefore the *local customization of the product*. Combining the use dimension with the customization dimension produces the scheme shown in figure 15.1. It contains three viable combinations (boxes 1,3,4) and one that represents failure (box 2).

A fast food restaurant in which the customers' only opportunity for customization is the combination of different menu items would occupy box 1.

Attempts at market differentiation of fast food restaurants notwithstanding, a burger is a standard commodity for many consumers. The standardization of operations is comprehensive and allows no looseness of operational responses to the performance metrics of individual outlets.

If there was looseness, the fast food restaurant would find itself in box 2. Standardization, not customization, would still be an objective. Loosely coupled operational responses to defined metrics would, however, introduce uncertainty in the process of selecting the right operational response. In box 2, uncertainty has no productive role to play. Uncertainty merely represents a cost to the business process or the consumer. This would constitute a poorly administered bureaucracy, a category, one would hope, that eventually gets eliminated.

Tightly connected metric-operational response links do not preclude product customization if enough information on the customer can be processed. The objective would be to interpret detailed performance metrics, compare them to learned models of customer preferences, and select one of the programmed responses. The outcome would be programmed customization, or mass-customization. Box 3 therefore comprises organizations that use information on individual customers to tailor offers for them. Recent initiatives in the financial services industry would be examples of programmed customization (Chapman and Gandy, 1997).

Box 4 represents customization without the investment in programmed responses to metrics. The task of customizing lies with individual operators who tailor the product in response to cues they receive about the customer's preferences. Depending on context, the same set of metrics read on two different occasions can give rise to different responses. Metrics are only loosely coupled to operational responses.

The benefits of loose coupling metrics and responses

In the case company we observed such loose coupling between performance metrics and operational responses. It provided scope for local restaurant managers and the operational management hierarchy to engage in nuanced discussions of the centrally generated performance information. The potential of loose coupling does not feature prominently in current debates on performance measurement. The overall trend in the performance measurement literature is towards advocating systems that integrate measures for various activities according to strategic priorities (Drucker, 1995; Eccles, 1991;

MacArthur, 1996; Meyer, 1994; Simons, 1994). Those systems would give rise to detailed analyses of multiple drivers of corporate success, supporting managers in their understanding of operations. The balanced scorecard (Kaplan and Norton, 1992, 1996a, 1996b) is an example. Kaplan and Norton recommend periodic revisions of the performance measures used because no comprehensive system can encapsulate a company's wisdom of successful management indefinitely. The coupling between metrics and responses is, however, not discussed.

Neither is the use of performance metrics much discussed in the contingency literature on management accounting. There is awareness that different market conditions, product characteristics, and organizational strategies would make different accounting systems designs advisable, but the failure to investigate the ways in which management accounting systems function is one main criticism of this literature (recent reviews include: Chapman, 1997; Fisher, 1998; Langfield-Smith, 1997). A combination of the contingency approach with a study of the uses of performance measurement systems would seem promising because accounting systems model and thereby simplify organizational contexts. By filtering information on the organizational context they buffer decision makers from the uncertainties that constantly arise from the developments surrounding their organization.

Hedberg and Jönnson (1978) in an early paper speculate about the connections between accounting systems design and use. According to them, in extremely unpredictable environments, organizations could benefit from "semi-confusing" information systems. These semi-confusing systems present structured views on complex environments without glossing over some of the key contradictions that are present in those environments, thus reducing the risk of managers believing they are monitoring the key variables of the environment, when in fact those key variables change much faster than internal information systems can be redesigned.

More recently, Ittner and Kogut (1995) explicitly concerned themselves with the benefits of keeping the metrics-response link flexible. They discuss the problems that rule-based management processes hold for the development of flexible capabilities. The policies, procedures, and measurements that make up formal control systems but also informal norms and evolved rules of thumb constrain the flexibility of managers' responses to contingencies. In companies where performance measurement readings are taken in diverse contexts this flexibility can be vital. In our case company the different localities of the restaurants provided somewhat diverse backgrounds, which managers had to consider before interpreting performance measurement information.

The case company

In this section we will explore those issues based on a longitudinal field study starting in autumn 1995. The case company is one of the largest chains of wholly owned, full-service restaurants in the UK. There were no franchises. It has consistently achieved returns on sales of about 20 percent. During the three years preceding 1998 year-on-year profit growth was above 7 percent and sales growth was 8 percent. This growth has been attained partly through acquisition but mainly through adding new units. More than 200 restaurants were organized as profit centers that report into areas and then regions of operational management. Between 25 percent and 50 percent of restaurant managers' remuneration was variable. The variable component depended on controllable restaurant profit, sales, and covers growth.

We carried out extensive interviews with all of the divisional board of directors, the entire executive committee, and selected head office staff. To complement our findings from head office we visited 15 restaurants where we interviewed all grades of operational staff and observed operational processes in kitchens and restaurants. We furthermore observed meetings between operational area management and restaurant operators as well as company-wide training sessions on implementing restaurant controls.

The case company brings to the fore issues of loose coupling in performance measurement because it combines a key characteristic of chain organizations: standard sets of performance metrics with the requirement to respond to diverse local operating conditions, because it offered a full waiting service to its customers. Its pricing was such that customers expected a high level of service, adding to the scope for customizing product delivery. We present some data from our field research in the case company in order to demonstrate three things. First, we report on the company's history of management concerns about their performance measurement practices and their failure to make system changes to address those concerns. Second, we describe the operational conditions to suggest that their loosely coupled system was in fact advisable. We use one central performance measure, the food margin, to illustrate this. In doing so we also show how the framework in figure 15.2 can help us to understand managers' discussions of their own organization. Finally, by making links to the main thrust of the performance measurement literature, we suggest some answers to the puzzle of managers who kept talking about modifying the performance measurement system when in fact it was serving their purposes well.

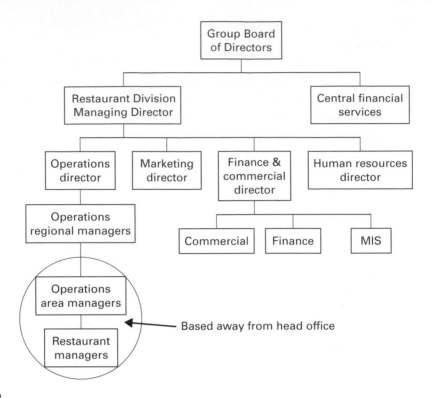

Figure 15.2.

A history of "failed" performance measurement system overhauls

Between 1995 and 1999 we tracked on-going discussions around the case company's performance measurement systems without observing any concrete changes to existing systems. At the beginning of the research period, the company had just introduced a new performance measurement initiative that was given a high profile throughout the organization. It was intended to focus management attention on the "13 key tasks." These tasks had been identified as being critical to the success of the case company, and were each matched with a quantified measure and a target level of achievement. This initiative was dropped after about six months since it was widely felt that, whilst no one disputed the significance of the issues addressed by the 13 key tasks, managers did not think about the management problems facing them in such a fragmented fashion. They found it difficult to think of performance metrics in the abstract, out of the practical context of their specific management problems.

None of our interviewees could recall all 13 key tasks without consulting a written list.

Performance measurement remained on the agenda of the board. Their discussions developed a new focus on the issue of the food margin. The cost of food represented a significant proportion of the overall cost base of the case company, yet it was felt in head office that this central performance measure, which connected the activities of all parts of the organization, was not well understood. Questions were also raised about the measure's calculative implementation through the central management information system. A working party was formed and given the task of resolving this issue.

Various issues were explored by the working party and led to another high-profile initiative within the company. A series of compulsory workshops for restaurant managers were established to reposition the role of centrally generated performance information within the case company. The workshops addressed the concerns of restaurant managers that a reform of performance evaluation systems would turn them into "glove puppets" controlled by head office. The findings of the working party did not result in any changes to the calculative or operational procedures involved in the measurement of the food margin, however.

Some six months after the workshops, at a meeting with the finance director, we were informed that he had set up another working party to clear up once and for all the issues relating to measurement and management of the food margin. Throughout the whole period of our research within the case company, the reform of performance measurement systems comprised various initiatives that were either aborted completely or produced piecemeal solutions that did little to change the status quo. Towards the end of the research period, the finance director denied that the board pursued an implicit strategy of keeping the flexibility that a loosely coupled performance measurement system might offer. He reinforced the message that systematic reporting and management was a fundamental aspect of "proper" management, and that the failure to address the issue beforehand was the result of a lack of focus and drive by the board. The finance director was subsequently promoted to another part of the corporate group before the working party could report any findings.

Why nothing changed – the example of food margin reporting

The finance director favored a technical solution to the difficulties of food margin reporting. In his view the restaurant management loosely coupled operational responses to performance metrics when in fact they should have been much more tightly coupled. Since he did not regard the product as highly customized, he wanted to move his organization from box 2 to box 1 (of our figure 15.1). He regarded past management's failure to effect this move as a mistake. Our analysis suggests that box 3 might more appropriately characterize the situation of the organization. Consequently, what he described as bad administration, one could reinterpret as beneficial given the organizational context of high local customization of product delivery. In order to illustrate this line of argument we will explain in more detail the issues around a key "unresolved" concern of the board: the food margin.

The food margin of a dish is the difference between its sales price and the cost of its component raw materials. Individual restaurant budgets were built up from assumptions about targets for covers, sales, and food margin. The case company's management information system allowed a comparison of achieved margin to target margin based on actual sales mix on a weekly basis. Achieved margin was calculated by dividing food purchases (adjusted for changes in inventory) by actual sales.

Planning for the delivery of food margin targets began anew with the design of every menu (up to two new menus per year). Menu design was a complicated process in which new dishes were designed, tested, and costed in the commercial function's test kitchen. The final decision to include or exclude a dish depended on its satisfactory integration into the menu as a whole. A menu had to deliver the desired target food margin percentage whilst offering a variety of tastes across a range of price points, and conform to the expectations of the brand concept.

Restaurants purchased all food through the central logistics operation at a price fixed for each menu period. The evaluation of food margin in restaurants was therefore based purely on food usage. Price variances were accounted for centrally. Head office prescribed standard procedures for food preparation in the restaurants. The predominant view at head office was that restaurant managers simply had to carry out operations according to the centrally determined parameters and that food margin reporting should police adherence to standards. However once the food margin reporting system is examined in detail and overlaid with an understanding of restaurant operation, the interpretation of a food margin deficit or surplus quickly becomes a complicated issue. This tension between expectation and reality was never resolved during our four-year research.

The standard dish specifications were the subject of mistrust and debate in restaurants. A major concern of restaurant managers was that standards were unrealistic since they were based on performance in a head office test kitchen that did not allow for the difficulty of simultaneous production of many different dishes in a busy and cramped restaurant kitchen. Head office staff felt that restaurant staff paid scant concern to central standards and routinely over-portioned. Restaurant staff, however, were concerned that standard portions could undermine customer expectations of value by leaving "white space" on the plate. Whereas head office staff were concerned with short-run food margin management, restaurant managers showed more concern for possible damage to long-term profitability.

Our observations in restaurants demonstrated that adherence to food preparation specifications was only a part of food margin management. Margin deficits could arise at any point between unloading food from the delivery lorry to consumption by customers. Restaurant managers felt that deliveries had to be supervised by a relatively senior member of staff to prevent theft. It was also necessary to check the quality of deliveries, particularly fresh produce, such as fruit and vegetables. Theft from junior staff occurred. One restaurant manager estimated that a single disgruntled employee had been responsible for the theft of over a thousand pounds worth of inventory over a three-month period.

In the kitchen chefs prepared some items (such as baked potatoes or chips) in advance in order to reduce guest's waiting time. Typically some of these would not be used during a session, but could not be kept until the next thus contributing to food deficits. In the storage area, failure to implement inventory rotation procedures resulted in food going off and being thrown away. Lapses in concentration during preparation might result in unserveable meals. Even appropriately prepared meals could be sent back by customers with particular tastes, or who had simply changed their mind. Staff feeding could amount to more than the specified allowances if left unmonitored. The final source of margin deficits was over-portioning. It could arise from the pace of action in a busy kitchen or the chefs' reluctance to serve "skimpy" portions. Over-portioning was also perceived to be a deliberate policy of some waitresses who connected an extra large desert with a large gratuity.

Adherence to food preparation standards was certainly a significant part of food margin management, however it was intricately tied up with other issues, such as managing guest experiences and expectations and staff expectations. Restaurant managers routinely considered the issue of margin deficits alongside wider issues of restaurant operation, such as staff and customer relations. For example, they clearly felt that theft was a problem. To a certain extent it was seen as an unavoidable aspect of running their kind of operation. Where wages were felt to be below a "living wage" a limited amount of theft was even seen as acceptable. In terms of customer relations, one manager consistently ran a food deficit that he justified in terms of the need to maintain customer expectations coupled with the level of activity of his kitchen that made a food deficit necessary for the success of his business.

The technical set-up of the food margin calculation implicitly supported restaurant managers who worked the system in those ways. Built into the system were allowances that affected a restaurant's food margin percentage but that were not connected to the efficient use of raw materials for the dishes. They included allowances for wastage, overestimates of standard food consumption, and unmonitored standard allowances for staff feeding. Another possibility for managers to manage the reporting system was the temporary mis-reporting of closing inventory.

Analysis and conclusions

As the operations director put it, customers resented being processed by the standard chain organization, they demanded to be treated as individuals. "Restaurant chain" conjures up too simplistic an image of the service process. The standard menu served only as a basis that restaurant managers had to build on to deliver a service tailored to customer expectations. This involved blending of the production and assembly functions in the kitchen with the service function at the tables. In addition to servicing individual tables, restaurant management also had to keep an eye on the atmosphere in the restaurant as a whole in order to provide an enjoyable eating-out experience.

The complexity and interdependence of factors that impacted on restaurant performance in the case company meant that specific metrics could not be tightly coupled to simple prescriptions for management action. Standard sets of metrics read in diverse local operational contexts characterized the performance measurement practice of this full-service restaurant chain. The operational managers for an area of ten to 14 restaurants had to adjust their judgment of the same standard set of performance measurements to the local context of every restaurant they visited.

Even looking at a much simpler measure than food margin, for instance, sales growth, we can see the benefits of loose coupling. In the case company, a restaurant's sales growth became the basis of detailed discussions, taking into account the wider context that influenced not just the individual restaurant's levels of activity but also the implications for operational capacity. They

		Looseness of the metric-operational response link	
		LOW	HIGH
Product customization	LOW	1. Programmed standartization "Restaurant managers become glove puppets"	2. Individual standardization "The problem with FOOD GP is just poor administration"
	HIGH	3. Programmed customization "We want to move towards intelligent waitresses"	4. Individual customization "Restaurant managers were king"

Figure 15.3.   Different managers categorized the case company differently.

would include the latest promotional activities and changes to the central logistics operations, the experience and capabilities of the waiting and kitchen staff, and local competition and demographics. As a result, the specific signal of stagnant sales growth could give rise to a variety of responses, concentrating for example on desert and starter penetration, local marketing, implementing service quality improvements, reducing guest experience time, starting a new training program for staff.

Our analysis, based on extensive observation of restaurant operation and discussion with restaurant managers suggested that the company's high level of financial performance was at least partly due to the flexibility that the loose coupling within existing performance measurement systems allowed restaurant managers. Whilst reinforcing the necessity to work within the predetermined chain–organization format, the performance measurement systems were used by restaurant managers to structure but not determine their responses to emerging contingencies and local operational considerations, such as staffing level (and capabilities). Restaurant managers were well aware of the drivers of performance within their businesses, but conceived of the various metrics as contributing to performance by setting out a framework within which managers could determine appropriate tradeoffs in the light of emerging contingencies.

Restaurant managers' flexibility to engage in tradeoffs was constrained by the chain format of the organization. This was borne out in various concerns and comments on the present state of the company and its future. Most managers saw the case company located somewhere between boxes 2 and 4 (figure 15.3). Pessimistic commentators saw the loosely coupled performance measurement system as a shortcoming. Optimists celebrated the restaurant managers' possibilities for entrepreneurial activity to deliver the challenging targets set by head office. Some restaurant managers recalled how in the early years "restaurant managers were king," before head office began to put more emphasis on developing, policing, and exploiting the brand concept.

Boxes 1 and 3 were referred to in discussion of the possible future of the organization. Box 1 was the restaurant managers' dystopian vision of a tight central control regime with no local discretion. Box 3 was various head office managers' dream of customized restaurant management based on centrally predetermined rules of service. For example, one rule of the brand concept stipulated that some minutes after serving, waiting staff had to ask customers if they enjoyed their meal. For many customers this enhanced the perception of service, but some customers who were deeply engaged in conversation resented the interruption. One training scheme was designed to teach waiting staff to distinguish when the question was appropriate.

The puzzle remains why managers in the case organization kept talking about solving their performance measurement system issues over all those years, apparently without getting closer to a solution. One obvious suggestion would be head office's inability to make their views felt amongst the restaurants. However, head office management did not have a reputation for weakness in dealing with restaurants. Our analysis would suggest two different points: One, the nature of the product made tight coupling rather difficult to achieve without significant investment in systems of rules and training. In a fast changing environment such investments might quickly become obsolete.[1] The second point is that by treating performance information as equivocal rather than concrete, the output of performance measurement systems triggered beneficial discussions and explorations of restaurant operation. We observed those in discussions between restaurant managers and head office staff and in training sessions.

The lesson of our case company for those interested in performance measurement systems is that, under conditions that favor local customization of product delivery, loose coupling in performance measurement may play an important role. For one thing, it can help bring about beneficial discussion of organizational priorities and how to manage operational inputs to achieve them. It also avoids wasting investment in formal decision rules when fast-moving environments create the risk that they might become obsolete, ossifying the organization's understanding of its situation. Given the pace of change

---

[1] Some recent support for the hypothesis that system "perfection" might be the exception rather than the norm in organizations that need to respond to demand variation in detail comes from Gosselin (1997). In his study of the adoption of activity-based costing he found that formal activitybased costing systems were mainly adopted by bureaucracies. Organizations that inhabited less-certain environments and that adopted prospector type strategies did not implement formal ABC systems, but halted the ABC adoption process at the stage of activity costs analysis.

of many business environments, box 3 must be a costly and difficult niche to occupy, and box 1 is not suitable for many organizations. Therefore box 4 would seem to cover the problems faced by a wide range of organizations. The issue of loose coupling in performance measurement has been largely ignored by the extant literature and merits much more detailed investigation.

REFERENCES

Bradach, J.L (1997). Using the plural form in the management of restaurant chains. *Administrative Science Quarterly*, **41**(1), 90–115.

Chapman, C. (1997). Reflections on a contingent view of accounting. *Accounting, Organizations and Society*, **22**(2), 189–205.

Chapman, C. and Gandy, T. (1997). Datawarehousing – unleashing the power of customer information. *Chartered Banker*, **3**(5), 10–42.

Drucker, P. (1995). The information executives truly need. *Harvard Business Review*, January–February, 54–62.

Eccles, R. (1991). The performance measurement manifesto. *Harvard Business Review*, January–February, 131–9.

Fisher, J.G. (1998). Contingency theory, management control systems, and firm outcomes: Past, present and future directions. *Behavioral Research in Accounting*, **10** (supplement), 44–64.

Gosselin, M. (1997). The effect of strategy and organizational structure on the adoption and implementation of activity based costing. *Accounting, Organizations and Society*, **22**(2), 105–22.

Hedberg, B. and Jönnson, S. (1978). Designing semi-confusing information systems for organizations in changing environments. *Accounting, Organizations and Society*, **3**(1), 47–64.

Kaplan, R. and Norton, D. (1992). The balanced scorecard – measures that drive performance. *Harvard Business Review*, January–February, 71–9.

Kaplan, R. and Norton, D. (1996a). Using the balanced scorecard as a strategic management system. *Harvard Business Review*, January–February, 75–85.

Kaplan, R.S. and Norton, D.P. (1996b). *The Balanced Scorecard: Translating Strategy into Action*. Boston, MA: Harvard Business School Press.

Ittner, C. and Kogut, B. (1995). How control systems can support organisational flexibility. In *Redesigning the Firm*, ed E. H. Bowman and B. Kogut. Oxford: Oxford University Press.

Langfield-Smith, K. (1997). Management control systems and strategy: A critical review. *Accounting, Organizations and Society*, **22**(2), 207–32.

Leidner, R. (1993). *Fast food, Fast Talk: Service Work and the Routinization of Everyday Life*. Berkeley, CA: University of California Press.

Love, J.F. (1987). *McDonalds – Behind the Arches*. London: Transworld.

MacArthur (1996). Performance measures that count: Monitoring variables of strategic importance. *Journal of Cost Management*, **10**(3), 39–45.

Meyer, C. (1994). How the right measures help teams excel. *Harvard Business Review*, May–June, 95–104.

Reiler, E. (1991). *Making Food Fast, from the Frying Pan into the Fryer*. Montréal: McGill–Queen's University Press.

Simons, R. (1994). How new top managers use control systems as levers of strategic renewal. *Strategic Management Journal*, 5(3), 169–90.

Wyckoff, D.D. and Sasser, W.E. (1978). *The Chain Restaurant Industry*. Lexington, MA: Lexington Books.

16   Redefining government performance

Ken Ogata and Rich Goodkey

Background

In 1993, the Province of Alberta initiated the development of a comprehensive business planning and performance measurement system, which is now considered a leader in Canada. This contribution examines theoretical models and practical experience for designing performance measurement systems, and compares the similarities and differences between Alberta's approach and three other prominent North American public sector models (Oregon, Minnesota, and Florida). Drawing upon the experiences of Alberta and these other jurisdictions, the contribution discusses the implications for the development and advancement of results-based public sector performance measurement.

Introduction

Performance measurement and quality management principles (e.g., re-engineering) came into vogue with North American governments following the release of *Reinventing Government* (Osborne and Gaebler, 1992). *Reinventing Government* provided a critical catalyst for mainstream experimentation by redefining the way government can and should operate. A central tenet of the book was the notion of results-oriented government, where the focus shifts to the outcomes of government policy actions, rather than the budget or programs delivered. *Reinventing Government*, combined with the United States Federal Government Performance and Results Act of 1993 motivated many jurisdictions to develop similar systems.

Among US state governments, some of the older, more prominent systems are: *Oregon Benchmarks, Minnesota Milestones, Florida Benchmarks, Texas Tomorrow,* and *Utah Tomorrow*. Performance measurement is gaining momentum in Canada. Alberta's system is the oldest, followed by Nova Scotia,

New Brunswick, and the Canadian federal government. Initiatives intended to measure quality of life such as the US Genuine Progress Indicator (Redefining Progress, 1998), and Human Resources Development Canada's Index of Social Health (Brink and Zeesman, 1997), are also attracting public interest.

As with many public sector reform initiatives, most jurisdictions embarking on performance measurement have learned from the experience of their predecessors. Although they may adopt elements of existing systems, situation-specific environmental, systemic, and cultural factors prevent mere duplication. Building from the experience of others is akin to benchmarking, where the fundamental tenets and underlying assumptions of existing systems must be examined prior to adapting elements to function within a different jurisdiction.

This contribution describes Alberta's experience implementing performance measurement, compared to that of Oregon, Minnesota, and Florida. By comparing these various jurisdictions' implementation experiences, this contribution will seek to identify critical success factors, variances between theory and practice, and implications for practitioners.

Methodology

In preparing this contribution, a literature review was conducted on the design of performance measurement systems and public sector reform. Based upon this review, a framework of key determinants of success for performance measurement was developed, incorporating both elements of theory and best practice. Practitioners in Oregon, Minnesota, and Florida were interviewed, and their publications and reports reviewed. Alberta's approach was compared to these three states using this framework to identify similarities and differences between the systems, and analyzed as to their potential implications for system design.

The *Balanced Scorecard* (Kaplan and Norton, 1992) represents the private sector equivalent of *Reinventing Government*. Notwithstanding its private sector popularity, the *Scorecard* was not used as a basis for comparison. Although public sector measurement suffers from a similar overweighting of financial measures, the scope of the *Scorecard* does not capture the greater diversity of public sector stakeholders. Moreover, the *Scorecard* focuses on factors considered within the organization's ability to control, whereas public policy addresses societal situations where the government frequently can only influence outcomes.

Theory and best practices

Early performance measurement systems were usually an extension of the organization's accounting system, and thus designed to function as cost control mechanisms. While cost information was vital for efficient program management, it was inadequate to meet the demands of a results-driven management structure. The cost emphasis of accounting-based performance measurement systems focused government attention on budget utilization, level of activity, and the cost efficiency of programs. This often resulted in organizations punishing managers for poor financial performance, irrespective of program effectiveness. This negative reinforcement climate rewarded managers that focused on short-term cost efficiency, sometimes to the detriment of longer-term policy outcomes.

Another set of performance indicators in widespread usage are economic indicators such as gross domestic product and the consumer price index. Economic indicators have traditionally been used to assess the economic "state of the union," particularly by governments. Strong economic growth, low inflation, and low unemployment are believed to be indicative of a healthy economic climate, and are expected to enhance the overall prosperity of the local citizenry. Although economic indicators are more effective than accounting measures in measuring the outcomes of government policy, economic prosperity does not necessarily translate into a higher quality of life. Economic and financial indicators can only provide a limited perspective of the overall well-being of society.

Current efforts to measure government performance attempt to assess the overall quality of life of society. These societal indicators typically focus on changes in the human condition and therefore are much less financially based. Difficulty quantifying aspects of societal health (e.g., equity, equality, safety) has restricted the use of such qualitative indicators in favor of more quantitative-based information. Results-oriented government has elevated the importance of qualitative societal indicators; however, measurement is complicated by the constantly evolving and frequently competing theories and philosophies of how best to achieve desired outcomes.

To provide a framework for comparing the four jurisdictions' performance measurement systems, we have constructed a list of key system design factors based upon a variety of sources (table 16.1). This list was synthesized from principles advocated by academics and practitioners (Osborne and Gaebler, 1992; Hatry, 1994; Kravchuk and Schack, 1996; Campbell and Fountain,

Table 16.1 System design elements

Dimension	Factor	Design elements
Environment	Political climate (public)	Public willingness to accept change (crisis climate). Public/stakeholder demands for increased accountability.
	Leadership	Top level support including "political" champion for the process.
Framework (system architecture)	Vision	System designed to provide information: to improve program performance. to improve planning and decision making. to improve accountability.
	Strategic planning	Define mission, goals and strategies. Measurement is part of larger managing for results process. Define logic chain of how strategies will influence outcomes and thereby achieve goals.
	Responsibility and accountability	Identify parties responsible for specific outcomes. "Contract" with delivery agents for the achievement of results. Organizational buy-in by program staff and managers.
Culture	Client centered service delivery	Consult with clients/public/stakeholders. Desired outcomes are consistent with client needs. Report on performance in user-friendly terms.
	High performing organization	Focus is on learning and results, not punishment. Information used to facilitate planning and resource allocation. Information supports decision making process. Need to have data analyzed/interpreted to identify required action.

1998), and findings from studies of best practices (OECD, 1997; National Performance Review, 1997; Epstein and Olsen, 1997).

Based upon these sources, performance measurement systems should be designed taking several key factors into consideration. The environment for change is critical to success. Top-level leadership is essential, while stakeholder support for change will facilitate the process. The actual structural design of the system will be based upon what type of information is desired, the context for measurement activities (as part of an overall strategic plan or stand alone initiative), and the accountability framework associated with measurement (who is responsible for each measure). The way in which performance information is utilized will depend upon the corporate culture. Client-focused organizations will involve stakeholders in the design of their systems, and tailor their measures to meet their clients' information needs. Learning organizations will use the information to manage their programs better, while others may try to manage the information to avoid negative stakeholder reaction.

Why results-based performance measurement?

In the past, government spending on programs was deemed to be sufficient evidence of results. Drucker (1989) notes that among non-profit organizations there is a temptation to equate good intentions or efforts with results. Emphasizing results requires a well-defined mission that focuses the organization on actions critical to achieving its goals, and defines success in terms of changes outside the organization. Similarly, governments need to re-examine why they are delivering certain programs and what outcomes they hope to achieve, including how their programs and strategies will be effective in producing results.

Osborne and Gaebler believe that by engaging in results-based performance measurement, governments will stop rewarding failure and focus on strategies that are successful in producing the desired results. The following key concepts from *Reinventing Government* capture the essence of their position:

1   If you don't measure results, you can't tell success from failure.
2   If you can't see success, you can't reward it.
3   If you can't reward success, you're probably rewarding failure.

However, determining the impact of public policy and programs is complicated by several factors. Inherent in outcome-based measurement is the lack of mathematical precision common to accounting and economic systems, and the associated foundational cause and effect logic models. Isolating the effect of government programs and policies from supporting and competing environmental forces, and quantitatively estimating their impact remains more art than science. Moreover, many programs have associated foundational supporting theories that represent an enormous challenge for translating outcome performance results into publicly accessible terms.

Outcome-based performance measurement also seeks to shift the discussion from program efficiency to program effectiveness. As noted by Osborne and Gaebler, "a perfectly executed process is a waste of time and money if it fails to achieve the outcomes desired." But what outcomes do government and citizens want? *Oregon Shines II* (Oregon Progress Board, 1997a), suggests that increasing economic prosperity shifts citizen concerns from more jobs, to better jobs, to better lives (see figure 16.1). Therefore, as citizens' economic status improves, their concerns about societal quality of life factors, such as

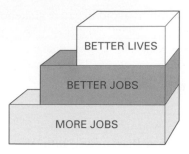

Figure 16.1.   Citizen aspirations rise as the economy improves
Source: Oregon Shines II – Oregon Progress Board (1997a).

the quality of education and health care and safety from crime, become more pronounced. This model of increasing societal aspirations conforms with Maslow's Hierarchy of Needs theory (1954), and Alderfer's ERG theory (1972). As lower-level basic/existence needs are satisfied (more jobs), people's attention shifts to higher-level safety and security concerns (better jobs) and relatedness/growth needs (better lives). Citizen concerns may not progress smoothly up the hierarchy as the intensity of citizen concerns at each level will often depend upon the overall state of the economy. The Alberta, Oregon, Minnesota, and Florida initiatives represent attempts to institute a new form of measurement based on societal outcomes.

The Alberta experience

In 1992, Alberta's future seemed dim. The 1992–3 provincial government deficit was $3.4 billion (budget of $16.8 billion), and economic growth was sluggish. Contributing to this overall malaise were several multi-million dollar losses on government-backed economic development ventures, eight straight years of budgetary deficits, and a weak oil and gas industry, a key driver of Alberta's economy. The province's poor fiscal and economic situation and growing public distrust of government provided a favorable "crisis" climate for change. The new government, led by Premier Ralph Klein and Provincial Treasurer Jim Dinning, seized upon this negative outlook and instituted sweeping reforms including: three-year business plans, a 20 percent reduction in government spending, privatization and downsizing of government services, transferring service delivery to publicly accountable community-based agencies, enhanced public accountability, and outcome-based performance measurement. Two major influences for these changes were *Reinventing*

Government and the New Zealand experience (Douglas, 1993). Performance measurement was instituted as part of the larger business planning process, with the intention of making government more open and accountable. By 1996–7, these reforms appeared to be bearing fruit. The Alberta government enjoyed a budget surplus of $2.5 billion (budget of $14.5 billion), aided in part by robust economic growth of 6.6 percent in 1996.

The 1993 Budget launched the process of three-year business planning for the government and each ministry. Business planning and performance measurement were coordinated by the Treasury department as part of the regular budget review process, which provided the necessary authority to "reinforce" ministry cooperation. However, these initiatives were not centrally controlled processes; only centrally coordinated. Ministries were allowed to draft their plans in accordance with broad overall guidelines to facilitate and encourage ownership over their plans and measures. Balanced budget and government accountability legislation were enacted in 1995; however, legislation served to reinforce political commitment rather than effect change.

In 1994, development began on a government-wide performance measurement system to monitor progress toward the goals stated in government and ministry business plans. In June 1995, the first annual *Measuring Up* report (Government of Alberta, 1995) was released containing 22 core government measures under 18 goals. *Measuring Up* contained a mix of economic, accounting, and societal indicators, intended to provide a snapshot of overall government performance.

Alberta's public accountability focus has shaped the content, presentation, and weighting of measures. *Measuring Up* was intended to be a user-friendly document, distilling complex policy issues into plain language. Graphical presentation of data was employed wherever possible, with additional explanatory and supplemental information to facilitate reader comprehension and interpretation of the results. In addition to economic indicators, *Measuring Up* featured numerous societal indicators for policy areas deemed to be within the government's sphere of responsibility. Measures of population health, crime rates, and air, water, and land quality reflect this emphasis on public accountability.

Alberta follows the parliamentary system of government, and the governing party held a majority position, thus there was less need to build broad political support. The concept of ministerial accountability under the parliamentary system also facilitated the definition and reinforcement of accountability relationships. Accountability relationships were extended from Cabinet through Ministers to community-based delivery agents, such as school boards and regional health authorities. Although some specific details

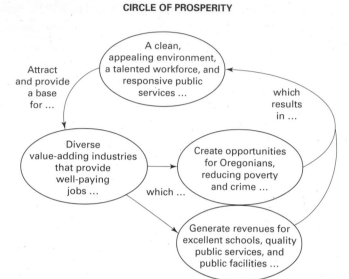

CIRCLE OF PROSPERITY

Figure 16.2.   Oregon circle of prosperity.

of accountability are still being defined, public expectations/notions of responsibility have served to frame the limits of each party's accountability and prescribe "ownership" over certain core measures.

Overview of Oregon, Minnesota, and Florida

In 1989, following several years of depressed economic performance, Governor Neil Goldschmidt unveiled *Oregon Shines* (Oregon Department of Economic Development, 1989), an economic development strategy intended to guide the shift from the state's traditional resource-based economy to a new information-based economy. *Oregon Shines* addressed not only economic diversification, but also the enhancement of citizens' quality of life through a circle of prosperity (see figure 16.2). The circle envisaged a diversified economy that created opportunities for Oregon citizens while protecting the environment and supporting quality public services, thereby attracting new businesses, leading to further economic growth.

Oregon Benchmarks (Oregon Progress Board, 1994) was developed to monitor the state's progress towards the goals identified in *Oregon Shines*. The 1990 *Oregon Benchmarks* contained 160 measures, which grew to 259 measures in 1994. Both the *Oregon Benchmarks* and *Oregon Shines* have been administered by the Oregon Progress Board, an independent agency created by the Legislature in 1989. The Progress Board and its mandate have survived two changes in leadership. Current Governor John Kitzhaber prompted the development of *Oregon Shines II* (Oregon Progress Board, 1997a), which significantly reduced the number of *Benchmarks* to 92 and focused attention on priority areas.

The weighting of measures in *Oregon Benchmarks* strongly reflects its roots in the *Oregon Shines* economic development strategy. Indicators of economic growth, balanced by protecting the environment, top the 1997 *Oregon Benchmarks* list, followed closely by knowledge/education measures, reflecting the importance of a highly skilled workforce, particularly in light of Oregon's desire to attract high technology industries.

Although the *Benchmarks* have been in existence since 1990, they have had minimal impact upon the state's budgeting/planning process until recently. *Oregon Shines II* acknowledged that the *Benchmarks* need to be part of a larger strategy for achieving results. To facilitate efforts to integrate *Benchmark* information into the planning process, a bluebook was published (Oregon Progress Board, 1997b), linking agencies to specific *Benchmarks*. Legislator interest in the *Benchmarks* as a planning tool has also increased, perhaps inspired in part by the reaffirmation of *Oregon Shines*.

Minnesota Milestones (Minnesota Planning, 1992) was initiated in 1991 at the direction of Governor Arne Carlson. The Governor was inspired by the *Oregon Benchmarks,* and charged Minnesota Planning, the state's strategic planning agency, with the task of developing a similar report. Minnesota started with an economic-based agenda similar to Oregon, but without a "crisis" climate. Although Minnesota had a significant budget deficit, the state's economy was reasonably healthy. *Minnesota Milestones* was intended to provide information to improve planning and decision making, as well as enhance public accountability.

Minnesota Milestones was first published in 1992, and contained 79 indicators under 20 goals to measure progress. Minnesota Planning recently reduced its list to 70 measures under 20 goals (Minnesota Planning, 1998). Given the economic development strategy roots of the *Milestones,* the lack of global economic measures was curious (the number was increased in the 1998 *Milestones).* Instead, the previous *Milestones* appeared to focus on personal income as an indicator of the effect of economic growth upon citizens. Two notable changes in the *1998 Milestones* were the deletion of specific targets for each *Milestone,* and the absence of recommendations on how to improve performance.

Minnesota legislators and state auditors have actually had significant exposure to performance information. Each agency was required to prepare a performance report for legislative committee review in 1994. However, the quality of information varied significantly, and many legislators found the process of limited value (Jackson, 1996). Although strongly endorsed at the time, interest has since waned. It is uncertain whether the *Milestones* will become an integral part of the state's planning process.

Florida Benchmarks (Florida Commission on Government Accountability to the People, 1998) was initiated in 1993 by Governor Lawton Chiles. The 1998 *Florida Benchmarks* contained 270 measures. A set of 57 critical benchmarks has also been identified (Florida Commission on Government Accountability to the People, 1997). The *Benchmarks* was developed as a report card on the "state of the state" to respond to low public trust in government. Like Minnesota, there was not a strong "crisis" situation driving the process. However, strong top-level political leadership was present, evidenced by the Governor creating the Florida Commission on Government Accountability to the People (GAP) through an executive order. Although motivated by a "crisis" of confidence in government institutions, the *Benchmarks* also reflect other priority issues for Florida citizens, such as the high level of crime (highest in the United States in 1994).

Florida's GAP Commission provides an interesting illustration of the effect of losing a political champion. With the Governor completing his final term, a legislative committee initially voted to eliminate the Commission's funding, but subsequently reinstated sufficient funding to maintain the Commission and preserve the database of information collected. Thus, it appears that Florida legislators have recognized the value of societal indicator information, but may be unsure how best to apply this knowledge. Florida officials have endeavoured to assist legislators in interpreting performance information, but further experience may be necessary before legislators are able to use performance information effectively.

Although *Florida Benchmarks* was created in response to low public trust in government, citizen interest has been limited. Within government though, performance measurement has garnered sufficient support that efforts are being made to implement a performance-based budgeting system for agencies. This would represent a significant achievement if performance information is used to facilitate and support the decision-making process.

Comparison of approaches

The Alberta, Oregon, Minnesota, and Florida systems were selected for comparison because of their innovative focus on ascertaining the societal impacts of public policy. All four systems are societal-outcome based, designed to monitor changes in citizens' quality of life. Other jurisdictions like Texas have designed their systems to monitor outputs, and thus are more operations focused (Southern Growth Policies Board, 1994). Given that Alberta, Minnesota, and Florida have modeled their systems in part on Oregon's outcome-based approach, we would expect them to exhibit similarities. However, regional priorities, differences in approach, and citizen demographics should still yield distinct systems. Identifying these similarities and differences may yield insights into potential best practices for outcome-based systems. Table 16.2 provides an overview comparison of the four jurisdictions' systems.

All four systems have a long-term perspective, measuring progress towards targets five to 30 years in the future. Annual fluctuations are less important than longer-term progress towards the stated targets. Adopting this perspective allows managers the opportunity to design and implement strategies that may take several years to generate results. Within this sort of culture, governments can focus on doing the right things, and doing them well, rather than reacting to the crisis of the moment. However, results are mixed on whether programs managers are adjusting to this longer time horizon.

All four systems were driven by top-level political leadership and supported by legislation. As with most change initiatives, a "political" champion, typically in a senior position of influence, is required to guide, advocate, and hold others accountable for change. Once formalized, the necessity of a champion or supporting legislation may decrease, but the absence of continued top-level support will reduce the effectiveness of the process and limit the rate of change. For example, Oregon has gone through two changes in leaderships during the lifetime of the *Benchmarks*, and has experienced a resurgence in the profile of the *Benchmarks* following the most recent change.

All of the jurisdictions engaged in a public consultation process during the development of their measures. While the nature of the consultation process differed with varying degrees of public participation, each jurisdiction deemed this an important step for selecting their measures. Curiously, although the importance of public engagement has been stressed, general public interest in these measurement initiatives has grown slowly. Given the limited media attention attracted by the release of these reports, continued public "education" about the role of performance information may be necessary to validate the process.

Each system was designed to address both public accountability and collect information for planning and decision making, although not with the same

Table 16.2 Comparison of systems

Factor	Alberta	Oregon	Minnesota	Florida
Technical				
Name of system	Measuring Up	Oregon Benchmarks	Minnesota Milestones	Florida Benchmarks
Number of goals	17	22	20	n/a
Number of measures	27	92	70	270 (57 critical)
Key target dates	2000/other	2000/2010	2020	2000/2010
Legislation	Yes	Yes	Yes	Yes
Environmental				
Separate board coordinating	No	Oregon Progress Board	No	Commission on Government Accountability to the People
Political climate (public)	Fiscal crisis, change in leadership and lack of public trust	Changing economy, change in leadership	Budget deficit and change in leadership	Change in leadership and lack of public trust
Leadership	Provincial Treasurer	Governor	Governor	Governor
Framework				
Vision – Primary information purpose	Government accountability	Improve planning and decision making	Improve planning and decision making	Government accountability
Overall strategic plan	Government Business Plan	Oregon Shines II	No	No
Accountability	Part of planning process	Part of planning process	Informal process	Part of planning process
Development process	By program officials and vetted by Treasury Board	By citizens and process participants	By citizens and process participants	By citizens, process participants and measurement experts
Culture				
Stakeholder consultation	Mail survey, consultation with stakeholders	Town hall meetings with business and community leaders	15 town hall meetings, over 1600 participants	Mail survey of 2000 citizens
Results publicly released	Yes	Yes	Yes	Yes
Information used in planning	Limited	Limited	No	Limited

Table 16.3 Number of measures by policy area

1998 Alberta Measuring up	#	1997 Oregon Benchmarks	#	1998 Minnesota Milestones	#	1998 Florida Benchmarks	#
Economy/Business	6	<u>Economy/Business</u>	14	**Protecting Environment**	14	Health/Wellness	11
<u>Government</u>	4	Protecting Environment	13	Health/Wellness	10	Protecting Environment	9
Protecting Environment	4	Knowledge/ Education	12	Income/Housing	9	Knowledge/ Education	8
Knowledge/ Education	3	Income/Housing	10	<u>Community Values</u>	9	Income/Housing	6
Crime/Public Safety	2	**Health/Wellness**	8	Families/Social Health	7	<u>Crime/Public Safety</u>	5
Health/Wellness	2	Infrastructure	8	**Knowledge/ Education**	6	Families/Social Health	5
Infrastructure	2	Families/Social Health	7	Economy/Business	6	Government	5
Community Values	1	Community Values	6	Government	3	Community Values	4
Families/Social Health	1	Crime/Public Safety	6	Crime/Public Safety	2	Economy/Business	2
Income/Housing	1	Government	5	Recreation/Culture	2	Infrastructure	2
Recreation/Culture	1	Recreation/Culture	3	Infrastructure	2	Recreation/Culture	0
Total	27		92		70		57

degree of emphasis. For example, the Alberta and Florida systems placed greater importance on accountability, partly in response to low public trust in government within their respective jurisdictions,. Oregon focused on the planning function, while Minnesota has attempted to use the information for decision making. Although the systems have enhanced accountability, limited success has been experienced using results information for future planning and decision making.

Perhaps most interesting is the coincident similarity and dissimilarity in the relative weighting of measures by policy area. Table 16.3 summarizes the weighting of measures by policy area for each jurisdiction. Although each system operates within unique environmental contexts, there is general "concurrence" on the top policy areas: protecting the environment, knowledge/education, and health/wellness (see bold entries). Although relative weighting is not necessarily indicative of the importance of these areas to each jurisdiction, and may be a function of their complexity, the similarity is striking. Given the differences in geography (north–south, east–west), economy, demographics, and history, we might expect less consistency.

Each system also exhibits its citizens' unique priorities (*see underlined entries in Table 16.3*). For example, Florida's list reflects its difficulties with crime and public safety, while community values are prominent in Minnesota. Alberta's list highlights government performance (government accountability/fiscal difficulties), while Oregon's list reveals its roots in *Oregon Shines* (state economic development strategy).

Perhaps the key difference between Alberta's approach and the others is the number of measures. Alberta reports on 27 macro-level measures (Government of Alberta, 1998), while Florida reports on 270 benchmarks and 57 critical benchmarks. Oregon has significantly reduced the number of benchmarks, while Minnesota has made a slight reduction. Part of the difference may be attributable to the hierarchical structure of Alberta's system. The 27 core measures are the focus of the system, but over 125 key ministry measures and other supporting information are utilized to provide an overall picture of performance. This difference may not be as pronounced in the future as the other jurisdictions are limiting the number of primary measures and encouraging agencies and community organizations to develop complementary measures. This should result in further convergence of systems.

Each jurisdiction experienced a different level of political urgency to undertake performance measurement, not only at the beginning, but over time as well. Alberta's experience suggests that the greatest advances in development occur under strong leadership within a crisis climate, although Oregon's experience suggests that a certain degree of maturity can also facilitate substantial change.

Other key differences include the purpose for which information is collected, and the existence of a global strategic planning framework. Public accountability is pre-eminent in two jurisdictions, though stated as important by all. Each jurisdiction also states that it collects information to support planning and decision making. Although all hope their system can support three functions, one function typically gains prominence. Regardless of primary system function capability, performance measurement will be an ineffective tool for planning in the absence of a global strategic planning framework. Currently, only Alberta and Oregon have such a framework.

Whither performance measurement?

A critical impediment to utilizing performance information for planning and decision making is the significant learning curve associated with outcome-based measurement. The steepness of the learning curve may be as much a function of the need to view the world through a different mental model, as the newness of the information. As we begin to analyze the results, the information often yields more questions than answers, thus generating even further investigation and analysis. Sometimes this information challenges conventional wisdom or indicates that alternative strategies are necessary. Results information which challenges conventional wisdom will likely be rejected unless information recipients are confident in the accuracy of the data and open to the possibility of change.

A further complication is the lack of a global strategic planning framework to provide a context for analyzing the performance results. Campbell and Fountain (1998) and Epstein and Olsen (1996) note that performance measures are not an end in and of themselves, but need to be part of a larger system of managing for results. By defining the overall strategic context, the implications of various strategies and their resulting effects can be assessed, which should indicate the options most likely to enhance program performance.

Jurisdictions that do not have an associated global strategic planning framework also often lack a formal accountability framework. Lead or responsible agencies have generally not been identified, except those that have volunteered. Unless agencies accept responsibility for specific outcomes, they are unlikely to work towards broader government goals without additional incentives. For example, Alberta operates under the parliamentary system, where the concept of ministerial accountability is foundational, and ministries usually cannot shirk their responsibility for specific social issues. Oregon and Florida have made progress in defining agency accountability requirements, which should advance the application of performance data for management planning.

An unresolved issue is whether systems emphasizing accountability need supplemental or supporting measures/systems to support the planning or decision-making function. Primary system focus appears to be symptomatic of inherent design parameter tradeoffs. A single system seems to be inadequate to support multiple functions simultaneously. Just as an operations management focus requires a different type of performance information, each of the main system functions will favor particular types of performance measures. If planning and decision-making processes encompass resource allocation decisions, they will likely require a blend of high-level information and program-specific performance information. In these situations, jurisdictions will likely require an expanded measurement system, or the development of parallel complementary measurement systems.

Conclusions

Based upon Alberta's and other jurisdictions' experiences, several performance measurement system design principles seemed to be substantiated.

Political leadership is critical. Each jurisdiction's process was championed by top-level political leadership. Changes in leadership may sustain, detract, or reinvigorate measurement initiatives. Leadership may also serve to prevent performance measurement from becoming another management reform that fails to realize its initial promise. However, longer-term success will depend upon management buy-in. Unless the value of performance information as a practical tool for enhancing programs is accepted by managers and even front-line staff, performance measurement may simply remain a reporting exercise.

Citizen feedback and participation is important. Each jurisdiction conducted public consultations prior to implementation. Sensitivity to local priorities is reflected by the different weighting of measures, even though these systems exhibit a fair degree of convergence for key policy areas. However, public demand for performance information may take time and effort to generate given the associated learning curve. Perhaps the crucial lesson learned to date is how much we still do not know about the complexity of achieving desired societal outcomes (Campbell and Fountain, 1998). Rather than being able to provide the public with answers, we may only be able to provide explanations for what went wrong. The challenge may then become explaining the limits of public policy and/or human knowledge.

An excessive number of measures, lack of legislation, or coordination by a separate board do not appear to restrict system implementation or effectiveness. Even the lack of a global strategic plan does not appear to impede implementation; however, lack of a strategic plan or an integrating/coordinating mechanism will limit overall system effectiveness. Although use of performance measurement as a public accountability vehicle may not be negatively affected, system applicability to planning and decision making will be impaired.

The most serious challenge to effective outcome-based performance measurement for use as a planning, resource allocation, and decision-making tool is the presence of a global strategic plan. Unless jurisdictions have sufficient vision, either collectively or through leadership that clearly specifies the desired societal outcomes, it will be difficult to mobilize concerted government effort in pursuit of enhanced societal well-being. Similarly, agencies within government responsible for achieving outcomes either need to be identified or accept their role, and strategies to be employed in pursuit of those goals developed.

Ultimately, however, the true benefits of performance measurement may be of a less tangible nature. In the case of Alberta, they were part of the catalyst for fundamental reform of the basic operating structure of government. As such, business planning and performance measurement may have symbolized the resulting management cultural change process. In Florida, they were the physical manifestation of an attempt to restore public faith in government. In Oregon, they were a focal point for mobilizing cooperation from broader society, recognizing that government alone could not effect the changes necessary to achieve the desired future espoused in *Oregon Shines*. Overall, they may represent the initial efforts of government changing its vocabulary to become more conversant with the public it is intended to serve. Governments can now discuss the effects of policies and programs in terms of their effect on the lives of citizens using the vocabulary of the people. If this is in fact true, performance measurement may have already fulfilled its purpose without realizing its greater management potential.

REFERENCES

Alderfer, Clayton P. (1972). *Existence, Relatedness, and Growth*. New York: Free Press.

Brink, Satya and Zeesman, Allen (1997). Measuring Social Well-Being: An Index of Social Health for Canada.

Campbell, Wilson and Fountain, Jay (1998). Service efforts and accomplishments – lessons learned. Paper presented through the National Centre for Public Productivity On-line Conference, November.

Douglas, Roger (1993). *Unfinished Business*. Auckland, New Zealand: Random House.

Drucker, Peter F. (1989). What business can learn from nonprofits. *Harvard Business Review*, July–August 88–93.

Epstein, J. and Olsen, R.T. (1996). Lessons learned by state and local governments. *The Public Manager*, Fall, 41–4.

Epstein, J. and Olsen, R.T. (1997). Performance management: Perspectives for today's public-sector manager. *PA Times*, January, Special Supplement.

Florida Commission on Government Accountability to the People (1997). Critical Benchmarks Goals.

Florida Commission on Government Accountability to the People (1998). The Florida Benchmarks Report.

Government of Alberta (1995). Measuring Up.

Government of Alberta (1998). Measuring Up.

Hatry, H.P. (1994). Findings and recommendations: Oregon benchmarks and associated performance measurement process. Unpublished paper.

Jackson, Marilyn (1996). Case study – Lessons learned from Minnesota's Government Performance Reports. Paper presented at the American Society for Public Administration National Training Conference, 30 June, 1996.

Kaplan, R.S. and Norton, D.P. (1992). The balanced scorecard – measures that drive performance. *Harvard Business Review*, January–February, 71–9.

Kearns, Kevin P. (1996). *Managing for Accountability: Preserving the Public Trust in Public and Nonprofit Organizations*, pp. 45–69. San Francisco, CA: Jossey-Bass.

Kravchuk, R.S. and Schack, R.W. (1996). Designing effective performance measurement systems under the government performance and results act of 1993. *Public Administration Review*, **56**(4), 348–58.

Maslow, A.H. (1954). *Motivation and Personality*. New York: Harper and Row.

Minnesota Planning (1992). *Minnesota Milestones*.

Minnesota Planning (1998). *Minnesota Milestones 1998: Measures that Matter*.

National Performance Review (1997). Serving the American Public: Best Practices in Performance Measurement.

OECD (1997). In Search of Results: Performance Measurement Practices.

Oregon Department of Economic Development (1989). Oregon Shines: An Economic Strategy for the Pacific Century.

Oregon Progress Board (1994). Oregon Benchmarks: Report to the 1995 Legislature.

Oregon Progress Board (1997a). Oregon Shines II: Updating Oregon's Strategic Plan.

Oregon Progress Board (1997b). Benchmark Blue Book: Linking the Oregon Benchmarks to State Government Activities.

Osborne, D. and Gaebler, T. (1992). *Reinventing Government*. New York: Plume Books, pp. 138–65, 349–59.

Redefining Progress (1998). The 1998 US Genuine Progress Indicator (GPI).

Southern Growth Policies Board (1994). Benchmarking Pioneers.

Part V

Performance measurement – specific measures

The aim of the fifth part is to explore how to measure specific dimensions of business performance and then how to use the data that are generated. The section starts with a contribution from Kristensen, Martensen, and Grønholdt that explores the measurement of customer satisfaction. Kristensen, Martensen, and Grønholdt begin their piece by discussing the importance of customer satisfaction in both the quality and marketing movements. They continue by introducing the rationale behind and the methodology underpinning the Swedish Customer Satisfaction Barometer, which has recently been rolled out to cover 12 member states in the European Union. Then they explore how data gathered through the Customer Satisfaction Barometer can be used both to form links between customer satisfaction and financial performance, and drive improvements in individual performance. Much of the data they use to do this are drawn from an application of the Customer Satisfaction Barometer in the Danish Postal Service.

The second contribution in this part builds upon the themes raised by Kristensen, Martensen, and Grønholdt and presents work which seeks to establish the links between employee satisfaction, customer satisfaction, and financial performance in a variety of case study companies. Neely and Najjar report the results of a three year study into the ways in which organizations can and do use measurement data. They illustrate how measurement data can be used to assess the validity of business models and identify some of the barriers that prevent organizations from making the best use of their measurement data.

The final contribution in this part comes from Katila who explores how innovation performance can be measured. Katila presents the results of an in depth investigation into whether patent citation analysis provide accurate insight into the impact of particular innovations. She finds that far too often the length of time over which patent citation studies are carried out is too short and argues that the impact of many patents can only be seen some ten years after they were originally registered.

17 Customer satisfaction and business performance

Kai Kristensen, Anne Martensen, and Lars Grønholdt

Introduction

The evaluation of the value of a company is traditionally based on financial performance measures. However, this type of information indicates what the company has achieved in the past, but the real value of the company must include future perspectives. What we need is non-financial performance measures, which can tell us about what is going to happen with the financial results in the future, so the evaluation of the value of the company can be based on actual financial success and forward-looking non-financial performance measures.

Also inside the company, managers require a measurement system, which provides forward-looking information, and by it early warning, and which makes it possible to carry out the necessary adjustments to the processes before they turn into unwanted business results. This is what modern measurement of total quality is all about.

This idea is in very good accordance with the official thoughts in Europe. In a working document on "A European quality promotion policy" from the European Commission, the following is said about quality and quality management:

> The use of the new methodologies of Total Quality Management is for the leaders of the European companies a leading means to help them in the current economic scenario, which involves not only dealing with changes, but especially anticipating them.

Thus, to the European Commission quality is primarily a question of changes and of early warning.

Improved business results are particularly due to an increase in customer loyalty stemming from an increase in customer satisfaction. Moving even further back we come to product and service quality, employee satisfaction, and internal structure, which depend on the business results. All these factors are related in a closed loop, which may be called the improvement circle. In this contribution we focus on the relationship between customer satisfaction, customer loyalty, and business results.

The importance of satisfied customers is emphasized by the European Business Excellence Model, developed by the European Foundation for Quality Management (EFQM). This model underpins the European and many national quality awards and includes nine criteria on which companies are evaluated. The criterion customer satisfaction is the weightiest criterion and accounts for 20 percent of the total points in the scoring system when companies assess and measure their own excellence. This means, that understanding the customers, and measuring customers' satisfaction is an important element in companies' continuous quality improvement, which leads to improved business performance, including economic performance.

Many companies are using some form of customer satisfaction measurement, but most companies find it difficult to demonstrate the link from customer satisfaction to economic performance. The primary reason for the difficulties is the traditional customer satisfaction measures' poor reliability, predictive validity, and the lack of explicit quantitative links to the desired economic results (Fornell, Ittner, and Larcker, 1995; Ittner and Larcker, 1996).

On this background there are still some areas that will need further work, e.g., we need customer satisfaction measures that are more predictive of the economic results of the quality program.

First, the contribution reports empirical evidence on the relationship between customer satisfaction and economic performance, documented by Swedish and American studies.

Second, the methodology behind the recently introduced European Customer Satisfaction Index (ECSI) is presented. The ECSI methodology has been applied at Post Denmark, both at a generic and a specific level, and the results of this successful measuring and managing of customer satisfaction, customer loyalty and their drivers are shown.

Finally, practitioner and academic implications of this new pan-European customer satisfaction measurement instrument ECSI are discussed. ECSI has recently been renamed EPSI which stands for "European Performance Satisfaction Index". This has been done in order to open up for other performance measures like employee satisfaction and society trust.

The impact of customer satisfaction: Swedish and American evidence

In 1989, Sweden became the first nation in the world to have a uniform, cross-company, cross-industry national measurement instrument of customer satisfaction and evaluations of quality of products and services, the Swedish Customer Satisfaction Barometer (SCSB). SCSB has been adopted and adapted for use in the American Customer Satisfaction Index (ACSI). Since Israel, Taiwan, and New Zealand have started similar national indices, and there are development efforts in other countries, including Canada, Brazil, Argentine, and several European countries (see the following section).

The basic model for estimating these indices is a structural equation model, developed by Professor Claes Fornell, the National Quality Research Center (NQRC) at the University of Michigan Business School, assisted by faculty colleagues there (Fornell, 1992; Fornell *et al.*, 1996). The model links customer satisfaction to its determinants namely perceived quality, customer expectations, and perceived value, and, in turn, to its consequences, namely customer loyalty and customer complaints. These six variables are seen as latent (non-observable) variables. The latent variables are operationalized using multiple questionnaire items, and the entire system is estimated using partial least squares (PLS) regression.

Input to the model comes from data collected through telephone interviews from a national, representative sample of customers who are recent buyers and/or users of specific products and services (about 25000 interviews in SCSB, and 50000 interviews in ACSI each year). For most companies interviews are conducted with about 250 of their customers.

The methodology produces an index for customer satisfaction and an index for the other latent variables (on a 0–100-point scale) at different levels: The model estimates company-level indices for each company in the sample (about 100 companies in SCSB, and 200 companies in ACSI), and these company-level indices are weighted to calculate industry indices (quite 30 industries in SCSB and ACSI) and national indices. SCSB has been published annually, and from 1997 it is continued as the Swedish Customer Satisfaction Index. ACSI is updated quarterly on a rolling basis, with one or two of the seven measured economic sectors updated each quarter.

For further details on the underlying methodology, including the questions that are asked, see Fornell *et al.* (1996).

The model estimation algorithm weights the questionnaire items such that the resulting customer satisfaction measure has maximum correlation with loyalty (operationalized by customer repurchase intention and price tolerance, Fornell, Ittner, and Larcker, 1995; Fornell *et al.*, 1996, p. 11). Therefore, in theory, this measure of customer satisfaction should be an economic indicator.

Now the question is: Empirically do results demonstrate this link between customer satisfaction, measured by SCSB/ACSI and economic performance?

Is increase in customer satisfaction actually related to economic returns and company value? The usefulness of the SCSB/ACSI methodology at the company level depends on whether this customer satisfaction measure actually shows a positive impact on economic results.

Combining specific companies' customer satisfaction index with economic data for each company makes it possible to study the association between customer satisfaction and economic performance. Time-series data of this type for Swedish and American company have been analyzed in different ways.

Based on 77 companies, covered by SCSB, Anderson, Fornell, and Lehmann (1994) have analyzed the relationship between customer satisfaction and return on investments (ROI) (that is, return on assets located in Sweden). Regression analysis indicates that, after controlling for past ROI and time-series trends, ROI is positively affected by customer satisfaction: the short-run elasticity between ROI and customer satisfaction is 0.40, i.e., for every percentage point change in satisfaction, ROI changes by 0.40 percent (p-value <0.01). This study "provides some of the first large-sample evidence that customer satisfaction and firm performance are related" (Ittner and Larcker, 1996, p. 18).

Anderson, Fornell, and Lehmann (1994, p. 62) illustrate the implications of their empirical results and calculate the value of an increase in customer satisfaction for the typical Swedish company represented in the SCSB. The typical company has a ROI of 10.8 percent (average for the sample), and the ROI is affected by an increase in the company's customer satisfaction index by one point in each of the next five years (cumulative increase of five points). Anderson, Fornell, and Lehmann (1994, p. 62) calculate the fifth-year ROI of 11.5 percent. This means an increase of 6.6 percent over the ROI level of 10.8 percent in the initial year.

Anderson, Fornell, and Rust (1997) have analyzed a database matching the customer satisfaction index with ROI and productivity for each company covered by SCSB from 1989 to 1992. Regression model estimation indicates that the coefficient for the direct relationship between customer satisfaction and ROI is positive (p-value <0.01). The marginal impact or "average elasticity" of ROI with respect to satisfaction for goods is 0.265, yet only 0.14 for services. ROI's relationship with productivity and the association between customer satisfaction and productivity is also analyzed, but these results will not be presented here.

Ittner and Larcker (1996) extend the study by using stock price as the dependent variable, because stock market return is a more relevant indicator of shareholder value. Most of the companies in the Swedish sample are not publicly traded, so the analysis is reduced to only nine large Swedish companies with actively traded stock. Based on a data set pooled across companies and over time, Ittner and Larcker (1996, p. 19) carry out regression analysis, where the dependent variable is percentage market-adjusted stock price return (raw return minus the return on the total Stockholm Exchange) over a two-year time period and the independent variable is the percentage change in customer satisfaction over the same two-year time period. The estimated regression slope coefficient is 7.36 (p-value <0.05). This result indicates, that a 1 percent change in the customer satisfaction index means about 7 percent change in shareholder value.

The same data set is also analyzed in a trading rule context. Also these results suggest that companies who score well on SCSB outperform the stock market index. For each year from 1991 to 1995, with the exception of 1993, companies that had improved their customer satisfaction index in the previous year normally achieve the best stock returns (Ittner and Larcker, 1996, pp. 19–21; EOQ, 1996, p. 22).

Ittner and Larcker (1996, pp. 21ff) carry out similar analyses for American companies. Their analyses are based on about 130 publicly traded companies, covered by the initial ACSI study in 1994, and with available accounting and stock price data. These results suggest that the customer satisfaction index, produced by the ACSI estimation, are economically relevant in that it is related to traditional economic performance measures: return on assets, market-to-book ratio, price–earnings ratio, and market value of equity. All four relationships between CSI and the selected performance measures are statistically significant in the expected direction at level 5 percent. For example, the results indicate that a one point change in the customer satisfaction index implies a $654 million increase in the market value of equity. This represents an approximately 5 percent increase in market value of equity for an "average" company in the sample (the average market value of equity is $13 374 million).

To examine the relationship between customer satisfaction and stock price among American companies, Ittner and Larcker (1996, pp. 23ff) conduct a study, similar to the above-mentioned trading rule study among Swedish companies. The study is based on the initial ACSI results during July 1994 and monthly stock price from August 1994 to January 1995 for about 130 companies. Also here, the conclusion is clear: The highest quartile companies (highest CSI) collectively outperform the stock market. These companies with the highest CSI earn, on average, return on stock price of 1–2 percent per month above the return on the market for somewhere between four and six months after the customer satisfaction measurement (Fornell, Ittner, and Larckner, 1995; Ittner and Larckner, 1996, p. 24).

The above-mentioned studies are based on individual companies and their stock performance. Also on an aggregate stock market level, there are very interesting results concerning ACSI. A significant correlation is found between percent change in the national customer satisfaction index in a given quarter and percent change in the Dow Jones industrial average in the following quarter, thus, "when customer satisfaction scores have moved up or down in recent years, stocks have followed three months later" (*Fortune*, 16 February 1998). However, the analysis is based on only 11 observations, namely quarterly data from the start of the ACSI in the fourth quarter of 1994 until the second quarter of 1997, and the correlation needs to be tested over a longer time period, for upturns and downturns in stock markets.

To sum up: The above-mentioned analyses of Swedish and American companies have demonstrated, that the SCSB/ACSI measure of customer satisfaction shows a statistically positive relation with selected economic performance measures. Increases in customer satisfaction actually affect increases in economic performance, here measured by ROI, stock price returns, market-to-book ratio, price–earnings ratio, and market value of equity. Customer satisfaction, measured by the SCSB/ACSI methodology, is forward-looking and provides insight into the company's future earning power and value. Therefore customer satisfaction is an economic indicator and provides useful information to the finance market about company value.

ECSI: A pan-European customer satisfaction measurement instrument

The successful experiences of the Swedish and American customer satisfaction indices have inspired recent moves toward creating a European Customer Satisfaction Index (ECSI), founded by the European Organization for Quality (EOQ), the European Foundation for Quality Management (EFQM), and the European Academic Network for Customer Oriented Quality Analysis, and supported by the European Commission (DG III). A pilot study in 1999 started in 12 European countries. The authors are responsible for developing and introducing the Danish Customer Satisfaction Index as a national part of the ECSI.

European experts have developed the ECSI methodology, based on a set of requirements (ECSI Technical Committee, 1998). The basic ECSI model (see figure 17.1) is a structural equation model with unobservable latent variables.

The model links customer satisfaction to its determinants, and, in turn, to its consequence, namely customer loyalty. The determinants of customer

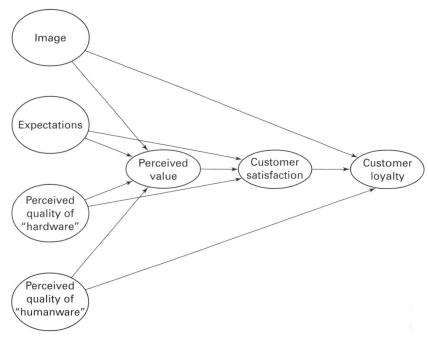

Figure 17.1.   The basic ECSI model.

satisfaction are perceived company image, customer expectations, perceived quality, and perceived value ("value for money"). Perceived quality is conceptually divided into two elements: "hard ware," which consists of the quality of the product/service attributes and "human ware," which represents the associated customer interactive elements in service, i.e., the personal behavior and atmosphere of the service environment. Main causal relationships are indicated; actually there can exist many more points of dependence between the variables.

Each of these seven latent variables is operationalized by a set of measurement variables, observed by questions to customers, and the entire system is estimated using a Partial Least Squares (PLS) method (Fornell and Cha, 1994).

Application of the ECSI methodology at Post Denmark

The ECSI ideas were introduced to the Danish business community at a relatively early stage and a large number of companies expressed interest not only

Table 17.1 Latent variables and measurement variables

Latent variable	Measurement variable
Image	Overall image Business practice Ethics Social responsibility
Customer expectations	Overall expectations of postal service Overall expectations of customer interaction
Perceived quality of postal service	Overall evaluation of quality experience Meeting the customer's requirements Comparison with competitors
Perceived quality of customer interaction	Overall evaluation of quality experience Meeting the customer's requirements Comparison with competitors
Perceived value	Value for money Comparison with competitors
Customer satisfaction	Overall satisfaction Fulfilment of expectations Comparison with ideal
Customer loyalty	Intention to buy again (remain as a customer) Intention to buy additional postal services Intention to recommend

to participate as sponsors for the Danish part of the project but also to adopt the model as a basis for their own specific customer satisfaction measurement. One of these companies was Post Denmark; a state-owned company with more than 33 000 employees.

During the autumn of 1998 data were collected for the first application of the ECSI model in Denmark. It was decided in the first place to apply the model to the private market, i.e. private parcel delivery, mail, and counter service.

Generic measurements

The generic questions which are given in table 17.1 were based upon the work done by the technical committee and the similar questions used in the Swedish and American studies. The latent variable company image is new in the ECSI

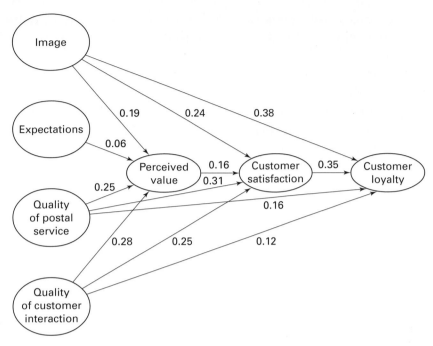

Figure 17.2.   The ECSI model for Post Denmark, the private market (unstandardized coefficients).

model compared to the SCSB/ACSI model, and our operationalizing is inspired by Naumann and Giel's (1995, pp. 219f) corporate image attributes: business practices, ethics, and social responsibility.

In total approximately 3000 respondents were interviewed about their attitudes toward Post Denmark. Data collection was performed in three different ways in order to study the consequences of different procedures. The methods were: (1) a direct postal survey, (2) a postal survey with pre-notification, and (3) a telephone survey. The difference between (1) and (2) was non-existent, while there was a small bias from the telephone survey, which tended to under-represent people with a higher education. Basically, however, the differences were small, and hence the choice of method could be based solely on economic considerations.

The estimation of the generic model, which is given in figure 17.2, showed that the ECSI structure gives a very good explanation of customer satisfaction. Furthermore it showed that the proposed split between "hard ware" and "human ware" quality was a good idea since the impact from these two areas is quite different in certain situations. In figure 17.2 the "hard ware" elements are called postal service and the "human ware" elements are called customer interaction. As mentioned the model deals with all kinds of postal services; both parcel delivery, mail, and counter services.

The ECSI Technical Committee has required that R^2 of customer satisfaction should be at least 0.65 (ECSI Technical Committee, 1998, p. 20). Furthermore, a 95 percent confidence interval for customer satisfaction should not be wider that ± 2 points. The Danish postal model for the private sector fully lives up to these requirements. Thus the R^2 is 0.79 and the confidence interval is much narrower than ± 2 points due to the very large sample size.

When compared to the basic ECSI model in figure 17.1 we see that there are some slight differences, i.e., quality of postal service also has a direct effect on loyalty, and expectations have only a significant effect on perceived value – not on satisfaction.

The indirect impact of expectations on customer satisfaction is low: a 1-point increase in the expectation index results in a $0.06 \times 0.16 = 0.0096$ point increase in the satisfaction index (all indices on 0–100-point scales). This impact is negligible when compared to the other exogenous variables. If we calculate all direct and indirect effects we see that a 1-point increase in either image, quality of postal service or quality of customer interaction results in an increase in the satisfaction index of 0.27 point, 0.35 point or 0.29 point respectively. The reason why the impact of expectations is as low as we observe is probably, that postal services are quite uncomplicated products, the quality of which is easy to assess. Furthermore the budget share is small. In such cases expectations usually play a minor role in the formation of customer satisfaction.

The estimated impact of the four exogenous antecedents on customer loyalty can be calculated by adding direct and indirect effects. Image has by far the largest impact on loyalty (0.47; i.e. a 1-point increase in image increases loyalty by 0.47) followed by quality of postal service (0.28), quality of customer interaction (0.22), and expectations with negligible impact (0.0034).

A rather surprising result is the impact of image. Image is by far the most important factor when it comes to the generation of loyalty and satisfaction. This conclusion is very important since competition is going to increase dramatically in the future.

Based on the model, the total customer satisfaction for Post Denmark in the private market may be estimated to 63. This result is close to the results obtained for USA, Sweden, and Germany where we find indices varying between 56 and 70.

Specific measurements

When introducing the specific measurements into the model two alternative strategies may be applied. One possibility is to substitute the generic questions by the specific questions and then run the model again. Another possibility is to estimate the model and the indices using the generic questions alone and then analyze the relationship between the estimated indices and the specific questions. The advantage of the first procedure is that you get an estimate of the full model. However, you get indices that are not necessarily identical to the indices obtained for the generic model. The advantage of the second procedure is that you only get one set of indices. For the case of Post Denmark it was important to obtain a model which could explain the generic results since the public will know part of the generic results. Hence the second procedure was chosen.

The procedure was as follows: All respondents answered both the generic and the specific questions. Using the generic questions, the ECSI model was estimated and the seven indices were computed once and for all. Subsequently a statistical analysis of the relationship between a computed index and its specific indicators was performed using a combination of principal component analysis and multiple regression analysis.

We will not go through all specific results in this contribution. Instead we will concentrate on image since this parameter was clearly the most important when it came to the creation of customer satisfaction and customer loyalty. In order to investigate the area in more detail the generic questions were supplemented by the following type of questions:

1 Is it an honest company?
2 Is it a company doing a good job for society?
3 Is it a professional company?
4 Is it a customer oriented company?
5 Is it an environmentally oriented company?
6 Is it an economically sound company?
7 Is it a company with a positive press?
8 Is it a good place to work.

These questions were then used as regressors with the estimated image index as dependent variable. In order to cope with multi-collinearity a principal component regression technique was used. As explained previously we did not run a full PLS estimation again due to the fact that we wanted to keep the estimated image index unaltered. The results of the estimation are given in figure 17.3 where the estimated importance scores and performance scores are shown.

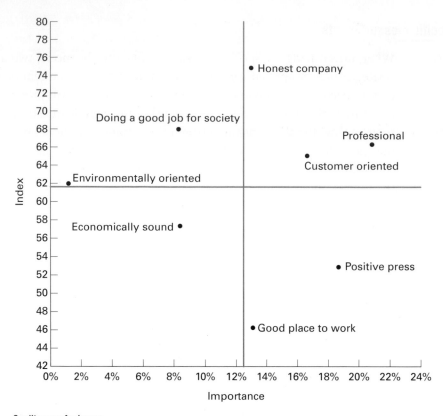

Figure 17.3.   Quality map for image.

From the quality map it appears that especially two image areas are critical to Post Denmark: The company as a working place and the company's relationship to the press. Both areas contribute significantly to the creation of image but they are both at a low level. These observations are critical to Post Denmark since they indicate that if nothing is done it could be problematic for Post Denmark to attract qualified people in the future. This is accentuated by the fact that the higher the education of customers the lower the image.

The ECSI model has also been applied to Post Denmark's business market. Also here the ECSI structure gives a very good explanation of customer satisfaction (R^2 is 0.78).

The general impression of the pilot study is very positive. The results are in accordance with expectations and people find the results easy to use in their daily work. Hence Post Denmark has decided to proceed with the ECSI model and use it as a full-scale customer satisfaction model.

Our experiences with this first application of the ECSI model have been very good. The model fits well and seems to be sufficiently flexible for different industries. Hence the model will be applied to other industries in the ECSI pilot phase during 1999. Telecommunication, financial services, and processed food will be among the industries measured.

Benefits of the ECSI: Practitioner and academic implications

As national customer satisfaction indices reliably and consistently measure customer satisfaction and quality perceptions for many companies within a variety of industries, the ECSI has the potential to be an excellent platform for comparisons between companies, industries, sectors, and countries. Benefits and practical implications of the ECSI would be evident both at company level, national level, and European level.

For individual companies, the ECSI will be a useful tool in three different ways:
- tracking performance over time;
- benchmarking;
- diagnosing the effects of various quality initiatives.

And the ECSI will be able to answer the key questions in today's business environment:

1 What are the customers' perceptions of quality of products and services? How satisfied are they? How loyal are they?
2 Is customer satisfaction and perceived quality improving or declining for the company?
3 How is the company performing relative to competitors in the industry? And relative to companies in other industries, sectors and countries?
4 What is the economic value of the customer base?
5 What are the drivers of customer satisfaction and customer loyalty? What is the impact of the different drivers?
6 What is the effect of different quality initiatives on customer satisfaction, customer loyalty, and the value of the customer base?
7 What is the optimal allocation of resources across alternative quality initiatives?
8 What will the consequence be to improve perceived quality and customer satisfaction?

When ECSI is used for tracking and benchmarking the basis is the generic measurements. But these measurements at the strategic level are not sufficient for diagnosing the need for quality improvement at the operational level. Here the basic ECSI model must be extended, incorporating company-specific drivers of quality of products and services (i.e., product/service range, attributes, accessibility, reliability, logistics, and facilities) and quality of customer interaction (i.e., professional skill, friendliness, time, complaints, and repairs). Each driver is associated with actionable alternatives, and this methodology can help the selection of quality initiatives that give the best effect on customer value.

In addition to this, the ECSI will also deliver useful information to the company's general measurement system, cf. the introductory discussion on the demand for performance measures and early warning.

Nationally, the ECSI will allow public authorities and organizations to provide useful information on customer satisfaction at the aggregate level (national, sectors) to complement the present macroeconomic measures, and will aid better understanding of the national economy, e.g., the dynamics and measurement of productivity, price, and inflation. The ECSI could lead to a sharper focus on quality and the customer, and could increase the welfare of customers and the competitiveness of the country.

At the European level, the ECSI also helps to answer questions about the European economy as a whole. Using ECSI measures, customer satisfaction inside specific industries can be compared with each other and with the European average, and this could lead to increased competitiveness, further development, and promotion of European quality, and a more complete picture of the European economy.

Futhermore, the ECSI will benefit European customers by giving voice to their evaluations of the products and services they buy and use.

The ECSI project and our study highlight the need for further research. Two important future research directions are: Firstly, developing tools and methods for the application of the ECSI methodology within the company in order to establish techniques of early warning and improved reporting in the company. Secondly, study of ECSI measurements at an aggregate level, which will make it possible to establish general conclusions concerning the relationship between customer satisfaction, customer loyalty, and the economic development.

More specifically, the first-mentioned research direction would include extension of the basic ECSI methodology, based on both generic and specific measurements, to individual companies. It would be interesting to develop general criteria for the transition from the generic to the specific level, which will serve as guidelines for the future application of the ECSI model at company level.

Conclusion

Many empirical studies support that customer satisfaction based on a structural equation modeling approach like SCSB/ACSI, has economic validity and this measure is therefore a forward-looking indicator of future economic performance.

The new developed methodology behind the pan-European customer satisfaction measurement instrument ECSI has been applied in Denmark, and there are interesting results providing insight about the satisfaction process and the impact of customer satisfaction on customer loyalty, which can indicate future economic performance. The basic ECSI model is also extended by incorporating company-specific measurements. This Danish study is one of the first applications of the ECSI methodology in the European pilot phase, and the analysis provides support for the proposed model. Our experiences with this application of the ECSI model have been very good. The model fits well and seems to be sufficiently flexible for different industries. Hence the model will be applied to other industries in the ECSI pilot phase during 1999. Telecommunication, financial services, and processed food will be among the industries measured.

The ECSI has the potential to be a new powerful customer satisfaction measurement instrument with benefits both at company, national, and European levels. After the pilot phase, the aim is to launch a full-scale ECSI as an annual index in all European countries, which could lead to a rise in quality activities in European companies.

REFERENCES

Anderson, E.W., Fornell, C., and Lehmann, D.R. (1994). Customer satisfaction, market share, and profitability: Findings from Sweden. *Journal of Marketing*, **58**(3), 53–66.

Anderson, E.W., Fornell, C., and Rust, R.T. (1997). Customer satisfaction, productivity, and profitability: differences between goods and services. *Marketing Science*, **16**(2), 129–45.

ECSI Technical Committee (1998). European customer satisfaction index: Foundation and structure for harmonized national pilot projects. Report prepared for the ECSI Steering Committee, October.

EOQ (European Organization for Quality) (1996). Customer forecast. *European Quality*, **3**(5), 20–4.

European Commission (1995). A European quality promotion policy. DGIII industry. January. Brussells.

Fornell, C. (1992). A national customer satisfaction barometer: The Swedish experience. *Journal of Marketing*, **56**(1), 6–21.

Fornell, C. and Cha, J. (1994). *Partial Least Squares.* In: *Advanced Methods of Marketing Research*, ed. R.P. Bagozzi, pp. 52–78. Cambridge, MA: Blackwell.

Fornell, C., Ittner, C.D., and Larcker, D.F. (1995). Understanding and using the American Customer Satisfaction Index (ACSI): Assessing the financial impact of quality initiatives. Paper presented at IMPRO 95: Juran Institute's Conference on Managing for Total Quality, Juran Institute, Wilton, CO.

Fornell, C., Johnson, M.D., Anderson, E.W., Cha, J. and Bryant, B.E. (1996). The American Customer Satisfaction Index: Nature, purpose, and findings. *Journal of Marketing*, **60** (October), 7–18.

Fortune (1998). As customers go, so goes the Dow. 16 February, p. 168.

Ittner, C.D. and Larcker, D.F. (1996). Measuring the impact of quality initiatives on firm financial performance. In *Advances in the Management of Organizational Quality*, ed. D.P. Fedor and S. Ghosh, Vol. 1, pp. 1–37. Greenwich, CO: JAI Press.

Naumann, E. and Giel, K. (1995). *Customer Satisfaction Measurement and Management: Using the Voice of the Customer.* Cincinnati, OH: Thomson Executive Press.

18 Linking financial performance to employee and customer satisfaction

Andy Neely and Mohammed Al Najjar

Introduction and background literature

Homilies such as "you can't manage, what you can't measure" and "you get what you inspect, not what you expect," encapsulate the traditional view of performance measurement. Namely that performance measures provide a means of tracking progress. Recent developments in the field, however, suggest that measures have hidden value as they can also help managers to (i) clarify strategy, (ii) communicate strategy, and (iii) challenge strategy.

Measures as a means of clarifying strategy

The process of deciding what matters to the organization and hence what should be measured is frequently cited by industrialists as a valuable one. Tony Singarayar, formerly director of process redesign at McNeil Consumer Products, part of Johnson and Johnson Inc., emphasizes this when he says:

> There are few today that know how to do this [build a balanced measurement system]. And fewer still that do it well. I'm not sure which is more proprietary in a scorecard – the data it contains, or the management process that went into creating it. (McWilliams, 1996)

The key benefit in the process of deciding what to measure appears to lie in the fact that the process forces management teams to be explicit about their priorities. No longer is it sufficient to say "we want to increase customer satisfaction," for customer satisfaction is an abstract concept. Without precise definitions and targets it is impossible to establish appropriate measures for customer satisfaction. Hence the act of deciding what to measure, forces management teams to clarify their language and make explicit what they mean when they say "we want to increase customer satisfaction."

Measures as a means of communicating strategy

One of the spin-off benefits of clarifying the language used to describe the organization's strategy is that it then becomes much easier to communicate that strategy throughout the organization. Numerous commentators, such as Rick Anderson from BP Chemicals and Martin Boaden, formerly with NatWest Bank, argue that the greatest benefit they see in measurement is the organizational alignment that results once the measures have been communicated.

Measures as a means of challenging strategy

While the practitioner community has concentrated on measurement as a means of clarifying and communicating strategy, several members of the academic community have raised the notion that perhaps measures, or more precisely measurement data, could be used to challenge the basis of an organization's strategy. Eccles and Pyburn (1992) were among the first to introduce this concept when they developed the notion that measurement systems should reflect organizational business models. Kaplan and Norton (1996) built upon this theme when they argued that core to the process of developing a robust balanced scorecard was the process of constructing a cause–effect map that illustrated the management hypotheses underpinning the strategy.

Take, for example, an operations strategy. The operations manager might believe that by reducing set-up times (s)he will be able to reduce batch sizes, and by reducing batch sizes (s)he will be able to reduce lead times, and by reducing lead times (s)he will be able to improve delivery performance, and by improving delivery performance (s)he will be able to improve customer satisfaction. At any point in time, and in any particular organization, this theory might or might not be valid. It might be that the reason for poor delivery performance is that the distribution network is inefficient, or the customer's goods inwards process is not functioning properly, rather than the fact that lead times are too long. The point is, that when formulating an operations strategy, managers are effectively being asked to make explicit their current theory of how their operation works. Authors have already recognized that aligning measures to this strategy is important, because measures affect the way people behave. Hence close alignment between measures and strategy can result in more efficient and effective implementation of strategy (Neely *et al.*, 1994). Now, however, authors have also recognized that perhaps the measures, or more precisely the data that they produce, can be used to challenge the strategy itself – i.e., the measures provide data that can be used by managers to explore whether the strategy they have chosen to pursue is valid.

This contribution reports the results of a three-year study that sought to explore this issue in detail. The questions underpinning the study were:

1 Can managers use measurement data to challenge the basis of their strategies?

2 Do managers use measurement data to challenge the basis of their strategies? And if not, why not?

The remainder of the contribution consists of three main sections. In the first the research methodology adopted in the study is explained. In the second the data gathered during the course of the research are presented and analyzed. In the third the implications of this research for both theory and practice are briefly reviewed.

Research methodology

As stated in the introduction the research reported in this contribution sets out to address two questions:

1 Can managers use measurement data to challenge the basis of their strategies?

2 Do managers use measurement data to challenge the basis of their strategies, and, if not, why not?

To answer these questions a two-phase research methodology was adopted. The first phase involved detailed case study research in British Airways and Company X.[1] Financial performance, customer satisfaction and employee satisfaction data were collected from these organizations for a five-year period. The data for each company were analyzed and links between the different dimensions of performance sought. Effectively the aim of this phase of the research was to establish whether statistically valid business models along the lines of those developed for Sears (Rucci, Kirn, and Quinn, 1996) and a UK supermarket chain (Barber, Hayday and Bevan, 1999) could be constructed on the basis of existing company data.

The second phase of the research involved a survey of 1800 large service operations based in the UK. The aim of the survey was to establish the extent

---

[1] The data gathered in company X were extremely sensitive in nature and hence the company has been disguised for the purposes of this paper.

to which firms claimed to explore the links between different dimensions of business performance (specifically customer and employee satisfaction for the purposes of this study). The survey also sought to identify what distinguished those who claimed they were exploring the links between different dimensions of business performance from those who were not.

Phase 1: Case Study Results

Both case study investigations demonstrated that it is possible to identify statistically significant relationships between different dimensions of performance, on the basis of existing company data. Furthermore, in both cases the identified relationships provided new insights into the inter-relationships between different dimensions of performance that had significant implications for the organization's strategies, policies, and priorities. Further detail on both cases are provided in the sub-sections that follow.

British Airways: The drivers of customer satisfaction

British Airways began systematically measuring customer satisfaction in 1983. Prior to the introduction of its customer satisfaction survey the airline held more than 4000 focus groups to identify the factors that appeared to matter most to customers. These factors were then structured into a customer processing blueprint, that highlighted the various moments of truth that customers experienced when interacting with the airline – i.e., ticket purchase, check-in, departure, in-flight service, arrival, and baggage reclaim. During the study data on each of these dimensions of service performance were extracted from British Airway's customer satisfaction measurement systems, along with data on sales turnover for the period January 1992 through to March 1997. Figure 18.1 identifies the specific pieces of data captured and their original source.

Multiple regression and correlation analyzes were then used to establish which of the various performance factors were related. These analyses, which are summarized in figure 18.2, identified that overall customer satisfaction is positively correlated with both willingness to recommend and sales turnover (0.747 and 0.653 respectively). The analyses also showed that cabin crew service had the highest influence on overall customer satisfaction. Further investigation revealed that, while meal rating and check-in service had positive relationships with cabin crew service, departure on time appeared to have negative relationship with cabin crew service. That is when planes depart late customers are more likely to be satisfied with cabin crew service. The question that this raises is why. The authors identified two possible explanations. First the airline has a well-designed service recovery process, which ensures that

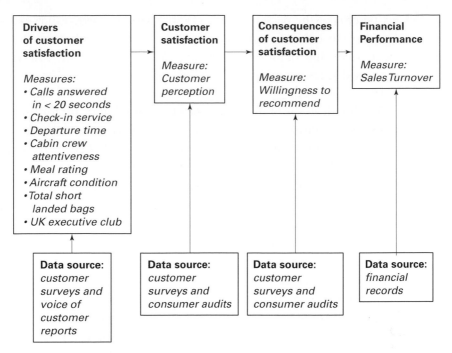

Figure 18.1. Data captured in British Airways.

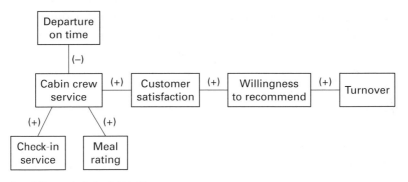

Figure 18.2. Correlation analysis for British Airways.

customers are kept fully informed of the reasons for late departure. Hence their expectations are carefully managed. Second it may be that cabin crew staff actually exert more effort when planes leave late, as they are aware that the customers are likely to be more frustrated and hence more prone to complain. These hypotheses were further investigated through a series of interviews with 38 passengers on both short and long haul flights. Preliminary analysis of the data gathered suggests that both hypotheses are valid. Seventy-six percent of the passengers interviewed said that when they experienced a late departure they felt that the cabin crew staff exerted more effort to satisfy their needs and requirements. Eighty-two percent of the interviewees also expressed pleasure about the way they were informed of the reasons for the delay.

The implications of these identified links are significant for British Airways as they illustrate that, while many of the theories held by the airline's management were correct, there are significant issues associated with the implementation of the firm's operations strategy. British Airways has traditionally focused on ensuring that planes depart on time. This makes sense as planes are extremely expensive assets and hence managing their utilization is key. Yet British Airways' data suggest that when planes depart late, customers tend to report that cabin crew service is better, and when customers report that cabin crew service is better, higher levels of customer satisfaction also tend to be reported. If correct, then this observation suggests that implementing an operations strategy that focuses on ensuring planes depart on time may not be the right thing for British Airways to do, at this point in time, especially as the airline is trying to differentiate itself through superior service. Of course, this does not mean that the airline should ensure planes depart late. Nor does it mean that all late departures are good. A 30 minute delay on a London to Paris flight is far more significant than a 30 minute delay on a London to New York flight. Instead the key issue the analysis raises for the airline's management is how can the airline ensure that the behaviors the customers appear to value, that come into play when planes leave late, are enacted on every flight. In essence this is the real power of using measurement to challenge strategy, as it forces management team's to question their theory about how their business runs.

Case Study 2: Links between employee and customer satisfaction in company X

The second case study involved the analysis of existing employee and customer satisfaction data in a second large service company. Both customer and employee satisfaction in this firm have shown a decreasing trend over a five-year period. Analysis of the data suggested that a 1 percent decrease in employee satisfaction was associated with a 0.25 percent decrease in customer satisfaction. Factor analysis of the employee satisfaction data allowed three broad categories of factors to be identified – work relationships, leadership and strategy and employee development. Specific statements within the employee satisfaction survey were linked to each of these sub-factors, e.g., "the business places the most competent people in management positions" and "the managers are interested in our well-being." Across the board employees were tending to disagree with the statements more and more as time passed. The one exception to this was that employees were tending to agree with the statement "my relationship with my immediate boss is good."

In interpreting these data the authors hypothesized that front line employees were openly sharing their frustrations about the organization with their senior managers. It appears as if the front-line employees were saying "this organization has no clear strategy," "senior management do not know what they are doing," "this is an awful place to work," "there is no future for me here." The response they received from their supervisors is "yes, I think you are right." Hence the supervisors and the front-line employees were building a relationship on the basis that neither believed that senior management in the firm knew what they were doing.

This interpretation may be right, or it may be wrong, but once again it illustrates how a theory about what is happening inside a business can be built on the basis of performance data that exists within the firm and that this theory can be used to challenge the organization's current strategies, polices, and priorities. When managers seek to do this they move beyond simply looking at trends in performance data. Instead they adopt a role more akin to that of a detective in that they seek to construct a case, based on the evidence (the performance data) they can access.

Phase 2: Survey of current practice

In the second phase of the research the authors undertook a postal survey of 1802 large service firms (employing over 250 people and with reported turnovers in excess of £10 million). Nineteen percent of the replies received were usable. While shortage of space precludes a full discussion of the data gathered through the survey, the key findings were:

1 Ninety-two percent of mass services, 84 percent of professional services, and 81 percent of service shops claimed to measure customer satisfaction.
2 Seventy percent of mass services, 66 percent of professional services, and 64 percent of service shops claimed to measure employee satisfaction.
3 Thirty-six percent of mass services, 36 percent of professional services, and 47 percent of service shops claimed to try and explore the links between employee and customer satisfaction, although the extent to which they do this on the basis of statistical analysis is less clear.

Six factors appeared to distinguish between those who sought to explore the links between employee and customer satisfaction and those who did not – motivation to collect data, desire to use the data strategically, confidence in the quality of the data, resources available to analyze the data, skills available to analyze the data, and a culture that valued and encouraged the use of the data.

Discussion and implications

This contribution makes three significant advances to performance measurement. First it explicitly recognizes the broader role of measurement in organizations and highlights the fact that managers can use measurement data to challenge the very basis of their strategies, policies, and priorities. Second it presents evidence from two case studies that there is real value for managers in using their measurement data to challenge the basis of their strategies, policies, and priorities. Third it presents new data that explains the extent to which managers use measurement data to challenge the basis of their strategies, policies, and priorities, and identifies the six factors that enable organizations to do this. Perhaps the most significant contribution, however, is that the data gathered through both the case studies and the survey illustrate how management teams can, and indeed are, seeking to use their measurement data in a much more sophisticated way than has traditionally been recognized in both the academic and practitioner literature.

REFERENCES

Barber, L., Hayday, S., and Bevan, S. (1999). From people to profits. IES Report 355.

Eccles, R.G. and Pyburn, P.J. (1992). Creating a comprehensive system to measure performance. *Management Accounting* (US), October, 41–4.

Kaplan, R.S. (1983). Measuring manufacturing performance: A new challenge for managerial accounting research. *The Accounting Review*, **58**(4), 686–705.

Kaplan, R.S. (1984). Yesterday's accounting undermines production. *Harvard Business Review*, **62**, 95–101.

Kaplan, R. and Cooper, R. (1997). *Cost and Effect: Using Integrated Cost Systems to Drive Profitability and Performance*. Boston, MA: Harvard Business School Press.

Kaplan, R.S. and Norton, D. P. (1996). *The Balanced Scorecard – Translating Strategy into Action*. Boston, MA: Harvard Business School Press.

Lynch, R. and Cross, K. (1991). *Measure Up – The Essential Guide to Measuring Business Performance*. London: Mandarin.

McWilliams, B. (1996). The measure of success. *Across the Board*, 16–20.

Miller, J. and Vollmann, T. (1985). The hidden factory. *Harvard Business Review*, September–October.

Neely, A.D., Mills, J.F., Platts, K.W., Gregory, M.J., and Richards, A.H. (1994). Realising strategy through measurement. *International Journal of Operations and Production Management*, **14**(3), 140–52.

Rappaport, A. (1998). *Creating Shareholder Value*. New York: Simon & Schuster.

Rucci, A., Kirn, S., and Quinn, R. (1996). The employee–customer profit chain at sears. *Harvard Business Review*, January–February.

Measuring innovation performance

Riitta Katila

Introduction

Patents and patent citations are increasingly used as measures of innovation performance. However, confusions exist over the applicability of these measures as well as the appropriate patent citation lag to be used. This study examines measurement of innovation performance through patents, especially focusing on how to measure the radicality[1] of innovations by using patent data.

Prior literature provides a wide array of definitions of radical innovation. In this study I propose that previous definitions of radicality can be arranged in four broad categories; industry, organization, user and technologically radical; each addressing a different dimension of radicality (see table 19.1). The first category of radical innovations defines radical as new or disruptive to the *industry*. Radical new products at the level of the industry dominate and make obsolete the previous products in established markets, can give rise to new industrial sectors (Achilladelis, Schwarzkopf, and Cenes, 1990), and affect the market power relations in the industry (Henderson, 1993).

The second category of radical innovations defines radical as new to the *organization*. Organizationally radical innovation may be defined as innovation which incorporates, for example, a technology that is new to the firm but may be well understood by others (Green, Gavin, and Aiman-Smith, 1995). Organizational radicality has also been described as the degree of change the innovation makes to the existing practices of the organization. The third category defines radical as new to the *users*. User-radical innovations fulfill customer needs much better than the existing products, but may require new skills to be used. Utterback (1994) defines radical innovation as one that has potential for delivering dramatically better product performance.

The fourth category of radical innovations defines radical as *technologically* new and significant. Technologically radical innovations include new know-

[1] Radical innovations have also been called path-breaking, discontinuous, revolutionary, new, original, pioneering, basic, or major innovations (Green, Gavin, and Aiman-Smith, 1995).

Table 19.1 Definitions of radicality of innovation

	Characteristics of each level of analysis
1 Industry	• Disruptive to the existing players of the industry • Requires incumbents to acquire new skills, practices and patterns of thinking
2 Organization	• Disruptive to the organization • Requires organization to acquire new skills – incompatible with existing practices
3 User	• Possibly disruptive and new to the users • Provides advantages over prior product forms, but also requires new skills from the user
4 Technology	• Disruptive to the experts of current technology • Requires new scientific and engineering knowledge and new problem-solving approaches

how: a new set of engineering and scientific principles, or a new problem-solving approach (Henderson and Clark, 1990). They require actors within a technological area to develop qualitatively new technological capabilities and incorporate technology that is a significant departure from existing technology (Henderson and Clark, 1990). This study focuses on technologically radical innovations and uses patent data to measure them.

I begin with the motivations for measuring innovation performance and its radicality, and discuss prior work in the area. I then present a study of biotechnology companies where patent-based measures of radicality are applied. The results of this study are further analyzed from the point of view of radical innovation measurement. Based on this analysis, several recommendations for future work are given. For example, researchers using patent-based measures are urged to check the validity of their results by experimenting with several different citation lags. Implications for theory and practice conclude the contribution.

Radical innovation performance

Why is radical innovation measurement important?

Studying measurement of radical innovations is important for at least three reasons. First, studies in technology management literature propose that radical innovations increase firm performance and competitive advantage. For example, industry leaders often produce incremental improvements and follow their core technologies to obsolescence and obscurity, while companies that are able to produce technologically radical innovations become the new leaders (Mitchell, 1989). Consequently, accurate and objective measurement of radical innovation is important for both managers as well as for performance researchers.

Second, despite the importance of radical innovation, and its wide use in the literature, there is relatively little work on how to measure radical innovation. For example, the different levels of analysis where radicality can be defined, and the continuous nature of radicality are poorly understood (Green, Gavin, and Aiman-Smith, 1995). There is a need for more work that helps firms measure the different types of radicality that result from their innovative efforts.

Third, the study on measuring radicality is motivated by the observation that the concept of radical innovation is increasingly used in new research areas. Previously, radical innovation has been a widely used construct in industrial organization economics and strategy studies. The general conclusion of this work is that incumbents have a somewhat reduced incentive to innovate radically because of their existing interests in the technology and market (Henderson, 1993). Recently, researchers on collaborative relations and networks, for example, have started to ask how the incumbents' lack of incentives to innovate radically affects the outcomes of collaborative relationships the incumbents are involved in. In all, both the theoretical and the practical importance of radical innovation motivates the study of reliable and valid operationalizations of this construct.

Measurement of radical innovation

Although radical innovations have been operationalized using several methods, there is no commonly accepted way to measure radicality of innovation. In this sub-section several measures used in prior work are discussed. I discuss the strengths and weaknesses of these measures, and specifically point out how operationalizations using patent data can address some of the central weaknesses of the other measures.

Radical innovation has been measured using several methods. Some authors have used qualitative methods, such as expert or manager interviews to determine the most radical innovations in the industry (see for example

Achilladelis, Schwarzkopf, and Cenes, 1990; Green, Gavin, and Aiman-Smith, 1995; Henderson, 1993). Other researchers combine qualitative measurement with quantitative data. Anderson and Tushman (1990) operationalize a radical design as an innovation which improves the product's current performance "frontier" by a significant amount; for example a significant improvement in the CPU speed of the computer. Also Christensen and Rosenbloom (1995) use performance improvement data to operationalize radical innovation.

The above-mentioned operationalizations of radical innovation have three main weaknesses. First, many studies use a binary categorization of radicality: innovations are either radical or incremental. This categorization, however, does not necessarily correspond to the more fine-tuned reality; radicality is a continuum. Second, in many studies evaluation of radicality is based on subjective and potentially partial assessment by managers, industry experts, or customers. Reliability of these measures can be context dependent (Pavitt, 1988). Third, prior operationalizations rarely distinguish between the four types of radicality discussed earlier in this contribution. Drawing definitive theoretical conclusions based on studies that fail to make these distinctions is difficult.

The three weaknesses of radical innovation measures discussed above can be, however, addressed by using patent-based measures of radicality. Patents and their subsequent citations provide a *continuous* and a relatively *objective* measure of technologically radical innovations. By definition, patents include *technologically novel*, useful, and distinct knowledge (Walker, 1995) and thus provide a good measure of technological radicality as defined above. Several studies have recently used patents as a measure of innovation performance (e.g., Dutta and Weiss, 1997; Henderson and Cockburn, 1994; Jaffe, Trajtenberg, and Henderson, 1993).

In addition to these methodological strengths of patent-based measures, also two other factors motivate the use of patent-based measures of innovation performance. Firstly, the use of patenting is increasing. Kortum and Lerner (1999) document a recent surge of approved patents in many high-technology industries, and Arora and Gambardella (1994) further argue that the importance of patents as innovation appropriability mechanisms will be increasing in many industries in the future, as several technological disciplines become more universal and the knowledge will be easier to articulate for patenting. Secondly, easier electronic access to patent data through for example European and US Patent Office databases has increased the possibilities for using patent data. Thus, patents are even more likely to be used as measures of innovation performance in the future in both R&D organizations as well as in innovation research.

Despite the above-mentioned benefits of patent-based operationalizations, these measures naturally also have limitations (see also Walker, 1995). Previous studies point out that the propensity to patent varies considerably across industries, and therefore patents provide the best, comparable measure of innovation when the analysis is restricted to one industry (Ahuja, 1996). Patents can also only measure a fraction of the research output, but, nevertheless, they seem to "provide one of the few direct quantitative glimpses into the innovation process available to us" (Griliches, 1984: 14).

Another issue with the use of patent measures is the differences among firms in their propensity to patent (Pavitt, 1988). One potential concern is the tendency of some companies to abuse the patent system, such as patenting only for the purpose of suppressing or preventing competition. However, patenting and renewal fees are designed to prevent this type of abuse (Walker, 1995). Finally, patents can vary in their qualitative importance. Recently, several researchers have proposed ways to distinguish and measure these qualitative differences. One of these methods, citation weighting is discussed below.

Citation-weighted patents as a measure of radicality of innovation

Several authors (see for example Jaffe, Trajtenberg, and Henderson, 1993; Trajtenberg, 1990) have argued that patents can vary enormously in their importance and value, and simple patent counts are thus unlikely to totally capture the qualitative differences in innovative output. Consequently, Henderson and Cockburn (1994) use granting of a patent in two of the three major geographical markets as an indicator of the patent's importance. Other authors have added citations to patent counts, i.e. citations that the focal patent receives in subsequent patents, to measure the radicality of a particular innovation (e.g., Dutta and Weiss, 1997). Receiving several citations, i.e. being the basis for a number of subsequent innovations is proposed to indicate the technological significance of the innovation. Citation-weighted measures are argued to indicate the technological, as well as the economic value of the innovation better than simple patent counts (Albert *et al.*, 1991; Dutta and Weiss, 1997).

Trajtenberg (1990) demonstrates that citation-weighted patents are a valid measure of radical innovation by confirming a significant relationship between citation-weighted patent counts and independent measures of eco-

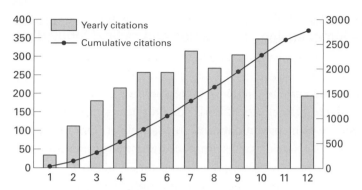

Figure 19.1.   Average citation pattern for 242 US biotechnology patents (patent applied in Years 1980–1987).
Notes: Patents citing the focal patents 0–12 years after application of each of the patents are illustrated.
Self-citations are excluded from these data.

nomic and social value of the same patents. Furthermore, Carpenter, Narin, and Wolf (1981) shows that patents that resulted in radical innovations (100 awarded products) received more than twice as many citations as a matching sample of random patents. Finally, Dutta and Weiss (1997) used citation-weighted patent data to discriminate between technologically significant and incremental innovations.

Figure 19.1 provides an example of citation-weighted patent analysis. This figure shows an average citation pattern for 242 biotechnology patents. As illustrated by this figure, citation data provide two main sources of information: the number of citations each patent receives, as well as the timing of these citations. In these data the 242 patents receive cumulatively almost 3000 citations in subsequent patents. Also two citation peaks are identified: first, the biotechnology patents are cited increasingly until seven years after their application, and, somewhat surprisingly, another citation peak is on average as late as ten years after the application of the patent.

While citation-weighted patent measures can reveal useful information about the innovation performance patterns of individual firms and industries, and the use of these measures is becoming more common (Walker, 1995), few studies have explored the issues relating to the construct validity of these measures. In the following sections I focus on two measurement validity issues: the correct citation lag (number of years included after the patent's application to count citations – in Figure 19.1 12 years were included), and, the potential differences in citation patterns between qualitatively different innovations.

Sample study – biotechnology companies and radical innovation performance

In this section empirical data on biotechnology collaboration performance is examined. I test the effects of R&D collaborations on radicality of innovation performance using patent data within a sample of 100 biotechnology companies. This study is used as an example of the use of patents for measuring innovation performance. Since the main focus of this contribution is on innovation performance measurement, I only briefly summarize the hypotheses of the sample study and the empirical results. In the following sections these sample data are further examined to test the validity of the patent-based radical innovation measures.

Main hypotheses

Main hypotheses of the sample study, and the empirical methods used, are summarized below. This sample study examines research and development (R&D) collaborations between small and large biotechnology companies. The study hypothesizes that collaboration can have negative effects on innovation performance. More specifically, collaboration with dissimilar partners – with older, larger, and foreign partners – is hypothesized to have a negative effect on the radicality of the innovation output of the smaller partner. The effects of the number of collaborative partners, and the complementarity of partner characteristics on the radicality of the smaller partner's innovation output are also examined. A more detailed description of the theoretical arguments leading to the hypotheses is available from the author, and similar arguments can also be found in other studies on R&D collaboration (for example Katila, 1997; Lane and Lubatkin, 1998; Shan, Walker, and Kogut, 1994).

Three main hypotheses are examined:

Hypothesis 1

The number of collaborative partners has a curvilinear (inverted u) relationship with the radicality of the innovation output of the smaller partner. Radicality of innovations increases up to point, but after this optimal point has been reached, additional increases in the number of partners is negatively related with the radicality of innovation output.

Hypothesis 2a

> The larger and the older the R&D collaborative partner, the less the radicality of the innovation output of the smaller partner.

Hypothesis 2b

> The foreign R&D collaborative partners have a negative effect on the radicality of the innovation output of the smaller partner.

Hypothesis 3

> The complementarity in the resources of the collaborative partners, such as complementary marketing and technological capabilities, has a positive effect on the radicality of the innovation output of the smaller partner.

Methods

To test these hypotheses, data on 100 biotechnology firms founded between 1980 and 1988 were gathered. The starting point of the study, year 1980, is a significant milestone in the US biotechnology industry: the first genetically engineered organism was patented in that year. The sample includes biotechnology companies listed in *PaineWebber* and *Genguide* biotechnology-specific directories and for which sufficient data were available during the period of study. Only biotechnology firms concentrating on human therapeutics and in-vivo diagnostics were included. This way the underlying technological setting and expertise requirements are relatively constant and the innovation outputs of the sample firms are comparable.

The dependent variable, radicality of innovation output, is measured by citation-weighted patent counts (*Patents*). To distinguish between companies that produce incremental improvements and those that focus on more radical innovations, I weight the number of patents with the citations the patents receive for six years after the application of the patent, or until the end of year 1997. Self-citations are excluded from these data. Patent information was obtained from the US Patent and Trademark Office documents and includes yearly counts of patents that the sample firms had applied for each year.

There are five independent variables in the study that measure different characteristics of biotechnology firms' collaboration behavior. The first independent variable, resource complementarity, measures the fit between the collaboration partners' resources. Resource complementarity is operationalized as an interaction between the larger partner's sales and marketing experience and the smaller partner's research capability. Research capability is measured as the cumulative number of the smaller partner's citation-weighted patents in three past years (years $t-3$ through $t-1$; see Henderson and Cockburn, 1995). The remaining partner characteristics are partner experience (*Partner age*), partner size (*Partner sales*), a binary variable indicating a foreign partner (*Foreign partner*), and the count of R&D collaborative partners (*Number of R&D partners*). Due to the time-series nature of the data, a lagged-variable design is used: data for the independent variables are collected a year before the dependent variable values. The data for this study were collected from several biotechnology-specific data bases and directories, 10-Ks and annual reports of these companies, as well as from the *US Patent Office* database. *PaineWebber* and *Genguide* directories, *Predicasts*, and various news databases were the sources of the cooperation data. Data regarding the collaborative partners were drawn from *Compustat* database, annual reports of the companies, and news articles in *Lexis Nexis*.

Poisson regression analysis was used to test the hypotheses. Poisson regression models have a number of attractive features for patent-based innovation measurement: these models are appropriate for integer data (counts of events), and they also account for counts that are aggregated over time periods (McCullagh and Nelder, 1989). In this study, the dependent variable, *Patents*, is a non-negative count of patents, and observations are combined to a time-series panel (yearly observations over a nine-year period for each firm). Poisson regression is thus an appropriate method to use.

Results

Innovative output of the sample companies was highly diverse: on average, these companies applied for 1.3 patents yearly, although some had no patents in any year (eight companies), and one organization applied for 18 patents in a single year. The number of R&D collaborations examined in this study was 246, resulting in 894 yearly observations. Yearly data for the companies were collected in 1980–90, including patent citations until the end of year 1997.

The results of the Poisson regression analysis are summarized in table 19.2. In all, the empirical results of this sample study show strong support for the above-mentioned hypotheses, and imply that unbalanced combinations between collaborative partners are likely to result in lower radicality of innovation output. Moreover, further analysis of the data demonstrated that patent citations play a significant role in the measurement: when raw patent counts instead of citation-weighted counts were used in testing the hypothe-

Table 19.2 Results of the Poisson regression analysis predicting Radicality of innovation. Last column gives parameter estimates

Variable	Proposed sign	Findings	Significance
H1 – Number of R&D partners	+/− (inverted U)	+/− (supported)	0.623*** (Number) −0.007*** (Number^2)
H2a – Partner sales	−	− (supported)	−0.0001***
H2a – Partner age	−	− (not significant)	−0.0006
H2b – Foreign partner	−	− (supported)	−0.245***
H3 – Complementary resources	+	+ (supported)	0.00001***

Note:
*** $p < 0.001$ (two-tailed tests).

ses, results become significantly weaker. More detailed results, as well as descriptive statistics, are available from the author.

Analysis of patent-based measures

The above-discussed study on biotechnology patenting gives an example of the use of patents as a measure of the radicality of innovation output. However, the use of citation-weighted patent measures raises two measurement issues which have not been discussed in the prior literature. First, I argue that prior work using citation-weighted patent counts has customarily used rather short citation lags. For example Dutta and Weiss (1997) use only five years of citation data. I argue that this lag may not be long enough to capture the differences in firm innovation performance. I know of no other work that has examined the effects of citation length on the validity of the empirical results.

Second, I ask whether the citation lags used in prior work are long enough to discriminate between incremental and radical innovations. If receiving more citations reflects the radicality of the patent, and the value of radical innovations is likely to be acknowledged relatively late after their introduction (Trajtenberg, 1990; Utterback, 1994), it is likely that the patents which eventually get most of the citations are cited relatively late. Short lags would not thus be likely to capture the majority of the citations radical innovations receive, and thus would not accurately reflect their radicality. I hypothesize

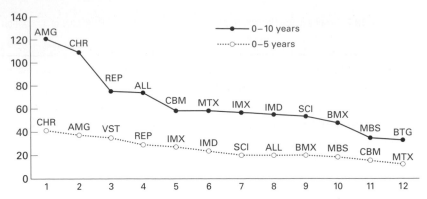

Figure 19.2. Most innovative biotechnology firms in 1985–1986 by citation weighted patent measures.
Notes: Companies in 0–10 year series: 1 Amgen, 2 Chiron, 3 Repligen, 4 Allelix, 5 Creative Biomolecules, 6 Matrix, 7 Immunex, 8 Immunomedics, 9 Scios, 10 Biomatrix, 11 Molecular biosystems, 12 Bio-technology general. Companies in 0–5 year series: 1 Chiron, 2 Amgen, 3 Vestar, 4 Repligen, 5 Immunex, 6 Immunomedics, 7 Scios, 8 Allelix, 9 Biomatrix, 10 Molecular biosystems, 11 Creative biomolecules, and 12 Matrix.

that the citation pattern of incremental innovation is skewed to the left, whereas radical innovations are likely to exhibit an opposite pattern.

To address these questions, two tests were conducted with the sample study data. The objective of these tests was to determine how sensitive the patent-based measure of innovation performance is to the citation lag used. In the first test I compared the average innovativeness of the sample companies in 1985–6 by using a citation-weighted patent count (see figure 19.2). A list of the most-innovative biotechnology companies in these years was first compiled using citations up to five years after the application of each patent. The second list was prepared using a period of ten years after application. As shown in figure 19.2, a comparison of the 12 most innovative companies in both lists leads to the conclusion that the length of the citation period has an effect on the innovation performance position of the company. Although many of the top companies changed relatively little in their positions as the citation period was extended, some companies such as Creative Biomolecules (fifth in 0–5 years vs. eleventh in the 0–10 years list) and Vestar in 1985 (fifteenth in the 0–5 year list vs. third in 0–10 year list) became fundamentally more or less innovative when the longer citation period was used. It is also interesting to note that the group of the most innovative four companies becomes increasingly distinguished from the rest of the firms as the longer citation period is used. This brief test gives an indication that the citation-weighted measure is possibly sensitive to the citation period, and that five years may not be a long enough citation period in many cases.

In the second test I selected a subset of patents, applied in years 1980–7, and calculated the average time period for these patents to receive all their citations. The sample was split in two parts based on the number of citations each company year had received. The purpose of the test was to find out whether years that had received above-average number of citations had longer citation periods. Two benchmarks were used, receipt of 30 percent and 80 percent of the citations.

I first tested the proposition that radical innovations (most cited) are recognized and cited later than more incremental innovations. Indeed, it took significantly ($p=0.019$) longer for those years that received an above-average number of citations to receive 80 percent of the citations, than for the less-cited years. On average, it took 9.5 years vs. 10.4 years for the less- vs. more-cited portfolios, respectively, to receive 80 percent of the total citations. Thus, more heavily cited, i.e. technologically more radical innovations tended to receive citations later than the technologically incremental. I also tested the same sample for the 30 percent benchmark. Surprisingly, less-cited patents got the first 30 percent of citations in later (3.7 years) than the more-cited patents (2.48 years) ($p=0.001$). In other words, the first citations for radical innovations were received early, but the majority of the citations were received relatively late.

In all, these two tests raise several empirical issues for performance researchers. Preliminary results on the sample of 100 biopharmaceutical companies for 1980–97 show that in most cases, a citation lag of five years is not adequate to reliably measure innovation performance. In case of biotechnology patents, for example, 80 percent of the citations were not received until on average ten years after the patent application. Furthermore, I found that radical innovations have longer citation lags than more incremental innovations. The results indicate that using short citation periods may result in exclusion of radical innovations from the sample. Consequently, researchers need to both assure that the length of citations used is long enough, as well as to experiment with the effects of different citation lags on their results.

Discussion

This chapter has three main contributions. First, from the theoretical standpoint, this study presents an overview of previous literature on innovation performance measurement and radical innovation. Four different categories of radicality are identified. Categorization is important for measuring radicality at the appropriate level of analysis that corresponds to the theoretical meaning of the construct. Patents and patent citations are suggested to be appropriate measures of innovation performance if the construct of interest is *technologically* radical innovation.

Second, this study contributes to the subsequent work on innovation measurement that uses patents to measure technological radicality of innovation performance. The chapter demonstrates the use of patent measures to analyze innovation performance. The main conclusion of the empirical analysis is that the length of the citation lag can dramatically change the picture of the innovativeness of firms. Moreover, the study shows how citation patterns of incremental and radical innovations differ: radical innovations tend to be cited later than incremental innovations. Consequently, short citation lags may not properly capture the value of radical innovations. Citation lags of ten years and longer are recommended for performance measurement.

Third, this study has managerial implications. The sample study on biotechnology collaboration presents evidence of the negative effects of collaboration on the radicality of innovation output. From the managerial perspective, these results complement those of a study by Lane and Lubatkin (1998) who find that the relative similarity in partner characteristics can enhance the smaller partner's innovative performance. Taken together, this study emphasizes the need for small organizations to carefully select their partners to obtain maximum radical innovation performance. The measurement issues discussed in this study can help in further clarifying the sources and measurement of radical innovation performance for these companies.

REFERENCES

Achilladelis, B, Schwarzkopf, A., and Cenes, M. (1990). The dynamics of technological innovation: The case of the chemical industry. *Research Policy*, **19**, 1–34.

Ahuja, G. (1996). Collaboration and innovation: A longitudinal study of interfirm linkages and firm patenting performance in the global advanced materials industry. Unpublished doctoral dissertation, University of Michigan.

Albert, M., Avery, D., Narin, F., and McAllister, P. (1991). Direct validation of citation counts as indicators of industrial patents. *Research Policy*, **20**, 251–9.

Anderson, P. and Tushman, M. (1990). Technological discontinuities and dominant design: A cyclical model of technological change. *Administrative Science Quarterly*, **35**, 604–33.

Arora, A. and Gambardella, A. (1994). The changing technology of technological change: General and abstract knowledge and the division of innovative labor. *Research Policy*, **23**(5), 523–32.

Carpenter, M., Narin, F., and Wolf, P. (1981). Citation rates and technologically important patents. *World Patent Information*, **3**, 160–3.

Christensen, C.M. and Rosenbloom, R.S. (1995). Explaining the attacker's advantage: Technological paradigms, organizational dynamics, and the value network. *Research Policy*, **24**(2), 233–57.

Dutta, S. and Weiss, A. (1997). The relationships between a firm's level of technological innovativeness and its pattern of partnership agreements. *Management Science*, **43**(3), 343–56.

Gilbert, R. and Newberry, D. (1982). Preemptive patenting and the persistence of monopoly. *American Economic Review*, **72**, 514–26.

Green, S., Gavin, M., and Aiman-Smith, L. (1995). Assessing a multidimensional measure of radical technological innovation. *IEEE Transactions on Engineering Management*, **42**(3), 203–14.

Griliches, Z. (1984). Introduction. In *R&D, Patents and Productivity*, ed. Z. Griliches, pp. 1–20. Chicago, IL: University of Chicago Press.

Henderson, R. (1993). Underinvestment and incompetence as responses to radical innovation: Evidence from the photolithographic alignment equipment industry. *Rand Journal of Economics*, **24**(2), 248–70.

Henderson, R. (1994). The evolution of integrative capability: Innovation in cardiovascular drug discovery. *Industrial and Corporate Change*, **3**, 607–30.

Henderson, R. and Clark, K. (1990). Architectural innovation: the reconfiguration of existing product technologies and the failure of established firms. *Administrative Science Quarterly*, **35**, 9–30.

Henderson, R. and Cockburn, I. (1994). Measuring competence? Exploring firm effects in pharmaceutical research. *Strategic Management Journal*, **15** (Special Issue), 63–84.

Jaffe, A.B., Trajtenberg, M., and Henderson, R. (1993). Geographic localization of knowledge spillovers as evidenced by patent citations. *The Quarterly Journal of Economics*, **108**(3), 577–98.

Katila, R. (1997). Technology strategies for growth and innovation: A study of biotechnology ventures. In *Frontiers of Entrepreneurship Research*, pp. 405–18. Babson College.

Kortum, S. and Lerner, J. (1999). What is behind the recent surge in patenting?, *Research Policy*, **28**(1), 1–22.

Lane, P. and Lubatkin, M. (1998). Relative absorptive capacity and interorganizational learning. *Strategic Management Journal*, **19**, 461–77.

Levin, R.C., Klevorick, A.K., Nelson, R.R., Winter, S.G., Gilbert, R., and Griliches, Z. (1987). Appropriating the returns from industrial research and development; Comments and discussion. *Brookings Papers on Economic Activity*, No. 3, 783–831.

McCullagh, P. and Nelder, J.A. (1989). *Generalized Linear Models*. Chapman & Hall.

Mitchell, W. (1989). Whether and when? Probability and timing of incumbent's entry into emerging industrial subfields. *Administrative Science Quarterly*, **34**, 208–30.

Pavitt, K. (1988). Uses and abuses of patent statistics. In *Handbook of Quantitative Studies of Science and Technology*, ed. A. Van Reenen, pp. 509–36. Elsevier.

Reinganum, J. (1983). Uncertain innovation and the persistence of monopoly. *American Economic Review*, **73**, pp. 741–8.

Rosenbloom, R. and Christensen, C. (1994). Technological discontinuities, organizational capabilities and strategic commitments. Working paper.

Shan, W., Walker, G., and Kogut, B. (1994). Interfirm cooperation and startup innovation in the biotechnology industry. *Strategic Management Journal*, 15, 387–94.

Trajtenberg, M. (1990). *Economic Analysis of Product Innovation – The Case of CV Scanners.* Cambridge, MA: Harvard University Press.

Utterback, J. (1994). *Mastering the Dynamics of Innovation.* Cambridge, MA: Harvard University Press.

Walker, R. (1995). *Patents as Scientific and Technical Literature.* Metuchen, NJ: The Scarecrow Press.

Part VI

Performance measurement – emerging issues and trends

The final part of the book contains two contributions that look toward the future. The first, from Rob Austin and Pat Larkey asks how should knowledge work be measured. The theme of this contribution is becoming increasingly important as more and more companies begin to recognize that they compete on the basis of their intellectual capital and intangible assets. Austin and Larkey explore the particular challenges associated with the measurement of knowledge workers, not the least of which is the fact that many of them are highly individualistic and entrepreneurial, characteristics which inappropriate measures can damp down.

The final contribution, from Neely, Marr, Adams, and Kapashi, explores the highly topical question of what should the dot.coms measures be, and what are they measuring. This contribution, which is based on research carried out in early 2000, builds on the measurement framework – the performance prism – introduced in the chapter by Kennerley and Neely. The research highlights the fact that there is massive interest in the dot.coms in measurement, but as yet there appears to be little agreement about which are the most crucial measures for the new economy. Indeed the reported levels of measurement in dot.coms suggest that many of them are simply "measuring everything that walks and moves." The question remains, however, are they measuring the things that matter.

20 The future of performance measurement: Measuring knowledge work

Rob Austin and Pat Larkey

Introduction

It has become widely accepted, as we approach the end of this century, that organizations' abilities to create, retain, communicate, and use knowledge are critical to their success (Davenport and Prusak, 1998; Nonaka-Takeuchi, 1995). Management of knowledge has become a frequently acknowledged source of "core competencies" (Prahalad and Hamel, 1990), which themselves give rise to sustainable competitive advantages (Leonard and Barton, 1995). The explosive growth of information-related sectors of industrialized economies has seen concomitant growth in the demand for products and services with potential to help organizations apply what they know more profitably. That same rapid growth has created entirely new occupational categories – web designer, network manager, software engineer, to name just a few – which produce economic value mostly by creating and manipulating thoughts, ideas, and symbols. Even in traditional occupations, ways of working have come to depend on intellectual activity, perhaps more than on physical activity. Factory workers invent and share process improvement ideas; salespeople develop novel ways to use the web to reach or retain customers.

One consequence of this shift in the nature of work is that the relationship between an organization's measured resources and its market success has become more tenuous. Unlike materials or equipment, core competencies are not listed on balance sheets; neither are the distinctive abilities of employees and teams, which can be an obviously significant reason for a firm's success. In some sectors of the economy, factors that contribute substantially to a firm's market success largely elude traditional means of quantification. This fact not only makes valuation of individual firms harder, it also complicates traditional analyses aimed at figuring out where to allocate resources, how to improve processes, and whom to reward. Existing notions of performance measurement and organizational control meet with substantial challenges in these settings.

In this chapter, we identify the distinctive characteristics of "knowledge work"[1] that impact on our ability to measure it, and briefly discuss the research challenges and practical implications associated with those characteristics. Conceptually, these characteristics can be placed in three categories.

First, knowledge work is less observable than physical work. The activities involved in loading coal into a railroad car are easier to see, understand, and evaluate than the activities involved in progressing toward a successful database design. Although the problem of observability has long been known and studied in measurement settings, it takes on new dimensions when the activity being measured is intangible "thought-stuff."

Second, the motivation of knowledge workers is arguably more reliably intrinsic than it is for many physical workers. Knowledge work is often idiosyncratic and oriented toward problem solving and, hence, intrinsically interesting for workers; physical work is more often repetitive and oriented toward compliance, and hence, less interesting.[2] The possibility that strong intrinsic motivation can be relied upon to direct workers' activities requires rethinking research based on less optimistic assumptions about human motivation (such as economic agency theory).

Third, it is the nature of knowledge work that a high degree of individual capability in the worker is often the critical factor in achieving successful outcomes, rather than, as with much physical work, his or her consistent compliance with a plan or efficient participation in a externally programmed system.[3] An excellent technical support person is excellent not because of his or her performance on well-known and well-understood tasks, but rather because he or she is good at the exploration, knowledge creation, and analysis needed to perform excellently on unprecedented problem solving or other vaguely defined tasks. In knowledge work, talent, skill, and knowledge differentials

---

[1] "Knowledge work" is, in many ways, an unsatisfactory phrase because it has become vague from overuse. We use the term because it is widely recognized and conveys some sense of what it means. For our purposes, knowledge work is work in which important value-creating transformations occur in the realm of ideas or symbols; or, alternatively, in which a substantial amount of productive activity is intellectual rather than physical. We assume that this work will tend toward conceptual complexity in ways that create disparities among work participants in the understanding of the work itself and of the events that occur in the course of completing the work.

[2] This is, of course, not always the case. An excellent carpenter no doubt does physical work that very much interests him, and his interest no doubt plays a vital role in developing his skills to a high level. However, we wonder if such an excellent carpenter is not also likely to have introduced a substantial element of knowledge work into his efforts, in the form of, say, creative improvements in methods or cabinet design. DeMarco has pointed out that the technologies we have available for automating routine or repetitive symbolic tasks are very good, much better than the technology for accomplishing the same kinds of physical work (Austin, 1996); hence we tend to quickly automate uninteresting knowledge work.

[3] This is not true for all physical work obviously. Professional athletes do work that is very physical and requires very highly developed individual capabilities in the worker.

(which we abbreviate "TASK" differentials) matter a lot; performance is much more about what a worker can do than it is about what you can get him or her to do. Identifying appropriately skilled individuals and inducing them to join the organization become very important; methods required to access fully the capabilities of these individuals may be quite different from those required in more physical settings.

There are sizeable literatures in fields as diverse as accounting, economics, industrial engineering, organization theory, psychology, and sociology that are useful in thinking about observability, motivation, and TASK differentials. Because of the sheer volume of this research, it is not possible to cover these subjects exhaustively. Rather, in this chapter, we draw selectively from various fields the findings that bear most directly on problems of observability, motivation, and TASK differentials in measuring knowledge work.

The problem of observability

Observability problems – that is, problems in actually discerning the essence of performance in a phenomenon we are attempting to measure – have been much studied in physical and generic organizational contexts.

Economic agency theories (Ross, 1973; Jensen and Meckling, 1976; Holmstrom, 1979; Holmstrom and Milgrom, 1987, 1991, 1994; Baker, 1992) constitute a recent and direct attempt to address issues of observability, which are notable for their growing prominence in research and practical contexts (they are, for example, increasingly used in discussions of how executives should be paid for their performance). The foundational model in this category was introduced by Ross (1973) and later refined by Holmstrom (1979). Essentially all subsequent theoretical models of this type are variations on the "Ross–Holmstrom" (R–H) model. Because the model attempts to distill observability problems into their simplest, most fundamental elements, it is a useful starting point for considering research on this subject.

The R–H model depicts an organization in drastically simplified form: two individuals and the contractual relationship between them. A principal has control over productive resources and seeks to hire an agent to do work that will transform resources into output with money value. The principal wants to maximize "profit" – the difference between the monetary value of the agent's output and the payment required to induce effort from the agent. The agent's motivations are equally self-interested and almost as simple: he wants to maximize his income while minimizing effort and risk.[4] The interests of the two are therefore opposed. The principal wants to extract as much value as possible from the agent and yet pay him as little as possible. The agent wants to do as little work and bear as little risk as possible and yet be paid as much as possible.

Observability problems enter into the model through an assumption that the principal cannot directly observe the agent as he works. The justifications of this assumption are as follows:

1 Often it is not feasible for a manager to watch an employee at every moment, and doing so would anyway obviate the efficiencies sought in hiring the agent; and

2 often workers are hired for specialized abilities that the principal does not possess and has only limited ability to understand and evaluate.

Because the principal cannot directly observe how much effort the agent is devoting to the task, she also cannot compensate him on the basis of how hard he works (i.e., his level of effort). There is available to the principal, however, a "signal" of the agent's effort level, that is complicated because it also includes a random component representing factors that are beyond the agent's control (e.g., rainstorms that depress a salesperson's performance in a given week). The random component of the signal has special distributional properties that ensure that unfavorable signal outcomes become less likely when the agent's effort level increases.[5] Hence, the outcome is statistically, although not directly, indicative of the agent's effort level and can serve as the basis of a compensation contract. There is also an assumption, sometimes implicit, that higher levels of effort by the agent will make more valuable work outputs more likely.[6]

An optimal compensation schedule based on the signal of agent effort can be derived from this setup. The schedule maximizes expected profits for the principal and expected utility for the agent, subject to a constraint that ensures that the agent expects enough reward to secure him from the labor market. Consideration of the properties of this schedule produces the following conclusions:

1 The agent demands additional compensation for bearing the probabilistic risk associated with the signal of his performance; thus, measuring and

---

[4] The principal is assumed to be risk-neutral, or, sometimes, less risk averse than the agent.

[5] This "Monotone Likelihood Ratio Condition" is important to the model's conclusions.

[6] This assumption is sometimes not explicitly stated because the signal and work output are considered to be the same. That is, the desired output is observable and is statistically indicative of the underlying effort level.

rewarding performance is more costly for the principal than if effort could be observed directly, because of the agent's risk aversion.

2   The outcome is *Pareto inferior* to the outcome that would result if direct observation of effort were possible; that is, the principal and agent would be collectively better off, and neither would be worse off, if effort were directly observable; hence there is economic value lost due to risk.

3   Resulting compensation will include a variable component that increases with the signal.

This last conclusion is frequently offered both as an explanation and an endorsement of increasing input–output payment schedules (such as sales commission systems).

Within this framework, Banker and Datar (1989) broadened the discussion of observability to include problems of *precision* and *sensitivity* of the stochastic signal, which may complicate discernment of underlying agent effort levels, thereby frustrating the creation of effective compensation schemes. Precision, roughly defined, is the degree to which movement in the signal indicates movement in the underlying quantity of interest (e.g., effort) rather than the random disturbance. A very low precision signal is not very useful because changes are due too much to random "noise."[7] Sensitivity, roughly defined, is the degree to which a change in an underlying quantity of interest (e.g., effort) tends to change an available measurement indicator. A signal that is very low in sensitivity is not very useful because even large movements in the underlying quantity of interest result in small, difficult to discern movements in the signal. The fields of statistical process and quality control (see, for example, Ishikawa, 1985) address related statistical issues involved in separating signal from noise in repetitive and stable industrial processes.

In contrast with the rigorous theorizing of agency economics, behavioral science has tended to approach measurement and observability via detailed empirical examinations. Early work in this area often focused on pathological phenomena. For example, Blau (1963) conducted field research on government bureaucracies and found well-intentioned organizational measurement programs were consistently dysfunctional. In one study, agents at an employment office reacted to a system that measured job applicant interviews by shifting most of their efforts to interviewing, away from locating new job opportunities. Consequently, the office made fewer job placements.

---

[7]   In such a situation, the agent will demand a very high risk premium to be exposed to the high level of uncertainty in the signal.

Realizing that the system was dysfunctional, office managers enhanced the system to include eight measures, some of them ratios, such as "percentage of interviews that resulted in job referrals." At first the enhanced system appeared effective, but a replication of the Blau study revealed that earlier dysfunctional behaviors had been replaced by more sophisticated dysfunctional behaviors. For example, agents "engaged in outright falsification . . . by destroying at the end of the day those interview slips that indicated that no referrals to jobs had taken place" (Blau, 1963, p. 50). Further attempts to fix this system by adding many more measures were to no avail; employees always adapted and dysfunction resulted.

In Blau's view, the pattern of dysfunction that resulted from observability problems had three unfortunate characteristics. First, dysfunction seemed inherent in the attempt to measure organizational activity. Regardless of the incentive effect, designers of a measurement system intended – regardless even of whether they meant to create any incentive effect at all – unintended incentive effects appeared.

Second, dysfunction was persistent. It resisted efforts to eradicate it by adjusting the measurement technology. Finally, dysfunction was invariably hidden from the designers and users of the measurement system, often until some catastrophic failure occurred.[8] The question "how do you know your system is not dysfunctional?" could not readily be answered. Ridgeway (1956) summarized the findings of this and other studies that reported a similar dysfunctional pattern by concluding that "quantitative performance measurements – whether single, multiple, or composite . . . have undesirable consequences for overall organizational performance."

This dysfunctional pattern has often been explained as resulting from *incompleteness* in measures (Lawler and Rhode, 1976). A measurement system suffers from incompleteness when measures do not capture all *critical dimensions* of productive work. A dimension of activity is critical when no value can be produced without devoting some effort to the dimension. In Blau's employment office example, searching for job opportunities was a critical dimension of the work being done by the office but it was not being measured. Workers shifted their efforts from searching for job opportunities to conducting interviews, a dimension that was measured. The result was dysfunctional.[9]

---

[8] In many cases disguising dysfunction relied on explicit deception, but not always. Dysfunctional activities also took more subtle forms of overly optimistic reports or convenient omission of detail.

[9] The problem of incompleteness has been independently documented in numerous contexts leading up to the present. For example: Measuring police work by percentage of crimes solved (i.e., "clearance

The R–H model offers no explanation for the pattern of dysfunction that results from incompleteness in measures because it assumes implicitly that measures are complete.[10] In fact, the increase in measured output payment schedules that seem implicated in the pattern of dysfunction identified by Blau (and others) seem to be specifically recommended by the R–H model. The two streams of research are at odds on this point.

Economists have modified their models to address the problem of incompleteness and consequent dysfunction. Holmstrom and Milgrom (1991) modeled a situation in which the agent allocates effort across tasks, some of which are measurable and some of which are not. They show that if one of the unmeasurable tasks is critical to value creation and rewards increase with measurements on measurable tasks, then dysfunction will result. If the agent is willing to do valuable work without measurement-linked rewards, then letting him work for a flat fee is the best you can do with incomplete measures.[11] Milgrom and Roberts (1992) concede that this result "imposes a serious constraint on the incentive compensation formulas that can be used in practice." Holmstrom and Milgrom (1994) have argued that the measurability of specific effort dimensions may be a determining factor in work efficiency, organization, and organizational structure.

Knowledge work and observability

As Holmstrom and Milgrom (1991) have shown for general settings, if you cannot solve the problem of completeness, then conventional solutions to the problem of risk from uncertainty in a signal of effort are dysfunctional. Furthermore, because knowledge work tends to be oriented toward innovation and problem solving, it may benefit from efforts on dimensions that were unanticipated. Knowledge work is multi-dimensional, and the criticalness of dimensions often evolves dynamically. To put this another way, in work that is all about "smartness," how smart someone works – that is, how cleverly one

rates") has been shown to result in some citizen's complaints not being posted, others being posted only after they are solved, and in minor crimes being worked on before major crimes (Skolnick, 1966). Measuring teachers on student test performance has been shown to result in narrowing of the educational mission to "teach the test" (Stake, 1971; Hannaway, 1991). Measuring tax collection rates has led US Internal Revenue Service employees to alter and falsify tax records (USA Today, 1997).

[10] Specifically, the assumption that more valuable work outputs will be more likely when the agent increases his effort is indicted. The problem of incompleteness reveals that *how* effort is allocated matters at least as much as *how m*uch is allocated.

[11] Baker (1992) arrives at a similar set of conclusions via a somewhat different route.

allocates effort across tasks – is necessarily of great importance. For these reasons (and others), the problem of completeness is especially prominent when the work being performed is knowledge work.[12]

Prescriptive works on the subject of organizational measurement often include recommendations that measures be as complete as possible. One popular treatment, for example, urges that organizational scorecards be "balanced" (Kaplan and Norton, 1992, 1996) by including non-financial as well as financial measures, in categories that more exhaustively cover what really matters to a business. Although balance might not be precisely the same thing as completeness, the evoked intuition is often the same. While recommendations of balance or completeness may be a step in the direction of improved practice, it remains important to understand when completeness can be achieved and in which work settings.

Observability issues that arise in physical settings have typically been framed in terms of asymmetry in *information* about workers' hidden acts. Knowledge work arguably generates more pronounced asymmetries, based not only on information asymmetries but also on knowledge (or even skill or talent) asymmetries between a manager and those she manages. A manager who has the same information as a worker can still lack the expertise needed to understand, attribute, evaluate, and act on what she observes. For this reason, observability problems that afflict knowledge work may be particularly severe and persistent.

It is important also to acknowledge that, like information asymmetries, knowledge asymmetries and resulting observability problems cannot necessarily be "designed away." Many prescriptive treatments of organizational measurement focus almost exclusively on the measurement technology – on "choosing the right measures" – as if observability were entirely dependent on the shrewdness of measurement system designers. In fact, observability problems derive ultimately from the totality of the organizational situation and specific setting of the measurement act, and not just from the measurement technology.

Persistent observability problems can be decomposed into three categories of more specific problems, all of which frequently appear in knowledge work settings, and any of which suffices to undermine performance measurement objectives:

Measurability is the degree to which important aspects of the observed work yield cognitively simple and relatively compact quantification. If you

---

[12] As we will argue in the next section, knowledge workers do tend to be intrinsically motivated and their motivation can be relied upon and productively directed. This fact makes inability to solve the completeness problem less painful and diminishes the relative importance of the issue of how *much* effort an "agent" is allocating.

cannot measure what you care about in a way that is meaningful, with acceptable confidence in the validity of the measure, then measurement necessarily becomes more complicated. In such situations, less direct proxy measures are often sought, which creates the potential for problems for the next two objectives. Software quality is, for example, notoriously difficult to measure. Defect counts, a common measure, are at best only suggestive of quality as a customer defines it, in terms of suitability for the customer's intended purpose.

Attributability is the degree to which a measurement can be attributed to some causal object – an individual, a group, or a process. Measuring something without knowing (or at least confidently hypothesizing) its relationship to a causal object is not very useful. Moreover, the ability to measure a thing does not assure that the thing can be easily or usefully attributed to an actionable underlying cause.[13] There tend to be, for example, important interdependencies in the production of knowledge work; it is rarely easy, even after the fact, to say who contributed what to the value in the final product.

Evaluability is the extent to which the normative adequacy of a measurement can be judged. Measuring and attributing without knowing whether the measurement reflects favorably or unfavorably on the object of attribution is also not very useful. Standards and benchmarks typically assist with evaluability issues. But the ability to measure and attribute a thing does not assure that the thing can be easily or usefully evaluated. Much knowledge work results in products that are distinctive and, in general, the greater the distinctiveness, the lower the evaluability.

Prescriptive treatments and economic models have often assumed away these problems, especially the second and third. The R–H model, for example, deals in a limited way with measurability in that the agent's effort expenditure cannot be directly observed. Because there is only one agent, however, there are no issues of attributability. Evaluability is assumed, in that signal and work outputs are usefully related and effort allocation occurs along a single dimension. More effort is good. Less effort is bad.

The situation can be considerably less simple and convenient in knowledge work settings. Because much of the work is intangible and conceptually complex, measurability problems are common. Proxy measures are not

---

[13] Ishikawa (1985) has dealt in detail with the attribution problem in the context of quality control, in his distinction between "true quality characteristics" and "substitute quality characteristics."

obvious, and there are usually questions about the attributability of the chosen proxy measures. The collaborative and interdependent nature of much knowledge work makes it difficult to draw lines of causality, especially when progress is evolutionary and proceeds at an uneven pace. Determining who or what was responsible for a favorable or unfavorable outcome can be difficult if not impossible for an idiosyncratic or poorly understood work process. These same difficulties complicate evaluability. Activities and outputs may be unprecedented. No obvious standard of evaluation may exist. Comparison with "last time" may not be meaningful because of changes in process and environment since then.

Measurability issues are a prerequisite for incompleteness. They necessitate the use of proxy measures in place of "true measures" – measures of what the organization truly values. Once proxy measures are introduced, questions about their relationship to true measures arise. Attributability concerns complicate attempts to establish persistent relationships between proxy and true measures, leaving workers latitude to engage in dysfunctional behaviors. Problems of evaluability hinder the detection of dysfunctional behaviors as the pattern unfolds.

Several characteristics of organizational situations that have often been observed to complicate work measurement create particularly difficult problems for knowledge work measurement. Measures of knowledge work are more likely to be incomplete due to factors such as:

Context Insensitivity Because measurement designers may lack vital knowledge about the work, contextual variables that have independent effects on proxy measures may remain unknown. Even if they are known, they may be ignored because of the conceptual complexity involved in measuring them. Ways of affecting proxy measures that are known to workers but not to managers create potential for incompleteness and dysfunction.

Inseparability Because of knowledge asymmetries and the highly collaborative nature of some knowledge work, measurement users may have difficulty in separating the work of one individual or group from that of another, because the work is (or seems) so interdependent (Alchian and Demsetz, 1972). Consequently, workers may have the ability to move proxy measures in what seems like a favorable direction by shifting work difficulties on to other workers. Needless to say, a system that rewards such behaviors does not foster cooperation among workers and may result in undesired outcomes from the overall collaborative activity.

Reliability For knowledge work that is rapidly changing, attribution and evaluation may become difficult because comparisons of an evolving process are obviously not valid. The degree to which measures succumb to problems of context insensitivity, inseparability, etc. may change over time. Empirically discovered correlations between measured quantities and underlying phenomena may not persist. If the measurement process is a statistical one, the problem manifests itself as a fundamental incoherence in the population definition.

Ex Post *Causal ambiguity* Knowledge asymmetries provide latitude for variation in *ex post* interpretation of events. If a complex computer error shuts down a production facility, for example, there may be only two or three people who truly understand what has happened. Parties involved may take advantage of this fact by lobbying for specific interpretations of measurements and events. This practice has a destabilizing effect on efforts to establish underlying causal attributions. In established or more physical measurement settings there is often consensus on the causal models that underlie measurement. In many knowledge work settings, no such consensus exists. Moreover, the extent to which such a consensus is realizable may be limited by the rapidly changing nature of knowledge work.

The problem of motivation

The assumption of Holmstrom and Milgrom (1991), that the agent might do some valuable work when paid only a flat fee because he is somehow internally[14] motivated to exert effort on another's behalf is not remarkable in the context of the behavioral literature, but it is non-standard in economic theory. Holmstrom and Milgrom do not explore other possible questions related to this kind of motivation such as "how might internal motivation be used to produce more value?" or "in what conditions might internal motivation be a viable control mechanism?" Behavioral scientists, however, have extensively studied human motivation and the conditions under which external and internal motivations can be used for organizational control (e.g., Eisenhardt,

---

[14] We use the expressions "internal" and "external" (or "intrinsic" and "extrinsic") to describe a specific distinction between types of motivation. External motivations are those that are linked to objectively discernable measured outcomes. Internal motivations are those for which the normative adequacy is determined subjectively by the individual whose performance is under consideration.

1985; Ouchi, 1979; Deci and Ryan, 1985; Ouchi, 1981; Vroom and Deci, 1970; Thompson, 1967; McGregor, 1960; March and Simon, 1958).

Thompson (1967) distinguishes between behavior and outcome-based measurement for the purposes of control. To the extent that behavior is observable, he argues, measures will be based on behavior. Similarly, outcome measures will be used when desired outcomes can be readily observed. Ouchi (1979) argues that when neither behavior nor outcomes are very observable, then socialization or "clan mechanisms" will be the only recourse. These mechanisms achieve control by increasing the congruence of objectives between the organization and individuals. The parallel to the Holmstrom and Milgrom (1991) model, in which value is produced without external reward via objectives that are assumed at least somewhat congruent, is apparent. More recent work by Holmstrom and Milgrom (1994) has taken an approach similar to that of Ouchi (1979) in suggesting that the choice between organizational and market coordination of production is contingent on measurability/observability conditions. A remaining difference between the two research streams, however, is in the degree to which internal motivations are assumed to be a viable means to control. For the most part, economics continues to treat the preferences of principal and agent as opposed and exogenous, while behavioral research has a long-standing tradition that explores ways of usefully altering worker preferences (e.g., Barnard, 1938; McGregor, 1960; Ouchi, 1979).[15]

Some researchers have argued that not only are worker preferences alterable but also that external motivation schemes themselves alter preferences to detrimental effect (e.g., Frey, 1993; Kohn, 1993; Deming, 1986; Deci and Ryan, 1985; McGraw, 1978). External motivations have been shown to "crowd out" internal motivations. Once offered rewards for taking specific actions, workers become unwilling to take actions that are not connected with specific rewards; the external reward system shifts the locus of control from worker to the external system, thus reducing the agent's sense of self-determination. Moreover, an offer of external reward for actions that would have been taken because of internal motivation can have an insulting or demeaning effect (Hirsch, 1976); the offer of a reward when none is required creates cognitive dissonance (Festinger, 1957).

---

[15] Leavitt and March (1988) summarize this difference between the two literatures in explaining Barnard's views on altering worker preferences: "In modern terms, Barnard proposed that an executive creates and sustains a culture of beliefs and values that would support cooperation. The appeal is not to exchanges, Pareto optimality, or search for incentive schemes; it is to the construction of a moral order in which individual participants act in that name of the institution – not because it is in their self-interest to do so, but because they identify with the institution and are prepared to sacrifice some aspects of themselves for it" (p. 13).

In apparent contradiction to the "crowding out" research, Simons (1996) points out that there do appear to be successful organizational control systems that combine external rewards and socialization in a way that facilitates particularly effective responses to environments in which observability problems are strongly present. These systems, which he terms *Interactive Control Systems* (ICSs), not only motivate employees but also serve as the primary mechanism for directing discussion around issues that are vital to the organization's survival.

ICSs embed measurement activities in intensive interpersonal processes. In a Harvard Business School case that illustrates an ICS in action, *Codman and Shurtlef*, a division of Johnson & Johnson, uses measurement intensively but invariably within the context of lengthy meetings between managers and those being managed. Underlying measurement activities are a set of norms about appropriate behaviors with respect to measurement uses that are widely known and accepted. Embedding measurement into social interaction in this way apparently engages the clan mechanisms referred to by Ouchi (1979).

Why the use of ICSs does not result in crowding out behaviors is not entirely clear. The socialization that occurs with successful ICSs may somehow prevent shifting of the locus of control from workers to the external system. In the *Codman and Shurtleff* case, the norm that places the right to change measurement targets solely with the person responsible for meeting the target is, for example, suggestive in this regard. Involvement of workers in the definition and operation of a measurement system may mitigate the potential "disempowering" effects of defining performance externally. Similarly, socialization may also sometimes, by a mechanism as yet unknown, diffuse the cognitive dissonance that comes from offering rewards for accomplishments that were internally motivated. Alternatively, and more pessimistically, ICSs that seem successful may simply be systems that have not yet revealed their dysfunctional tendencies.

Knowledge work and motivation

The prominence of the problem of incompleteness in measures of knowledge work has implications for motivation to which we have already alluded. In the presence of incomplete measures, Holmstrom and Milgrom (1991) suggest paying the agent a flat fee and relying on any partial congruence between the objectives of principal and agent to produce value. If we assume that incompleteness of measures is the norm for knowledge work, then we are forced into consideration of internal motivation as a primary means of directing and controlling agent action. Methods of engaging clan mechanisms (Ouchi, 1979) or ICSs (Simons, 1996) become extremely important. The likelihood of creating successful systems that rely on external reward and compliance with plans is reduced, not only because performance verification is frustrated by incompleteness in measures, but also because plans may be unstable in knowledge work settings.

This news is not so bad as it might seem, however, because it is commonly observed that knowledge workers are highly motivated. Knowledge workers tend to self-select into their professions because they like the work. Obtaining effort from such workers is less an issue than direction of the effort. The problem of objective congruence is not so much about workers' aversion to effort or risk as it is about independently minded workers, whose performance cannot be verified, having different ideas about what ought to be done.

The CEO of a startup software company recently related the problem of managing one of her most talented developers. This developer, in addition to taking a strong interest in the success of the company, was also a "free software" activist, ideologically opposed to software patents and the ownership of ideas as expressed in software. At a time when the company was working under a deadline for a client, struggling for its very life, this developer was working on a program to generate random patent applications, ostensibly to frustrate patent authorities. The developer also finished work for the client on time, but his "extracurricular" activities were non-optimal (to say the least) from the perspective of the management team. This same CEO, however, conceded that there was little to be done about this problem, and that such knowledge workers were uncontrollable in any traditional sense.[16]

The potential for crowding out is a particular concern for knowledge work. If external motivation crowds out internal motivation, actually reducing workers' willingness to do more than exactly what they are paid to do, then it reduces tendencies toward self-direction and initiative that are crucial in knowledge work. Furthermore, external reward systems may interfere with communication by encouraging workers to censor and adjust information flows to managers. Workers worried about how their measures "look" may not share information as willingly or as effectively.[17] This is likely to present a significant problem since it has often been argued (e.g., Eisenhardt and Brown,

---

[16] This CEO also noted that it often proved useful that the workers were not controllable: "When the business shifts, often you'll find the seed for the shift in that group because they're not really paying attention to you all along anyway – they've been worried about some way-out-there trend."

[17] Narayanan and Davila (1998) have dealt with aspects of this problem in an agency theory context.

1997; Leonard-Barton, 1995) that effective communication is a key element of success in knowledge work, which requires coordination of concepts that are to a great extent only tacit in the work environment.

Austin and Gittell (1999) have suggested that the act of explicitly sacrificing control-oriented performance measurement can both increase internal motivation and align the preferences of individuals with those of the organization. They describe situations in which control-oriented performance measurement instituted by management is then subverted by management in a way that is highly visible to workers. The act of subverting the measurement system serves as a symbolic gesture that conveys to workers the message "see, we trust you, now be worthy of our trust." Faced with situations in which managers have seemingly intentionally made themselves vulnerable to opportunistic behavior by workers, the workers are – in direct contrast with the assumptions of economic models – unlikely to take advantage and, in fact, are more likely to perform "heroically" in the interests of the organization. In this way, performance measurement indirectly facilitates, via its symbolic sacrifice, high performance and open communications.

The problem of TASK differentials

Like performance measurement, the subject of talent, skill, and knowledge differentials draws historically from numerous fields. Differential capabilities in problem solving have, for example, been treated extensively in developmental and cognitive psychology (see, for example, Simon, 1989). The field sometimes referred to as "complex adaptive systems" has explored the manner in which algorithmic behaviors of organisms or automata evolve differentially in response to environmental conditions (see, e.g., Kalai, 1990). Economists have dealt with TASK differentials as the basis for adverse selection problems; differentials are assumed exogenous and the challenge becomes distinguishing level of capability in agents being selected.

But, as we have observed elsewhere (Larkey *et al.*, 1997), there has been surprisingly little substantial research into the nature of differential inherent capabilities. Differential capabilities in a basketball game between Michael Jordan and the average college faculty member would be the primary determinants of the outcome of a contest between the two. Yet we lack, for the most part, any theoretical framework that would predict or account *ex post* for the outcome. To some extent, we lack this theory because capability differentials are context specific. Skill in basketball is specific to basketball. Unless the context is worth researching on its own (as, for example, organizational capability to innovate is – see, e.g., Leonard-Barton, 1995), then research on skill lacks the generalizability that researchers value in their products.

The absence of theoretical representations of skill become very relevant to performance measurement in that much of its underlying analysis, particularly in economics, is game theoretic in nature. Agency theory is based on the notion that equilibria will emerge as the result of mutual optimization by principal and agent. There is an implicit assumption that all participants in the game can and will optimize. Capability differentials are not present in this representation at all. This is unfortunate for contexts in which these differentials are primary determinants of outcomes (think of our basketball contest between Michael Jordan and Joe Q. Faculty member). Binmore (1990) provides a sweeping, critical review of game theory and concludes that the absence of specific representations of players abilities and tendencies is a glaring hole in applicability of game and economic theories. It similarly poses a challenge to the relevance of performance measurement.

Knowledge work and TASK differentials

Curtis, Krasner, and Iscoe (1988) have documented tremendous disparities in the productivity of software developers. It has become a common belief in the knowledge work fields related to high-tech that inherent capability of individual workers is one of the most important factors in the success of an organizational initiative. The CIO of a major Silicon Valley hardware manufacturer recently estimated that there are only 1000 or so world class software developers in the world, and that his firm was dedicated to holding onto theirs and acquiring more.[18] Increasingly, companies like Trilogy Software, in Austin, Texas, are fashioning their competitive strategies around acquiring the very best technical talent emerging from universities and then facilitating their work with a minimum of obtrusive structure (see Austin and Gittell, 1999).

---

[18] When TASK differentials are pronounced, selecting appropriately skilled workers becomes as important as directing and controlling them once selected. The programmer who can perform a critical task with 5 percent of his effort is always preferable to the programmer who cannot perform the same task with 100 percent of his effort. Economists have dealt with the problem of how performance measurement interacts with worker selection. Lazear (1986), for example, demonstrates that higher piece rates are relatively more attractive to better workers, ostensibly because they give better workers the opportunity to exhibit their greater abilities. He concludes that strong linkage between performance and reward will attract better workers. A potentially serious flaw in this analysis as it applies to knowledge work contexts, however, is that workers are judged to be "better" primarily by their ability to perform on measured outcomes. As has been discussed, if measures are incomplete, strong measurement performers may not be "better" at all, just more inclined to exploit the problems in the measurement system.

Top-tier consulting firms have long used this strategy, as do universities in hiring faculty.[19]

Conventional performance measurement frameworks have very little to say about managing TASK differentials and can often have dysfunctional effects in contexts where TASK differentials are known to be important. Understanding why this is so requires examining the intended uses of performance measurement in organizational settings. Intended uses of measurement can be usefully divided into two categories:

Motivational Measurement is explicitly intended to affect the people who are being measured. An example of measurement in this category is sales tracking linked to a sales commission system. Used in this way, measurement is an attempt to control individual activity which, it is assumed, will not be congruent with organizational objectives, absent the measurement. This is the use of measurement that is implicit in most conventional measurement frameworks.

Informational Measurement is valued primarily for the logistical, status, and research information it conveys, which provides insights, supports organizational learning, and allows better short-term management and long-term improvement of organizational processes. An example of measurement in this category is data gathering for the purpose of understanding how to redesign a business process. This use of measurement has little to do with control and much to do with learning.

In knowledge work settings, motivational uses of measurement are unlikely to be helpful for many reasons. Incompleteness in measures, if present, will likely result in distortion of effort allocations that is not constructive. The silver lining in all this, however, is that the informational uses of measurement are likely to be very helpful in knowledge work settings. Knowledge workers have an appetite for measurement information that can help them do their jobs or improve their own performance. The idiosyncratic resourcefulness that knowledge work requires can be greatly enhanced by effective use of informational measurement, much as a sprinter's performance can be enhanced through training with a stop watch.

It would seem to follow that organizations engaged in knowledge work would be well served by instituting purely informational measurement

---

[19] V. G. Narayanan of the Harvard Business School has observed [private communication] that the job markets in such settings do not "clear" in the economic sense. In markets where top talent is regarded as the determining factor, firms battle furiously for the top-quality workers and refuse to extend offers at any price to those who are not perceived as top quality.

systems and avoiding motivational uses of measurement. Avoiding motivational responses to preserve the validity of informational measurement can be very difficult, however. Because the distinction between the two categories of measurement use is not inherent in the information itself, but rather in how the information is used, it is nearly impossible to credibly assure workers that the purpose of a measurement system is purely informational. The transformation of an informational system of measurement to a motivational one can be triggered by seemingly minor events.

In an interview from an earlier study (Austin, 1996), one subject described an organization engaged in knowledge work in which workers were measuring their own job processes, posting and comparing measurement information, and using it to refine processes and improve performance:

> Then one day, a very high-level president . . . was taken through the hall . . . he saw [measurement information posted on a wall] and said "What's this all about?" They told him and he said "This is wonderful." He took out a red pen . . . and circled [one group's numbers] . . . and he wrote "great work" and signed his name . . . He put the pen away and walked off. Literally the next day, the graphs came off the walls. No one ever put any graphs up again.

It is worth noticing that the act that caused the system to be abandoned was not a punishment, but a reward. The red pen reward, although well intentioned, changed a system conceived to facilitate self-directed work (an informational system) into an explicit external reward mechanism (a motivational system) and in the process destroyed the system.

Given that informational measurement systems can so easily become motivational, it would seem difficult to avoid dysfunctional effects of performance measurement in knowledge work settings. That there is hope, however, is demonstrated by the fact that the measurement system in place in the above "red pen" example did work well until the intervention by senior management. Through use of clan mechanisms (Ouchi, 1979), ICSs (Simons, 1996) or some other means, it may be possible for measurers with informational aims to diffuse unintended motivational effects.

There is some irony here in that the incentive design problem is turned on its head relative to its formulation in agency economics. Rather than *defining* explicit incentives that are expected to be the only way of productively motivating self-interested agents, the informational measurement challenge is to *diffuse* implicit incentives that might tempt self-interested agents. The principal tools to accomplish this are instruments of socialization, aimed at modifying worker preferences. Explicit incentives, such as the one introduced by the red pen, encourage reductions or falsifications in vital communication.

Research challenges

The challenges for research in the area of knowledge work extend naturally from its distinctive characteristics:

1 Research frameworks must emphasize the completeness problem and explore the potential for problems of measurability, attributability, and evaluability to complicate and make dysfunctional any attempts at performance measurement. Knowledge work is primarily about "working smart." The research on measuring knowledge work should not, therefore, be primarily (if at all) about working hard.

2 Because of the prevalence of the problem of incompleteness of measures in knowledge work, the degree to which workers can be internally motivated to create value must be endogenously included in performance measurement models. For knowledge work, marginal returns from investments in improving worker conditions, motivations, or skills may be greater than marginal returns from investments in performance verification. The latter sort of investment is the focus of much of the traditional research in this area.

3 TASK differentials must be somehow included in representation of measurement and behavior. Success in knowledge work has more to do with what workers are capable of than with how hard workers are working. Differential capabilities are not at all present in most performance measurement frameworks, but must be introduced.

Practical implications

The primary practical implications of the distinctive characteristics of knowledge work concerning performance measurement have to do with the very different picture of how measurement interacts with work in the knowledge work setting. If the traditional organizational model was "organization as machine with interchangeable parts," the knowledge work model is "organization as theatrical ensemble." The parts are selected for their roles and are not interchangeable. Talent, skills, and knowledge are too individual and knowledge is too often tacit to accommodate traditional notions of performance comparability.

The presence of TASK disparities necessitates a shift from traditional feedback control to *measurement-facilitated discovery*. Of vital importance in using the measurement in the latter sense is that workers, not managers, become the primary consumers of the information. Managers give up their roles as primary keepers and analyzers of measurement. While this has been advocated as a desirable arrangement in many physical work settings, knowledge work settings may offer no alternative (other than dysfunction).

The most important duty managers have under this model of measurement is to convince workers to participate willingly in the measurement and distribution of information that could potentially be used against them. We consider this a fundamental principle of measuring knowledge work: *that it requires that workers engage in a behavior that is fundamentally irrational on a self-interested individual basis.* Every day, knowledge workers are confronted with choices between actions that will make them "look good" according to incomplete performance measurements, and other actions which will have less favorable impact on measured performance but will in fact create more value. The success for performance measurement in knowledge work settings hinges on which choice the worker consistently takes.

BIBLIOGRPAHY AND REFERENCES

Alchian, A. and Demsetz, H. (1972). Production, information costs, and economic organization. *The American Economic Review*, **62**(5), 777–95.

Austin, R.D. (1996). *Measuring and Managing Performance in Organizations.* New York: Dorset House.

Austin, R.D. (1998). *Trilogy Software, Inc.* Case No. N9–699–034, Boston, MA: Harvard Business School Press.

Austin, R.D. and J. H. Gittell (1999). Anomalies of high performance: Reframing economic and organizational theories of performance measurement. Working paper.

Baker, G.P. (1992). Incentives contracts and performance measurement. *Journal of Political Economy*, **100**(3), 598–614.

Banker, R.D. and Datar, S.M. (1989). Sensitivity, precision, and linear aggregation of signals for performance evaluation. *Journal of Accounting Research*, **27**(1), 21–39.

Barnard, C.I. (1938). *The Functions of the Executive.* Cambridge, MA: Harvard University Press.

Berry, S. and Larkey, P.D. (1998). Aging and athletic performance. In *Science and Golf III*, ed. Alastair Cochran and Martin Farrally, E. & F.N. Spon.

Binmore, K. (1990). *Essays on the Foundations of Game Theory.* Cambridge, MA: Basil Blackwell.

Blau, P.M. (1963). *The Dynamics of Bureaucracy: A Study of Interpersonal Relations in Two Government Agencies.* Chicago, IL: The University of Chicago Press.

Caulkins, J. and Larkey, P.D. (1993). All above average and other unintended consequences of performance evaluation systems. John Heinz III School of Public Policy and Management Working Paper 92–41.

Curtis, B., Krasner, H., and Iscoe, N. (1988). A field study of the software design process for large systems. *Communications of the ACM*, 31(11), 1268–87.

Davenport, T.H. and Prusak, L. (1998). *Working Knowledge: How Organizations Manage What They Know*. Boston, MA: Harvard Business School Press.

Dawes, R.M. (1991). Social dilemmas, economic self-interest, and evolutionary theory. In *Recent Research in Psychology: Frontiers of Mathematical Psychology: Essays in Honor of Clyde Coombs*, ed. D.R. Brown, and J.E.K. Smith, New York: Springer-Verlag.

Deci, E.L., and Ryan, R.M. (1985). *Intrinsic Motivation and Self-Determination in Human Behavior*. New York: Plenum Press.

Deming, W.E. (1986). *Out of the Crisis*. Cambridge, MA: MIT Press.

Eisenhardt, K.M. (1985). Control: organizational and economic approaches. *Management Science*, 31(2), 134–49.

Eisenhardt, K.M. and Brown, S.L. (1997). *Competing on the Edge*. Boston, MA: Harvard Business School Press.

Festinger, L.A. (1957). *A Theory of Cognitive Dissonance*. Evanston, IL: Row, Peterson.

Florac, W.A., Park, R.E., and Carleton, A.D. (1997). Practical software measurement: Measuring for process management and improvement. Software Engineering Institute (CMU/SEI-97–HB-003), Pittsburgh, PA.

Frey, B.S. (1993). Motivation as a limit to pricing. *Journal of Economic Psychology*, 14, 635–64.

Hannaway, J. (1991). Higher-order thinking, job design and incentives: an analysis and proposal. Working Paper.

Hirsch, F. (1976). *The Social limits to Growth*. Cambridge, MA: Harvard University Press.

Holmstrom, B. (1979). Moral hazard and observability. *Bell Journal of Economics*, 10, 74–91.

Holmstrom, B. and Milgrom, P. (1987). Aggregation and linearity in the provision of intertemporal incentives. *Econometrica*, 55, 302–28.

Holmstrom, B. and Milgrom, P. (1991). Multi-task principal-agent analyses: incentive contracts, asset ownership, and job design. *Journal of Law, Economics, and Organizations*, 7, 25–52.

Holmstrom, B. and Milgrom, P. (1994). The firm as an incentive system. *The American Economic Review*, 84(4), 972–92.

Ishikawa, K. (1985). *What is Total Quality Control? The Japanese Way*. Trans. by David J. Lu, Englewood Cliffs, NJ: Prentice-Hall.

Jensen, M.C. and Meckling, W.H. (1976). Theory of the firm: managerial behavior, agency costs, and ownership structure. *Journal of Financial Economics*, 3, 305–60.

Kalai, E. (1990). Banded rationality and strategic complexity in repeated games. In *Game Theory and Applications*, ed. T. Ishiishi, A. Neyman, and Y. Tauman, pp. 131–54. San Diego, CA: Academic Press.

Kaplan, R.S. and Norton, D.P. (1992). The balanced scorecard: measures that drive performance. *Harvard Business Review*, January–February, 71–9.

Kaplan, R.S. and Norton, D.P. (1996). *The Balanced Scorecard: Translating Strategy into Action*, Boston, MA: Harvard Business School Press.

Kohn, A. (1993). Why work incentives fall down on the job. *USA Today*, December 16, A13.

Larkey, P., Kadane, J., Austin, R., and Zamir, S. (1997). Skill in games. *Management Science,* **43**(5), 596–609.

Lawler, E.E. III and Rhode, J.G. (1976). *Information and Control in Organizations,* Santa Monica, CA: Goodyear.

Lazear, E. (1986). Salaries and piece rates. *Journal of Business,* **59**(3), 405–31.

Leavitt, B. and March, J.G. (1988). Chester I. Barnard and the intelligence of learning. *Annual Review of Sociology,* **14**, 319–40.

Leonard-Barton, D.A. (1995). *Wellsprings of Knowledge: Building and Sustaining the Sources of Innovation.* Boston, MA: Harvard Business School Press.

March, J.G. and Simon, H.A. (1958). *Organizations.* New York: John Wiley & Sons.

McGraw, K.O. (1978). The detrimental effects of reward on performance: A literature review and a prediction model. In Lepper and Greene, 33–60.

McGregor, D. (1960). *The Human Side of the Enterprise.* New York: McGraw-Hill.

Merton, R.K. (1968). *Social Theory and Social Structure.* New York: The Free Press.

Milgrom, P. and Roberts, J. (1992). *Economics, Organization and Management.* Englewood Cliffs, NJ: Prentice-Hall.

Narayanan, V.G., and Davila, A. (1998). Using delegation and control systems to mitigate the trade-off between the performance-evaluation and belief-revision uses of accounting signals. *Journal of Accounting and Economics,* **25**, 255–82.

Nonaka, I. and Takeuchi, H. (1995). *The Knowledge Creating Company: How Japanese Companies Create the Dynamics of Innovation.* Oxford: Oxford University Press.

Ouchi, W.G. (1979). A conceptual framework for the design of organizational control mechanisms. *Management Science,* **25**(9), 833–48.

Ouchi, W.G. (1981). *How American Business Can Meet the Japanese Challenge.* Reading, MA: Addison-Wesley.

Prahalad, C. and Hamel, G. (1990). The core competence of the corporation. *Harvard Business Review,* May–June, 79–91.

Ridgeway, V.F. (1956). Dysfunctional consequences of performance measurement. *Administrative Science Quarterly,* **1**(2), 240–7.

Ross, S.A. (1973). The economic theory of agency: The principal's problem. *The American Economic Review,* **63**(2), 134–9.

Simon, H. (1989). *Models of Thought.* New Haven, CT: Yale University Press.

Simons, R. (1996). *How Managers Use Innovative Control Systems to Drive Strategic Renewal.* Boston, MA: Harvard Business School Press.

Simons, R. (1987). Codman and Shurtleff, Inc.: Planning and Control Systems. Harvard Business School case number 187-081.

Skolnick, J. (1966). *Justice Without Trial: Law Enforcement in Democratic Society.* New York: John Wiley & Sons.

Stake, R.E. (1971). Testing hazards in performance contracting. *Phi Delta Kappan,* June, 583–9.

Sugarman, C. (1990). US produce standards focus more on appearance than quality. *The Pittsburgh Press,* August 5, E1.

Thompson, J.D. (1967). *Organizations in Action.* New York: McGraw-Hill.

Vroom, V.H. and Deci E.L. (1970). *Management and Motivation.* eds., Middlesex: Penguin Books, England.

Measuring eBusiness performance

Andy Neely, Bernard Marr, Chris Adams, and Neha Kapashi

Measuring eBusiness performance: Key findings

In the first quarter 2000 members of both Accenture's Managing With Measures team and the Centre for Business Performance at Cranfield School of Management began a study of performance measurement in the new economy. During the course of the investigation senior managers from over 70 bricks-and-mortar, clicks-and-mortar and dot.coms offered their views and opinions on the strengths and weaknesses of their organization's performance measurement systems. The ten key findings of the study were:

1 Everyone wants to improve their organization's measurement systems. Despite the vast time and effort that many management teams have exerted on their measurement systems over the last few years, still there is immense frustration. Survey respondents from 96 percent of bricks-and-mortar, 96 percent of clicks-and-mortar, and 100 percent of the dot.coms said they wanted to improve their measurement systems.

2 When it comes to performance measurement, the dot.coms have different improvement priorities to the bricks-and-mortar and clicks-and-mortar firms. While everyone wants to develop more comprehensive strategic measurement systems, the dot.coms are also particularly interested in using technology to track performance – especially for click stream analysis and customer relationship management.

3 Everyone understands the importance of measuring customer satisfaction. One hundred percent of those surveyed said either that they measured customer satisfaction or that they should measure it.

4 Satisfied customers are not enough. Today's thought leaders talk of loyal and profitable customers. The argument being that there is no point having satisfied customers that are not profitable (or likely to become profitable) and that do not come back to buy again. The dot.coms appear to have taken this message on board, with 89 percent of them claiming that they measure whether they are getting what they want and need from their customers. This contrasts quite markedly with the 26 percent of

bricks-and-mortar and 41 percent of clicks-and-mortar that claimed the same.

5 The war for talent is being taken seriously, although apparently not as seriously by the dot.coms. 74 percent of bricks-and-mortar, 70 percent of clicks-and-mortar, but only 50 percent of dot.coms claim to measure employee satisfaction.

6 The dot.coms are more interested in shareholder satisfaction than either the bricks-and-mortar or clicks-and-mortar firms. Thirty-nine percent of bricks-and-mortar firms claim to track shareholder satisfaction, compared with 44 percent of clicks-and-mortar and 56 percent of dot.coms, which in itself is a surprisingly low figure given the dot.coms incredible reliance on their investors.

7 Across the board demand is greatest for measures of new measures of supplier satisfaction and the effectiveness of the demand generation process. Numerous organizations said that they wanted to measure these dimensions of performance, yet few claimed to have decent measures in place.

8 The biggest reported barrier to improving measurement systems was lack of time. Other frequently cited barriers include availability of data, availability of technology, the cost of developing and implementing measurement systems and the frequency of organizational change.

9 Overall the dot.coms appear to measure more and be more confident in their measurement systems than either the bricks-and-mortar or the clicks-and-mortar firms. The interviews and other research, however, suggest that some of this optimism is misguided, as there are numerous studies that show that the dot.coms are failing to deliver the service their customers expect. So, even if they have the data, they are failing to act on it.

10 Too many of the dot.coms are obsessed with measurement rather than management. As the dot.coms grow in size their managers perceive that they are losing control. Hence they begin to introduce measures. The danger is that they will not stop. There is a limited set of measures that the dot.coms should track (see measures prescriptions). To date, however, the managers of the dot.coms have not learnt the lessons from bricks-and-mortar firms that have introduced too many measures and now find themselves floundering with complicated measurement systems, designed for an age of command and control.

The eRevolution: State of play

Start-up B2C dot.com businesses are appearing and disappearing everywhere and threatening long-established businesses' market share. Long-established businesses, the so-called bricks-and-mortar companies, are reacting by creating new sales channels using the Internet – some more successfully than others – to become clicks-and-mortar firms. Other established businesses are giving eCommerce a wide berth (or, in some cases, they are being forced to do so) and leaving it to their distributors and retail customers to develop these new sales channels. They may, however, benefit from Internet purchasing rather than selling.

Online auctions – and so-called reverse (or Dutch) auctions – are rapidly changing the way many consumers buy certain goods and services (Zapna *et al.*, 2000). At the same time, dot.com businesses are creating new B2B websites, which threaten established intermediary businesses, such as brokers, wholesalers, merchants, dealers, and distributors. Long-established businesses are beginning to "bury the hatchet" with their direct competitors and are clubbing together with each other (and with technology partners) to form their own rival Internet exchanges. Almost certainly, there are already more B2B exchanges than are sustainable in the longer term. Several industries have multiple exchanges, where there would appear to be room for only one or, at most, two players in the longer term. Inevitably, there will be survivors, failures, and mergers. Many industries have local, national, or regional purchasing needs, while others are more global in the nature of their procurement requirements. Yet, in some of the more esoteric industries, no one has yet come forward with a B2B exchange from either side, but it seems a fair bet that someone is working on it somewhere and that it is only a matter of time before they do emerge.

The struggle between the so-called New Economy and the Old looks likely to continue for a while. Some dot.coms will carve out a viable market niche and become profitable, others will not. Davids can slay Goliaths in this knowledge-based economy, but there are almost certain to be some major start-up casualties (e.g. Boo.com), and some disappointed shareholders and venture capitalists too. Equally, some established businesses will pour millions of dollars into trying to see off the new intruders only to fail – whereas others will vanquish their foes and become even stronger. No one can be certain whether it will be the keen "first-movers' who will hold on to their tenuous initial advantage or the smart "fast-followers" who will learn from the pioneers' mistakes and come through to be the real winners.

The only real "definite" is that no one can afford to be complacent. Every company needs to have a strategy that addresses the eRevolution. That strategy then needs to be supported with the appropriate business processes and capabilities. Given this premise then: How are executives supposed to manage in this turbulent environment? What are the critical business issues they need to address? And what are the particular implications for performance measurement?

This and the related contributions in this series set out to address these questions, but importantly to address them on the basis of data rather than subjective opinion. During the course of a six-month study, executives from over 70 bricks-and-mortar, clicks-and-mortar and dot.coms were surveyed and interviewed. Answers were sought to several substantive questions, including:

1 What are the similarities and differences between the measurement systems used by bricks-and-mortar, clicks-and-mortar, and dot.com firms?
2 Are managers in these firms happy with their measurement systems. If not, why and what is preventing them from improving their measurement systems?
3 In an ideal world, what should managers in bricks-and-mortar, clicks-and-mortar, and dot.coms be measuring?

The sections that follow expand upon these themes and provide answers to the three questions raised above, with particular emphasis on the eBusinesses.

What are eBusinesses measuring?

At the outset of the research we had to chose a measurement framework around which to base our investigation. While numerous such frameworks exist, they all offer partial perspectives on performance. The balanced scorecard (Kaplan and Norton, 1992, 1996), with its four perspectives, focuses on financiers (shareholders), customers, internal processes, plus innovation and learning. In doing so it downplays the importance of other stakeholders, such as suppliers, alliance partners, and employees. The business excellence model (EFQM, 1993) combines results, which are readily measurable, with enablers, some of which are not. Shareholder value frameworks incorporate the cost of capital into the equation, but ignore everything (and everyone) else. Both activity-based costing and cost of quality, however, focus on the identification and control of

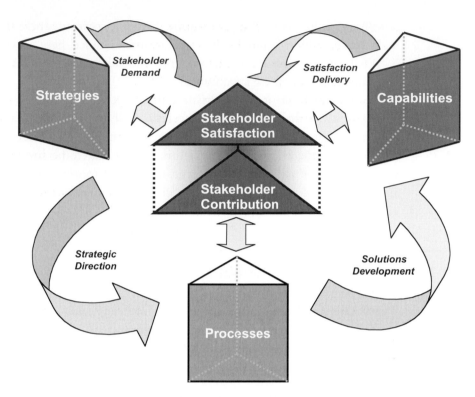

Figure 21.1.

cost drivers (non-value-adding activities (see Deming, 1986 and Kaplan and Cooper, 1997) and failures/non-conformances respectively), which are themselves often embedded in the business processes. But this highly process-focused view ignores any other perspectives on performance, such as the opinion of shareholders, customers, and employees. Conversely, benchmarking tends to involve taking a largely external perspective, often comparing performance with that of competitors or other "best practitioners" of business processes. However, this kind of activity is frequently pursued as a one-off exercise towards generating ideas for – or gaining commitment to – short-term improvement initiatives, rather than the design of a formalized on-going performance measurement system. For this reason we chose to adopt a new measurement framework, which we call the Performance Prism (Neely and Adams, 2001). The Prism (see figure 21.1) has been deliberately designed as a comprehensive measurement framework and in application it allows five key questions to be addressed:

1 Who are the key stakeholders and what do they want and need?
2 What strategies do we have to put in place to satisfy the wants and needs of those key stakeholders?

3 What critical processes do we require if we are to execute these strategies?

4 What capabilities do we need to operate and enhance these processes?

5 What contributions do we require from our stakeholders if we are to maintain and develop these capabilities?

We used this Performance Prism framework as the basis of a research survey, firstly, to find out what eBusinesses actually <u>do</u> measure today and, secondly, what they are not measuring but believe that they definitely <u>should</u> be measuring in the future. To analyze this, we segregated the survey's respondents into three categories: dot.coms, clicks-and-mortar, and bricks-and-mortar. Table 21.1 that follows summarizes the results for the two eBusiness categories – clicks-and-mortar and dot.coms.

The improvement agenda: priorities and barriers

The opening question on the survey was "are you seeking improvements to your measurement systems." Ninety-six percent of bricks-and-mortar, 96 percent of clicks-and-mortar, and 100 percent of dot.coms claimed that they were. When the data are probed in more detail some unexpected findings emerge. Firstly, we had anticipated at the outset of this research that dot.coms, being – by definition – young, immature, and entrepreneurial businesses, might be somewhat antagonistic or, at least *laissez-faire*, towards performance measurement. We were wrong – generally they could hardly be keener or indeed more enthusiastic about making further improvements.

We also thought that clicks-and-mortar enterprises would perceive that they had inherited much of the "best practice" performance measurement and management culture of their parent companies, but that they might be wishing that they did not have to carry quite so much "corporate baggage" around with them. Wrong again – generally they did not think that they were as good as their dot.com counterparts in this respect and wanted to make significant improvements.

Lastly, we thought that the bricks-and-mortar companies would probably perceive that they already have the most sophisticated performance measurement systems and practices. After all, unlike their counterparts, they have had years and years to practice getting this right, even if things have moved on a bit recently. Just how wrong can you be? They generally confessed to being quite slovenly in their approach to many performance measurement aspects and thought that they ought to do a much better all-round job of it.

Table 21.1 Measuring eBusiness Performance

Points of View (2)	Research Results			
	Dot.coms		C-&-M	
	Do	Should	Do	Should
Stakeholder satisfaction Big improvements in key stakeholder satisfaction measures are desired – dot.coms think this a more urgent need than clicks-and-mortar firms.				
• Customer satisfaction is a "mission critical" performance measure. Each aspect of the customer experience needs to be addressed – not just the web-technology front-end. All organizations either already *do* or agree that their performance *should* be measured.	83%	100%	85%	100%
• Measures of investor satisfaction are perceived by dot.coms to be more important than in clicks-and-mortar businesses – this may be due to their particular requirement for sequential external funding.	56%	100%	44%	80%
• Employee satisfaction measures are high on the agenda of dot.com companies, but more frequently practiced by clicks-and-mortar organizations (probably due to practice transfer from parent companies).	50%	100%	70%	75%
• We contend that many eBusinesses have so far underestimated the importance and value of measuring both Supplier satisfaction and Alliance partner satisfaction – the organizations on which they are often *extremely* dependent. Dot.coms recognize the gap most.	28% 28%	92% 85%	33% 30%	78% 63%
• Measures of Regulator satisfaction are not seen as important today, but are highly likely to become an increasingly important aspect of eCommerce – we believe both groups underestimate this.	22%	57%	33%	56%
Stakeholder contribution Improvement in key stakeholder contribution measures are imperatives for both groups – again they are most prevalent within dot.coms.				
• Dot.com companies seem to be generally far more aware of the need to have measures of Customer contribution than clicks-and-mortar organizations. They need to prove their business model.	89%	100%	41%	75%
• Measures of Employee contribution are recognized as important by the majority of both dot.com and clicks-and-mortar companies. All dot.coms think it is a "must measure" item, but only two-thirds do so today versus three-quarters of clicks-and-mortar firms.	61%	100%	74%	86%
• Clicks-and-mortar firms are naïve if they believe that they can do without measures of both Supplier contribution and Alliance partner contribution. Their dot.com counterparts seem to have a far greater awareness of this need for improvement.	33% 39%	92% 91%	48% 19%	79% 55%

Table 21.1 (*cont.*)

	Research Results			
	Dot.coms		C-&-M	
Points of View (2)	Do	Should	Do	Should
Stakeholder contribution (cont.)				
• All dot.coms think that measuring <u>Investor contribution</u> is very important (although only one-third of them claim to do so already), whereas only around half the number of clicks-and-mortar firms share this view – probably because of parent company funding.	33%	<u>100%</u>	19%	50%
Strategies				
It's hard to imagine why any organization would disagree with the simple need to measure achievement of its strategic intent in terms of performance targets set – although not quite all agreed that they did so, it is the number 1 strategy measure for both types of eBusiness.	<u>83%</u>	<u>100%</u>	<u>78%</u>	67%
• Dot.com companies are concerned to have measures that reflect whether their <u>strategies need to be changed</u>, while clicks-and-mortar firms want to know if they have the <u>right strategies in place</u> (which are only very subtly different requirements).	<u>78%</u> 61%	<u>75%</u> 71%	41% <u>67%</u>	69% <u>89%</u>
• Both groups – particularly dot.coms – also identified the need for data about whether their <u>strategies are being implemented</u>.	<u>72%</u>	<u>100%</u>	56%	<u>83%</u>
• Clicks-and-mortar companies are particularly concerned about *improving* the measures which tell them whether their <u>strategies are understood</u> (and, to a lesser extent, this applies to dot.coms too – perhaps the more so as they grow in size).	39%	<u>82%</u>	52%	<u>92%</u>
Processes				
Business Process measures are perceived as a big issue by dot.com organizations, while clicks-and-mortar firms value them less highly.				
• Both dot.coms and clicks-and-mortar firms want to improve measures of the <u>effectiveness</u> – and also the <u>efficiency</u> – of their <u>Fulfill demand</u> processes, but the former appear further advanced.	<u>83%</u> <u>78%</u>	<u>100%</u> <u>100%</u>	48% 52%	<u>100%</u> 69%
• Dot.com organizations appear to be *significantly* more demanding in their requirements for improving measures of other business processes than their clicks-and-mortar counterparts (who seem to value efficiency above effectiveness) – particularly in the areas of:				
<u>Generate demand effectiveness</u>	67%	<u>100%</u>	48%	73%
<u>Generate demand efficiency</u>	44%	<u>90%</u>	37%	<u>76%</u>
<u>Develop new products and services effectiveness</u>	67%	<u>100%</u>	33%	<u>78%</u>
<u>Develop new products and services efficiency</u>	56%	<u>88%</u>	19%	<u>82%</u>
<u>Plan and manage the enterprise effectiveness</u>	56%	<u>100%</u>	26%	70%
<u>Plan and manage the enterprise efficiency</u>	50%	<u>89%</u>	22%	<u>76%</u>

Table 21.1 (*cont.*)

	Research Results			
	Dot.coms		C-&-M	
Points of View (2)	Do	Should	Do	Should
Capabilities While dot.coms have the edge today in Technology and People Skills measures, everyone agrees improved capability measures are needed.				
• Dot.coms are far more concerned about measuring whether they have the <u>Technologies</u> and <u>People Skills</u> their organization requires than their clicks-and-mortar counterparts.	<u>83%</u> <u>61%</u>	67% 71%	48% 41%	<u>86%</u> <u>88%</u>
• Dot.coms most want to improve the <u>Infrastructure</u> and <u>Best Practices</u> components of their Capabilities measures – whereas clicks-and-mortar firms recognize the need to improve all four components of their capabilities from their current low base.	50% 22%	<u>100%</u> <u>100%</u>	44% 41%	<u>73%</u> <u>75%</u>

Table 21.2 Top three improvements required – priority order

Bricks-and-mortar	Clicks-and-mortar	Dot.coms
Develop/introduce a more comprehensive measurement system	Integrate various systems and integrate new technology with legacy systems	Improve click stream analysis
Enhance our analysis capabilities – establish what really drives business performance	Benchmark against good practice	Improve the entire company's performance measurement system
Link pay to performance	Make our measurement systems more comprehensive	Introduce more sophisticated CRM and data warehouse

Across the board managers reported that they wanted to improve their measurement system, so naturally the next question was: "What aspects of your measurement systems do you want to improve." For the bricks-and-mortar firms the number one priority was to develop a strategic measurement system. While both the clicks-and-mortar and the dot.coms identified this as a high priority, the number one priority for the dot.coms was to improve their methods of customer tracking – i.e., click stream analysis (see table 21.2).

The contrast between traditional businesses (bricks-and-mortar) and dot.coms is stark. Traditional business are much more concerned about

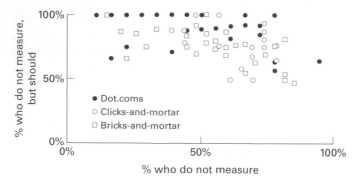

Figure 21.2.   Figure measurement needs.

developing balanced measurement systems and moving into more sophisticated analysis. Dot.coms, on the other hand, are still striving to establish specific technology related measures associated with issues such as "web page stickiness" and "click stream patterns." While all of the respondents appear to have concerns about the process of capturing data, it is also interesting to note that the dot.coms are much more concerned about how to use technology to access data, than either the bricks-and-mortar or the clicks-and-mortar businesses.

Another way of cutting the data is to look at which of the dimensions of performance that are not currently measured managers want to measure. Figure 21.2 above shows the summary data for the bricks-and-mortar, clicks-and-mortar, and dot.coms. The *x*-axis is based on the percentage of respondents who claimed not to measure a particular dimension of performance. The *y*-axis is based on the percentage of respondents who claimed not to measure a particular dimension of performance, but said that they should. Each symbol on the chart refers to a particular dimension of performance.

The way to read the chart is to look at the patterns of identical symbols. Symbols falling in the top right-hand quadrant have scored high on both counts – that more than 50 percent of the sample said they did not measure that specific dimension of performance and more than 50 percent of the sample said they wanted to measure that dimension of performance. Hence symbols falling in the top right-hand quadrant highlight areas of greatest need.

By a similar logic, symbols falling in the top left-hand quadrant represent opportunities for transfer of best practice. Less than 50 percent of the sample claimed not to measure that particular dimension of performance under examination, while more than 50 percent of those who did not, wanted to.

Hence it should be possible for those who do not have measures in place to "borrow" ideas from those who have.

Continuing around the chart in an anti-clockwise manner, symbols falling in the bottom left-hand quadrant are symptomatic of areas where those who want the measures have them. This is because less than 50 percent of the sample claim not measure the item under examination and less than 50 percent of those who do not have a measure in place wish to introduce one.

Finally the bottom right-hand quadrant highlights areas for which there is no demand. Over 50 percent of the sample say they do not measure the item under examination, yet less than 50 percent of the sample say they wish to.

Before specifying which are the specific areas of greatest demand it is worth reviewing the chart at an aggregate level. Doing so enables some important conclusions to be drawn. Firstly, it is possible to see that for all 31 of the measurement areas identified in the Performance Prism at least 50 percent of those firms who did not have measures in place felt that they should introduce them. This suggests that the Performance Prism framework enables many managers to identify some significant gaps in their existing measurement systems, which in turn supports our assertion that it is a more comprehensive framework than those already in existence. Secondly, the groups with the greatest measurement needs appear to be the clicks-and-mortar and bricks-and-mortar firms. Of the 31 different measurement areas identified in the Performance Prism, over 50 percent of the clicks-and-mortar firms said that they needed help with 22 of them, while over 50 percent of the bricks-and-mortar firms said they needed help with 21 of them (hence the dense clustering of "clicks-and-mortar" and "bricks-and-mortar" symbols in the top right-hand quadrant of figure 21.1). Thirdly, there appears to be significant scope for sharing best measurement practice among the dot.coms. Seventeen of the 31 different measurement areas identified by the Performance Prism, fall in the top left-hand quadrant for the dot.coms. The implication of which is that many of the dot.coms claim to have measures in place, so there is significant scope for those who do not to learn from their peers.

At a more detailed level, it is also worth reviewing the data to explore which measurement topics fall where for each of the sub-groups. For the dot.com firms this more detailed view revealed the following major findings:

1 The dot.coms greatest measurement needs lie in the areas of best practice transfer, investor contribution, supplier satisfaction, local community contribution, supplier contribution, and alliance partner satisfaction and contribution.

Table 21.3 Measurement needs of bricks-and-mortar, clicks-and-mortar and dot.coms

Bricks-and-mortar	Clicks-and-mortar	Dot.coms
Strategies understood (74%, 94%)	Develop new products effectively (81%, 82%)	Best practices in place (78%, 100%)
Plan and manage effectively (74%, 94%)	Plan and manage effectively (78%, 76%)	Investor contribution (67%, 100%)
Best practices in place (65%, 100%)	Fulfill demand efficiently (52%, 100%)	Supplier satisfaction (72%, 92%)
Customer contribution (74%, 88%)	People skills in place (59%, 88%)	Local community contribution (94%, 65%)
Technologies in place (57%, 100%)	Supplier satisfaction (67%, 78%)	Supplier contribution (67%, 92%)
Plan and manage efficiently (74%, 82%)	Develop new products efficiently (67%, 78%)	Alliance partner satisfaction (72%, 85%)
Infrastructure in place (74%, 82%)	Plan and manage efficiently (74%, 70%)	Alliance partner contribution (61%, 91%)
Strategies need changing (78%, 78%)	Strategies understood (48%, 92%)	Employee satisfaction (50%, 100%)
Supplier satisfaction (74%, 76%)	Generate demand – effectively (63%, 76%)	Infrastructure in place (50%, 100%)
Generate demand effectively (74%, 76%)	Technologies in place (52%, 86%)	Generate demand – effectively (56%, 90%)

2 There is significant scope for best practice measurement transfer between dot.coms, especially for those measurement areas associated with the efficiency and effectiveness of process execution.

Table 21.3 contains a summary of the detailed analysis for and highlights the top ten areas of greatest measurement need for them.

It is worth noting that only two of these different measurement needs appear across the board – supplier satisfaction (ninth for bricks-and-mortar, fifth for clicks-and-mortar, and third for dot.coms) and generate demand effectively (tenth for bricks-and-mortar, ninth for clicks-and-mortar, and tenth for dot.coms). Once again, then, the implication is that there must be considerable scope for best practice transfer, this time between rather than within categories.

Having identified the massive demand for improved measurement systems and having gathered views on improvement priorities, the final question asked was: "What stops you from improving your measurement systems." On this issue there was considerable agreement, with time being identified as the number one barrier across the board. Other frequently cited barriers include availability of data, availability of technology, the cost of developing and implementing measurement systems, and the frequency of organizational change. The time barrier, however, was so significant that it lead us to the next phase of our research, which involved developing some measures prescriptions – i.e. attempting to identify what the minimum set of measures for a firm operating in the new economy should be.

The measures prescriptions

As already mentioned, the research reported in this and the accompanying contributions was structured around a new measurement framework, the Performance Prism. Given the level of interest in the Performance Prism and the fact that it highlighted some significant gaps in the existing measurement systems of the bricks-and-mortar, clicks-and-mortar, and dot.coms (see previous section, especially chart 1), it seemed appropriate to structure our measurement prescriptions around the same framework. This is not to suggest that all eBusiness should measure all of the items listed in the measures prescriptions that follow. Rather the measures prescriptions are designed to provide a template that can be used to assess the comprehensiveness of an eBusiness' measurement system. Table 21.4 illustrates the set of measures for new economy organizations.

Conclusions and moving forward

The survey provided one over-riding conclusion. There is a significant trend to suggest that the dot.com group of companies believe that they are better equipped to manage their business with the measures they are using than either of the other two groups – although they admit that they could and should do an even better job.

So why should this be so? After all, these are all relatively young companies with essentially little experience of performance measurement and management practices. Playing the devil's advocate, there could be several reasons:

1 "They are naïve optimists" – performance measurement is much more complex than they perceive it to be. Their companies are too young to have experienced the mistakes that can be made introducing measures and

Table 21.4 Prism-based eBusiness measures: Illustrative examples

Stakeholder Satisfaction: Who are our key stakeholders and what do they want and need?

Customer satisfaction	*Investor satisfaction*
Online customer satisfaction surveys	Progress to stated business plan milestones
Competitive perception surveys [incl. most appreciated website features and perception of alliance partner(s) quality surveys]	Market capitalization out-/under-performance trend [vs. sector]*
# Customer complaints/resolutions [by type]	Investor turnover [vs. sector]*
Level of product returns [w/a]	Actual performance vs. Analyst expectations*
Level of customer cost savings achieved	Share price response to announcements*

Alliance partner satisfaction	*Employee satisfaction*
Alliance Partner satisfaction surveys	Employee satisfaction surveys
# Alliance Partner disputes/resolutions	Training satisfaction feedback
	Employee turnover trend [by reason for leaving categories at exit interview]

Regulator satisfaction	
Level of regulatory non-compliances	

Note: *Post-IPO only

Strategies: What strategies are we pursuing to satisfy these wants and needs?

Business unit strategy	*Brands, products and services strategy*
Progress towards strategic intent milestones	Direct Product/Service sales revenues trend
Business Unit cashflow [vs. plan]	Indirect Product/Service sales revenues trend
Sales growth/decline through each channel*	Advertising/Commission revenues trend
Margin trend [through each channel*]	Level of new/repeat business sales trend
Level of existing customer conversions to new channel*	Percent of customers placing repeat orders
Cash revenue vs. Barter revenue	Change in market share [vs. plan]
Level of advertising and promotions spend	Public/Trade brand recognition surveys
	Demographic analysis of brand awareness
	Cost of attracting new customers
Note: *Clicks-and-mortar only	Cost of retaining existing customers

Table 21.4 (*cont.*)

Processes: What processes to we need to put in place to achieve these strategies?

Generate demand	*Fulfill demand*
Level of website visits: direct/cross-referrals	On-time delivery-to-promise performance
% of repeat visits to website	Requested delivery-window refusals
Conversion rate: Level of website visits consummated [with sales]	Assisted service demand vs. capacity
	Delivery leadtime and charges benchmarks
Competitor price comparison tracking	Level of stock-outs [vs. stock-turns]
Advertising response rates [by source]	Level of product substitutions [w/a]

Develop New Products & Services	*Plan and Manage The Enterprise*
No. of channel-specific products/services	Headcount vs. plan
No. of new product/service lines introduced	Capital investment vs. plan
Level of extended product/service line sales	Working capital vs. plan

Capabilities: What capabilities do we require if we are to operate these processes?

Practices	*Technology*
Website navigation best practice benchmarks	Website downtime
Order confirmation best practices adoption	Peak demand vs. server capacity
Level of mid-purchase/checkout abandons	Average download times at peak demand
Customer behavior patterns (clickstream analysis)	Systems integration achievement [vs. plan]
Level of security accreditation [vs. plan]	Website revisions backlog
Best practice privacy policy benchmarks	Time to execute website updates

People	*Infrastructure*
Skill-sets inventory vs. plan	Facilities and equipment vs. plan
Recruitment achievement vs. plan	[*e.g. call center, distribution center, delivery*
Compensation benchmarks [by job type]	*fleet, hardware capacity upgrades, etc.*]
Training provided vs. plan	

Stakeholder Contribution: What do we want and need from our stakeholders?

Suppliers	*Customers*
Service level agreement performance of supplier(s)	Customer loyalty
Level of spend by supplier	Customer profitability

Table 21.4 (*cont.*)

Stakeholder Contribution (*cont.*)	
Alliance partners	*Employees*
Alliance Partner contribution to revenues	Employee improvement suggestions implemented
Alliance Partner improvement suggestions implemented	
	Investors
	Level of Institutional Investor/Venture Capital Support

Note:
The term 'vs. plan' here refers to latest business plan agreed by the executive team (as opposed to an annual or long-term plan)

measurement systems. They think that they are doing a "good job" with it, but maybe they are not really.

2 "They are more techo-sophisticated" – they actually use modern information technologies more effectively to collect and collate their measurement data than their more "mortar-based" brethren.

3 "They have better business models to guide them" – to get to where they are today they had to develop business models in order to obtain the funding they needed to keep them alive. So, they needed to have appropriate broad-based measures in place to make that happen, while the "mortar-based" companies are driven more by accounting measures.

4 "They have relatively simple business models" – compared with other businesses, most of the dot.coms have a greater level of focus as to what they need to achieve and how to go about getting there. By creating organizations that are more virtual with fewer people and management layers, complexity is reduced but inter-relationships become more important.

5 "They have a greater immediacy of purpose" – since they are pioneers and live on a less secure platform of continued existence, they need to have enhanced "radar systems" that will allow them to react much faster than their more-established and better-funded counterparts.

6 "They don't carry any 'corporate baggage' with them" – they have no pre-conceived notions or imposed performance measurement practices dictated by their parent companies in the name of "standardization."

Alternatively, perhaps we should not be looking for excuses. Are we "in denial" here? Is it possible that these companies that were created just the day before yesterday have genuine performance measurement and management lessons for their clicks-and-mortar and bricks-and-mortar counterparts? After all, quite plausibly, they have had the opportunity to build their measurement practices from scratch, prioritizing only the stuff that really matters and putting it in place.

Clearly, further research will be needed in order to identify the particular causes of the dot.coms perceived strengths in this area. The current research study has identified this somewhat unexpected phenomenon, further research should focus on getting a better understanding of whether it is arrogance and "puff," or genuinely better measurement systems and practices. If it is the latter, what then are the lessons that can be learned by the clicks-and-mortar and bricks-and-mortar companies about improving their systems and practices? Furthermore, given that the dot.coms in our sample have indicated (despite their perceived superiority) that they believe they still have considerable room to improve their measurement systems and practices too, this study should also try to identify what – specifically – they are planning to improve, find out which particular performance measures they are attacking and discover how they are intending to measure and use the data to manage their businesses more effectively in the near future.

One further observation needs to be made in relation to the bricks-and-mortar organizations. The eBusinesses seemed to be highly attuned to the more "modern" enterprise measurement agenda set by the Performance Prism's facets and sub-sets, whereas the traditional businesses seemed to be caught "off-guard" by these. Perhaps this could be because the Performance Prism seeks some alternative criteria not specifically addressed by other commonly applied frameworks that they are more accustomed to using today? If so, they should consider whether they need to update the content and application of their scorecards.

The ultimate conclusion from this research study, however, is that the vast majority of respondents – whether they be dot.coms, clicks-and-mortar, or bricks-and-mortar companies – have, with a considerable degree of solidarity, indicated that they would like to do a better job of managing with measures than they do today. Some perceive that they have a considerable way to go to reach the levels of "common practice" they believe that they should achieve, while others are striving towards becoming the "best practice" leaders. Each type, though, appears to recognize the need to change in order to be more successful and that measures are a vital component of creating that environment.

BIBLIOGRAPHY AND REFERENCES

Atkinson, R.D. and Court, R.H. (1998). The new economy index: Understanding America's economic transformation. Progressive Policy Institute, Washington DC. www.neweconomyindex.org

Bapna, R., Does, P., and Gupta, A. (2000). A theoretical and empirical investigation of multi-item on-line auctions. *Information Technology and Mangement*, 1, 1–23.

Brown, M.G. (1996). *Keeping Score: Using the Right Metrics to Drive World-Class Performance.* New York: Quality Recourses.

Crosby, P.B. (1972). *Quality is Free.* New York: McGraw-Hill.

Davis, S.M. and Meyer, C. (1998*). Blur: The Speed of Change in the Connected Economy.* Oxford: Capstone Publishing Ltd.

Deming, W.E. (1986). *Out of the Crisis.* Boston, MA: MIT.

Eccles, R.G (1991). The performance measurement manifesto. *Harvard Business Review*, January–February, 131–7

European Foundation of Quality Management (1993). *Total Quality Management: The European Model for Self-appraisal.* Brussels: EFQM

Hagel, J. and Amstrong, A. (1997). *Net Gain.* Boston: MA: Harvard Business School Press.

Johnson, H.T. and Kaplan, R.S. (1987*). Relevance Lost: The Rise and Fall of Management Accounting.* Boston, MA: Harvard Business School Press.

Kaplan, R.S. and Cooper, R. (1997). *Cost and Effect: Using Integrated Cost Systems to Drive Profitability and Performance.* Boston, MA: Harvard Business School Press.

Kaplan, R.S. and Norton, D.P. (1992). The balanced scorecard – measures that drive performance. *Harvard Business Review*, January–February, Boston, MA: Harvard Business School Press.

Kaplan, R.S. and Norton, D. P. (1996). *Balanced Scorecard – Translating Strategy into Action.* Boston, MA: Harvard Business School Press.

Keegan, D.S., Eiler, R.G., and Jones, C.R (1989). Are your performance measures obsolete? *Management Accounting (US)*, 70(120), 45–50.

Leadbeater, C. (2000). *New Measures in the New Economy.* London: Chartered Institute of Management Accountants.

Lynch, R. and Cross, K. (1991). *Measure Up – The Essential Guide to Measuring Business Performance.* London: Mandarin.

Malone, M.S. (2000). The most valuable companies in the eEconomy, Value Creation Index, http://www.forbes.com/asap

Neely, A. (1998). Measuring business performance – why, what and how. *The Economist.* London: Profile Books.

Neely, A. and Adams, C. (2001). The Performance Prism perspective, *Journal of Cost Management*, 15(1), 7–15.

Sink, D.S. (1991). The role of measurement in achieving world class quality and productivity management, management strategies. *Norcross*, 23(6), 23–9.

Webber, A.M. (1993). What's so new about the new economy? *Harvard Business Review*, January/February.

Index